Ethical Investigations

General Editor

Lawrence C. Becker

Professor Emeritus

College of William & Mary

A ROUTLEDGE SERIES

Contents of the Collection

Rights and Duties

Volume 5

Welfare Rights and Duties of Charity

Edited with introductions by

Carl Wellman

University of Washington, St. Louis

ROUTLEDGE

New York/London

Published in 2002 by
Routledge
29 West 35th Street
New York, NY 10001

Published in Great Britain by
Routledge
11 New Fetter Lane
London EC4P 4EE

Routledge is an imprint of the Taylor & Francis Group.

Printed in the United States of America on acid-free paper.

10 9 8 7 6 5 4 3 2 1

Library of Congress Cataloging-in-Publication Data

Rights and duties / edited with introductions by Carl Wellman.
p. cm. — (Ethical Investigations)
Includes bibliographical references.
Contents: v. 1. The concept of a right and a duty — v. 2. The rational foundation of rights and duties — v. 3. Natural rights and duties—v. 4. Against rights and duties—v. 5. Duties and obligations to others—v. 6. Property as a right, distribution as a duty.
ISBN 0-415-93982-8 (set : alk paper) — ISBN 0-415-93983-6 (vol. 1 : alk. paper) — ISBN 0-415-93984-4 (vol. 2 : alk. paper) — ISBN 0-415-93985-2 (vol. 3 : alk. paper)—ISBN 0-415-93986-0 (vol. 4 : alk. paper)—ISBN 0-415-93987-9 (vol. 5 : alk. paper)—ISBN 0-415-93988-7 (vol. 6 : alk. paper)
1. Natural law. .2. Obedience (Law) .3. Duty. 4. Law and ethics I. Wellman, Carl II. Series.
K460.R46 2002
340'.112—dc21 2002020621

Contents

Duties of Charity

Series Introduction

This volume is part of an ambitious series designed to collect English language journal articles and book chapters of enduring philosophical interest in the field of ethics. The articles are published here in their original formats and pagination, without editorial changes of any sort. They are thus primary bibliographic documents as well as philosophical ones.

The series is organized into multivolume collections. The first of these is the six-volume collection called *Rights and Duties*, edited by Carl Wellman, of which this volume is a part. Future collections, with their projected publication dates, include *Justice and Equality* (2002); *Ethics and Public Policy Issues* (2003); *Environmental Ethics* (2003); *Moral Responsibility* (2004); and *Feminist Ethics* (2004).

For obvious reasons the series cannot reasonably aim to be comprehensive. The English language journal literature in ethics is vast, and although the common wisdom is that much of it is ephemeral, a good deal of it is clearly better than that—and there is more of that than we can possibly republish here. Moreover, we have not chosen articles simply because they are, or are likely to be, of interest to historians of philosophy. Rather, we have confined ourselves to topics of continuing philosophical interest, and articles on those topics that are either of continuing importance in themselves or of special use in orienting readers with respect to the wider literature. In addition, we have included some material from serials published in book form, and in unusual cases, we have included chapters from monographs. The focus, however, has been on the journal and serial literature, not monographs.

In an ideal world, all important journal articles in ethics would effortlessly enter into the institutional memory of professional philosophers. Our world falls short of that ideal, of course. For one thing, Anglo-American philosophers are notoriously stingy with citations, and many, on principle, resist attempts to create anything that might be misused as a closed, canonical list of worthy philosophical texts or topics. Those traits, combined with a propensity for closely focused argument on tightly defined problems, can induce a form of professional negligence in which, say, a young philosopher working on property rights in the final third of the twentieth century, circulating drafts of his manuscripts widely, can easily fail to come across Morris Cohen's useful articles on the subject. Moreover, literature searches are of limited use if the literature is difficult to access or too large to survey effectively—especially if one is unconsciously convinced of the false proposition that "If it is important, and if I don't know about it already, one of my critics will point it out to me soon." One of the aims of this series is to address the problem of professional amnesia, by pointing some things out.

Lawrence C. Becker

Volume Introduction

This is one of six volumes of collected articles and chapters on rights and duties. The others are *Conceptual Analyses of Rights and Duties*, *Rational Foundations of Rights and Duties*, *Possible Possessors of Rights or Duties*, *Human Rights and Universal Duties*, and *Property Rights and Duties of Redistribution*. Each is intended to be a coherent collection that presents a set of closely related debates concerning rights and duties. Together they represent the most important themes in the twentieth century theory of rights and duties. In addition to the articles and chapters that had to be omitted from each volume in order to hold them down to publishable size, there are other important publications that are not included because they do not fit neatly into any of these volumes. As I have attempted to fulfil my duties as an editor, I hope that I have not violated any right of authors I have reluctantly excluded from my selections.

Most moral philosophers take welfare rights to be a species of what D. D. Raphael called rights of recipience and others call claim rights, rights logically correlative with duties of some second party. Thus, Martin P. Golding conceives of a welfare right very broadly as a morally justified claim to some good, some element of or means to one's personal welfare. Rodney Peffer defines welfare rights as rights to those goods or services necessary to meet one's basic needs. Allen Buchanan defines a welfare right as a right to be provided with cash or with material goods or services, either without charge or at a subsidized rate below their market value. James P. Sterba suggests that in addition to claim-rights of these kinds, there are welfare liberty-rights of the poor to take from the rich the resources they need to satisfy their basic needs.

What are the grounds of moral welfare rights? Golding suggests that justifying one's claim to some welfare benefit requires the recognition that it is an element in or means to the personal good of the right-holder and the acknowledgement that it is a genuine good, also a good for the duty-bearer and other members of the moral community. William Aiken grounds the moral right for food of those who through no fault of their own cannot get enough to eat upon the right to be saved from starvation that is in turn grounded on the general right to be saved from preventable death due to deprivation. Presumably the same reasoning would ground welfare rights to any other goods or services required to prevent one's death. Peffer grounds welfare rights, in the sense of rights to those goods or services necessary to meet one's basic needs, directly upon the human worth of the right-holder, especially the human capacity to enjoy well-being that Gregory Vlastos argues implies a prima facie human right to well-being. He grounds other rights usually called welfare rights in a broader sense, such as the rights to an education or to social security, upon the principles of distributive justice that would be accepted in a Rawlsian social contract. Buchanan grounds positive rights to be provided with welfare benefits upon the negative rights not to be interfered with by violence or threat of violence. The libertarian rights to freedom of expression, to the benefits of the legal system and to political participation are denied or at least severely limited to those deprived of the economic resources needed to take advantage of them. It is unfair that the deprived members of a society can enjoy the benefits of these rights to a very limited extent if at all while the affluent members of a society can enjoy them much more fully. Hence, the principle that the institutions of a society ought to provide fair equality of opportunity to all its members requires welfare rights to overcome this injustice. Although A. I. Melden denies that there are any human rights to welfare benefits, he argues that the disadvantaged members of any society have moral rights to welfare benefits because without such benefits they would be unable to enjoy their other more fundamental human rights. Sterba grounds welfare liberty-rights upon a more fundamental general right to liberty. He points out that the liberty of the affluent to prevent others from using their property conflicts with the liberty of the poor to take what they need from the wealthy. But the liberty to act to meet one's basic needs is more important than and takes moral priority over the liberty to use one's wealth to provide luxuries for oneself or those one favors. Hence, the libertarian commitment to liberty grounds the moral liberty-right to take what is required to meet one's basic needs over the liberty-right of the affluent to prevent one from doing so. Raymond Plant grounds welfare rights on respect for human dignity, specifically respect for the capacity to form a view of the good and to follow it. This requires more than that one not prevent others from pursuing their ideal of a good life because their pursuit can be harmed by inaction as well as by action. Hence, respect for human dignity grounds positive rights to those resources necessary for agency, although not those needed to achieve every particular goal one chooses, as well as negative rights that others not act to destroy or damage one's agency. David Copp grounds a moral right to be enabled to meet one's basic needs, to acquire those things one needs as a rational autonomous agent, upon the duty not to harm others. If something is a basic need, then to lack it is to suffer harm. Thus, either to prevent one from meeting her basic needs or to fail to enable her to meet them is to harm that person. And the urgency of one's interest in meeting one's basic needs gives the duty to enable others to meet such needs the stringency required to imply a correlative right.

Advocates of welfare rights face many challenges. Maurice Cranston denies that the social and economic rights declared by the United Nations can be real human rights. Any human right must meet the tests of practicality, universality and paramount moral importance. (1) If there were a right of all human beings to an adequate standard of living, then all societies would have a correlative duty to ensure an adequate standard of living to their members. But there cannot be any such duty because there cannot be any duty to do the impossible and some societies lack the resources to ensure an adequate standard of living to all its members. (2) The alleged human right to holidays with pay or even to just remuneration cannot be a universal right, a right of all human beings, because it applies only to those who are employed. (3) The alleged human right to social security is not of paramount moral importance because one may be deprived of it without a grave affront to justice. D. D. Raphael replies that the human rights to work or to social security are not entirely impracticable because they can be implemented to some degree in every society. These are also universal moral rights in that they are rights of all human beings, although they are not universal in the sense of holding against all human beings; welfare rights hold only against other members of one's society. And meeting the basic needs of human beings is of paramount moral importance. David Watson also responds to the challenges posed by Cranston. Although there may be societies that at present lack the resources to enable all their members to enjoy an adequate standard of living, human rights impose duties upon all human beings and, given the resources of all the human beings in the world, it would be practicable to ensure an adequate standard of living to everyone. Cranston admits that there is a paramount duty to relieve great distress. Presumably the logical correlativity of rights and duties implies that there is a paramount right to be rescued from great distress, including the distress of being deprived of necessary goods and services. Finally, the test of universality fails to distinguish between the traditional civil and political human rights that Cranston accepts and the social and economic rights that he rejects. The right to freedom of religion applies only to those who belong to some religious group or are religious, just as the right to just remuneration applies only to those who are employed. And not all human beings have any right to a fair trial, only those who have been indicted or sued before some court.

An even more fundamental challenge to welfare rights is the charge that so-called welfare rights cannot be genuine rights because they lack the defining characteristics of rights in any strict sense. Rodney Peffer responds to three such challenges. (1) Rights are permissions to act with correlative obligations not to interfere. Hence, rights imply only negative duties, duties not to prevent or hinder one from acting by any form of coercion. But the alleged welfare rights would imply positive duties to provide goods or services to the disadvantaged. Peffer responds that some paradigm examples of rights fail to fit this definition of rights as permissions. If John promises Richard ten dollars, then Richard has a moral right to be given ten dollars. This right is not a permission for Richard to act in some manner but a right to be given something, a right implying a positive duty of John to give ten dollars to Richard. Thus, Joel Feinberg's definition of rights as valid claims captures our conception of a right better than that assumed by this challenge. (2) H. L. A. Hart and others argue that moral rights belong to that special area of morality concerned with the distribution of freedom. But the alleged welfare rights are concerned with something quite different, the distribution of goods and services. Hart observes that the phrase "I have a right to . . ." is most often used either to claim some special justification for interference with another's freedom or to resist some interference with one's own freedom. Peffer replies that this linguistic evidence does not necessarily exclude other uses of the language of rights. He agrees that rights do belong to some special area of morality, but suggests that what is special about rights could be explained as Feinberg does in terms of the activity of claiming. (3) Any claim-right by definition implies some correlative duty, and most advocates of welfare rights assume that they impose positive duties to provide goods or services. But the alleged welfare rights either impose no real obligations, as that of an impoverished society do the impossible by providing welfare benefits to all its citizens, or burden us with innumerable intolerable obligations, as that each of us contribute to the welfare of every disadvantaged person in the world. Peffer, like H. J. McCloskey and others, rejects the thesis that it is a conceptual feature of rights that they always imply correlative obligations. In particular, some rights to well-being and some social contract rights imply no correlative duty.

The most vehement opponents of welfare rights are libertarians who typically assume that rights are liberties of individual action protected by duties of others not to interfere. Buchanan attempts to undermine this challenge by deriving welfare rights from rights central to libertarian theories. Tara Smith argues that any such derivation suffers from two fatal flaws. First, it wrongly assumes that to possess a right one must be able to enjoy it. But to possess a right is simply to be entitled to claim it. To exercise a right includes more, to actually make use of it. But a person may possess a right even when she is unable to exercise it. And she may exercise it without achieving the benefit she intends to achieve as a result of its exercise. Hence, the lack of goods and services may prevent one from exercising a right or exercising it successfully, but it does not thereby deprive one of that right. Second, such derivations confuse the freedom to seek and obtain goods with either the ability to obtain goods or the entitlement to possess goods. Only the former is and ought to be protected by legitimate moral rights.

Assuming that there are moral welfare rights, upon whom do they impose duties? Theories of welfare rights imply various answers. (1) Some imply that the corresponding duties fall primarily upon all other human beings. Aiken argues that the right to be saved from starvation is a right *in rem* that imposes a duty to save upon anyone who is aware of the right-holder's need and who has the resources to prevent her death. He adds that everyone also has a duty to become aware of the needs of others. Watson responds to the challenge of scarce resources by suggesting that the combined resources of all the persons in the world are adequate to provide the goods and services demanded by welfare rights. Hence, he must suppose that any welfare right of one human being imposes duties upon all other human beings. Plant also argues that welfare rights imply duties upon all other individuals. He suggests, however, that these are not duties to provide resources from their personal wealth, but duties to support public institutions adequate to meet needs of the poor. (2) Other theories imply that welfare rights impose duties primarily upon other members of one's society. Raphael maintains that although social and economic rights are rights of all human beings, the corresponding responsibilities rest on the members of one's society and that their government has a duty to carry out these responsibilities on their behalf. He also suggests that any moral responsibilities to help people in need in other societies would be duties of charity not a matter of implementing rights. (3) Some theories impose the corresponding duties directly upon the government of the right-holder's society. Copp asserts the right to be enabled by one's society to meet one's basic needs insofar as it is possible for the society to do so. Because he grounds this moral right partly on an appeal to the justice of social institutions and because a society would have to be efficiently organized to promote effectively people's ability to meet their basic needs, he argues that the corresponding duty falls upon the state. And because Buchanan grounds welfare rights on the principle that justice requires that social institutions ensure a fair equality of opportunity as well as on libertarian rights, he similarly concludes that they impose upon one's government the duty to provide a fair system of procedures including welfare rights.

Are the duties to provide goods and services to those in need duties of justice or duties of charity? Traditionally duties of justice have been defined as duties with logically correlative rights and duties of charity as duties without any correlative right. Corollaries have usually been assumed to be that duties of justice are perfect duties that may legitimately be enforced while duties of justice are imperfect duties that ought not to be enforced. Libertarians even infer that duties of justice must be purely negative while duties of charity might be positive. Buchanan challenges all four of these theses. The assertion that duties of justice must be purely negative begs the question of whether there are any positive moral rights. One reason to believe that there are positive rights is that one important concern of morality is the harmfulness of many human actions. Thus, there is at least a presumption that there are some positive rights, rights to aid that prevents harm. Second, there are sound moral reasons for enforcing duties to provide collective goods, and some of these are arguments for enforcing duties of charity. Without an effective enforcement mechanism, strictly voluntary duties to aid those in need may be ineffective because some rational individuals will defect in order to enjoy their wealth while avoiding the costs of aiding the poor. Again, duties of charity are supposed to be imperfect because both the individuals the duty-bearer is obligated to aid and the amount and kind of aid required are indeterminate. But duties of charity can be rendered determinate in both respects by the morally justified institutions of society. Finally, Buchanan argues that whether duties of charity have correlative rights is a question of great theoretical complexity. Therefore, to simply assume that they do not will be of very little use in constructing a theory of rights; and because duties of charity may legitimately be enforced, it will be of little practical significance also. Onora O'Neill constructs the distinction between duties of justice and duties of charity along Kantian lines. Duties of justice are required by moral principles that must be adopted by rational agents of any sort who act only on principles that could be adopted by all rational agents. Duties of charity, duties to aid those who need assistance in order to become and remain rational agents, are required by moral principles that must be adopted by human beings, given their vulnerabilities, who act only on principles that could be adopted by all human beings. Thus, obligations are logically prior to rights so that duties of charity may not correspond to any welfare rights, unless social institutions establish special relations that allocate duties to aid identifiable right-holders.

Moral philosophers often defend duties of charity independent of any welfare rights. Peter Singer, an act-utilitarian, argues that because the suffering and death from the lack of food, shelter and medical care are very bad, acts of preventing them wherever and whenever one can are duties, not merely supererogatory acts of generosity. Robert E. Goodin maintains that the special responsibilities of parents to their children and of the members of a society to fellow citizens are based on the vulnerabilities of children or of fellow citizens to their actions. In any society, these responsibilities might be imposed either on individuals or collectivities, but ultimately they devolve into the duty of individuals to organize and implement a scheme, a welfare state, to protect the interests of the most vulnerable. James W. Nickel suggests that between duties to aid correlative to welfare rights and acts of giving not required by any right or duty are duties to aid, for example the duties of families to meet the needs of family members who are immature, sick, or unemployed. He then argues that in modern societies the inadequacies of private charity and family duties call for the implementation of welfare rights. Keith Burgess-Jackson attempts to resolve the paradoxical moral status of charity by redefining duties of charity. Rather than conceiving of them as imperfect duties to perform actions of aiding those in need, he conceives of them as duties to be a charitable person. Richard Stith rejects the logical correlativity of rights and duties. The language of rights adds something to the language of duties, the right-holder's power of claiming something from the duty-bearer. But duties of generosity presuppose no such power.

Some moral philosophers remind us that many acts of aiding those in need are not required by duty in any strict sense. Jeffrey Obler asserts that public welfare programs compel people to do what private morality does not demand. When private persons help poor strangers voluntarily, they do what is morally praiseworthy but not required. And if they choose to ignore poor strangers, they do no wrong. John M. Whelan, Jr., argues that although there is no moral duty to give to charity, giving to charity is not morally optional in the way that giving to the local symphony is. He argues that although one could not possibly relieve all suffering, completely neglecting the suffering of other people when one could do something about it is a bad thing. Therefore, those who have money to spend on inessentials ought to give some of that money to charities which reduce suffering. Although Loren E. Lomasky defends some welfare rights, he suggests that charity ought not to be conceived of in terms of the jurisprudential paradigm of rights and duties. Charity is a virtue we have reason to prize irrespective of anyone's rights. A social order graced with individuals disposed to act compassionately toward their unfortunate fellows will seldom need to resort to welfare rights. Charitable giving is superior to reliance on welfare rights both because rights define only the moral minimum and because there is a moral presumption against the coercion needed to sustain a system of rights.

A Short List of Related Articles

A. Campbell Garnett, "Charity and Natural Law," *Ethics* 66 (1956), pp. 117–122.

Frank I. Michelman, "Constitutional Welfare Rights and *A Theory of Justice*," in *Reading Rawls*, Norman Daniels (ed.), New York: Basic Books, 1975, pp. 319–347.

Onora Neill, "Lifeboat Earth," *Philosophy & Public Affairs* 4 (1975), pp. 273–292.

John Arthur, "Rights and the Duty to Bring Aid," in *World Hunger and Moral Obligation*, William Aiken & Hugh LaFollette (eds.), Englewood Cliffs, NJ: Prentice-Hall, 1977, pp. 37–48.

David Miller, "Social Justice and the Principle of Need," in *The Frontiers of Political Theory: Essays in a Revitalized Discipline*, Michael Freeman & David Robertson (eds.), New York: Saint Martin's Press, 1980, pp. 173–197.

Carl Wellman, "The Grounds of Ethical Rights," in Carl Wellman, *Welfare Rights*, Totowa, NJ: Rowman and Littlefield, 1982, pp. 149–182.

Allen E. Buchanan, "The Right to a Decent Minimum of Health Care," *Philosophy & Public Affairs* 13 (1984), pp. 55–78.

Robert E. Goodin, "Welfare, Rights and Discretion," *Oxford Journal of Legal Studies* 6 (1986), pp. 232–261.

Jeremy Waldron, "Welfare and the Images of Charity," *Philosophical Quarterly* 36 (1986), pp. 463–482.

Alan Gewirth, "Private Philanthropy and Positive Rights," in *Beneficence, Philanthropy and the Public Good*, Ellen Frankel Paul, Fred D. Miller, Jr., Jeffrey Paul, & John Ahrens (eds.), Oxford: Basil Blackwell, 1987, pp. 55–78.

Thomas A. Horne, "Welfare Rights as Property Rights, "in *Responsibility, Rights and Welfare: The Theory of the Welfare State*, J. Donald Moon (ed.), Boulder, CO: Westview Press, 1988, pp. 107–132.

Desmond S. King and Jeremy Waldron, "Citizenship, Social Citizenship and the Defence of Welfare Provision," *British Journal of Political Science* 18 (1988), pp. 415–443.

Phillip Montague, "Rights, Obligations, and Easy Rescue," *Pacific Philosophical Quarterly* 72 (1991), pp. 235–245.

James W. Nickel, "A Human Rights Approach to World Hunger," in *World Hunger and Morality*, 2nd edition, William Aiken & Hugh LaFollette (eds.), Upper Saddle River, NJ: Prentice-Hall, 1996, pp. 171–185.

James P. Sterba, "Reconciling Liberty and Equality, or Why Libertarians Must Be Socialists," in *Liberty, Equality, and Plurality*, Larry May, Christine Sistare, & Jonathan Schonsheck (eds.), Lawrence, KS: University Press of Kansas, 1997, pp. 38–57.

James Griffin, "Welfare Rights," *Journal of Ethics* 4 (2000), pp. 27–43.

FOUR

MAURICE CRANSTON

Human Rights, Real and Supposed

IT is said that when that remarkable American jurist Wesley Newcomb Hohfield tried to make the students at Yale Law School discriminate carefully between different uses of the term 'right' in Anglo-American law, he earned himself considerable unpopularity; his pupils even got up a petition to have him removed from his Chair.[1] If the analysis of positive rights is thus resisted by law students we should not be surprised if the analysis of human rights is ill-regarded by many politicians, publicists, and even political theorists. Some politicians, indeed, have a vested interest in keeping talk about human rights as meaningless as possible. For there are those who do not want to see human rights become positive rights by genuine enactments; hence the more nebulous, unrealistic, or absurd the concept of human rights is made out to be, the better such men are pleased.

I shall argue in this paper that a philosophically respectable concept of human rights has been muddied, obscured, and debilitated in recent years by an attempt to incorporate into it specific rights of a different logical category. The traditional human rights are political and civil rights such as the right to life, liberty, and a fair trial. What are now being put forward as universal human rights are social and economic rights, such as the right to unemployment insurance, old-age pensions, medical services, and holidays with pay. I have both a philosophical and a political objection to this. The philosophical objection is that the new theory of human rights does not make sense. The political objection is that the circulation of a confused notion of human rights hinders the effective protection of what are correctly seen as human rights.

One distinction which seems now well established in people's minds is that between human rights or the Rights of Man or natural rights (I take these expressions to mean the same thing) and positive rights, a distinction which corresponds to the distinction between natural law (or justice, or the moral law) and positive law. The distinction has been made better understood by the critics of natural rights, by men like Edmund Burke who could understand what was meant by the rights of Englishmen but not by the Rights of Man, and Jeremy Bentham who said 'Right is the child of law; from real laws come real rights, but from imaginary law, from "laws of nature", come imaginary rights. . . . Natural rights is simple nonsense, natural and imprescriptible rights [an American phrase] rhetorical nonsense, nonsense upon stilts'.[2]

I do not think Bentham's remark is true, but it was worth saying, because it obliges those of us who think natural rights is *not* nonsense to explain what sort of sense it is. For Bentham — and for Burke — the only test of a right was 'Is it actually enjoyed?', 'Is it really enforced?' In other words, 'Is it a positive right?' On this analysis, any right which is not a positive right is not granted the name of a right at all. For Burke the Rights of Man were mere abstractions: the rights of Englishmen were realities — a 'positive recorded hereditary title to all that can be dear to the man and the citizen'.[3] Real rights, again, were positive rights.

Both Burke and Bentham had a political as well as a philosophical interest in this question. Both regarded talk about the Rights of Man as mischievous as well as meaningless. Burke, the conservative, objected to such talk because it stimulated revolutionary sentiments, it injected 'false ideas and vain expectations into men destined to travel the obscure walk of laborious life'. Bentham, the radical, objected to talk about the Rights of Man because it produced declarations and manifestos that had no real significance in positive law, declarations which took the place of effective legislation for the public welfare. Burke disliked the rhetoric that led to public unrest and Bentham disliked the rhetoric that enabled politicians to fob off the public with words instead of deeds. Being thus attacked from Right and Left, it is no wonder that the idea of the Rights of Man, and of Natural Law, became unfashionable in the nineteenth century.

The present century has seen a marked revival of consciousness of what is now generally known as human rights — a term which has the advantage over the older expression 'natural rights' of not committing one too ostentatiously to any traditional doctrine of Natural Law. The reason for this revival is perhaps to be sought in history, first, in the great twentieth-century evils, Nazism, fascism, total war, and racialism, which have all presented a fierce challenge to human rights; and secondly, in an increased belief in, or demand for, equality among men. When the United Nations was set up by the victorious powers in the Second World War, one of the first and most important tasks assigned to it was what Winston Churchill called 'the enthronement of human rights'. The efforts that have been made at the United Nations to fulfil this promise have much to teach a political theorist.

At the inaugural meeting of the Economic and Social Council of the U.N. in May 1946, a Commission on Human Rights was appointed to submit to the General Assembly recommendations and reports regarding an 'International Bill of Rights'. English-speaking delegates on this Commission promptly put forward a draft 'Bill of Rights' in the form of a draft convention or treaty which both named the specific rights to be recognized and provided for the setting up of international institutions to deal with any alleged breach of those rights. The English-speaking delegations not unnaturally interpreted the expression 'Bill of Rights' as meaning an instrument of positive law, and therefore understood the duty of the Commission to be that of finding a formula for making human rights positive rights by making them enforceable. The Russian representative objected to these proposals. He said that it was premature to discuss any measure of a binding or judicial nature; the Soviet Union was willing to support a 'Bill of Rights' only if it was understood as a manifesto or declaration of rights. Some years afterwards the United States followed the Russian example, and announced that it, too, would not commit itself to any legally binding convention for the international protection of human rights.

In the U.N. Commission on Human Rights a compromise was settled on. The Commission agreed first to produce a manifesto or declaration of human rights, and then afterwards begin to work out 'something more legally binding' which it was decided to call a Covenant. The manifesto did not take long to produce. It was given the name of Universal Declaration of Human Rights and proclaimed by the General Assembly of the United Nations in December 1948 (see Appendix, p. 143). The 'more legally binding' Covenant of Human Rights, however, is still, after many years, at the stage of discussion.

One of the difficulties of translating the Universal Declaration of Human Rights into any kind of positive law is that the Declaration contains so much. It has no fewer than thirty articles. The first twenty spell out in detail the sort of rights that were named in the various classical statements of the Rights of Man: the rights to life, liberty, property, equality, justice, and the pursuit of happiness are articulated as, among other things, the right to freedom of movement; the right to own property alone as well as in association with others; the right to marry; the right to equality before the law and to a fair trial if accused of any crime; the right to privacy; the right to religious freedom; the right to free speech and peaceful assembly; the right to asylum. Among the institutions outlawed are slavery, torture, and arbitrary detention.

The Universal Declaration of 1948 did not, however, limit itself to this restatement of the familiar Rights of Man; it includes a further ten articles which name rights of a new and different kind.[4] Article 21 states that everyone has the right to take part in the government of his country, and further articles affirm the right to education; the right to work and to form trade unions; the right to equal pay for equal work; the right of everyone to a standard of living adequate to the health and well-being of himself and his family; the right to security in the event of unemployment, sickness, disability, widowhood, old age, or other lack of livelihood; the right to enjoy the arts and to share in scientific advancement and its benefits; and, what is even more novel, the right to rest, leisure, and 'periodic holidays with pay'.

The difference between these new rights and the traditional natural rights was not unnoticed by those responsible for drafting the Declaration. In the records of the Commission, the first twenty articles are called 'political and civil rights' and the further rights 'economic and social rights'. These later rights appear to have been included under pressure from the Left; but there are many humanitarian people, apart from those on the Left, who (in my belief, unwisely) agree with their inclusion.[5]

So far as the United Nations is concerned, the Commission on Human Rights soon discovered, when it came to draft the 'more legally binding' Covenant, that the two kinds of rights did not mix together well; and the Commission was therefore obliged to draft *two* covenants, one concerning the political and civil rights, the other the social and economic rights. Neither draft has so far proved acceptable to the General Assembly. In the meantime altogether more progress has been made in the field of human rights by another international organization, the Council of Europe. In 1950 a European Convention for the Protection of Human Rights was signed by the member States of the Council of Europe at Strasbourg. This time the so-called 'social and economic rights' were omitted; the rights that were named were the traditional 'political and civil rights'. Moreover, in this case, a European Commission and a European Court of Human Rights were set up with full judicial powers to investigate and remedy any alleged breach of the rights named in the Convention. Here, clearly, is a tangible attempt to translate the human rights into positive rights on an international scale. The only weakness of the European Convention is that some leading European powers, France, Italy, Greece, and Turkey, have refused to recognize the jurisdiction of the European Court or to grant the right to individual petition to the Commission or the Court. Nevertheless a dozen other nations *do* recognize these institutions; so that changes in positive law have helped in those places to make men's 'human rights' positive rights.[6]

One of the objections to regarding the 'social and economic' rights as authentic human rights is that it would be totally impossible to translate them in the same way into positive rights by analogous political and legal action. There are other objections: but the time has now come to consider more carefully what is meant by a right, and then what kind of right a human right is. We have already noted the distinction between human rights and positive rights; I propose now to rearrange rights into two other categories; the one I shall call legal rights, the other moral rights.

(1) Legal Rights may be distinguished as follows:

(*a*) *General positive rights:* the rights that are enjoyed and fully assured to everyone living under a given jurisdiction or constitution.

(*b*) *Traditional rights and liberties:* Burke said that the English people had risen against James II because he had taken away their traditional rights and liberties as Englishmen. The Vichy government took away many of the traditional rights and liberties of Frenchmen. This class of rights includes lost positive rights as well as existing positive rights.

(*c*) *Nominal 'legal' rights:* Even the least liberal nations tend to have 'façade' constitutions[7] which 'guarantee' freedom of speech, movement, assembly, and other such rights to their inhabitants. But where these nominal rights are not enforced, they cannot, of course, be classed as positive rights. We nevertheless see the demand in some such places for the nominal 'legal' rights being made positive rights. One example is the demand of certain Polish intellectuals for that freedom of expression which their constitution assures them. An even more publicized example is the demand of the Negroes in the United States for the nominal legal right to vote, enter State schools, and so forth, to be translated into positive rights.

(*d*) *Positive rights, liberties, privileges, and immunities of a limited class of persons:* Under this category we should have to include all rights which are attached to membership of a given category, e.g., the rights of clergymen, of peers, of doctors, of graduates of the University of Oxford, and of freemen of the City of London. The twentieth century has become impatient of privileges, and rights which were once enjoyed by a limited class of persons are often now claimed by all the inhabitants of a country. For example, the privileges of citizenship, the rights of ratepayers, as they were known in nineteenth-century England, are now enjoyed by all adult British subjects. A demand for the extension of rights within a political society is often confused with the demand for human rights. But the two are quite distinct.

(*e*) *The positive rights, liberties, privileges, and immunities of a single person:* Here the examples are few, because the cases are few: the rights of the President of the United States, of the Chairman of the Senate; the rights of the King, or the Lord Chancellor, or the Archbishop of Canterbury, are examples. Since the decay of the doctrine of the Divine Right of Kings, this class of rights does not present much of a problem.

The foregoing classes cover the category of legal rights. Next in turn is the category of moral rights. In this case it will be convenient to reverse the order of generality.

(2) MORAL RIGHTS

(*a*) *Moral rights of one person only:* We remember Bradley's famous phrase 'my station and its duties': we can equally speak of 'my station and its rights'. I, and I alone, have a network of rights which arise from the fact that I have done certain deeds, paid certain monies, been elected to certain places, and so forth. Some of these rights are legal rights as well as moral rights. But in considering them as moral rights the question is not 'Does the law uphold them?' but 'Have I just claim to them?' Not all my moral rights may in fact be enjoyed. Often we become most conscious of our moral rights precisely when they are *not* upheld. I am inclined to say 'I have a moral right to be told what is going on in my own house' when I realize I am not being told. So just as the crucial question with legal rights is 'Are they secured and enjoyed?', the crucial question in a moral right is 'Is there a just title?' Is there a sound moral claim? *Justification* is the central question.

(*b*) *The moral rights of anyone in a particular situation:* This is the class of moral rights which belongs to everyone who comes into a certain specific category, e.g., that of a parent, or a tutor, or an *au pair* girl. So we can say of a person, if he is a member of this class, he is entitled to so and so. Claims to have such moral rights are pressed by proving that one does belong to the appropriate category.

(*c*) *The moral rights of all people in all situations:* Because these rights are universal we should naturally expect them to be few in number; and we should expect them to be highly generalized in their formulation. It is easier to agree, for example, about the kind of deed which violates the right to life than it is to agree about any philosophical expression of the right to life. Moreover, it is inevitable that such a right as that to liberty will be somewhat differently understood in different societies, where the boundary between liberty and licence will be differently drawn. Again, our understanding of the right to property will differ according to the meaning we give to that richly ambiguous word.

The place which human rights occupy in my classification is readily understood. Human rights are a form of moral right, and they differ from other moral rights in being the rights of all people at all times and in all situations. This characteristic of human rights is recognized in the first paragraph of the preamble to the Universal Declaration of 1948, which says: 'Whereas recognition of the inherent dignity and of the equal and inalienable rights of all members of the human family is the foundation of freedom, justice and peace in the world. . . .'

Part of the difficulty of justifying human rights is their very universality. Moral rights of classes (2) (*a*) and (2) (*b*) above are justified by reference to the definite station or situation of the claimants. I claim a right to be told about the health of Nicholas Cranston by showing that I am his father. I do not think anyone else (except his mother) has the same right. But human rights do not depend in any way on the station or the situation of the individual. This is part of what is meant by saying they are 'rights that pertain to a human being merely because he is a human being'. If the validity of a moral right is commonly established by reference to the station or situation of the claimant, it is not altogether easy to see by what tests one could validate the rights which are *not* considered in relation to any definite situation.

Nevertheless there are some tests for the authenticity of a human right or universal moral right. Rights bear a clear relationship to duties. And the first test of both is that of practicability. It is not my duty to do what it is physically impossible for me to do. You cannot reasonably say it was my duty to have jumped into the Thames at Richmond to rescue a drowning child if I was nowhere near Richmond at the time the child was drowning. What is true of duties is equally true of rights. If it is impossible for a thing to be done, it is absurd to claim it as a right. At present it is utterly impossible, and will be for a long time yet, to provide 'holidays with pay' for everybody in the world. For millions of people who live in those parts of Asia, Africa, and South America where industrialization has hardly begun, such claims are vain and idle.

The traditional 'political and civil rights' can (as I have said) be readily secured by legislation; and generally they can be secured by fairly simple legislation. Since those rights are for the most part rights against government interference with a man's activities, a large part of the legislation needed has to do no more than restrain the government's own executive arm. This is no longer the case when we turn to 'the right to work', 'the right to social security', and so forth. For a government to provide social security it needs to do more than make laws; it has to have access to great capital wealth, and many governments in the world today are still poor. The government of India, for example, simply cannot command the resources that would guarantee each one of the 480 million inhabitants of India 'a standard of living adequate for the health and well-being of himself and his family', let alone 'holidays with pay'.

Another test of a human right is that it shall be a genuinely universal moral right. This the so-called human right to holidays with pay plainly cannot pass. For it is a right that is necessarily limited to those persons who are *paid* in any case, that is to say, to the *employé* class. Since not everyone belongs to this class, the right cannot be a universal right, a right which, in the terminology of the Universal Declaration, 'everyone' has. That the right to a holiday with pay is for many people a real moral right, I would not for one moment deny. But it is a right which falls into section (2) (*b*) of the classification of rights which I have set out above; that is, a right which can be claimed by members of a specific class of persons *because* they are members of that class.

A further test of a human right, or universal moral right, is the test of *paramount importance*. Here the distinction is less definite, but no less crucial. And here again there is a parallel between rights and duties. It is a paramount duty to relieve great distress, as it is not a paramount duty to give pleasure. It would have been my duty to rescue the drowning child at Richmond if I had been there at the time; but it is not, in the same sense, my duty to give Christmas presents to the children of my neighbours. This difference is obscured in the crude utilitarian philosophy which analyses moral goodness in terms of the greatest happiness of the greatest number: but common sense does not ignore it. Common sense knows that fire engines and ambulances are essential services, whereas fun fairs and holiday camps are not. Liberality and kindness are reckoned moral virtues; but they are not moral duties in the sense that the obligation to rescue a drowning child is a moral duty.

It is worth considering the circumstances in which ordinary people find themselves invoking the language of human rights. I suggest they are situations like these:

A black student in South Africa is awarded a scholarship to Oxford, and then refused a passport by the South African government simply because he is black. We feel this is clear invasion of the human right to freedom of movement.

Jews are annihilated by the Nazi government, simply because they are Jews. We feel this is a manifest abuse (an atrocious abuse) of the human right to life.

In several countries men are held in prison indefinitely without trial. We feel this is a gross invasion of the human right to liberty and to a fair trial on any criminal charge.

In considering cases of this kind, we are confronted by matters which belong to a totally different moral dimension from questions of social security and holidays with pay. A human right is something of which no one may be deprived without a grave affront to justice. There are certain deeds which should never be done, certain freedoms which should never be invaded, some things which are supremely sacred. If a Declaration of Human Rights is what it purports to be, a declaration of universal moral rights, it should be confined to this sphere of discourse. If rights of another class are introduced, the effect may even be to bring the whole concept of human rights into disrepute. 'It would be a splendid thing', people might say, 'for everyone to have holidays with pay, a splendid thing for everyone to have social security, a splendid thing to have equality before the law, and freedom of speech, and the right to life. One day, perhaps, this beautiful ideal may be realized. . . .'

Thus the effect of a Universal Declaration which is overloaded with affirmations of so-called human rights which are not human rights at all is to push *all* talk of human rights out of the clear realm of the morally compelling into the twilight world of utopian aspiration. In the Universal Declaration of 1948 there indeed occurs the phrase a' common standard of achievement' which brands that Declaration as an attempt to translate rights into ideals. And however else one might choose to define moral rights, they are plainly *not* ideals or aspirations.

Rights have been variously defined by jurists and philosophers. Some have spoken of them in terms of 'justifiable claims' or 'moral titles'; others have analysed rights in terms of duty ('what we have an overwhelming duty to respect'); others again have preferred to speak of right conduct or obligation or of ought ('a man has a right whenever other men ought not to prevent his doing what he wants or refuse him some service he asks for or needs'). All these words — 'right', 'justice', 'duty', 'ought', 'obligation' — are the key terms of what Kant called the 'categorical imperative'. What ought to be done, what is obligatory, what is right, what is duty, what is just, is not what it would be nice to see done one day; it is what is demanded by the basic norms of morality or justice.

An ideal is something one can aim at, but cannot by definition immediately realize. A right, on the contrary, is something that can, and from the moral point of view *must*, be respected here and now. If this were not so, we should have to agree with Bentham; if the Rights of Man were ideals, to talk of them as rights at all would indeed be rhetorical nonsense. We can give sense to human rights only because we can reasonably claim that men have moral rights, and that among the moral rights which each man has are some that he shares with all other men.

To deny that the 'economic and social rights' are the universal moral rights of all men is not to deny that they may be the moral rights of some men. In the moral criticism of legal rights, it is certainly arguable that the privileges of some members of a certain community ought to be extended to other members (and perhaps all members) of that community. But this matter is correctly seen as a problem of *socialization* or *democratization* — that is, the extension of privileges and immunities — rather than as a problem about the universal rights of all men: and the case for any such specific claims to an extension of legal rights must be argued on other grounds.

FIVE

D. D. RAPHAEL

Human Rights, Old and New

THE concept of Human Rights, as they are called in the English text of the Universal Declaration of 1948, is of course a revival of the eighteenth-century concept of the Rights of Man. According to Mrs. Eleanor Roosevelt, who was Chairman of the United Nations Commission on Human Rights, the old phrase was changed because of an interpretation given to it, at an early stage of international discussion, by a delegate from some benighted country. 'I assume', he blandly remarked, 'that when we speak of the rights of man, we mean what we say. My government, of course, could not agree to extend these rights to women.' The French text of the Universal Declaration retains the traditional '*droits de l'homme*', perhaps because the French can count on a general appreciation of legal as of other niceties concerning the relations between the sexes, and are familiar with the dictum that, in the language of the law, 'the male is presumed to embrace the female'.

In the eighteenth century, when there was no place for Mary Wollstonecraft on an official commission, it was not thought necessary to express the universality of these moral rights by the adjective 'human'. But in order to show that their moral force is independent of positive law, they were described by more pompous adjectives — 'natural', 'inherent', 'inalienable', 'imprescriptible' — that were to be deflated by Bentham in a well-known jibe (already quoted by Mr. Cranston): 'Natural rights is simple nonsense, natural and imprescriptible rights rhetorical nonsense, nonsense upon stilts.' Let us lay aside the stilts and look at the 'simple nonsense' as it first showed itself in the history of political theory. The notion of Natural Rights finds its chief expression in Locke and is a development from the theory of Natural Law.

The traditional doctrine of natural law does not give any particular prominence to the idea of individual rights. Law implies both duties and rights, and it is no doubt fair to say that the ancient and medieval theories of natural law were more concerned with the foundations of moral, legal, and political duty than with the foundations of rights. Nevertheless, Hobbes is quite wrong when he says that traditional theorists have confused '*jus* and *lex*, *right* and *law*' (*Leviathan*, Ch. 14). In English we do not speak of a system of right, as we speak of a system of law, but Latin and various modern European languages find it natural to use the noun 'right' as more or less synonymous with 'law' when referring to a legal system as a whole. Consequently the expression '*ius naturale*' means the system of natural law. The reason for this usage is that a system of law is at one and the same time a system of duties and a system of rights. For example, a law which requires *A* to fulfil his contract with *B*, or a law which forbids *A* to assault *B*, lays a duty on *A* and confers a right on *B*. Indeed, this last clause is just saying the same thing in two different ways. The statement, '*A* has a duty to fulfil his contract to *B*', means the same as the statement, '*B* has a right against *A* to the fulfilment of his contract'; and the statement, '*A* has a duty to refrain from assaulting *B*', means the same as the statement, '*B* has a right against *A* to freedom from assault'. Consequently, a system of law, 'natural' or positive, is a set of rules which may be regarded either as listing duties which men have towards each other, or as listing rights which they have against each other. And since positive law in fact tends to begin from the notion of rights to be protected, it is intelligible that such a set of rules should be called a system of *ius* (or *droit*, etc.) more readily than it is called a system of *lex* (or *loi*, etc.).

The fact is that the meanings which Hobbes gives, both to natural law and to natural right, are radically different from the meanings which these terms have in the traditional doctrine and which they retain in Locke. By 'radically different' I mean not only different in content but different in conception. It is often said, for example, that Hobbes, like Locke, holds that there is a natural right to life. This is a mistake — but not on the ground that Hobbes gives a different content to a right of the same character. According to Hobbes, every man will inevitably endeavour to preserve his life; his natural right is to do whatever he thinks is a means to this inevitable aim of self-preservation. Natural right for Hobbes is a right *to act*, it is not a right *to have* something or a right *against* other persons. Again, natural law, according to Locke and earlier tradition, lays down duties which largely consist of duties *towards* others. According to Hobbes, however, the requirements of natural law are not duties to others.

We speak of 'a right' in two different senses. The first sense I call a right of action (not to be confused with a technical use of this term in the law). Here we speak of a right to do something. Such a right is equivalent to an absence of obligation. If *A* has a right to sing in his bath, to cultivate his garden, or to give away his inheritance, this means that he has no obligation to refrain from these actions. In doing such an action, he is doing nothing wrong. He is morally and legally free to do the action, i.e., he is not morally or legally bound to refrain. This is how Hobbes uses the term 'natural right'; it is, as Hobbes calls it, a liberty, a freedom from the impediment of obligation imposed by any law.

The second sense of 'a right' I call a right of recipience. Here we speak of a right against someone else, i.e., a right to receive something from him, even if the something is simply the facility of being left alone. Such a right is equivalent to the existence of an obligation on the part of the other person against whom one has the right. If *A* has a right against *B* to have a contract fulfilled or a debt paid, this means that *B* has an obligation to *A* to fulfil the contract or pay the debt. And if *A* has a right to be left free from interference by *B*, this means that *B* has an obligation to *A* to leave him alone. A right to be left alone is a right *to liberty*, i.e., a right to freedom from interference by other people; but this should not be confused with a right of action, which can itself be called *a liberty*, i.e., a freedom from obligation.

E. F. Carritt (*Ethical and Political Thinking*, p. 77) denied this distinction on the ground that a right to act is simply a right to freedom from interference with one's action, and so is what I call a right of recipience. In my view, a man who has a right of action, a freedom from obligation, has *in addition* a right of recipience to freedom from interference. To say that he has the first right is to say that his proposed action is itself not wrong or unlawful, and it is only when this is true that he has the second right to freedom from interference. The second right depends on the first, but not *vice versa*. It seems at first sight plausible to deny that the first, the right of action, exists independently, because people do not normally speak of their rights of action unless someone else hinders them or at least interferes to the extent of querying the propriety of their action. If Lewis Carroll's Father William were not only incessantly to stand on his head, but were incessantly to declare that he had a right to do it, he would be called senile, not just old. He justifies his acrobatics only when the youth queries whether, at his age, it is right. Thus it seems sensible to say that one who speaks of his right to act is telling others that they have no business to interfere. But consider the meaning of a statement denying a right to act. Suppose Father William were to kick his son downstairs without the provocation that he receives in the poem, and suppose a spectator were to say, 'You have no right to kick the boy'. According to Carritt, a statement that a man has no right to act means simply that 'nobody has the duty not to prevent him'. Our spectator, then, would mean only that he and others were not obliged to stand by while Father William did his kicking, i.e., that their interference would not be wrong. But this is too weak to express the force of the spectator's statement, which means that something else, the action of Father William himself, is quite definitely wrong.

In the traditional doctrine of natural law, rights are rights of recipience, rights against other people. These rights correspond to, or rather they are simply another way of looking at, the duties of those other people to the persons who are said to have the rights. The rights are rights against other people, and the duties are duties to other people. Thus a system of natural law, a system of duties which all men have to others, is at the same time a system of rights which all men have against others.

The traditional doctrine of natural law, when speaking of duties, does not in fact confine them to duties towards other men. Theological versions of the doctrine usually refer to three categories of duty: duty to God, duty to self, and duty to other men. Exponents of the doctrine in this form might go on to say that ultimately all duties are duties to God; duties to self and duties to other men are ultimately duties to God because all men are created by God and belong to God. However, in so far as men have rights against each other, these rights correspond to their duties to each other.

In the theory of Hobbes, on the other hand, the obligations of natural law are not obligations to other men. For one who believes that the laws of nature are commands of God, the obligations imposed by natural law are obligations to God. But both for the believer and for the atheist, the so-called laws of nature are rules for self-preservation, i.e., maxims of prudence. One could say that they are therefore duties to self (and ultimately, for the believer, duties to God), but they are not duties to other men. Consequently they do not correspond to rights of recipience held by other men. There are no *natural* rights of recipience in Hobbes's theory. Rights of recipience for Hobbes (though Hobbes does not call them 'rights' — he speaks of what is 'due'), and likewise obligations to other men, are artificial, not natural. If *A* makes a promise to *B*, *A* thereby imposes upon himself an artificial obligation, an obligation *towards B*, and this is tantamount to saying that he sets up an artificial right for *B*, a right of recipience against *A* himself. Since there are no natural rights of recipience, Hobbes has to give a different interpretation to the notion of natural right. For him, natural right is right of action, the absence of obligation. That is why he opposes natural right and natural law.

Locke is not altogether consistent in his usage, but on the whole he follows the tradition. The obligations of natural law include obligations to other men, and therefore natural rights are, by and large, rights of recipience against other men. My natural right to life is a right against other men that they should not deprive me of my life; it corresponds to their natural obligation not to kill me. My natural right to liberty is a right against other men that they should leave me in peace; it corresponds to their natural obligation to leave me in peace. My natural right to 'estate' (property in the narrower sense of the word) is, I think, a mixture of right of action and right of recipience. On the one hand, I am, in certain conditions, free from obligation to leave land and its products available for common use; I have a right of action, a right to consume and appropriate. On the other hand, appropriation is not just simple action; it implies a right of recipience. When I fence in a piece of land with which I have 'mixed my labour', I thereby declare that I *alone* have the right to use it; this implies that others have an obligation not to use it, i.e., I have a right of recipience that they should keep out.

Hobbes's idea of natural right is an aberration from the tradition that led to the concept of human rights. Human rights are rights of recipience, not rights of action. Some of the rights in the Universal Declaration are framed in a way that perhaps suggests rights of action. For example, Article 14 speaks of a right *to seek* asylum from persecution, Article 21 of a right *to take part* in government, and Article 23 of a right *to work*. But of course the meaning of these Articles is not that it is morally permissible for a man to seek asylum from persecution, to participate in government, or to work. Nobody needs to be told that. When the American Declaration of Independence spoke of a natural right to pursue happiness, it was not arguing against ascetics and killjoys that there was nothing wrong in pursuing happiness. And when Louis Blanc enunciated a right to work, he was not arguing against any advocates of the virtues of idleness. All these rights are rights of recipience. The right to pursue happiness, and the right to seek asylum, are claims *to be allowed* to do these things. Likewise, the right to work, and the right to participate in government, are claims *to be given the opportunity* for work and for political activity.

Someone may say that here at least there is no real difference between a right of action and a right of recipience. It would indeed be silly to understand Article 14, for example, as a statement that it *is morally* permissible to seek asylum from persecution; but it is not silly to understand the Article as a statement that it *ought* to be *legally* permissible to seek asylum from persecution. Therefore, the objector may say, the Article enunciates a right of action in the sense of a liberty that ought to be allowed by law. Similarly the right to pursue happiness, in the American Declaration, may be interpreted as a claim that individuals ought to be legally free to pursue happiness.

This objection is misplaced, for two reasons. First, the statement that it *ought* to be legally permissible for any man to seek asylum from persecution means that governments have a moral obligation to their subjects to make this legally permissible; and to say that governments have a moral obligation to their subjects is the same as saying that the subjects have a moral right against the governments. Consequently the objector has admitted that Article 14 of the Universal Declaration is a statement that everybody has a *recipient* right to be permitted by law to seek asylum. A right to be allowed to act (as distinct from a right to act) is a right of recipience, because it corresponds to an obligation on the part of other people to refrain from interference when one exercises a right of action. It is a right *to liberty*, whereas the right of action itself is *a liberty*.

The second reason why the objection is misplaced is that certain of the rights under discussion are rights to more than liberty, so that the proposed identification with rights of action as liberties does not apply to them anyway. The right to seek asylum and the right to pursue happiness are recipient rights to liberty, claims to be simply left free or allowed by law to do what one wants to do. But the other two examples mentioned earlier are different. Take first the right to participate in government. Is this simply a claim to be *allowed* by law to participate? To be sure, it is not a claim to be *required* to vote, still less to be *required* to stand for election! But it is not simply a claim for a liberty either; it is a claim for an opportunity. There is no point in urging that the laws should not forbid me to vote or to stand for election, unless the laws also make positive provision for people to vote and to stand for election. The difference is even plainer with the right to work. A declaration of a right to work would be silly, not only if it meant that there was nothing wrong in working, but also if it meant that there should be no law forbidding work. To speak of a right to work is to claim that a positive opportunity to work should be provided.

It is therefore a mistake to think that some human rights are rights of action and others rights of recipience. What I have just said about liberties and opportunities, however, points to a real and important difference among human rights. Some are rights to liberty, rights to be *allowed* something, while others are rights to opportunity or more than opportunity, rights to be *given* something. We come here to the distinction between the older concept of Civil Rights (or Rights of Liberty) and the relatively more recent concepts of Political, Economic, and Social Rights. When a man has a right to liberty, the obligation of those against whom he has the right is a *negative* obligation, an obligation to leave him alone, to leave him free to do as he thinks fit. But when he is said to have a right to participate in government, or a right to work, and even more when he is said to have a right to social security, the obligation of those against whom he has the right is a *positive* obligation, an obligation to provide him with something which he could not achieve by himself. When we say, for example, that a man has the right to participate in government, we mean that those who organize the political life of the country are obliged to give him the opportunity to vote and make his opinions known, and that they are further obliged to have regard to his opinions when they take their political decisions. The right to work means that the government has a duty to prevent unemployment so far as it can. The right to social security means that the community as a whole has a duty to provide its needy members with the means of subsistence and with essential services such as schools and hospitals.

Locke summed up the content of his concept of natural rights as a right to property, giving the word 'property' an extended meaning so as to cover life and liberty as well as 'estate'. He had his own reasons for this peculiar usage. It would be more appropriate to pick out the word 'liberty' as a compendious term to cover the content of Locke's three natural rights to life, liberty, and property. In Locke's conception, natural right is a right to be left free to live (or, if one is unlucky, to die), to be left free to do as one chooses, and to be left free to enjoy the fruits of one's labour.

Mr. Maurice Cranston, writing on p. 46 of the preceding essay about economic and social rights as 'rights of a new and different kind', includes among them the right to take part in the government of one's country (a right which I have preferred to call political). Earlier, in his book, *Human Rights Today*, p. 38, he said, rather incautiously, that 'economic and social rights were unknown to Locke and the natural rights theorists of the eighteenth century', and there too (on p. 37) he coupled the political right to participate in government with economic and social rights, all of these being contrasted with the older conception of 'civil rights' or rights of liberty. He would probably now agree that his generalization about the *eighteenth* century needs to be qualified. Locke certainly confined himself to rights of liberty (life, liberty, and property); and 'the pursuit of happiness', which the American Declaration of Independence substituted for 'property', is still a right of liberty. It might be said also that the addition of 'security', in the Virginian Declaration of Rights, and in the French Declaration of 1789, does not substantially change the conception of rights of liberty or civil rights. Both these declarations, however, go on to speak of the political right to take part in government by way of voting for representatives. Nor is this all. There are also suggestions, even in the eighteenth century, of what are now called economic and social rights. Mr. Cranston has referred, in note 4 of the preceding essay, to an article by Professor Carl J. Friedrich ('Rights, Liberties, Freedoms: A Reappraisal', *American Political Science Review*, lvii, Dec. 1963), drawing attention (p. 843) to statements, by Turgot in 1776 and by Robespierre in 1793, of a right to work, and, in the French Declaration of 1793, of a right to education. So far as France is concerned, we may add the *Manifeste des Égaux* of the Babeuf Conspiracy of 1796, which spoke of a universal right to education (and a universal obligation to work). In one of the English theorists of the time, furthermore, there is a far more detailed conception of what we now call economic and social rights. Thomas Paine, in Part I of *The Rights of Man* (1791), enunciates and discusses the general principles of the French Revolutionaries; but in Chapter 5 of Part II (1792), he applies these principles in a carefully thought-out plan of what we should now call social security. It included, for all who needed them, a State system of education, children's allowances, old-age pensions, maternity, marriage, and funeral allowances, and a scheme of publicly endowed employment for the poor of London. In *Agrarian Justice* (1797), he sets out a revised plan, with a different method of financing a simpler system of benefits, available this time to all, whether rich or poor. He says emphatically, in both works, that he is speaking of a right and not of charity.

Of course all these suggestions of economic and social rights come towards the end of the eighteenth century and are pointers to socialist theory of the nineteenth century, though only one of the men so far mentioned, Babeuf, could be called in any sense a socialist. In general it is true that the advocates of the rights of man in the eighteenth century thought chiefly, like Locke, of civil rights or rights of liberty, rights to be left in peace by other men and by governments except in so far as governments were fulfilling their task of keeping the peace and preserving men's liberties. The functions of government were regarded by most men at that time as negative functions, to protect individuals in the enjoyment of what they already possessed, and to leave them free to fend for themselves so long as they did not encroach upon the established legal rights of others. The idea that a government also has the positive duties of increasing welfare and of redistributing wealth more justly is a product mainly of nineteenth-century socialist thought. In so far as this idea of the positive duties of government was expressed under the notion of rights, of the just claims of need, it owes most to French theorists of the period, especially Louis Blanc and Proudhon.

Mr. Cranston argues that it is a mistake to class economic and social rights with the older 'natural' rights of liberty. Human rights, he says on pp. 49–51 of his essay, are universal moral rights, and in addition to being genuinely universal they must satisfy two further tests, of practicability and of paramount importance. I agree with Mr. Cranston that these are appropriate tests, but they do not in fact draw a clear line between the earlier and the later concepts of human rights. Tom Paine evidently understood the natural right to life as implying not only laws against homicide but also laws to provide a bare subsistence. Will anyone say that he was wrong in terms of paramount importance? Nobody would accept Clough's satirical couplet:

> 'Thou shalt not kill, but need'st not strive
> Officiously to keep alive.'

Importance, like practicability, is of course a matter of degree, and no doubt the prevention of murder is of more paramount importance than the prevention of starvation. Yet the degrees of paramountcy do not place all the rights of liberty before all the economic and social rights. If a man is subject to chronic unemployment in a depressed area, he will not thank you for the information that he has the basic rights of liberty. Locke's right of freedom to amass property is of little interest to such a man when it goes along with 'freedom to starve'. J. S. Mill's plea for absolute freedom of expression cuts little ice with labourers who do not know whether they will have a job next month.

I have not forgotten practicability. Tom Paine's plan for social security was eminently practicable for the England of his day, as he took care to show, but even his modest scheme would not be feasible universally. Yet this is not to say that poorer nations are unable to organize any aid at all for the needy; a sort of system of social security is to be found in the Old Testament laws about leaving harvest gleanings for the poor, the periodic cancellation of debts, and so forth. Again, while unemployment is among the greatest of evils for those who are subject to it, no amount of reading Lord Keynes will produce a golden key for full employment everywhere. Yet there is some possibility nowadays of some control of unemployment by governments, as there was not in former times, and therefore it is justifiable to speak of a duty of governments to do what they can. After all, no amount of criminal legislation or of police forces will be able to prevent *all* homicides; but that is no reason for saying that the right to life must be struck out of our list of human rights as not being universally practicable. Nobody suggests that the right to work or the right to social security can be implemented to the same degree everywhere. Article 22 of the Universal Declaration, in introducing economic and social rights, recognizes that the entitlement has to be 'in accordance with the organization and resources of each State'.

Mr. Cranston justifiably derides the extravagance of Article 24 in calling holidays with pay a universal right. But we could also deride the extravagance of Article 19 in speaking, without any reservations, of a universal right to seek, receive, and impart information through any media and regardless of frontiers. On the face of it, this Article would justify the transmission to a foreign power of secret military information, the tapping of telephone conversations, the opening of private correspondence, or the prying by any newspaper reporter into the private lives of individuals. Of course the Article does not in fact intend these consequences. It needs to be read in conjunction with Article 12, which forbids arbitrary intrusion upon privacy, and with Article 30, which limits the exercise of any right so as not to aim at the destruction of other rights. Likewise Article 24, with its provision for holidays with pay, needs to be read in the light of Article 22, which sets a general limit on economic and social rights so as to accord with the resources of each State. I should agree, nevertheless, that the inclusion of holidays with pay is an absurd extravagance. It is so, however, not because the alleged universal right to holidays with pay is an economic or social right, but because holidays with pay are a luxury. The general principle of Article 24, the right to rest and leisure, is a perfectly proper element in a list of basic rights and duties. If I may refer to the Old Testament again, the Mosaic Decalogue included a day of rest along with the prohibition of elementary crimes like murder and theft. To the manual worker (and that means to two-thirds of the working population even in advanced societies), some security of employment and a reasonable limitation of working hours mean more than certain (I do not say all) parts of the classical rights of liberty.

I have said that the inclusion of holidays with pay is an extravagance because holidays with pay are a luxury. To call something a right (of recipience) is to say that it is morally necessary. A luxury is an enjoyment that goes beyond necessity. There is, however, no fixed principle for drawing the line between those wants that are regarded as 'needs' (a species of moral necessity) and those that are not. Ideas of what is due as a matter of moral necessity for human personality vary from one age to another and from one society to another. In general, material and moral progress produces a continuous expansion of the conception of needs. It is therefore to be expected that a twentieth-century declaration of rights should include more than an eighteenth-century declaration, and what is thought to be a luxury today may be regarded as a necessity tomorrow.

I have argued that Mr. Cranston's tests of practicability and paramount importance do not afford a criterion for distinguishing the rights of liberty from economic and social rights. There is a sense, however, in which it is correct to say that the rights of liberty are universal moral rights while political, economic, and social rights are not. The expression 'a universal moral right' may be used in a stronger sense or in a weaker sense. In the stronger sense it means a right of all men against all men; in the weaker sense it means simply a right of all men, but not necessarily against all men. In the weaker sense, all men may have a right which is, for each of them, a right against some men only. An example or two will make this clear. Every man has a moral right against every man not to be killed; i.e., every man has a duty to every man not to kill him. This is a universal right in the stronger sense. By contrast, every man has a right, when a child, to parental care, but this is not a right against every man; i.e., it is not the duty of every man to give to every child the care of a parent. Now the economic and social rights, and likewise the political right of participation in government, are universal rights in the weaker sense. When the Universal Declaration says that every man has the right to work, or the right to subsistence, it does not imply that the corresponding responsibility to provide any particular man with work or subsistence rests on every other man or every group of men; it implies that this responsibility rests on the members of his own State, and that the government of that State has a duty to carry out the responsibility on behalf of all its members. We do of course speak of a responsibility to help people who are in need in other parts of the world, but such help is an act of benevolence or charity, and not a matter of implementing a right. Similarly, the political right of participation in government applies only within one's own State. An Englishman has the right to participate in the government of Great Britain but not to participate in the government of France; and since there is no World State, it makes no sense to speak of a right to participate in the government of mankind as a whole.

There is therefore a genuine difference between the rights of liberty on the one hand and political, economic, and social rights on the other. It is well expressed by the French distinction between 'the rights of man' and 'the rights of the citizen'. One has the rights of liberty simply as a member of the human race, and they are rights which link every man with every other man. One has political, economic, and social rights as a member of a particular civil society, and these rights link each man with all the other members of his society.

While this distinction limits 'the rights of man' or 'human rights' to the rights of liberty, it does not justify any suggestion that the rights of the citizen, i.e., the political, economic, and social rights, should not be included in an international declaration. Although the Universal Declaration has led to the establishment of a regional international court, the European Court of Human Rights, and may well lead to further international institutions, nevertheless the main purpose of the Declaration is to encourage national governments to promote legislation and administrative measures for securing the rights of individuals within their own States. Legislation by governments of course encompasses the rights of men as citizens and not merely the rights which they have as human beings. Some people may say that the Universal Declaration taken by itself, without international machinery for implementation, can have no effect on the actions of national governments. I myself do not share this view. Despite the lack of realism in some of the annual reports made by governments, I think that the influence of the Declaration and of the reports, by the force of example, is not negligible. However, this is a practical question, on which the theorist had best hold his tongue. So far as the analysis of concepts is concerned, I have tried to show where there is not, and where there is, a difference of principle between two kinds of rights in the Universal Declaration.

Social Philosophy & Policy Vol. 1 Issue 2 ISSN 0265-0525

THE PRIMACY OF WELFARE RIGHTS

MARTIN P. GOLDING

This paper deals with three topics: (1) types of rights, (2) the development of the terminology of rights, and (3) the question of the primacy of welfare rights. Because these topics are interrelated, my exposition does not observe rigid boundaries among them. There is no pretence at all that any of these subjects is fully covered here; nor is it proposed, except for one writer, to touch upon the contemporary literature on rights, as noteworthy as some of that literature is. In order to gain entrance into the field, on which the writing has grown to massive proportions, I shall begin with an interesting historical phenomenon, some of whose philosophical import I want to explore.

I should say at the outset, however, that the general motivation of this paper is the problem of the significance of the language of "rights." Does it really make a difference, for instance, to speak of the "rights of man" rather than the "common duties of humanity"? Does the term "rights" add anything of special significance or is its only significance rhetorical and ideological? Can we dispense with the language of rights and still say everything we need to say about our moral relations? I confess to a moderate skepticism about the necessity of the language of rights in the last analysis. At any rate, this paper is intended as a contribution, however small, to this problem. The historical phenomenon with which I am going to begin will enable us to bring into focus the issue of the meaning of "rights."[1]

In the first chapter of his study, *John Locke and Children's Books in Eighteenth Century England*, Samuel F. Pickering traces the development of a genre of literature – not John Locke Comics – written for young ladies and gentlemen which was, as the title of one such book put it, an attempt to amend the world, to render the society of man more amiable.[2] This genre – animal books – was

[1] My interest in the specific, non-reducible functions of rights language – if there are any such functions – is part of a larger interest in the specific functions of the various terms of moral discourse and appraisal. This subject begins with Plato (Socrates?), *e.g.*, in the *Euthyphro*, which discusses the relationships and differences holding between "piety" and "justice." It is carried on in Aristotle's discussion of "justice" and the various virtues. On the other side, though, we may note the tendency to subordinate the various forms of moral appraisal to a single moral standard or bring them all under a single moral concept.

[2] Samuel F. Pickering, Jr., *John Locke and Children's Books in Eightteenth-Century England* (Knoxville: University of Tennessee Press, 1981), 15.

based on the premise that "first impressions" have an especially powerful influence on the mind and that proper habits of conduct are therefore to be inculcated in the early years. Furthermore, it was concluded, in order to instill the social virtues it is particularly important to wean children away from cruelty to animals, for cruelty to animals leads to a hardening of the heart which will later show itself in one's dealings with one's fellows. If the number of books devoted to the subject is a reflection of the pervasiveness and seriousness of the problem, one may fairly judge that cruelty to animals was, for the eighteenth-century English child, the moral – or perhaps immoral – equivalent of watching violence on television.

By the end of the eighteenth century a new and rather controversial note began to be introduced into the educational theory underlying this literary genre. It was not enough, it was said, to teach compassion to animals because of its character-building effects. To be sure, as one writer argued, "many of those brought to the scaffold for capital crimes" began their "progress in wickedness" as children who mistreated animals. What needed to be recognized, however, was that animals have rights, for the rights of animals like the rights of man are "deduced from the Light of Nature."[3] As another writer of animal books states, the time would soon come when men would "acknowledge the RIGHTS; instead of bestowing their COMPASSION upon the creatures, whom, with themselves, GOD made, and made to be happy!"[4]

The idea that animals have rights clearly was a minority position, and it met with sharp rejection. The most vigorous opponent seems to have been Mrs. Sarah Trimmer, perhaps the period's leading writer of children's books and also the leading Lockean educational theorist. The ascription of rights to animals, she held, was a confusion of the order of nature. Now the issue of animals' rights, itself, is not of interest to me here. What does interest me, rather, is the historical phenomenon of the emergence of a seemingly new moral claim and the attitude with which it was met. I say "seemingly" because the claim that animals have rights may well have been asserted before the end of the eighteenth century. Nevertheless, in that English context the claim provoked both anger and surprise. For the overwhelming majority of rights thinkers it was an entirely unanticipated claim.

The anger, I think, is easily understood. As indicated by one of the quotations I mentioned, the argument for animals' rights seems to have been this: Humans have rights because God made them to be happy; God made animals to be happy; therefore animals have rights. While this is a simplistic formulation it expresses the orthodox seventeenth and eighteenth centuries' view that rights have a theological underpinning, a view which, I believe, was

[3] Thomas Young, *An Essay on Humanity to Animals* (1798); cited in Pickering, 37.
[4] E. A. Kendall, *Keeper's Travels in Search of His Master* (1798); cited in Pickering, 38.

also held by Locke. The response to the argument, therefore, was along theological lines: the argument is mistaken because it overlooks the fact that God made animals for human use. Were the upholders of animals' rights seriously claiming that it is wrong to shear the wool of sheep?, that it is wrong to own animals? It certainly was readily agreed that it is *wrong* to torture animals and that men have a *duty* to be compassionate toward animals. But the assertion of animals' *rights* was perceived as carrying with it a definite danger, for it involves a "levelling" of man and beast, as Mrs. Trimmer wrote.[5] The ascription of rights to animals, therefore, could easily be seen as threatening the panoply of the natural rights of man; for instance, such rights as the right of property and those political liberties claimed as natural rights.

But why the surprise? The surprise was of course not occasioned by any unfamiliarity with the terminology in which the assertion of animals' rights was expressed: it was formulated in the familiar and accepted language of "rights." This situation should be compared with its mirror image, namely, the use of new moral terminology to express accepted and familiar claims. In this latter case it would appear that a kind of conceptual, and I think ultimately moral, reorientation is actually occurring and it is understandable that some surprise should ensue. But why in the former case?

Moral surprise is not an entirely unusual event. T. H. Green describes the case of the Greek slaveholder who becomes disabused of the Aristotelian doctrine of natural slavery when he enters into conversation with his slave on the basis of a common language.[6] By means of this special kind of interaction, prejudice and ignorance are broken down, and "moral progress," one might say, is achieved. Still, that the barbarian slave should come to be regarded as having a moral status equal to that of his Greek owner is something initially unanticipated.

The structure of the situation, however, is a familiar feature of moral and legal discourse. Certain normative qualities are ascribed to some person, action, thing, or circumstance on the basis of the possession of various properties. When it is shown that some other person, action, thing, or circumstance has these properties, it is then argued that it too has similar normative qualities. The conclusion, nevertheless, can be as surprising as it often is unwelcome. There is no doubt that the ascription of equality of moral status to the slave involves a considerable "reordering" of nature for the Greek as well as a revision of particular moral claims. Aside from the rejection of the doctrine of natural slavery, however, it is not clear how much of a shift is produced in the conceptual system of the accepted ethical theory.

[5] *Guardian of Education*, 1802, 1; cited in Pickering, 38.

[6] See T. H. Green, *Lectures on the Principles of Political Obligation* (New York: Longmans, Green and Co., 1941), sec. 140.

The surprise occasioned by the assertion of animals' rights is in a different case from the above. The novel ascription of rights to animals partly incorporated old moral prescriptions – that it is wrong to torture animals and that there is a duty of compassion to animals – in (by then) old moral language, but it must have gone beyond these prescriptions in some way. It was clear to the majority of eighteenth-century English rights thinkers that animals could not possibly have the rights that men have. And this was true independently of the theological claim that animals were made for human use. Despite the "territorialism" of animals, beasts cannot own property; they have no *animus domini*, intention to own, though they may have an intention to exclude others from their nests and dens. The extension of the terminology of rights to animals, it was feared, could have the effect of contracting its normative range – hence, the angry tone of the rejection.

But the surprise was partially the result of the received tradition of rights thinking and the particular concept of rights that it explicitly employed. The received tradition had left the eighteenth-century rights thinkers unprepared to consider whether there was a *kind* of right that animals would have, if they did have rights. In fact there was a more antique tradition of rights thinking that did recognize a different sort of right than the received conception, but it had slipped from ken. Although the eighteenth-century thinkers may ultimately have come to reject the proposition that animals do have this other sort of right, even if they had had this type of right in view, they might also have been led to consider whether there is any difference between saying, for instance, that it is wrong to torture animals or that there is a duty not to torture animals, on the one side, and saying that animals have a right not to be tortured, on the other: that is, the problem of the significance of rights language.

The natural rights tradition did, of course, assert that there are a variety of different rights that men have. In expounding what these rights are, the theorists probably were influenced by particular rights that were recognized in their own legal systems. Rights naturally fell into certain categories: for instance, the right to transfer property fell under the right to own property, from which the former was derived. Oftentimes the Latin terminology of jurisprudence was employed in expounding these rights, e.g., *ius in personam*, a term that, incidentally, was not used by the classical Roman jurists. Yet the received concept of what a right is, the explicitly acknowledged concept of rights, broadly took rights as being basically of one kind, namely, as *option* rights.[7]

Option rights correspond to spheres of individual sovereignty, as it were, in

[7] For the terminology of "option" and "welfare" rights see M. P. Golding, "Towards a Theory of Human Rights," *The Monist*, October 1968, 52(4), 521–49.

which the individual is morally free to act on the basis of his own choices. Depending on what the rights are, these spheres, and hence the rights, generally are conceived of as limited. Possession of an option right, furthermore, implies some kind of rightful control over the actions of others. Why anyone has option rights (if anyone has them), what these rights are, whether any of them are natural or human rights, what the limits of one's sphere of sovereignty are, are all questions of ethical theory. The concept of an option right of itself does not imply, for instance, that no one has the right to injure himself or others. It is a question of ethical theory whether or not this is the case.

The notion of option rights, as an explicitly recognized concept, was inherited by the natural rights theorists from the definition of "rights" given in the late middle ages and the Renaissance. These definitions do not express the oldest explicitly formulated conception of rights, but they were the ones which were influential. I have traced the development of these definitions elsewhere and shall not go into details here.[8] These definitions conceive a right in terms of *potestas*, power, or *facultas*, capacity or power, and they emphasize the "active" character of rights. The epitome of this tradition is a statement of Sir William Blackstone's in his *Commentaries on the Laws of England* (1765 et seq.):

> The absolute rights of man, considered as a free agent, endowed with discernment to know good from evil, and with the power of choosing those measures which appear to him most desirable, are usually summed up in one general appelation, and denominated the natural liberty of mankind (I, 125). . . . The rights themselves . . . will appear from what has been premised, to be no other, than that *residuum* of natural liberty, which is not required by the laws of society to be sacrificed to the public convenience; or else those civil privileges, which society has engaged to provide in lieu of the natural liberties so given up by individuals (I, 129).

From the phrases "power of choosing" and "residuum of natural liberty" and such phrases as "power of acting" and "free will" used in nearby places in the text, the historical roots of Blackstone's conception of rights are apparent, and this is an option-rights conception. It is also clear why it might be thought that beasts cannot have rights.

But option rights, arguably, are not the only kind of right: there also may be *welfare* rights. Welfare rights are entitlements to goods. They imply that the possessors of these goods have desires and/or interests, but the concept itself

[8] Martin P. Golding, "Justice and Rights: A Study in Relationship," in E. Shelp (ed.), *Justice and Health Care* (Dordrecht, Holland: D. Reidel, 1981), 23–36. See also the useful book by Richard Tuck, *Natural Rights Theories* (Cambridge: Cambridge University Press, 1979), and my review in *Political Theory*, February 1982, 10(1), 152–57.

does not entail that one has a right to everything one desires or that one has no right to what one does not desire. It is a substantive question of ethical theory whether or not one may relinquish or waive a welfare right, though of course one may refrain from claiming the object of such a right. Like an option right, possession of a welfare right implies some kind of rightful control over the actions of others. Questions of ethical theory parallel to those mentioned earlier arise here too: why anyone has welfare rights (if anyone has them), what these rights are, and so on.

Although any concrete right is likely to be a composite of welfare and option elements, the failure to distinguish between them can lead to moral confusion. It is claimed, for instance, that a woman has the moral right to abort the fetus she is carrying. Is this merely an option right, something she is morally free to do if she so chooses? If it is, it entails no claim to the provision of facilities or financial assistance to have an abortion, anymore than my right to drive a car implies a claim to be provided with gasoline. Clarification of the *kind* of right the alleged right to an abortion is, or of the elements of this alleged right, would be helpful in the present social context.

It is fairly plain, I think, that *if* animals have rights, these are welfare rights or something very much like them; and so, also, are the alleged rights that more recently have been claimed for trees and other natural objects. (I confess to being puzzled by the relative rights of the pine tree and the pine-tree beetle: which ones have precedence?) If the eighteenth-century rights thinkers had had welfare rights as clearly in view as option rights, they might not have been taken aback by the assertion of rights for animals, though they still may have rejected the claim. Their attention, however, was so fixated on option rights, partly because of the tradition they had received, that they overlooked the possibility of animals' rights as welfare rights. And this happened despite the fact that some of the rights recognized by many of these theorists could have been put into the welfare category. But the conception of a welfare right had failed to chrystalize for them.

The broad notion of welfare rights, in fact, is represented in an older tradition in the development of definitions of "rights." These other definitions are found primarily in the Glossators on Roman legal texts, which may partially explain why an explicitly recognized conception of welfare rights was lost until the nineteenth century, when it became clear that the claims that were being pressed in society as matters of alleged rights could not all be subsumed under an option-rights notion.

These older definitions[9] are interesting because they connect rights with justice; in fact they primarily occur in comments on the definition of "justice" given by Ulpian, a third-century Roman jurist, and contained in the first

[9] For a fuller discussion see my paper, "Justice and Rights."

sentence of Justinian's *Institutes*: "Justice is the constant and perpetual will of giving to each his own right (*ius suum*)." Placentinus expresses the prevailing twelfth-century view that rights flow from justice *tanquam ex fonte rivuli*, just like rivulets from a spring.[10] And *ius* is identified with *dignitas*, worth, or more often with *meritum*, desert or worth. This approach derives from Cicero, whose definition of "justice" is cited by Placentinus with approval: "Justice is that condition of the mind which, with the common utility being preserved, gives to each his own *dignitas*" (*De Inventione*, II, 53, 160).

I think it is no surprise that the oldest definitions of "rights" occur in legal texts. Although law and ethics contain a number of overlapping concepts, rights are the most legalistic of our moral notions because they cover the domain of *interpersonal claims* in a way that such notions as right, wrong, good, and evil do not. (The problematic notion is that of duty, which I shall discuss later.)

The fact that definitions of "a right" do not appear until the middle ages does not mean that the concept of rights was "discovered" or "invented" in that period. Nor does it mean that the term *ius* was not employed in option and welfare senses until it was defined in one or the other way. It is the case, rather, that the Roman jurists and moral philosophers did not take the trouble to define the rights-sense of *ius* because the concept did not have for them the systematic importance that it later attained in law and ethical theory. (The only definition in the classical sources is that of the jurist Celsus, in Justinian's *Digest*, 1.1, 1: "Ius is the art of the good and the equitable." But this is a definition of *ius* in the sense of "law" not in the sense of "a right.") It is important to recognize, I think, that much of what *we* would express in the terminology of rights was not expressed that way in the early sources. I want to illustrate this point and then remark on its theoretical significance.

The legal context can be illustrated by translations of the Bible. Genesis, chapter 23, tells the story of Abraham's purchase of a gravesite for Sarah, who had just died. "Give me," he says to the children of Ḥeth, "*aḥuzath* burying-place with you" (v. 44). Literally the Hebrew means "the possession of," which is adhered to in the Vetus Latina, *possessionem monumenti*. Jerome's fourth-century Vulgate, however, reads *ius sepulchri*, the right of a grave. This terminological development is reflective of a tendency in law – and I suspect in moral discourse, too – to move from relatively concrete concepts to more abstract ones, in this case from possession to a right. (Compare, also: mine and thine, property, the right of property, and property in rights.)

This tendency is present, for example, in Jewish law. The classical texts of the third through the sixth centuries hardly seem to know the abstract concept

[10] Cited in H. Kantorowicz, *Studies in the Glossators of the Roman Law* (Darmstadt, Germany: Scientia Verlag Aalen, 1969), 10.

of a right, while the mediaeval and especially the later sources employ it more freely. Interestingly, the notion first begins to turn up in Franco-German eleventh-century juristic rabbinic sources as something close to an option-right idea: the term is *koaḥ*, the equivalent of *potestas* (power).[11] It is nearly astounding, though, that the later term for a right, *zekhuth*, means "merit" in classical rabbinic Hebrew.

To revert back to my Biblical illustration, I find it fascinating that the sixteenth-century Spanish philosopher, Francisco Suarez, explains that Jerome's *ius sepulchri* means *facultas sepliendi*, the capacity or power of burying.[12] Thus, Jerome first reads "a right" into the Biblical text and Suarez then reads this expression in terms of his own "active," option-rights conception. This "reading in" is something we all do; sometimes it is quite harmless, but sometimes it can be misleading – especially in the case of "rights," if the terminology of rights has special significance.

An old illustration of this phenomenon (interpreting a source that lacks an explicit concept of rights in terms of a rights notion) is Socrates' situation in the *Crito*. Socrates wants to know whether it is just or unjust, right or wrong, to escape his sentence. We easily translate his question into rights terminology: Does he have the right to escape his sentence? When we do this we are going from an "objective" notion of rightness to a "subjective" notion of rights possessed by individuals, to use the nomenclature of continental jurisprudence. I do not particularly care for this terminology, but I think it hints at a very fundamental distinction and helps in identifying the domain of morality to which rights are unique – if there is such a domain. I shall return to this issue shortly.

The word "right" has a dual use and, therefore, an ambiguity that can bedevil the ethical theorist. A similar duality is had by the Latin word *ius*. While Roman legal texts generally employ the word in an objective sense (in which *ius* means "the law" or "the right") they also employ it in the sene of "a right" that someone has, though less frequently so in the earlier sources. The Roman moral philosophers, on the other hand, very rarely use the term in a subjective or personal sense. The outstanding example is Cicero's important work – it is said to have influenced Kant – *De Officiis*, concerning duties, which is based upon Stoic sources. The term *ius* occurs well over 100 times in this book, and in at most a few cases is it ever used to refer to "a right" rather than "the right."

One of these cases is instructive. Cicero states that only the Stoics, Academicians, and Peripatetics have anything to teach us about duty. Certain

[11] See, e.g., Rashi's comment on *Makkoth*, 3a, s.v., *kaytzad shamin* (in standard editions of the Babylonian Talmud).

[12] Francisco Suarez, *De Legibus* (Madrid: Consejo Superior de Investigaciones, 1971), 24.

skeptical philosophers, on the other hand, would "have the right" (*tamen haberunt ius suum*) to discuss duty if they had left us any power of choosing between things, so that there might be a way of finding out what duty is (I, 6). This reference to a right sounds very much like what Professor Alan Gewirth calls an "intellectual right," but I do not think that this really is the case. Until I read Professor Gerwith, I confess, I had never heard the expression "intellectual right."[13] I like the term, but it seems to me to be an entirely unnecessary addition to our language. Whether or not a particular conclusion follows from given premises is a matter of objective standards of reasoning, and there is no need whatever to speak of someone's "having the right" to draw some inference. On the other hand, it is a matter of moral right, and not any so-called intellectual right, whether or not someone has the right to express the conclusion to others, or whether others have the right to prevent him from expressing it. The notion of an intellectual right is parasitic on the idea of "what is right."

In the last analysis this proposition may also be true of moral, natural, or human rights. The problem of the significance of rights language would thereby be compounded. Still, it may be possible to locate the domain of morality proper to rights. My earlier illustrations, from a legal and a moral context, of the importation of rights into sources in which they do not initially appear raise the question of the indispensability or dispensability of rights-discourse. The emergence of the terminology of rights in the law seems to be virtually inevitable because of the law's concern with interpersonal claims. This fact provides an important clue to the nature of rights language generally.

Before proceeding with this point, I want to go back to our eighteenth-century English friends and animals' rights. I earlier maintained that the surprise with which the assertion of animals' rights was met was partially due to the negelect or unawareness of the possibility of welfare rights. Another factor, I think, was the belief that other moral notions than that of a right are quite adequate to govern man's behavior toward animals. This circumstance is exemplified in Samuel Pufendorf's *De Iure Naturae et Gentium* (*Of the Law of Nature and Nations*, 1672, expanded edition 1674). This large tome, written by a seventeenth-century writer born in Saxony, was published in English translation in 1710, and was a great success. (It had been available earlier in a French translation.) Before Pufendorf gets to a treatment of rights, he has extensive discussions of man's duties, to himself and to others. Of particular interest is his expression of grave doubts on whether the killing of animals is permitted. He concludes that the killing and use of animals is allowed, but he says that it nevertheless is beyond dispute "that the Abuse of this Power, and especially such as is attended with foolish Cruelty and Barbarity, deserves to

[13] Alan Gewirth, *Reason and Morality* (Chicago: University of Chicago Press, 1978), 69f.

come under Censure" (IV, iii, 6).[14] The English rejectors of animals' rights fully agree with this statement. The fact that they also agree that such abuse of animals also "tends to the prejudice of men" (i.e., has detrimental effects on character) as Barbeyrac, the French translator, notes, does not at all derogate from the separate wrongfulness of mistreating animals.

Putting aside the case of animals and focusing instead on the moral relations of human beings, I think it is noteworthy that such an important natural rights theorist as Pufendorf was able to write a book on ethics in which the notion of rights plays a very subsidiary role. I refer here to his 1673 book *De Officio Hominis et Civis* (*On the Duty of Man and Citizen*), the French translation of which appeared in many editions from 1707 on. Topics in which one might expect "rights" to be the key term are instead expounded in terms of "duty." For example, Pufendorf talks about the duties attendant upon the ownership of property rather than about the rights of ownership. (I suspect that the title of the French *Declaration of the Rights of Man and Citizen* was deliberately chosen in opposition to Pufendorf's title.)

I think it is clear that moral discourse can go quite a distance without employing the quasi-legal conception of rights. This also is evidenced by the great ethical systems of the ancient world in which the notion hardly appears, though I should concede that it sometimes is lurking below the surface. It is plain, at any rate, that these antique systems are conceptually very far from any kind of "rights-based" morality and that their transmutation into such a morality would have constituted an ideological shift of a radical sort. To the extent that these sytems did employ a notion of rights, which was almost not at all, they tended to cash it out in terms of such "objective" ethical notions as "the just," "the right," and "the good." (A good example is Cicero's *De Officiis.*) It cannot be denied that it is only with the coming of the middle ages, and in fact more towards the end of that period, that we find the upsurge of rights thinking and a tendency to displace other ethical concepts by that of rights. This upsurge, I believe, is partly due to the infusion of legal ideas into ethics and political philosophy and partly due to the concomitant rise of individualism and the nation-state. Still, even though the ancients managed quite well without the concept or terminology of rights, one is justified in wondering whether they thereby also left part of the domain of morality fallow.

If we focus attention on the idea of duty I think a bit of progress can be made toward understanding the nature of this domain and the significance of rights language. Let us put aside so-called duties to oneself and begin with duties to (or of) humanity, as they were termed. These duties obviously are other-regarding; or to put it a bit differently, they govern conduct that is other-

[14] Samuel Pufendorf, *Of the Law of Nature and Nations* (London: 3rd edition, 1717), trans. by Basil Kennet, with the notes of J. Barbeyrac, Bk. IV, 144.

affecting. Of course, this is also true of other moral concepts. For instance, it would be unjust or wrong for Socrates to escape his sentence, and the wrong committed would be a wrong *to* the *polis*. But it is quite impossible, here, to go through the gamut of other-affecting applications of our moral notions. The focus on duty is sufficient and also the most germane.

Now, it is important to recognize that there can be other-affecting duties that are *not* correspondent to a right held by the affected party, that is, the beneficiary of the duty. "Duties of humanity" is an apt description of them. Since I want to use it to make a point, I offer the following as an example. According to Jewish law, an individual is duty-bound (*ḥayyav*) to rescue someone in danger of loss of life, if there is no substantial risk to his own.[15] This is a *personal duty* of the would-be rescuer's, and there is no suggestion that the would-be victim has a right to be rescued. This duty should be compared with another one that the individual has, namely, the duty to rescue someone's possessions that are in danger of being lost (e.g., by being swept away by a river), if there is no danger to oneself. In this case, the owner may waive the rescue of his possessions, and thereby absolve the would-be rescuer of the duty. The case, therefore, has a feature often associated with one's having a right, namely, the power to waive it if one so chooses. (Compare, however, "inalienable rights.") And it would not be misleading to say that the owner has a right to the rescue of his possessions were it not for the fact that the emphasis would be misplaced: the duty is still conceived of as a personal duty. (In the former case, the duty of rescue cannot be waived. There is a duty to let oneself be rescued, so to speak).

It appears that an other-affecting personal duty, a duty that is not rights-related, is possible insofar as such a duty is imposed by law or is a *naturalis obligatio*, a natural duty imposed by morality or "objective right." Other-affecting duties, however, have no application in a universe inhabited only by a single, isolated person. On the other hand, the *concept* of a personal duty, itself, is perfectly intelligible for such a universe, and could have applications as long as deliberate activity were possible therein. A single person could have duties in respect of himself. (Such a being may only be able to engage in mental acts. I suppose it could then have the duty to think "clear" or "clean" thoughts.)

Personal duties, of whatever kind, might not exhaust the domain of dutiful conduct, however. They would not exhaust it if there were duties that had as their *ground* the rights of the recipients or beneficiaries of the dutiful conduct. If we choose to speak in the modern way and talk of other-regarding personal duties as being correlated with the rights of other parties, we should be clear that these rights are *normatively subsequent* to the duties; while in the case of the

[15] For an extensive treatment see Aaron Kirschenbaum, "The 'Good Samaritan' and Jewish Law," *Diné Israel*, 1976, 7, 7–86.

other other-affecting duties, the duties are normatively subsequent to the *rights*. In more general terms, the distinction between personal duties and rights-related duties turns on the way each type is justified.

It is just this area of rights-related duties which was given short shrift in ethical theory until the emergence of an explicitly defined notion of a right. Until that time the tendency was to conceive of duties in personal terms and to subordinate them to "objective" notions. The best example of this is Stoicism, as presented in Cicero's *De Officiis*. The general tendency, as I argued earlier, was to bypass the language of rights at large. Even in the law, where the use of the language of rights and duties would be natural, the opportunity to employ it was often passed up. Thus, in Roman law "obligation" (*obligatio*) is defined as "a tie of law which binds us according to the rules of our civil law to render something" and it arises, as Gaius says, through consent or commission of injury (*Institutes*, III, 88). The use of the langauge of correlated rights and duties would be natural here, but "obligation" is taken as designating the parties' situation as a whole and as arising through law.

Of course, rights-related duties, duties that are grounded on the rights of others, lurk below the surface of the classical theories. Aristotle's idea of the virtue of particular justice, which concerns fairness in one's dealings with others, comes very close to the concept, though it is not explicitly construed as deriving from a right of others to a given share or a given conduct. Yet it seems more than an accident that Aristotle's discussion of distributive justice probably was the *urtext* of the earliest explicit definitions of *ius*, which were given in terms of *dignitas* and *meritum* (worth and desert). These definitions derive from Cicero, whose own definition of "justice" as giving to each his *dignitas* stems from Aristotle's principle of "each according to his *axion*" (worth or merit). As I noted, these early definitions are close to a welfare notion of rights – a suggestive if not a theoretically determinative fact.

The distinction between personal duties and rights-related duties, as I said, turns on the way in which each type is justified. In trying to spell out the difference, it is important to keep in mind that the concept of a personal duty has sense for a universe of a single, isolated individual (though there may not actually be any duties in such a world), while the concept of rights-related duties has no sense for such a universe – and neither does the concept of rights. The question of whether or not Robinson Crusoe has rights does not arise before the arrival of Friday. It would be completely idle to speak of Robinson's rights, and *a fortiori* of his rights "against the world" (assuming that the actions of those who have no contact with him have no affect on him). The concept of rights is inherently interpersonal; it presupposes claimers and claimants. These considerations have important theoretical consequences.

First of all, rights, and rights-related duties, can arise only in a social context, and that context may even have to be of a fairly specific sort, which is a subject I cannot go into here. In asserting the necessity of a social context, I perhaps am prejudicing the question of animals' rights, because humans and animals hardly stand in the same "social" relations that humans can toward each other. (In older language, there is no "common right" between humans and animals.)[16] This thought, I believe, underlies the occasional statement in the classical natural rights literature that humans have no rights *against* things or animals; our rights *in* things or animals are rights against other humans. It is clear, in any case, that if the case for rights as between humans cannot be made, we will never succeed in establishing animals' rights against humans, and I think that the necessity of a social context of some sort is an element of this case.

For this reason I would take exception to Professor Alan Gewirth's attempt to derive rights from the generic features of action, if I understand it correctly. Consider the situation of Robinson Crusoe before the arrival of Friday. Robinson of course acts, and I am willing to grant that freedom and well-being are necessary conditions of his action: they are necessary goods for Crusoe, to use Gewirth's terminology. Still, it cannot be maintained that Robinson either has or does not have rights to freedom and well-being, for the question does not arise. The "dialectically necessary method" whereby Gewirth argues that a prudent, self-interested agent *must* claim rights[17] has no foothold in the situation of Robinson Crusoe. It may be true that the "necessary content of morality is to be found in action and its generic features,"[18] but rights cannot be derived from the generic features of action alone. Once Friday arrives the situation changes and Robinson now *can* claim rights, and perhaps he also must claim them. I think, in any case, that the more important issue is why Friday should concede any rights to Robinson.

The inherently interpersonal character of rights is a clue to the significance that rights language has as a minimum, namely, that rights language exists as a device for making claims and demands against others. (The fact, however, that people *make* claims doesn't mean that they *have* claims.)[19] This is a feature that moral rights language shares with legal rights language. The quasi-legal character of moral rights explains, I think, why some writers have thought that rights belong to that part of morality which can be physically enforced. Although I am not sure that one may not be rightfully compelled to perform one's other-affecting personal duties, I think it plain that one's possession of a right, whether welfare or option, does imply some kind of legitimate control

[16] See, e.g., St. Augustine, *The Catholic and Manichaean Ways of Life* (Washington: Catholic University of America Press, 1966), trans. by D. A. and I. J. Gallagher, Ch. 17, 102. This translation reads "common rights," but see the original in J. P. Migne (ed.), *Patrologiae Latinae* (Paris: 1844–), v. 32, 1368.

[17] *Reason and Morality*, 42–47.

[18] *Ibid.*, 25.

[19] See my paper "Towards a Theory of Human Rights," cited above, n. 7.

over others. So, while someone's having a duty does not necessarily entail that anyone else has a right, having a right does entail that someone else has a duty, the special kind of duty I have called "rights-related." Unless this were the case it is hard to see what special function would be served by the introduction of the terminology of rights into moral discourse. Admittedly, welfare rights pose a problem in this connection, for it is not always clear on whom it is incumbent to fulfill a welfare-rights claim. Perhaps, though, welfare rights impose some sort of duty on everyone.

In any case, the archetypical option right, the Hobbesian-Seldenian "right of nature," a right that passes no obligation,[20] is a phony right. The proposition that men have rights but do not stand in moral relations to each other (as in the "natural condition of mankind") undercuts the use of rights language. It is only by equivocating on the term "a right" that Hobbes is able to move his argument forward. The objection to Hobbes is well-stated by Pufendorf:

> . . . not every Natural License, or Power of doing a Thing, is properly a *Right*; but such only as includes some Moral Effect, with regard to others, who are Partners with me in the same Nature. . . . For 'tis ridiculous Trifling to call that Power a *Right*, which should we attempt to exercise, all other Men have an *equal Right* to obstruct or prevent us.[21]

Once we move from the situation of the isolated individual to that of human beings (or beings like humans in certain significant respects) in social interrelationship the question of rights becomes meaningful. At this point it becomes possible to assert and to deny that men have various specific rights and also to deny that they have any rights at all. At this point we can ask, Why should Friday concede to Robinson any of the rights the latter happens to claim? Why should he not, instead, deny these claims and even deny that Robinson has any rights at all?

Caution is required in approaching these questions. For there are at least two different respects in which rights claims can be conceded and two different ways in which a rights claim can be denied.

First of all, a rights claim can be conceded without its being acknowledged as a claim of right. It may, for instance, merely be *acceded to*. Friday thus may have good prudential reasons for acceding to Robinson's rights claims as claims or demands while not admitting them as rights claims. If Robinson and Friday each need and desire the cooperation of the other in order to achieve his own ends, they might enter into trade-offs that would be advantageous to each, these trade-offs being dependent upon imaginable variations in their respective circumstances. But, again, the bargained concessions need not be

[20] See the book by Richard Tuck (cited above, no. 8), at 111.
[21] *Of the Law of Nature and Nations*, III, 5, 3; in Kennet trans., Bk. III, 48.

acknowledgements of moral rights. In addition, a claim can be conceded as a matter of *grace*. David Hume speculates[22] that we would not be under restraints of justice to creatures who are very much weaker than we are, "nor could they possess any right," but I suppose that we could be gracious towards them. It is partly to forestall this possibility that Hobbes postulates a natural equality of strength among men in the construction of his rights theory. (In the legendary Wild West, the equivalent of the Hobbesian state of nature, the Smith and Wesson .44 was called the "Equalizer.") And in more orthodox constructions of rights theories an equality of moral status is postulated in order to forestall the merely gracious accession to a rights claim. This postulate, again, would prejudice the case of animals' rights. I probably should own up to the fact that I don't think that animals and other natural things, and also artificial things like buildings and art objects, have rights.[23] But I am not certain that the postulate of moral equality is required for a rights theory. Finally, of course, a rights claim can be conceded because it is acknowledged *as such*. Whether this occurs depends upon the special kind of reason for the concession, which I shall take up shortly.

A rights claim can be denied in two ways: in a *weak* way and in a *strong* way. Denial, as I conceive it, is a combined pragmatic-semantical notion. The weak denial of a proposition merely says that the proposition is *not true*, and it does not commit the denier to the assertion of some counter-claim. The strong denial of a proposition, on the other hand, does so commit him. This distinction, I believe, is important in the area of normative discourse, in which the notion of commitment plays a role, in the sense of what a person is committed to as a result of accepting or denying various claims. Thus, the weak denial of a proposition of the form

(R) *A* has a right to interfere with *B*'s liberty

merely states that (R) is not true. The weak denial of (R) does not entail (does not commit one to) the counter-claim

(S) *B* has a right not to be interfered with by *A*

or the counter-claim

(T) *A* has a (rights-related) duty of non-interference toward *B*.

I take it that the moral skeptic, who denies that there are any rights and duties at all, is prepared to deny all three of these propositions; that is, he weakly

[22] David Hume, *An Inquiry Concerning the Principles of Morals* (New York: Library of Liberal Arts, 1957), 21 (Sec. III, Pt. 1).

[23] See M. P. and N. H. Golding, "Why Preserve Landmarks? A Preliminary Inquiry," in K. E. Goodpaster and K. M. Sayre (eds.), *Ethics and Problems of the 21st Century* (Notre Dame, Ind.: University of Notre Dame Press, 1979), 175–90.

denies them; he declares that none of them is true. The strong denial of a normative proposition, however, does entail (does commit one to) the assertion of a counter-claim. Thus, the strong denial of (R) entails (S) and (T).

If we now ask why Friday should concede any of Robinson's rights claims (or vice versa) or why he should not deny any of these claims (or vice versa), our concern must be with concession *as* a rights claim and with denial in the strong sense. Anything less will not take us fully into the realm of moral discourse and would leave us unprovided with a basis for moral rights. The focus of our attention, nevertheless, must be on the question of why a rights claim should be conceded as such, for this is the more fundamental issue.

Now, it is important here to keep in mind the distinction mentioned earlier between personal duties and rights-related duties. For it might be maintained that Friday should concede a rights claim of Robinson's because Friday accepts some personal duty-proposition that commits him to conceding some rights-proposition. This may very well be the case in the last analysis. But if it is the case, we should probably have to admit that the terminology of rights has no special significance and does not mark out a particular domain of moral conduct. Secondly, I do not think it adequate to say that Friday should concede a rights claim of Robinson's because Friday makes rights claims against the latter. This conventional and generally proper move in moral argument is inadequate because Friday might not make any rights claims; he may merely make claims and demands that he expects or hopes will be acceded to for any of a number of reasons, and he may deny Robinson's rights claims in the weak sense of the term. This assertion is contrary to Professor Gewirth's thesis that rationally self-interested individuals must make rights claims, against which thesis I have expressed objections elsewhere.[24] In any case, underlying our initial question is the further question, Why rights at all?, Why isn't the rest of our moral language enough?

In order to answer the question of why Friday should concede Robinson's rights claim as a rights claim, I think it is useful to consider how he might come to so conceding it. In order to grasp this process, we must be careful not to confuse it with any of the other ways in which a rights claim purportedly can be accepted.

It seems to me that there just is one way in which this concession can come about (aside from its being entailed by another rights claim which he concedes), a way that has two analytically separable steps. The first step consists of the recognition that the object claimed by the other as a matter of right is an

[24] Martin P. Golding, "From Prudence to Rights: A Critique," in J. R. Pennock and J. W. Chapman (eds.), *Human Rights*, NOMOS XXIII (New York: New York University Press, 1981), 165–74. I have not succeeded in convincing Professor Gewirth of the error of his ways. See his reply in *idem, Ethics, Economics, and the Law*, NOMOS XXIV (New York: New York University Press, 1982), 178–88.

element of, or a means to, the other's *personal good*. The second step consists of the acknowledgement that this good is genuinely *a good*, that is, the good-of-Robinson's is a good-to-Friday. By this I, of course, do not mean that it is good for Friday to acknowledge Robinson's personal good or that Robinson's good is something that Friday necessarily has a stake in.

It is the combination of these two steps which provides the clue to the special kind of justification that marks off the domain of rights-related duties from other other-affecting duties. The ground of Friday's duty is located in Robinson's personal good that is also taken to be a genuine good. This, however, is not to say that Robinson's personal good is a genuine good because it is his personal good. For Friday can be as mistaken in the second step as he can be in recognizing that the claimed object is an element in, or a means to, Robinson's personal good. Nevertheless, having taken these two steps Friday has committed himself to conceding Robinson's rights claim as such. These steps mark out the domain of "subjective right."

Admittedly, the above account, which for purposes of the present exposition has had to focus upon a simple, two-person situation, is a highly abbreviated description of the process that is uniquely involved in the concession of rights claims. (The account also can explain what is meant in saying that someone "implicitly" has a concept of rights even though rights language is not available to him.) Much remains to be filled in. In particular, further clarification is needed regarding the idea of a personal good. The important point, however, is the centrality of this idea in the concession, as such, of rights claims.

Strictly speaking, taking the described steps commits one only to conceding a *presumptive* right to the claimed objects. Much more is required before it can be maintained that the other party *has* an unqualified right to those objects. Plainly, an object claimed by one person as a matter of right might also be claimed by another person, so these conflicting claims will have to be arbitrated in some way. There is, in fact, a long list of items that need to be established before it can be maintained that anyone has rights. Most of these items are the traditional matter of ethical theory. The above steps provide a clue as to the starting point of the inquiry. They are only the beginning of wisdom on the subject. And much filling in needs to be done to take care of rights against the government, so-called group rights, and so on. (I am not announcing any of this as if it were news.)

One thing nevertheless can be said. If there are any rights at all, there are welfare rights. This assertion, I think, follows from the location of the ground of rights in a personal good that also is a genuine good. Furthermore, it follows, I think, that the notion of welfare rights has a theoretical primacy, conceptually and normatively, over option rights. I have no doubt that liberty is an element in, and a means to, a human being's personal good. So, if there are any human rights at all, there are also option rights. Still, I see no reason whatsoever for respecting liberty as such, or for conceding option rights as such, that is, as something separate from an individual's personal good. (Of course, there can be prudential reasons and reasons of political or social expediency for respecting individual liberty.) The primary notion that underlies any theory of rights is that of welfare. I do not think that this idea is very far from those early definitions of "rights" given in terms of *dignitas* and *meritum*. Welfare rights, therefore, also appear to have historical priority.

I realize I have not said anything at all about the content of rights, if there are any rights. This issue, however, was not the subject of my paper. It is my strong suspicion, if I may say so, that many currently asserted rights claims, both welfare and option, are at best presumptive rights.

This paper has proceeded on the assumption that the language of rights has a special significance within moral discourse and marks out a special domain of morality. This assumption may be false, and perhaps we do not require the terminology of rights in order to say all we need to about our moral relations. It could be argued that there is a personal duty to promote the personal good of another if it is a geniune good, so that the need for the language of rights is obviated. We can weakly deny rights claims without being moral skeptics. But I rather doubt that I should give up claiming rights for myself.

There is a story told about John Dewey. Dewey was an ardent supporter of women's suffrage. He went to participate in a suffragist parade, picked up a sign, and marched along. Everytime he passed a group of men, he noticed that they would break out in howls of laughter, and this became quite embarrassing. When he put down the sign at the end of the parade, he saw the reason for the laughter. The sign read: "If men can vote, why can't I?" If other people claim rights, why shouldn't I?

Philosophy and Law, Duke University

WILLIAM AIKEN

Aiken maintains that persons have a moral right to be saved from starvation, which is derived from the general right—the right to be saved from preventable death due to deprivation. Recognition of this right, he claims, would substantially alter the moral debate on world hunger.

1. *He suggests that the normative mode of reference to rights is more fundamental than the descriptive mode. Is this true?*

2. *How strong is this right? Does it ever override other moral or legal rights?*

3. *What changes in our normal beliefs would recognition of such a right entail?*

4. *Should we recognize this right in a world already overcrowded?*

William Aiken teaches philosophy at Chatham College. He recently completed his doctoral dissertation, "Starvation, Morality, and the Right to Be Saved."

The Right to Be Saved from Starvation

I

Human beings who have the same needs, fears, pains, and wants as you and I are starving to death. The advocates of triage, the Neo-Malthusians, and the lifeboat "ethicists" seem to forget this obvious fact. Those "hopeless masses" of the Hungry World are just individual persons who are hungry, sick, and dying. They need help. Through no fault of their own they cannot get enough to eat. They can do nothing but ask for help from

This article has not been previously published.

persons of the Affluent World. And if they do ask for help, are they merely begging for charity? Are they merely pleading for us to be benevolent? Are they merely crying out for some merciful supererogatory crumbs from our overabundant tables?

The belief that a person in dire need has no stronger claim against those who can help him or her than a plea for benevolence (which is no real claim at all) is unacceptable. Dire need creates obligations and rights. Starving persons have a moral right against those who are in a position to help them. Their suffering is not simply a harmful by-product of a morally permissible omission on the part of others. It is a *wrong* committed against them. It is a violation of their moral right. It is a reprehensible neglect of moral duty.

The right to be saved from starvation is derived from the more general moral right, the right to be saved from preventable death due to deprivation. This general right is based on human need. A person involuntarily undergoing extreme deprivation which would lead to his or her death has a moral right to the goods and services required to prevent that death. The sufferer has this right against any and all who are in a position to provide the necessary goods and services, since the sufferer's need puts them under an obligation to prevent his death.

II

No doubt many readers will find the above assertions controversial. It will be argued that moral rights result from promises or from special roles and relationships—not from human need alone. In fact, some will argue that a 'need right' is either a misuse of the term 'right' or, if not a misuse, then a frustratingly vague use which can only muddy the waters of good clear analysis. In section III, I will show that a need right as a moral right is not problematic. I will show this by making it clear exactly what is and what is not being said when a need right is claimed as a moral right.

Other critics of need rights will argue that any formulation of a proposed need right is doomed to failure because of inherent vagueness; that careful specification of conditions of ascription and the determination of stringency are impossible. However, basing a moral right on the criterion of need does not necessarily condemn us to wishy-washy generalizations which are impractical, inflexible, and inapplicable. The problem which has arisen with the lack of specificity is not due to the nature of need rights, but to the lack of careful analysis of this type of right by moral philosophers. In section IV, I will discuss the relevant considerations involved in specifying one type of need right, the right to be saved from preventable death due to deprivation.

Finally, some critics may object that the ascription of the right to be saved[1] to dying persons will not benefit them. It would be maintained by these critics that even if we ascribe such a right, we still would not know what to do about deprivation situations like world hunger. Why, they would ask, confound the moral issue with talk of nonenforced "moral" rights—why not simply concentrate on what we ought to do? In section V, I will address this criticism and argue that talk of rights is significant for moral deliberation (and ultimately personal action) on deprivation situations.

III

According to some critics, to say there is a right to be saved from preventable death due to deprivation is to misunderstand the meaning of the term 'right.' A right, it would be maintained, involves public rules, prescriptive institutions, and enforcement procedures with specified sanctions. The paradigm use of the term 'right' is in the expression 'legal right' in which a power, immunity, liberty, or privilege is specified under a valid legal rule and enforced by legal sanctions. This paradigmatic use of rights talk functions solely from within the descriptive mode; it speaks of those rights which *are* ascribed by rules. Any moral rights there might be must conform to this paradigm; that is, A has a right to x only if public rules ascribe x to A and enforce A's right to x. For example, the right a child has to loving support from his parents is a right generally acknowledged by popular moral rules and enforced by public opinion. Since the right to be saved is not ascribed and protected by law or popular moral rules, then it would not be a right at all.

Often claims of right are made which are not rights actually ascribed or protected by public rules. For example, the right to have an abortion was claimed before this right was recognized by either popular moral rules or legal rules. Currently, the right to privacy, the right to adequate health care, and the right to death with dignity are all being claimed independently of the actual public rules. There are four ways to account for this apparent nondescriptive mode of reference to rights.

The first way is just to say that this is a misuse of the term 'right.' A second way is to label claimed rights mere 'claims of right' which are *not* rights until so designated by public rules. They are possible candidates for rights but they are not rights; for example, the right to privacy is really only a possible candidate for the right to privacy. If a law is passed which ascribes and protects a candidate for right, then it will become a legal right.

[1]The elliptical expression, 'the right to be saved', will be used interchangeably with the expression, 'the right to be saved from preventable death due to deprivation'.

It may also become a moral right (in the sense of being ascribed and protected by a popular moral rule), but this process is more complicated. It is mysterious how mores, morals, and popular moral opinions which ascribe some claims as moral rights (but exclude many others) become accepted as moral rules in the first place; but it is even more mysterious (even baffling) to try to explain how newly proposed candidates for rights would become ascribed and protected by these popular rules. Does it just happen? Is an expensive advertising campaign the most effective way to transform a candidate for a right into a right? But how they become ascribed is not important to this account. All that matters is that claims of moral right are not rights until they are ascribed and protected by public rules.

A third way to account for the apparent nondescriptive modes of referring to rights is to argue that the appearance is often illusory. Some claims of right (though not all) which are not ascribed by human rules (legal or moral) are ascribed by Natural or Divine Law. These rights, Natural Rights, are enforced by Nature, Providence, or eschatological rewards and punishments. So at least some of the claims of right which appear not to be ascribed and protected by rules are, in fact, ascribed and protected by some 'higher law.'

There is a fourth way to account for these claims of right and that is to say that they are *not* rights in the descriptive mode of reference, but they *are*, nonetheless, rights in another mode—the normative mode. The normative mode refers to rights which ought to be protected by public rules, conditions permitting. The human rights listed in the United Nations Declaration of Rights are rights in this normative sense.[2] Rights which are ascribed by public rules may or may not be rights in the normative sense. The right of a slave owner to dispose of his 'human property' at will is not, in my opinion, a right which ought to be protected by public rules; rights like the right to adequate health care are. This fourth way to account for these references to rights does not, like the other three, relegate all legitimate talk of rights to the descriptive mode. The right to be saved from preventable death due to deprivation (like the right to death with dignity) is a moral right in this normative sense and not in the popular morality sense.

In an important way the normative mode of reference to rights is more fundamental than the descriptive mode. Founding Fathers, reformers, judges, and even legislators (to some extent) must consider which claims of right *ought* to be protected by public rules and which rights presently protected by rules *ought not* to be so protected (e.g., should the right to own handguns or the right to unlimited procreation be removed from the list

[2]UNESCO, *Human Rights* (Westport, Conn.: Greenwood Press, 1973) pp. 273–80.

of rule-protected legal rights?). Positive law and popular moral rules need not be interpreted anew, criticized, or changed. But when they are and when the interpreter, criticizer, or changer appeals to what ought to be the case regarding rights—then the normative mode is being used to make judgments about rights in the descriptive mode. The normative mode must be used to determine which rights we should protect by rules.

Determining which claims of right ought (morally) to be protected by rules is difficult. Not every claim of right is a claim that can be morally justified (e.g., I have a right to rule the world). To determine if a claim is a justified one we must appeal to moral principles. If a binding moral principle justifies my claim to x, then I have a moral right to x (in the normative sense) which ought to be protected by rules. Once this right is protected by rules, I have a right to x in the descriptive sense. Naturally, persons differ as to which moral principles are binding: are Liberty principles, Equality principles, Benevolent principles? Thus, they will differ as to which claims are morally justified and so which moral rights persons have.

In the normative mode all claims of right (both those presently protected by public rules and those not protected) are on an equal footing. All claims of right are justified by appeal to moral principles. The claim of right is only as strong as its justifying principle. Many of our legal and popular moral rights are based on the negative *in rem* right (a general right of noninterference) to liberty which is justified by appeal to a moral principle that promotes maximal individual liberty for all. The right to be saved (which is not presently protected by rules) is a positive *in rem* right (a general right of entitlement *to* certain goods) which is justified by appeal to a moral principle that promotes maximal individual welfare for all. Since life (which the right to be saved is designed to preserve) is required for the exercise of the right to liberty, I would place priority upon the welfare principle over the liberty principle, making it, in many cases, the binding principle when the resultant rights come into conflict. But this need not be maintained in order to argue that some welfare rights ought to be protected. As long as both principles are understood to be good ones, then rights based on liberty (like the right to privacy) and rights based on welfare (like the right to adequate health care) ought to be enforced by public rules (either popular moral or, in some cases, even legal rules).

I have shown that the right to be saved from preventable death due to deprivation (a need right) is a moral right—albeit, in the normative, not descriptive, mode of reference. Speaking of rights in the normative mode does not result in a misuse of the term 'right,' nor does it result in a misunderstanding of the concept of right. It is different from the paradigmatic use (in the descriptive mode) but it is, nonetheless, a proper one. In fact, it appears to be more fundamental.

IV

It is not uncommon for persons who assert that there are human rights which are based on need alone to avoid specificity or careful discussion of these rights. It is as if they would have us just "look at that mother's face" or just "listen to that child's cry" and we would know (intuit? grasp? infer? feel?) that needy persons do have a right to our assistance. Critics are correct to level the charge of vagueness at these assertions. They would ask a list of questions: How are needs distinguished from wants and wishes? How needy does one have to be in order to have such a right? Who, if anyone, is this right correctly claimed against? Why should your need obligate me—I didn't put you in that condition? How is this right balanced against other rights—like my right to control my property?

Even to maintain that the right to be saved from preventable death due to deprivation is a plausible candidate for a moral right which ought to be protected by rules, the typical vagueness surrounding rights based on need must be avoided. In this section, I will demonstrate the manner in which such a right can be specified. I do not intend for this to be a complete specification, but at least it should show that vagueness is not inherent in claims of right based on need.[3]

The right to be saved from preventable death due to deprivation can be justifiably claimed by or on behalf of any individual in a condition of extreme deprivation such that without assistance from others that individual will die as a result of the deprivation.[4] Pure cases of death due to deprivation are rare because in typical cases, like starvation, the sufferer is gradually weakened by the deprivation and eventually dies from a deprivation-related disease (pneumonia, dysentery, etc.). However, if the deprivation is the *dominant factor* leading to the sufferer's death, then the sufferer may claim relief from this deprivation as a moral right.

The right to be saved from preventable death due to deprivation differs from other rights based on need (e.g., the right to adequate housing, the right to employment, etc.) in that identifying it does not require distinguishing needs from wants and wishes. This need right is clearly grounded upon a need—the need for the goods or services *necessary* to stay alive.

However, the sufferer cannot justifiably claim this right if he has voluntarily placed himself in a condition of deprivation by knowingly refusing to prevent foreseeable and preventable consequences of his actions. Thus if he *could*, but willingly does *not*, obtain the goods required to maintain

[3]See William H. Aiken, Jr., "Starvation, Morality, and The Right To Be Saved" (Ph.D. diss., Vanderbilt University, 1977).

[4]I will not consider here the problems involved with fetuses' rights. Individuals, as identified in this essay, are *born* persons.

himself (by work, for example) then he has voluntarily placed himself in the condition of deprivation and thus cannot justifiably claim the right to be saved from preventable death due to deprivation (though he may ask for charity). This allows for suicide by deprivation (e.g., a hunger strike or a refusal of medical treatment) as well as prevents abuse of the claim of a right to be saved. It is important to realize that the *sufferer* must have voluntarily placed himself in the condition of deprivation. If another person places the sufferer in that position, then failure to save the sufferer is a violation of his right to be saved. This is an important distinction for it rebuts the common argument that we have no duty to save starving children if their parents knowingly overprocreate with the foreseeable consequence that at least some of their children will die of starvation. If parents knowingly place their child in a condition of dire need (by having an excess of children), we nonetheless have a duty to that child to save him from starvation.

The right to be saved from preventable death due to deprivation is a right against others. It is a general positive right and so is claimable against all persons who satisfy three minimal conditions: an epistemological condition, an 'ought implies can' condition, and an 'equivalent need' condition. If *no one* satisfies these conditions, then the claim of right cannot justifiably be made.

In order to be obligated to provide the goods and services to the sufferer one must be aware of the sufferer's condition of extreme need. A person starving to death on a desert island whose plight is unknown to the rest of the world cannot claim the moral right to be saved from starvation. The right to be saved and the obligation to save are, like other rights and obligations, concepts dependent in meaning upon there being a social context (of at least a minimal form). There must be knowledge of a person's need before one can be obligated to help that person. However, we have at least some moral responsibility to become aware of the needs of others. The intentional cultivation of ignorance of the needs of others for the purpose of avoiding the obligation to save them is as reprehensible as the cultivated ignorance of an investor who buys into a loan shark operation and then says, "I don't want to know how you get it—as long as my profits are high, I'm happy."

The second minimal condition is the 'ought implies can' condition. In order to be obligated to save the sufferer one must have the means to remedy his condition, that is, have the goods or the capability to render the services required to alleviate the condition of the sufferer. I can only be obligated to save you if I *can* save you. Thus, if you are dying for need of a blood transfusion of a very rare type of blood and I am available for a transfusion, but my blood type is incompatible with your blood type and thus of no use to you, then no matter how severe your need is, I have no duty to save you because I cannot provide you with the goods you need. However, any person of the right blood type who knows of your condition and who is available to provide a transfusion has a moral duty to save you.

"Having" goods normally means "possessing" goods—or at least, having legal access to those goods. Thus, if I do not have legal access to the goods required to save you, I cannot save you. However, since the 'ought implies can' condition is a logical one, and since I *could* steal to acquire the necessary goods, then theft is not *formally* excluded. "Robin Hoodism" is sometimes morally justified, especially when those who possess and own the goods have, like the Sheriff of Nottingham, acquired them unjustly. I may also be justified in taking others' goods if those who have the goods are exceptionally neglectful of their moral duties to save others. For instance, suppose a natural disaster destroys a village, leaving only one large house; the owner refuses shelter for the seriously injured on the grounds that it is, after all, *his* house. In this instance, the townspeople may, with moral justification, take over the house. However, the normal association of 'have' with 'possess' or 'have legal access to,' should be maintained in most cases.

The 'ought implies can' condition is often used to defend inaction in the world hunger situation since, it is claimed, we simply cannot feed everyone. If it becomes true that persons cannot be saved from starvation (that is, if the world population outruns the *world's* food-producing capacity), then there can be no moral right to be saved from starvation. Naturally, this level of "impossibility" involves several complicated issues, for example, the distribution of food, the strength of property rights over moral rights, the unequal quality of diet among peoples of different regions of the world, the amount of food inefficiently utilized on meat production, etc. The point of "impossibility" may be rapidly approaching if the present increase in birth rate in the famine-stricken areas of the world continues and if the affluent nations continue to improve their diets by increasing the consumption of inefficiently produced animal products. But the point of impossibility is far off if an equitable means of production and redistribution is effected.

This 'ought implies can' qualification is included as a formal condition. However, it should be noted that it does not mean 'ought if convenient' or 'ought if I feel charitable.' It means 'ought if at all possible.'

The third condition is the equivalent need condition. It states that a person is not obligated to save another if he cannot render the service or supply the goods without involving himself in a position of equivalent or more extreme need than that of the sufferer for whom the services and goods are granted. This is called the 'equivalent need' condition. If the only way to save you of dying of dehydration is to give you my canteen of water and thus bring about my own death by dehydration, then obviously I have no duty to save you. Similarly, if to save you from feeezing to death I must give you my only coat and thus freeze to death myself, then I have no moral duty to save you. This condition prevents the appeal to lifeboat situations of *extreme* scarcity from serving as counterexamples to the right to be saved from death due to deprivation. The ethics of extreme scarcity is perhaps different from the ethics of moderate scarcity or moderate abundance. Be that as it may, there are *very* few situations in which the scarcity is so extreme as to warrant appeal to "lifeboat ethics" (which is, in my opinion, the same as prudent self-interest). One situation of such scarcity might be the case of the clotting factor for hemophiliacs. Another might be the use of a dialysis machine for those with kidney failure. But very few cases demonstrate this extreme scarcity. The world hunger situation is not yet—*pace* the opinion of many—a lifeboat situation. It is more of a problem of distribution, use, and waste of food than it is of scarcity of food.

Until it is true that I cannot help another without putting myself in an equivalent position of need (that is, dying of deprivation), I have a *prima facie* obligation to honor others' right to be saved from preventable death due to deprivation.

Some have maintained that there is a fourth minimal condition which a potential helper of a person in need must satisfy in order to be obligated to act—the condition of being the 'last resort'. Richard Brandt suggests such a condition in his book, *Ethical Theory*.[5] He specifies that it is only in cases where "we are the only one in a position to help" that we have a moral obligation to assist a person in dire need and that the person in need has a right to our assistance.

There is a danger in adopting this 'last resort' condition since it poses an additional epistemological difficulty, that is, the determination of whether or not I am the last resort. Beyond this, it is an undesirable condition because it will justify inaction where more than one person *could* act but where no one *is* acting. In most emergency situations there is more than one potential assistor. For instance, five persons may simultaneously come across a drowning child. Each would be obligated to act if he were the last resort, but since no single one *is* the last resort, then all five may refuse to act, claiming that it is not their duty to act any more than it is the duty of the other four and so each one would be justified in not acting. If this condition is placed on the right to be saved, the child could drown and none of the five spectators could be held morally accountable. But surely the presence of another person at an accident site does not automatically relieve me of a moral duty to assist the victim in need, any more than

[5]R. B. Brandt, *Ethical Theory* (Englewood Cliffs, N.J.: Prentice-Hall, 1959), p. 439.

the presence of one police officer called to the scene of a bank robbery relieves other officers in the area from attempting to apprehend the suspects. The condition of last resort is too strong; it is not a minimal condition for obligation.

The moral right to be saved from preventable death due to deprivation is not an absolute right. Rights which are not absolute are sometimes called '*prima facie* rights' or 'rights *prima facie*.' I will call them '*prima facie* rights,' meaning only that such rights are not absolute. This right to be saved is a claim which, other things being equal, and provided that there is no conflict of it with another right or obligation, is one that we ought to act in accordance with or honor. Of course, the difficult cases are those in which there is a conflict of rights or obligations; for instance, when your right to be saved from preventable death due to deprivation comes into conflict with my right to control my goods in the way I desire. There are two ways to describe rights in conflictual situations.

One way is to make all *prima facie* rights "maybe rights." When one "maybe right" is judged to override another, then it becomes a right. In effect, this approach says that two conflicting *prima facie* rights at first glance both look like rights—but later we see that one really is a right and the other is not. The overridden "maybe right" ceases to have any claim upon us. So if my "maybe right" to control my goods overrides your "maybe right" to my assistance, then I have a right and you no longer have anything—you cease to have a legitimate claim against me.[6] Rights are, in effect, determined by right actions.

The second way to approach the conflict of *prima facie* rights is to see *prima facie* rights as legitimate moral claims. When these claims come into conflict and we must choose to act on one, the other (overridden) one remains a legitimate claim even though it would be wrong, in this circumstance, to act on it. Although it is a legitimate moral claim, it is not a justified moral claim in this circumstance. Thus *prima facie* rights are not "maybe rights"; and even though they are rights that are defeasible, when they are defeated, they remain legitimate claims. Honoring one *prima facie* right may excuse us from honoring other conflicting ones. But though we are excused, the conflicting claims remain legitimate claims.[7] For instance, if I am forced to hit and kill you with my car in order to avoid hitting a dozen children, then your *prima facie* right not to be killed remains a legitimate claim upon me—only in this instance, I am excused from honoring it. The former position would result in your "maybe right" not to be killed disappearing altogether.

[6]This, or something like it, is suggested by W. D. Ross in *The Right and the Good* (Oxford at the Clarendon Press, 1930), Chapter II.

[7]I derive this position from A. I. Melden's views in "The Play of Rights," *Monist*, 56 (1972), 479–502.

The right to be saved from preventable death due to deprivation is a *prima facie* right in the second sense, and so I can be excused from acting on a sufferer's legitimate claim to assistance. There are excusing conditions to my obligation. If we lived in a world where our obligations did not conflict with other obligations and rights, then there would be no excuse for failing to save others in need. But we do not live in that type of moral world. Obligations conflict. Some obligations are less stringent than others; some are overridden and some are defeated. The obligation to save others from death due to deprivation also comes into conflict with other obligations. Sometimes it is overridden and we are excused from acting on it. There are, it seems, at least two conditions which can excuse us from providing others with the goods and services required by them to be saved from preventable death due to deprivation—although both of these conditions are difficult to describe precisely.

The first excusing condition is this: if rendering the goods and services required to save another from death involves an *unreasonable* amount of cost to the giver, then the giver is excused from aiding the sufferer. By cost I do not mean only expense, but also effort, risk, and sacrifice. The obvious difficulty with this condition is the unfixed nature of the 'unreasonable' criterion. What is an unreasonable amount of cost? Surely if I am not a good swimmer, then risking my life in the pounding surf to save you from drowning would be an unreasonable risk. So too, if by helping you I place myself in a similar, but not quite equivalent, position of deprivation, then this too would be an unreasonable amount of cost. But at what point, precisely, does a cost become unreasonable and thus provide me with an excusing condition to fail to act on your claim against me? Some would suggest that the cut-off point is the point of marginal utility. Others would suggest that it is not until the point of complete egalitarian distribution. Others would suggest the point is the level of slight inconvenience. This cut-off point may not be determinable outside of the context of an actual situation. But some suggestions can be made.

The stringency of the obligation to save others, and thus the strength of the right to be saved, should be seen as standing in inverse proportion to the cost of the goods or services to the actor. Thus, if all that I need do to save you from drowning is to reach out my hand, then my duty to save you is more stringent and your claim of right stronger than if I must swim to reach you. The greater the cost to the actor, the less stringent the duty. Once the actor reaches a state of equivalent need, the obligation has ceased altogether.

As the claim against me decreases in strength according to the cost of the action to me, the duty to honor that claim (by acting upon it) becomes more easily overridden by my other moral duties. For instance, my duty to provide for my family would override my duty to save your starving family if by saving your family I seriously endanger my family's health. The greater the cost to me, the more easily my duty is overridden by my other moral duties.

Perhaps the determination of the degree of cost to me which is an unreasonable amount of cost could be made by finding that point in a particular situation where any other conflicting moral duty I have overrides the duty to save the person in need. At this point of cost I would be excused from the obligation because any conflicting duty would override it. It would still be debatable as to whether or not this point of cost is above or below the point of marginal utility; but at least this criterion allows for flexibility. Flexibility in this matter is desirable because different persons have different moral duties, some of which do and some of which do not conflict with the duty to save persons in dire need. For those persons with few conflicting moral duties, the point where the cost becomes unreasonable (and thus the point where one is excused from performing the saving act) will be higher than for those who have many conflicting moral duties. A greater amount of effort, risk, sacrifice, and expense will be required of that person with fewer conflicting moral duties because there will be less to justify his being excused from acting.

This flexible criterion of unreasonable cost accounts for the general impression that persons who have much in the way of goods but little in the way of moral responsibilities ought to give more to assist persons in need. It also allows for the performance of acts beyond the call of duty (that is, supererogatory acts), for if a person takes an unreasonable risk or sacrifices an unreasonable amount, then he is truly acting nobly or even saintly. It is important to allow for the distinction between obligations and acts of supererogation since without it all persons would be required, by duty, to be moral saints. This would make morality unattainable by the majority of humans—and perhaps even irrelevant to human action.

There is another excusing condition to the obligation to save persons from preventable death due to deprivation. If one has no access to an effective method of making the goods and services available to the sufferer, then one is excused from the obligation to save the sufferer. For example, if a government intentionally prevents the delivery of food relief to starving persons within that nation, then one possible method of delivering the food would be to destroy that government by declaring war on it. Another would be to smuggle the food in with the knowledge that most of it would be confiscated. Another would be to drop packages from high flying aircraft with the hope that at least some of them reached the ground undamaged and were then received by those who need them. Each of these methods is a *possible* means of delivering the food but none of them is particularly *effective*. In this case, where no effective means of distributing the food is available, we would be excused from the obligation to save the starving persons in that nation. Of course, it might be that we have other moral responsibilities to find or to establish an effective method. We might even be required to coerce that government into permitting us to distribute the food necessary for the lives of persons within that nation; but this would be another type of moral responsibility, and justification of it would require a separate argument.

The term 'effective' is an evaluating notion and as such it creates in this excusing condition, as in the previous one, a flexible criterion. The stringency of the obligation to save persons in dire need is proportional to the effectiveness of the available method of providing the goods and services required by the persons in need. But this flexibility is not necessarily undesirable. For instance, there is a general opinion among moral philosophers that distance provides a relevant moral consideration; that is, if a person is starving on your doorstep he has a stronger claim to assistance from you than does someone who is living on the other side of the world. Although the claim that distance alone makes a difference is popular, it is difficult to justify other than by appeal to moral intuitions. But with the effectiveness of the method of distribution playing a role in determining the strength of the duty to save persons in dire need, it is easily seen that the duty to the man on your doorstep is stronger than the duty to the person across the world. All that is required of you to deliver the necessary food to the man on your doorstep is to walk to the kitchen and bring back some food from the refrigerator. But to deliver the food to the person in India, for example, you must depend upon a complex network of international relief; however, since there are effective relief organizations (CARE, Ox-Fam, etc.), we are not *entirely* excused from our obligation. There are other elements, in addition to distance, involved in determining effectiveness (e.g., political sovereignty); but it certainly is one element. Although voluntary organizations like CARE are effective methods, they are not very effective. Much more effective methods of food distribution are needed if all those dying of hunger are going to be saved. As suggested before, we may have some responsibility to see to it that obstacles impairing the effective commission of our obligations are removed—be they obstacles presented by our own or another government's action.

The flexibility of the effectiveness condition also accounts for the insight expressed in the proposed 'last resort' condition for obligation mentioned above. If I *am* the last resort, for instance, if I am the only person near enough to a pond to save a drowning child, then I have a more effective method of acting (owing to my physical proximity) than do others. So I cannot be excused from acting. If there are others with more effective methods, I may be excused. But if there are other persons with *equally* effective methods of providing goods or services, then none of us is excused from his or her obligation to act (by the effectiveness condition). Not being the last resort does not necessarily excuse me from by obligation, but it may.

In this lengthy section, I have tried to show that moral rights based on need are not necessarily doomed to failure because of vagueness—that at least one such right is specifiable, the right to be saved from preventable death due to deprivation.

V

Recognition of the right to be saved from preventable death due to deprivation would clarify many traditional problem cases for moral philosophers. In addition to the 'drowning child' case and the 'accident victim' case, it would also be useful in deciding on cases of euthanasia like the Karen Quinlan case, where the issue seems not to be whether the right violated by unplugging a respirator is the right to life (that is, the right not to be killed unjustly), but is rather the right to be saved from preventable death due to deprivation. As the instruments for keeping people (both terminal patients and newborns) alive improve in technological capability, the deliberations of ethicists will increasingly be confused without the recognition of this moral right.

But the one area where recognition of this moral right will have the most impact on moral deliberation is the world hunger issue. Since starving to death is a form of death due to deprivation, and since death due to this cause is preventable (at least at present), then persons who are starving to death have a *prima facie* moral right to be saved. There *is* a moral right to be saved from starvation.

But has any benefit been gained by admitting that there is such a moral right? Does the recognition of this right tell us what we *ought* to do about the problem of world hunger and the massive death toll that famine is reaping in the sub-Sahara and in India? Certainly, the recognition of this right by itself will not solve the difficult problem of making moral choices. But it does, I believe, substantially change the moral arena in which such decisions must be discussed. In order for us to know that we *ought* to provide someone with the goods and/or services he needs to stay alive, we must know that his *prima facie* moral right overrrides all other rights in this circumstance and that we are not excused from honoring his right. Unfortunately, we have no automatic procedure to discover what we ought to do when there is a conflict of *prima facie* rights. But even though recognition of this right to be saved will not tell us, *a priori*, what we ought to do in every circumstance, it does have several important implications for the world hunger situation.

Giving aid to persons who are in need is not always merely an act of charity to which the recipient should respond with gratitude. That people are starving is not merely a signal to exercise our duties of benevolence and thereby become better persons (that is, persons with better moral characters). Those starving people have a claim of right against us. As the situation is seen today by affluent nations like the United States, giving aid to starving peoples is a matter of charity. And so, when Third World Nations demand assistance from us in the world food conferences, we scream with indignation about the ungrateful beggars. After all, one cannot demand charity. All one can do is plead for it. Recognition that there is a moral right to be saved from starvation would at least rid us of any illusions about our "good deeds."

With recognition of the moral right to be saved from starvation, it will be seen that the world hunger problem cannot be solved simply by appeal to prudential considerations. For instance, it is in the grain-producing nations' best economic interest to control carefully the amount of grain that is sold on the world market in order to insure that the prices remain high. Since the demand for food is rapidly becoming as high as the demand for petroleum products, the grain-producing nations have an exceptionally valuable resource with which to balance trade deficits, to utilize as a political tool to insure friendly governments, and with which to gain power over potentially threatening nations. It is definitely not in their prudential interest simply to give food away or to sell it at less than competitive prices, for this would be to waste a valuable commodity from which great profits could be made. This dual use of the food weapon as an economic and political tool becomes questionable if persons have a moral right to be saved from starvation. If failing to assist starving persons is a neglect of a moral obligation, then we cannot, without proper justification of our omission, avoid being morally reprehensible for following prudential guidelines.

Recognition of this right to be saved from starvation would transform the debate about aiding hungry people from one of charity-in-abundance to one of conflicting *prima facie* moral rights. The arena for moral decision would become the adjudication of conflicting claims. This shift of arena alone would substantially affect the world hunger issue. For example, the popular 'population explosion' argument, which does not see the issue as a conflict of rights, would be seen to be inadequate. This argument runs something like this: if you feed x number of starving persons now they will, in some period of time, procreate at such a rate that the population will be doubled and so too will the total amount of human misery due to starvation. So failure to feed people now will diminish the total amount of human suffering.

Besides the difficulties involved in predicting a continued geometrical increase in population according to present trends, this approach is misguided. It addresses the problem as one would the rat population in a city slum: if we kill x number of rats now we can avoid having to kill 2x number next year. Except for appeal to the omission–commission distinction and the supposed crucial moral distinction between the two, the case of people in the first argument is the same as the case of rats in the second. Since it is immoral to simply exterminate several million starving people (it violates their right not to be killed unjustly), it is best to "let nature take its course"—that is, it is right to let these people die even though we could prevent their deaths. By ignoring the right to be saved from starvation and thereby avoiding the conflict of rights, the 'population argument' suggests that the intentional reliance on starvation as a means of population control is a moral alternative. But it is *not*, other things being equal, a moral alternative. It is a violation of a moral right which must be justified. The real moral difficulty that underlies the population problem is a fundamental conflict of two moral rights: the right to procreate (which is deduced from the generally recognized right to freedom) and the right to be saved from starvation. If the population exceeds the food supply, then either the right to procreate must be overridden by the right to be saved or vice versa. I would advocate mandatory birth control (say, after the birth of two children) before I would support the intentional reliance upon starvation as a means of population control. But I need not defend this position in order to make the general point that there is a conflict of rights here which must be resolved by offering good moral reasons why one right should override another.[8] If the moral arena of the world hunger debate were the arena of conflicts of rights (as it should be), the 'population explosion' argument would not be as sheltered from criticism as it presently is.

Another argument which would be eliminated by the recognition that the issue is a matter of a conflict of rights is what I shall call the 'it's mine' argument. The revival of the deification of property rights with its distinguished prophets is of no small consequence for the world hunger issue. The 'it's mine' argument simply says, "the goods in question are *mine* and I may do as I please with them without thereby incurring moral blame." This theory can only be maintained seriously if it presupposes that property rights are absolute rights. But it seems absurd (without the sophistical backing of Natural Law) to claim that any moral right is absolute. If

[8]Some leaders in famine-stricken nations may not see that the right to procreate conflicts with the right to be saved from starvation. They need to be convinced of this. However, if they persist in avoiding population control programs, I do not think that tying food relief to population control is the most moral alternative. An inducement with favorable trade agreements or developmental assistance would be better alternatives. Other goods than food should be used to bribe neglectful governments into action to curb population growth.

property rights are *not* seen as absolute rights, then there will be situations in which my *moral* claim (we are not talking about legal entitlement nor about what extent of coercion is justifiable) to goods in my possession can be overridden by others' moral claim to those goods. My property rights may come into conflict with another's need right and may be overridden by it. One could maintain that property rights always override need rights without the supposition of property rights being absolute, yet this would need a very sophisticated *moral* defense. Since there is a conflict between property rights and need rights, the standard of measurement of the strength of each right must be morally defensible. The suggested inflexible priority of property rights over need rights would require its advocates to defend it against a host of counterexamples. (For example: Does my right to possess a gold-plated toilet seat override someone else's right to a survival quantity of food? Does my right to own all the oxygen in, around, and above New York City, if I could figure out a way to capture it and bottle it, override the residents of that city's right to be saved from death due to deprivation of oxygen? Etc.)

The problems cited in the above paragraph result from considering the world hunger issue as a conflict of rights. But the 'it's mine' argument would not even require us to examine this problem. By ignoring the conflict of rights, the 'it's mine' argument supposes that the only moral issue involved is the goodness of the moral character of the person who could, if he chooses, aid the starving. The starving have absolutely no claim (moral or otherwise) to aid; refusing to give aid is morally permissible, though it is perhaps being "less than a Minimally Decent Samaritan" (as Judith Thomson would say).[9]

The final and most important aspect of recognizing the moral right to be saved from starvation and of seeing the world hunger issue in terms of a conflict of moral rights, is that the burden of proof has been shifted from those in need of food to those who could give food. The needy no longer must supply reasons why they should be helped (e.g., by promising favorable trade, by making compromising political concessions). Rather, those who can assist the hungry must explain why they are *not* acting. It would no longer be morally acceptable merely to let people die and then claim moral innocence. Not honoring the right to be saved from starvation by giving the required goods and services would require giving excusing reasons and offering moral justifications for inaction. This would involve weighing moral duties and balancing claims. No longer would it be taken for granted that as long as you do not harm someone directly, you are morally blameless. This applies to the drowning child case, the accident

[9]Judith Thomson, "A Defense of Abortion," in J. Feinberg, ed., *The Problem of Abortion* (Belmont, Calif.: Wadsworth Publishing Co., Inc., 1973), pp. 121–39.

victim case, and especially to the world hunger issue. Inaction, the omission to act, must be justified when the need of another is extreme (to the point of death). The question is not "Why should I send money to save starving people?" but rather "If I am not sending money, why am I not?" I must offer reasons. I must show that there are excusing conditions which apply. I must justify my inaction.

Welfare Rights and Human Rights*

DAVID WATSON†

ABSTRACT
Recent discussions of a 'welfare rights' approach in social work have suggested that the European Convention on Human Rights might provide a useful framework, a list of service objectives against which present provision might be assessed. In the present paper the author argues that the United Nations Universal Declaration of Human Rights is to be preferred, because of its inclusion of social and economic rights. However, there are philosophical and political objections to such a wide-ranging list of human rights. The author attempts to answer these objections in order to release the Universal Declaration as a viable framework for a welfare rights approach.

1

It has long been recognized that social work is at least in part regulated by moral principles. Textbooks[1] regularly list such things as individualization, acceptance and self-determination as casework values, professional bodies generate codes of ethics for social work,[2] and teachers of social administration 'attempt a clarification of the ideals of social welfare'.[3]

The importance of moral principles has continued to be stressed in the development of a 'welfare rights' approach in social work. Moral principles held relevant to casework are not abandoned, but at the same time there is evidence in social work literature of a new emphasis. Rosalind Brooke[4] argues that if we are to pursue a welfare rights approach 'we need some framework within which to examine rights within the social services'. Brooke suggests that 'one useful frame of reference can be found within

* Roger Montague, Tom Campbell, David-Hillel Ruben and many others have provided helpful comment on an earlier draft of this paper.
† Lecturer in Moral Philosophy, Glasgow University.
[1] See for example, F. P. Biestek, *The Casework Relationship*, London: Allen & Unwin, 1961, and Jonathan Moffett, *Concepts in Casework Treatment*, London: Routledge & Kegan Paul, 1968.
[2] For example, 'A Code of Ethics for Social Work', Discussion Paper No. 2, British Association of Social Workers, 1973.
[3] Cf. Robert Pinker, 'Social Policy and Social Justice', *Journal of Social Policy*, 1974, vol. 3, no. 1, pp. 1–19.
[4] Rosalind Brooke, 'Social Administration and Human Rights' in Peter Townsend and Nicholas Bosanquet (eds), *Labour and Inequality*, London: Fabian Society, 1972, p. 247.

certain articles of the European Convention on Human Rights' and goes on in her essay to employ this framework in just such an examination. Wayne Vasey[5] and R. G. Walton[6] have also recently stressed the importance of human rights as goals for a welfare rights approach because of their relation to our idea of social justice: a just society guarantees human rights.

Both Vasey and Walton have in mind human rights as listed in the United Nations Universal Declaration of Human Rights, proclaimed in 1948.[7] Brooke, as I have said, recommends the European Convention. Does it matter which we choose? I think it does, and for the following reasons.

We may draw a broad distinction between 'civil and political' rights and 'social and economic' rights. The rights to life, freedom of movement and freedom of opinion fall into the first class, the rights to work and to social security fall into the second class. The European Convention concentrates primarily, though not exclusively,[8] on civil and political rights. Brooke quotes article 6(1), which begins: 'In the determination of his civil rights and obligations or of any criminal charge against him, everyone is entitled to a fair and public hearing within a reasonable time by an independent and impartial tribunal established by law.' Such civil and political rights have an important place in a welfare rights approach. In this case, as Brooke points out,[9] we are led to ask whether particular services are being fairly administered, whether the recipient is being given adequate notice of a hearing to curtail his benefit, whether reputable evidence is being used as a basis for allocating or curtailing benefit, and so on.

Even so, I think we should choose the Universal Declaration rather than the European Convention as the framework for a welfare rights approach to social work. All the civil and political rights proclaimed in the European Convention are included in the Universal Declaration[10] but the latter also includes additional social and economic rights. No framework for a welfare rights approach in social work could be adequate if it did not, for example, recognize that 'Everyone has the right to a standard of living adequate for the health and well-being of himself and his family, including food, cloth-

[5] Wayne Vasey, 'Social Welfare as a Human Right', in *Social Work Values in an Age of Discontent*, Council on Social Work Education, 1970.

[6] R. G. Walton, 'Welfare rights and social work: ambivalence in action' in Howard Jones (ed.), *Towards a New Social Work*, London: Routledge & Kegan Paul, 1975.

[7] The Universal Declaration and the European Convention are reprinted as Appendices A and B, respectively, in Maurice Cranston, *What are Human Rights?*, London: Bodley Head 1973.

[8] Articles 8 and 9 mention the protection of health, article 11 proclaims the right to form and join trade unions, presumably for the protection of economic interests, and article 2 of the first Protocol to the Convention adds the right to education.

[9] Brooke, *op. cit.*, p. 248.

[10] Brooke's examples, articles 6(1) and 8(1) of the European Convention, are articles 10 and 12, respectively, of the Universal Declaration.

ing, housing and medical care and necessary social services, and the right to security in the event of unemployment, sickness, disability, widowhood, old age or other lack of livelihood in circumstances beyond his control' or that 'Everyone has the right to rest and leisure, including reasonable limitation of working hours and periodic holidays with pay', respectively articles 25(1) and 24 of the Universal Declaration. As Wayne Vasey put it, 'The Universal Declaration included economic, social, and cultural, as well as political and civil, rights. Who more than the people engaged in social welfare should recognize the validity of this scope of rights?'[11]

If human rights are to provide a framework within which to examine rights within the social services, our list of human rights must include social and economic rights as well as civil and political rights, and the Universal Declaration seems the obvious choice. However, objections have recently been raised even to the *possibility* of a framework proclaiming such a range of human rights. Professor Maurice Cranston[12] has recently put forward philosophical and political objections to the classification of certain social and economic rights, including those proclaimed in articles 24 and 25(1) of the Universal Declaration quoted earlier, as human rights. Cranston sets out three 'tests for the authenticity of a human right'[13] which, though passed by the traditional civil and political rights, he argues, the social and economic rights in question fail. Cranston uses the tests to distinguish rights in these two classes. Only the civil and political rights pass these tests, so only they are human rights. This philosophical criticism of the Universal Declaration is backed by a political point: 'the circulation of a confused notion of human rights hinders the effective protection of what are correctly seen as human rights'.[14]

Brooke chooses not to discuss 'the philosophical basis of rights'[15] but, faced by a philsophical objection to a framework which includes social and economic rights, if we wish to employ such a framework we *must* enter into the philosophical debate. We might avoid this terrible fate by denying the value of employing such a framework, but I do not think anyone seriously concerned with a welfare rights approach in social work would offer such a denial. The aim of the approach is legal recognition of welfare rights. Since, as Cranston puts it, 'a human right is something of which no one may be deprived without a grave affront to justice',[16] the framework in question

[11] Vasey, *op. cit.*, p. 84.
[12] M. Cranston, 'Human Rights, Real and Supposed', in D. D. Raphael (ed.), *Political Theory and The Rights of Man*, London: Macmillan, 1967. The arguments, recur in Cranston 1973, *op. cit.*, and in R. S. Downie, *Roles and Values*, London: Methuen, 1971, p. 49.
[13] 1967, *op. cit.*, p. 50.
[14] *Ibid.*, p. 43.
[15] Brooke, *op. cit.*, p. 248.
[16] 1967, *op. cit.*, p. 42.

provides us with a strong moral argument which may be deployed in defending and extending legal entitlement to welfare rights.[17]

I turn, then, to the philosophical debate. If I can show that the social and economic rights in question pass Cranston's three 'tests for the authenticity of a human right', the Universal Declaration is released as a framework for a welfare rights approach.

2

Cranston's three tests test are practicability, paramount importance and universality. As we shall see, the first test is presented in a way which suggests that it must be passed if what is claimed is to be a right of any kind, unlike the second and third tests, which are tests of being a *human* right. Further, since Cranston concludes in the case of *each* test that a certain right does not qualify as a human right simply because it fails that test, it seems that each test provides a *necessary* condition for being a human right. That is, any right purporting to be a human right must pass all three of these tests.

'Rights bear a clear relationship to duties', says Cranston, 'and the first test of both is that of practicability. It is not my duty to do what it is physically impossible for me to do. You cannot reasonably say it was my duty to have jumped into the Thames at Richmond to rescue a drowning child if I was nowhere near Richmond at the time the child was drowning. What is true of duties is equally true of rights. If it is impossible for a thing to be done, it is absurd to claim it as a right. At present it is utterly impossible, and will be for a long time yet, to provide "holidays with pay" for everybody in the world. . .The government of India, for example, simply cannot command the resources that would guarantee each one of the 480 million inhabitants of India "a standard of living adequate for the health and well-being of himself and his family", let alone "holidays with pay".'[18]

In Cranston's example of the drowning child it *is* impossible for me to rescue the child and, therefore, I cannot be said to have a duty to do so. Given the correspondence rights bear to duties, in this case the child correspondingly cannot be said to have a right against me to be rescued. It is worth noting, however, that in Cranston's example the impossibility is a *logical* impossibility. Given the employment of spatio-temporal criteria in the identification of particular people, it is logically impossible for the same person to be in different places at the same time. Given the employment of these criteria it is inconceivable that I might at one and the same time be

[17] Cf. Walton, *op. cit.*, p. 104.
[18] 1967, *op. cit.*, pp. 50–1.

both 'nowhere near Richmond at the time the child was drowning' *and* jumping in the Thames at Richmond to rescue him. It is worth noting this feature of the example because it is a serious weakness. If only the logically impossible fails the test of practicability, then the social and economic rights in question *pass* the test. We can certainly *conceive* of everybody in the world being guaranteed 'a standard of living adequate for the health and well-being of himself and his family' and 'holidays with pay'.

However, this weakness is built into the test by mistake. This is shown in Cranston's account of the test when he says 'It is not my duty to do what it is *physically impossible* for me to do' (italics mine) and 'At *present* it is utterly impossible, and will be for a long time yet, to provide...' (italics mine). A logical impossibility does not become a possibility *in time*. It is not Cranston's view, then, that all logical possibilities pass the test of practicability, but only those it is *at present* possible to realize; it is these possibilities which generate significant claims to rights. This is confirmed when he later says 'A right...is something that can, and from the moral point of view must, be respected here and now.'[19]

It seems to me that a test of practicability which is passed only by claims it is at present possible to realize is a reasonable test. But Cranston would add a further qualification, which prevents all such claims qualifying. When he says 'The government of India, for example, simply cannot command the resources that would guarantee each one of the 480 million inhabitants of India "a standard of living adequate for the health and well-being of himself and his family" ', Cranston implies that what is claimed is a right *of* all men, but not necessarily *against* all men; in the case in question, the right is implied to be a right only against other inhabitants of India. Cranston's test of practicability is passed only by claims it is at present possible for every state to guarantee *its own* inhabitants. Naturally, the social and economic rights in question fail this test.

There seems no good reason why we should accept so tough a test of practicability, why we should accept that the social and economic rights in question should not be claimed by all men *against* all men. Further, in setting such a test Cranston is inconsistent with a position he later expounds.[20] He adopts a distinction between rights of all men against all men and rights of all men but not necessarily against all men, allowing only the former to be classed as human rights. If his test of practicability is to discover human rights, he should surely pass as human rights all which are practicable as rights claimed by all men *against all men*, and to be consistent with his later view, he must.

[19] *Ibid.*, p. 53.
[20] 1973, *op. cit.*, p. 96.

If the social and economic rights in question are claimed against all men, it is plausible to suggest (and I take the United Nations' Declaration to assume) that it *is* at present possible to guarantee the new social and economic rights to everybody in the world, and so significantly claim them as human rights. As claims of all men against all men, the new social and economic rights *pass* the test of practicability.

According to Professor David Raphael,[21] 'When the Universal Declaration says that every man has the right to work, or the right to subsistence, it does not imply that the corresponding responsibility to provide any particular man with work or subsistence rests on every other man or every group of men; it implies that this responsibility rests on the members of his own State, and that the government of that State has a duty to carry out the responsibility on behalf of all its members. We do of course speak of a responsibility to help people who are in need in other parts of the world, but such help is an act of benevolence or charity, not a matter of implementing a right.'

I see no reason to accept either of these statements and Raphael offers no arguments in their support. Of course, it may be admitted that a social or economic right of all men against all men *would* fail the test of practicability if it implied that a *personal* responsibility to provide any particular man with work or subsistence, or whatever, rests on every other man; it is of course not possible at present for every other man, independently of every other man, to provide these things. On the other hand if this were implied in the test of practicability, the *traditional* human rights to life, liberty and a fair trial would also fail. It is not possible at present for every other man independently to guarantee these rights for any particular man. However. a right of all men against all men does *not* fail the test of practicability if what is implied is that a responsibility to provide what is claimed rests on all men collectively rather than singly, since I believe it is possible at present for all men collectively to provide these things. I conclude from this discussion, then, that as claims of all men against all men collectively, the new social and economic rights *pass* the test of practicability.

This assumes of course that *as a matter of fact* at present all men collectively possess adequate natural resources, and administrative ingenuity, to guarantee these rights to all men. At various times it may not be possible to guarantee the new social and economic rights in full, but surely men are able to guarantee the new rights *in part*. As Raphael says, 'a sort of system of social security is to be found in the Old Testament laws about leaving harvest gleanings for the poor, the periodic cancellation of debts, and so forth. Again, while unemployment is among the greatest of evils for those

21 D. D. Raphael, 'Human Rights, Old and New', in Raphael, *op. cit.*, pp. 65–6.

who are subject to it, no amount of reading Lord Keynes will produce a golden key for full employment everywhere, yet there is some possibility nowadays of some control of unemployment by governments, as there was not in former times. . .',[22] and therefore it is justifiable to speak of a duty to do what we can, and a right that it be done. If Cranston holds that rights which at present it is possible to guarantee only *in part* fail the test of practicability for human rights, then social and economic rights may fail to qualify as human rights, but so do such traditional rights as the rights to life, liberty and a fair trial, which he wants to say *are* human rights. As Raphael points out, 'no amount of criminal legislation or of police forces will be able to prevent *all* homicides; but that is no reason for saying that the right to life should be struck out of our list of human rights as not being universally practicable'.[23] If practicability requires the possibility of at present meeting obligations *in full*, then Cranston applies this test inconsistently; if practicability requires only the possibility of at present meeting obligations *in part*, then both the new social and economic rights and the traditional civil and political rights are practicable: the test of practicability provides no ground for denying that the social and economic rights in question are human rights.

There are two further points I should like to make about the test of practicability in the revised form I accept. First, I would use the test to discriminate between rights and ideals. But then, it may be objected, even in its revised form the test is too easily a defence of the *status quo*. Reforms which take a year or more will be not 'at present possible', classed as ideals, and thus filed away and forgotten. Cranston too has this view of ideals. In reply I would simply point out that it does not follow, from the fact that we do not expect ideals to be fulfilled at present, that we do not expect a government, say, to take all necessary steps for their fulfilment as soon as possible. Though not at present possible, an ideal is precisely something that is *pursued* and not forgotten.

Second, I should make the point that as a way of discriminating between rights and ideals, the test of practicability draws no sharp boundaries. 'At present' is clearly vague, and, I think, usefully so, leaving room for some debate about what can be done, what claims can at present be satisfied.

3

Next the test of *paramount importance*. 'Here the distinction' between human rights and social and economic rights, says Cranston, 'is less definite,

[22] *Ibid.*, pp. 63–4.
[23] *Ibid.*, p. 64.

but no less crucial. And here again there is a parallel between rights and duties. It is a paramount duty to relieve great distress, as it is not a paramount duty to give pleasure. It would have been my duty to rescue the drowning child at Richmond if I had been there at the time; but it is not, in the same sense, my duty to give Christmas presents to the children of my neighbours. . .Common sense knows that fire engines and ambulances are essential services, whereas fun fairs and holiday camps are not.'[24] Cranston then suggests that 'ordinary people find themselves invoking the language of human rights' in defence of the traditional human rights, say where there is an invasion of the human right to freedom of movement. 'In considering cases of this kind', he says, 'we are confronted by matters which belong to a totally different moral dimension from questions of social security and holidays with pay. A human right is something of which no one may be deprived without a grave affront to justice.'[25]

This discussion seems to me quite unsuccessful. Cranston admits that there is a paramount *duty* to relieve great distress; given the correspondence between rights and duties which he again emphasizes, there must then surely be a paramount *right* to the relief of great distress. Or rather there must be a group of paramount rights each to the relief of a different form of great distress, and including, surely, paramount rights to the relief of great social and economic distresses. Cranston can avoid this conclusion only if he denies that social and economic distresses are great distresses. This, in effect, he does in saying that a human right, but not a social or economic right, 'is something of which no one may be deprived without a grave affront to justice'.[26] The denial is implausible.

Raphael presses this point when he says, 'Tom Paine evidently understood the natural right to life as implying not only laws against homicide but also laws to provide a bare subsistence. Will anyone say that he was wrong in terms of paramount importance? Importance, like practicability, is of course a matter of degree, and no doubt the prevention of murder is of more paramount [*sic*] importance than the prevention of starvation. Yet the degrees of paramountcy do not place all the rights of liberty before all the economic and social rights. If a man is subject to chronic unemployment in a depressed area, he will not thank you for the information that he has the basic rights of liberty.'[27]

We may conclude that the test of paramount importance does not in general distinguish traditional human rights from the social and economic rights in question; nor does it, then, provide grounds for denying that the welfare rights these include are human rights.

[24] 1967, *op. cit.*, p. 51.
[25] *Ibid.*, p. 52.
[26] *Ibid.*, p. 52.
[27] *Op. cit.*, p. 63.

4

Next, the test of genuine *universality*. 'This,' says Cranston, 'the so-called human right to holidays with pay plainly cannot pass. For it is a right that is necessarily limited to those persons who are *paid* in any case, that is to say, to the *employé* class. Since not everyone belongs to this class, the right cannot be a universal right, a right which, in the terminology of the Universal Declaration, "everyone" has. That the right to a holiday with pay is for many people a real moral right, I would not for one moment deny. But it is a right which. . .can be claimed by members of a specific class of persons *because* they are members of that class.'[28] Cranston would no doubt raise the same objection to a claim to a social (welfare) right to unemployment benefit as a human right. Since not everyone belongs to the class of the *unemployed*, the right cannot be a universal right, it is rather a right which can be claimed by members of a specific class of persons *because* they are members of that class.

In parallel with Cranston's argument we might say that 'this so-called human right to a fair trial plainly cannot pass the test of universality. For it is a right that is necessarily limited to those persons who are *on trial* in any case, that is to say the *accusé* class; since not everyone belongs to this class, the right cannot be a universal right, a right which "everyone" has; it is rather a right which can be claimed by members of a specific class of persons *because* they are members of that class.' By the same form of argument the traditional rights to leave any country, including one's own, to freedom of religion and freedom of peaceful assembly, are excluded from the class of human rights, since each is 'necesarily limited' to those persons who are leaving a country, religious, and peacefully assembling, respectively.

Indeed, it is difficult to think of any of the traditional civil and political rights which satisfy this test of universality. It is not true that everyone's life, liberty or security of person is threatened and so it is not true that everyone is now in circumstances appropriate to the exercise of these rights, and so they are not universal rights. Cranston cannot be happy with this consequence. He makes it quite clear at the beginning of his paper that his objective is the effective protection of the traditional human rights: 'The traditional human rights are political and civil rights such as the right to life, liberty, and a fair trial.'[29] It is a consequence of his own application of the test of universality that precisely these rights are not universal rights and so are not due the effective protection due to human rights.

[28] 1967, *op. cit.*, p. 51.
[29] *Ibid.*, p. 43.

Thus applied, the test of universality fails to distinguish between traditional human rights and the social and economic rights in question. If this test, thus applied, supplies Cranston's ground for denying that social and economic rights are human rights, he must apply it inconsistently. On the other hand, it seems clear that the test is misapplied. The test is a test of whether or not everyone has the right, but we pass only rights which everyone is now in appropriate circumstances to exercise. As a result the rights to periodic holidays with pay and to a fair trial, and the others, are not universal rights. It is time to start again.

The test of universality is passed by rights which everyone has. Cranston argues that the right to periodic holidays with pay (and, no doubt, others of the social and economic rights in question) is not a right which everyone has, because it is a right which 'can be claimed by members of a specific class of persons *because* they are members of that class' (where 'a specific class' is less than all men). The force of this description is to suggest that the rights in question are rights of the kind attached to a *social role*. We may, for example, say of the right of a father to discipline his child, that he can claim it just because he is a member of a specific class of persons: he is a father. Such rights are not universal, and are not *human* rights.

But what of the rights of those in employment? Is 'being employed' a social role? There are many types of employment each itself a social role; each constituted by its own set of rights and duties: teacher, cook, carpenter, barman, and so on. Can all these different roles be said to be part of one role – being employed – to which attach a set of rights?

We might be led to think that this is so by suggested examples of such rights, suggestions such as 'the right to periodic holidays with pay', 'the right to reasonable limitation of working hours', and so on. But I think that, in these cases at least, we would have been, and Cranston is, *mis*led. This emerges in the form of justification offered. A man's right to discipline his child would be justified by saying 'he is a father'. The same form of justification does not suffice in these other cases.

Why should that man enjoy reasonable limitation of his working hours? Because he is in employment. This reply simply will not do as a justification. To be a father is, amongst other things, to have the right to discipline your children. But to be in employment entails nothing about the limitation of your working hours. The reply we need, I suggest, is 'Because he is an employed *man*.' We justify a reasonable limitation of working hours by referring not to the fact that the man is employed, but to the fact that he is a *human being*. This is true of the right to periodic holidays with pay, and it is even more obviously true of the right to a fair trial: Why should that man be given a fair trial? Because he is accused? No, because he is an accused *man*.

We *may* say that the social and economic rights in question, and the civil and political rights mentioned in my parallel argument, 'can be claimed by members of a specific class of persons *because* they are members of that class'. But we must *beware* of saying that therefore they are not rights which 'everyone' has. This again is to presume 'being employed', 'being on trial' 'being religious', and so on, to be social roles. Certainly, in the case of rights attached to social roles, we can identify all the possessors of the rights as all those in that role. Every father, and no one else, has the distinctive rights of a father. This is not true for rights justified *not* by reference to the social role of the claimant, but by reference to his humanity. To say that a man possesses a right to a fair trial just because he is a human being implies that he possessed that right *before* being accused. Rights justified by reference to being human are rights possessed before becoming a member of any specific class of persons (and they are retained).

If we say that such rights 'can be claimed by members of a specific class of persons *because* they are members of that class', this must simply express the point that these are rights which can be exercised only when one is in a certain situation, a situation which not everyone is in. Only a man on trial can exercise his right to a fair trial; and not everyone is on trial. But *anyone* might be in a situation in which these rights can be exercised. They therefore remain rights which *everyone* has. They may be rights 'necessarily limited' to members of a specific class of persons, in the sense that only certain people are in the situation in which these rights can be exercised, but they are, nevertheless, rights *possessed* by all men.

Cranston demands of a universal right that everyone belong to the class of people for whom it is an occasion appropriate to its exercise; I have sketched some consequences of this demand. Recognizing that one may be a possessor of a right without being a person for whom it is an occasion appropriate to its exercise, we can alternatively demand of a universal right only that everyone possess it simply in virtue of being human.

This demand retains the distinction between rights which are universal and rights which are not; the right not to be held in slavery or servitude is, on this test, a universal right, the right of arrest is not. The right of arrest is justified by reference to satisfaction of further conditions than simply being human, such as, say, being a member of the police forces. Further, the traditional civil and political rights to life, liberty, a fair trial, and so on are also universal rights; they are rights possessed simply in virtue of being human. However, on this test the social and economic rights in question are also universal rights; these too are possessed simply in virtue of being human. The Universal Declaration says that human rights are validated by reference to the 'inherent dignity. . .of all members of the human family'.

It seems to me that this form of justification is available equally to the civil and political and the social and economic rights in question. The rights to reasonable limitation of working hours and to periodic holidays with pay, though exercisable only on specific types of occasion, are possessed, and may be exercised on such occasions, by everyone, it may plausibly be argued, simply in virtue of being human; such rights recognize the inherent dignity of man.

If this is correct, the revised test of universality fails to supply grounds for denying that the social and economic rights in question are human rights.

The adjustment I have proposed for the test of universality is particularly relevant to welfare rights. Over recent years there has been, and indeed there still is, a debate about whether social welfare services should be universal or selective. One might assume that services labelled 'universal', like health and education, pass the test of universality; one might also assume that services labelled 'selective' do not pass this test. *Selective* services provide benefits to people who 'fit into a number of common categories of need, by virtue of sickness, old age or unemployment'.[30] It is therefore important to notice that much selective as well as universal provision corresponds to rights which *pass* the test of universality; 'concentrating help on those whose needs are greatest' does not prevent our claiming the welfare rights in question as human rights. The welfare rights corresponding to selective services are usually rights which may be exercised only on specific types of occasion – in sickness, old age or unemployment, say; but we may still claim that they are social rights which are possessed and may be exercised on the appropriate occasion by all men. The claim that they are human rights is not undermined even if it is true that as a matter of fact not all men are in the circumstances which qualify one for the benefit or service in question, since any man might be, and would be entitled simply in virtue of being human; the test of universality is passed.

Much selective treatment is like this, but not all. We may all hope or expect to live to old age and draw our old age pensions, but, since a large part of our population is not female, we cannot plausibly claim that a right to a *widow's* pension is possessed and may be exercised by all mankind on the appropriate occasion. Entitlement is not *simply* in virtue of being human. Such rights thus fail the revised test of universality, though even in these cases being human is a necessary condition of possession. At least, such rights fail the revised test of universality when they are thus specified.

30 Cf. Michael J. Hill, 'Selectivity for the poor', in Townsend and Bosanquet, *op. cit.*, and P. R. Kaim-Caudle, 'Selectivity and the Social Services', *Lloyds Bank Review*, no. 92, April 1969.

Welfare rights may express human rights in a particular historical and social setting, and rights such as that to a widow's pension may be seen as the human right to 'a standard of living adequate for the health and well-being of himself and his family' expressed in relation to bereaved women in a certain society. At different times different groups will need attention drawn to their possession of certain human rights and this may result in legislation recognizing rights which refer only to the endangered group, as in this case. Such welfare rights are not human rights on the revised test of universality, but they may be supported by reference to human rights since they defend the human rights of a particular group. The human rights framework is again useful.

It is my conclusion, then, that the three tests of practicability, paramount importance and universality, though appropriate types of test, quite fail to provide grounds for distinguishing the social and economic rights from the civil and political rights in question, and fail to provide grounds for denying that the welfare rights included in the former are human rights. The tests are:

(1) To pass the test of practicability it must at present be possible for men collectively to guarantee all men the right in question, at least in part;
(2) To pass the test of paramount importance the right in question must be one of which no one may be deprived without a grave affront to justice;
(3) To pass the test of universality the right in question must be possessed by all men simply in virtue of being human.

5

It might be admitted that Cranston's tests, even in their revised forms, fail to supply *philosophical* grounds for placing social and economic, and civil and political rights in different categories. Nevertheless, it might be said, there is still *political* point in holding the two groups apart. It will be recalled that I said earlier that Cranston raised political as well as philosophical doubts about including social and economic rights in a list of human rights, and both may not fall to the same philosophical arguments. Towards the end of his paper, Cranston[31] says that if the social and economic rights in question are also proclaimed as human rights, 'the effect may even be to bring the whole concept of human rights into disrepute. "It would be a splendid thing", people might say, "for everyone to have holidays with

[31] 1967, *op. cit.*, p. 52.

pay, a splendid thing for everyone to have social security, a splendid thing to have equality before the law, and freedom of speech, and the right to life. One day, perhaps, this beautiful ideal may be realized. . ." '

Cranston is here drawing the distinction between rights and ideals. Even if one admitted that the social and economic rights in question passed the revised test of practicability and were rights rather than ideals, one might be tempted to suggest that social and economic rights are more like ideals than are civil and political rights. And in that case one would think it politic to keep the two groups of human rights apart – for the effective protection of the civil and political rights. One might be so tempted if one thought of civil rights as 'designed to guarantee the individual against arbitrary treatment', and political rights as 'designed to relate the government to the consent of the governed', but social and economic rights as 'rights which require that something be done if they are to be secured for their recipients'.[32] On this view civil and political rights are presented as implying only that a *negative* obligation falls upon others, an obligation not to interfere with your exercise of these rights; the social and economic rights, on the other hand, place a *positive* obligation upon others. A positive obligation is more difficult to fulfil than a negative obligation, social and economic rights are thus closer to (distant) ideals than civil and political rights, and for the effective protection of the latter should be kept distinct in practice even if they are not significantly distinct in theory.

To use a disreputable phrase, I think that on reflection this objection is seen to be ill-founded.

For one reason, the courts, legislature, police force, defence services and administrative services involved in government do not compare all that favourably in terms of expense and effort with provision for the social and economic rights in question. In these terms social and economic rights in general seem no closer to ideals than civil and political rights.

A different political argument for keeping the two groups of rights apart is offered by those who argue that because the social and economic rights are 'rights which require that something be done if they are to be secured for their recipients', the promulgation of these rights has 'brought them into conflict with civil and political rights, for the planning and control essential to the former impinge on some of the freedom of choice and action that had seemed defensible under the latter'.[33]

Two points might be made in reply. First, such conflict can arise even between rights within just one of these groups. For example, a man with a

[32] Cf. Richard McKeon, 'Human Rights in the World Today', in *Human Rights*, Comments and Interpretations, UNESCO, 1949.

[33] McKeon, *op. cit.*, p. 44.

potentially fatal allergy to raw meat might have his right to life secured by having his right to freedom of movement diminished in the vicinity of butcher's shops.

Second, although rights in the two groups sometimes conflict, they also must often *co-operate*. This objection and Cranston's discussion of course assume that the traditional civil and political human rights can be secured quite independently of the social and economic rights now claimed. This assumption may be challenged. I earlier quoted Raphael as saying that 'if a man is subject to chronic unemployment in a depressed area, he will not thank you for the information that he has the basic rights of liberty'. I would suggest that such a man should not thank you, not because what he lacks is equally as important as or more important than liberty, but because his liberty is seriously at risk if he does not enjoy certain social and economic rights. In general, as Luc Somerhausen has put it, 'traditional human rights will not become a reality until they have been completed by a social organization which makes it possible for man to protect himself against exploitation'.[34] According to R. H. Tawney this co-operation is even more extensive: 'political rights afford a safeguard and significance to civil rights...economic and social rights provide means essential to the exercise of political rights...rights of communication and thought may prepare the resolution of differences concerning economic and social rights'.[35]

Article 3 of the Declaration proclaims the right to life. As Raphael notes, life is not secured merely by ensuring that no one takes it. Means of subsistence must be available, the usual means being employment or unemployment benefit. Article 7 says, 'all are equal before the law and are entitled without any discrimination to equal protection of the law'. If the means to this protection is to be bought from lawyers, the wherewithal must be available as of right to all – there must be some scheme for legal aid. The right to freedom of opinion and expression declared in article 19 is secured only if education, and indeed a certain kind of education, is available.

The assumption which seems to underly the view that the traditional civil and political human rights can be secured quite independently of the social and economic rights now claimed is that civil and political rights require from a government only that (1) it shall not actively interfere with their exercise, and (2) it shall prevent others actively interfering with their exercise. It seems to me that many (at least) of these human rights are secured only if the government also (3) guarantees the social and economic rights which permit all men to exercise them. Otherwise, these civil and

[34] L. Somerhausen, 'Human Rights in the World Today', in UNESCO, 1949, *op. cit.*, p. 32.
[35] R. H. Tawney, *The Acquisitive Society*, London: Methuen, 1937.

political rights will not be practicable, all men will not in fact be able to exercise them.

6

So much for Cranston's philosophical and political objections to the inclusion of social and economic rights in a list of human rights. Cranston would not deny that *some* welfare rights are human rights – the traditional rights to liberty and a fair trial are plausibly described as welfare rights. But he would deny that certain other, social and economic welfare rights are human rights. I have tried to meet his arguments to this conclusion because they seem to me to hinder the effective, that is, statutory, protection of all these welfare rights. Where human dignity is used in moral justification of social welfare provision, we assume welfare entitlement to be a human right. It is this assumption which it has been my purpose to clarify and defend. It points us towards the Universal Declaration, and a framework for the welfare rights approach matching its ambitions.

RODNEY PEFFER

A Defense of Rights to Well-Being

Many value theorists, especially those adhering more closely to classical liberalism, refuse to recognize rights to well-being. For one reason or another they assert that rights are basically rights to freedom, that is, rights *against* others who have correlative obligations not to interfere with all but certain classes of our actions rather than rights *to* certain types of goods or services or rights to be in certain social or economic positions. The latter may be called rights to well-being or welfare rights. Whereas rights to freedoms are traditionally said to arise from our respect for a person's autonomy (and hence may be referred to as autonomy rights), rights to well-being arise from our concern for human welfare. Furthermore, I should like to distinguish a third kind of right which includes whatever rights to freedom and rights to well-being we may legitimately be said to have, but is not limited to them. These rights, which I shall call social contract rights, accrue to individuals by virtue of their being members of a particular society at a particular time.[1] They are defined as the rights which we, as members of that society, can justly claim, the rights that a just society, given its concrete conditions of production and so on, deems us to have. I contend that social contract rights are those rights which derive from the application of such principles as guarantee the structure of society to be just (on Rawls' theory, those principles which would be arrived at in the original position) to the concrete conditions

1. The inspiration for this concept comes from J. G. Murphy's excellent article "Rights and Borderline Cases." However, as we shall see later, my notion of social contract rights differs in several important ways from his.

Philosophy & Public Affairs 8, no. 1.
0048-3915/78/030065-23$01.15/1

of a particular society at a particular time. We do not possess these rights merely by virtue of being persons; given the principles of distributive justice and other such basic principles, they are rights that must be guaranteed by the particular society in which we live. Examples are the right to a free education, to adequate health care, to a fair trial and, I think it can be argued, the right to own property. Even a cursory glance at various manifestos on human rights will reveal they contain rights of each of these three kinds. "The Universal Declaration of Human Rights" adopted by the United Nations General Assembly in 1948 contains, for example, "the right to freedom of opinion and expressions," "the rights to . . . food, clothing, housing," "the rights to rest and leisure, including reasonable limitation of working hours and periodic holidays with pay."

My theses in this essay are (1) that there are no a priori reasons to reject the notion that we have rights to well-being as well as rights to freedoms (that we are not, for example, making a linguistic or conceptual mistake in speaking of such rights); (2) that classical liberal social and political theory and its most backward descendent, libertarianism, are untenable in that they maintain that violations of rights are the *only* legitimate ground for coercion and that rights to freedom are the *only* rights we have; and (3) that recognizing rights to well-being and social contract rights is justified because it helps us to better account for our considered moral judgments in certain types of moral situations. Further, such recognition allows us to construct a systematic moral, social, and political theory that is more in harmony with our considered moral judgments than any of its competitors. I might note at this point that the account of human rights offered here should be viewed as a supplement to Rawlsian theory and framework rather than as a rival. Rawls has little to say about human rights or rights of any kind and relies entirely on natural duties to account for situations in which, though coercion is justified, no rights to freedom are at stake. Therefore, an explication of the concept of rights and the construction of a theory of human rights is useful, even for those who consider Rawlsian theory to be basically correct.

During the course of this essay I shall attempt to refute several of the major objections to the notion that we have rights other than the traditionally recognized rights to freedom. These are that

(1) rights are permissions to act and correlative obligations not to interfere. Since welfare rights must be construed as entitlements or valid claims to certain sorts of things they cannot be genuine rights.

(2) rights are concerned only with the restriction or distribution of freedom; they come from this realm of moral discourse. Hence to speak of rights to well-being is to muddle the distinction between the concept of rights on the one hand and the concept of obligation or the rightness or wrongness of an act on the other.

(3) rights, by definition, have correlative obligations. Since rights to well-being and social contract rights either do not entail correlative obligations or burden us with innumerable obligations of a positive variety, they cannot be genuine rights.

I shall also offer a characterization of rights per se and of each of the three types which I assert we possess and show how this account of rights fits in with theories of distributive justice.

I

Locke and other classic liberals were the first to stress the existence and sanctity of natural rights of human beings, that is, rights we have without being in any special circumstances. Though they spoke of both natural law and natural rights it is clear that, insofar as they worked with the concept of rights, they construed them as permissions to act in certain ways and correlative obligations of others not to interfere. The underlying ideas were that persons ought to be free "to order their actions and dispose of their possessions and persons as they see fit," and that "all men may be restrained from invading one another's rights."[2] Robert Nozick, a contemporary libertarian who sees himself as being very much within the Lockean tradition, explicitly states that rights are "permissions to do something and correlative obligations of others not to interfere."[3]

2. John Locke, *Two Treatises of Government* (Cambridge, England, 1960), pp. 309, 312.

3. Robert Nozick, *Anarchy, State, and Utopia* (New York, 1974), p. 92.

This is an adequate characterization for some rights but not for others. Many of our civil liberties–such as the right of free speech, of assembly, the press, and political association–can be readily construed as permissions to act entailing correlative obligations of others not to interfere. The right of free speech does not entail that I must be provided with a soap box or be given equal time in the mass media to express my point of view (though one might argue for this on other moral grounds). Rather, it entails that one cannot stop me from climbing atop the soap box and speaking what I will–unless, of course, I speak obscenely or so loudly that I disturb the peace. But this merely serves to point out that no right is absolute in the sense of being indefeasible in the face of any and all other moral considerations. In this sense all rights are prima facie.

There are other rights however, rights which almost anyone would admit to, that do not fit easily into this characterization. Take special rights that arise from promises. If John Doe promises to give Richard Roe ten dollars, then Roe has the prima facie right to hold Doe to his promise. But how is this to be construed in terms of permissions to act? What actions has Richard Roe permission to do? It seems to be a question, not of Roe being permitted to *do* anything, but rather of him being *entitled to have something*, namely the ten dollars. There is, to be sure, a correlative obligation on the part of Doe in this case to give Roe the money. Perhaps there are even prima facie permissions accruing to Roe to act so as to make Doe give him the money, but the permissions analysis still seems defective.

Or consider the right to a fair trial. Can this right be construed simply in terms of permissions of the accused to act in certain ways? I think not. It is not just a right of the defendant to act in certain ways–such as acting as his own attorney, being able to make phone calls, or being able to perform any number of other possible actions. It is also a right to have or receive certain things or to have certain things done in his behalf. The right includes being provided a fair jury and, if necessary, an attorney, and to have the proper courtroom procedures observed. Thus an analysis of rights, even within the realm of civil liberties, shows the permissions characterization to be untenable.

A more promising approach is to characterize rights as entitlements or valid claims. McCloskey adopts the first approach, Feinberg the second. According to McCloskey, "a right is an entitlement. It may be an entitlement to do, to demand, to enjoy, to be, to have done for us. Rights may be rights to act, to exist, to enjoy, to demand. We speak of rights as being possessed, exercised, and enjoyed." In support of this conclusion McCloskey offers examples similar to those I have previously given. He states, for example: "My legal right to marry consists primarily in the recognition of my entitlement to marry and to have my act recognized. It indirectly gives rise to claims on others not to prevent me so acting, but it does not primarily consist in these claims."[4]

Furthermore, McCloskey rejects the correlativity thesis, the thesis that it is a conceptual feature of rights that they always have correlative obligations.

> My right to life is not a right against anyone. It is my right and by virtue of it, it is normally permissible for me to sustain my life in the face of obstacles. It does give rise to rights against others in the sense that others have or may come to have duties to refrain from killing me, but it is essentially a right of mine, not an infinite list of claims, hypothetical and actual, against an infinite number of actual, potential, and as yet non-existent human beings.
>
> When a right is attributed, we cannot always significantly ask "Who has the corresponding duties?" And, when a duty is postulated, we cannot always find someone who possesses a corresponding right.[5]

The latter claim in the preceding paragraph is relatively noncontroversial. Most of us are willing to recognize imperfect duties, such as duties to be charitable or duties to realize one's own potentialities. The former claim is the one disputed. Feinberg offers an analysis of rights which turns out to be compatible with McCloskey's.

Feinberg accepts the correlativity thesis and stresses the respects

4. H. J. McCloskey, "Rights," *Philosophical Quarterly* 15 (1965): 117, 116.
5. McCloskey, pp. 118, 122.

in which rights are tied up with claims and the activity of claiming. His position is as follows:

> To have a right is to have a claim against someone whose recognition as valid is called for by some set of governing rules or moral principles. To have a claim in turn, is to have a case meriting consideration, that is, to have reasons or grounds that put one in a position to engage in performative and propositional claiming.[6]

Rather than argue against McCloskey's entitlement analysis, Feinberg suggests the two are perfectly compatible.

> Whether we are speaking of claims or rights, however, we must notice that they seem to have two dimensions, as indicated by the prepositions "to" and "against" . . . all rights seem to merge *entitlements to* do, have, omit, or be something with *claims against* others to act or refrain from acting in certain ways. If we mean by "entitlement" that *to* which one has a right and by a "claim" something directed at those *against* whom the right holds (as McCloskey apparently does), then we can say that all claim-rights necessarily involve both, though in individual cases the one element or the other may be in sharper focus.

However, Feinberg accepts the thesis of correlativity.

> As far as I can tell, the only reason McCloskey gives for denying that in rem rights are against others is that those against whom they would have to hold make up an enormously multitudinous and "vague" group, including hypothetical people not yet even in existence. Many others have found this a paradoxical consequence of the notion of in rem rights, but I see nothing troublesome in it. If a general rule gives me a right of noninterference in a certain respect against everybody, then there are literally hundreds of millions of people who have a duty toward me in that respect; and if the same general rule gives the same right to everyone else, then it imposes on me literally hundreds of millions of duties—or duties towards hundreds of millions of people. I see nothing paradoxical

6. Joel Feinberg, "The Nature and Value of Rights," *Journal of Value Inquiry* 4, no. 4 (Winter 1970): 257.

about this, however. The duties, after all, are negative; and I can discharge all of them at a stroke simply by minding my own business.[7]

Unfortunately this is not a solution to what I shall refer to as the problem of near innumerable positive obligations (those obligations which require acts of commission rather than mere inaction), but rather a denial of the problem. It is clear, however, that the problem exists even on Feinberg's account of rights. True, he speaks of a special "manifesto sense" of "right" in which rights are not correlative to duties and is thereby liberated from the responsibility of accounting for obligations which might have been correlative to this class of rights. But a careful reading of Feinberg reveals that rights to well-being in the "manifesto sense" are those claims which someone is "in a position to make . . . even when there is no one in a corresponding position to do anything about it." But what of those rights to well-being which some or all of us are in a position to do something about? Feinberg clearly recognizes such a class of rights or at least the potentiality of the evolution of such a class of rights. He speaks of "claims, based on need alone" which are "permanent possibilities of rights, the natural seed from which rights grow."[8] Feinberg is able to "solve" the problem of almost innumerable positive obligations only by the sleight of hand of ignoring a class of positive rights to well-being which his own theory of human rights recognizes. Thus he neither solves nor dissolves the problem. On the account of rights I shall offer, this problem is solved by denying the correlativity thesis in the case of certain classes of rights to well-being and social contract rights. The thesis is denied on grounds that (1) the concept of rights is a cluster concept and thus the meaning of the term "rights" need not be restricted by the correlativity thesis and that (2) we have good systematic reasons to recognize both rights to well-being and social contract rights.

II

It is clear, I think, that the "entitlement," or "valid claim" characterization of rights is more in harmony with our linguistic intuitions than

7. Feinberg, pp. 256-257.

8. Feinberg, p. 255.

is the "permission" characterization. The former can account for cases in which we assume rights are at stake, while the latter cannot. Accepting this account of the concept of rights does not, however, entail that there are rights to well-being. It may be the case, as Hart suggests, that rights concern only the limitation or distribution of freedom. In that case, though we may have a rhetorical license to speak of rights to well-being, there really are no such rights at all.

It is true that the concept of rights originated with classical liberalism and has historically dealt with problems of the limitation of freedom. But simply to assert that rights are concerned only with freedom or that the concept of rights to well-being is a linguistic error begs the question. Further, if this claim is based on an appeal to the ordinary usage of contemporary populations it is quite likely false. And even if it were true as a descriptive claim about usage, this consideration would not settle the issue. From a systematic point of view we may have good reason to adopt one usage rather than another, regardless of ordinary usage.

Hart also argues that we ought not recognize rights to well-being because anything we want to say about the cases in which we might appeal to such rights can be equally well described by other terms or phrases. Since this is the case, the argument goes, we should not conflate the different realms of moral discourse. To do so may bring about considerable confusion and put us in a worse position to construct coherent, viable moral theories. If, however, it can be shown that the important distinctions Hart wishes to preserve can be preserved within an expanded theory of human rights, then Hart's argument is considerably weakened. Further, if it can be shown that the expanded theory of human rights ties in with other theories that one might want to accept (for example, theories of human worth or of distributive justice), then one might have good reason to adopt such a theory. I should like to argue for both these claims.

First, however, let us consider Hart's claim that the concept of rights is linked to the concept of freedom. Hart states that

> . . . the concept of a right belongs to that branch of morality which is specifically concerned to determine when one person's freedom may be limited by another's and so determine what action may ap-

> propriately be made the subject of coercive legal rules. . . . it is I think a very important feature of a moral right that the possessor of it is conceived as having a moral justification for limiting the freedom of another and that he has the justification not because the action he is entitled to require of another has some moral quality but simply because in the circumstances a certain distribution of human freedom will be maintained if he by his choice is allowed to determine how that other shall act.[9]

The evidence Hart offers for his hypothesis consists in appeals to the common usage of the term "rights" in our moral discourse. He claims the phrase "I have a right to . . ." is used in two main types of situations:

> (A) when the claimant has some special justification for interference with another's freedom which other persons do not have ("I have a right to be paid what you promised for my services"); (B) when the claimant is concerned to resist or object to some interference by another person as having no justification ("I have a right to say what I think").[10]

This is probably correct as a descriptive statement concerning our ordinary discourse. Appeal to rights is probably most common in the kinds of situations Hart describes, but this can be accounted for in terms of the amount of time the usage has been in the language, the fact that many of the rights to freedoms have been institutionalized in the legal system, and the fact that some concrete situations naturally give rise to claims of interference or non-interference. However, claims concerning well-being are seldom called forward by concrete situations because there is seldom a determinate individual to make the claim against. In an age of humanistic manifestoes it is not uncommon, however, for people to claim rights to well-being, such as the right to a job or the right to health care. Hart's analysis does not establish that it is a conceptual error to speak of such rights.

The stronger argument, I think, is the one concerning the advan-

9. H.L.A. Hart, "Are There Any Natural Rights" in *Human Rights*, ed. A. I. Meldon (Belmont, CA, 1970), pp. 63, 64.

10. Hart, p. 68.

tages of not conflating the different realms of moral discourse. Hart suggests this position in the following passages:

> These considerations should incline us not to extend to animals and babies whom it is wrong to ill-treat the notion of a right to proper treatment, for the moral situation can be simply and adequately described here by saying that it is wrong or that we ought not to ill-treat them or, in the philosopher's generalized sense of "duty" that we have a duty not to ill-treat them. If common usage sanctions talk of the rights of animals or babies it makes an idle use of the expression "a right," which will confuse the situation with other different moral situations where the expression "a right" has a specified force and cannot be replaced by the other moral expressions which I have mentioned.
>
> The characteristic function in moral discourse of those sentences in which the meaning of the expression "right" is to be found . . . is to bring to bear on interferences with another's freedom, or on claims to interfere with freedom and characteristically different from the moral criticism of actions made with the use of expressions like "right," "wrong," "good," and "bad."[11]

I shall not take up the "rights of animals, babies, and idiots" controversy. I should like to point out, however, that Hart's suggestion that we can adequately describe those moral situations in which we are tempted to speak of rights to well-being by means of speaking about what one ought to do or what is right and wrong is not above suspicion. The problem with this suggestion is that to attribute a right to an individual affords grounds for coercion—we can legitimately force someone to not violate or cease from violating another person's rights. In contrast, to speak only of what someone "ought" to do or of what it would be "right or wrong" for someone to do in a moral situation does not generally afford grounds for coercion.

Consider an example given by Judith Jarvis Thomson. You are abducted during the night and plugged into the kidneys of an ailing but greatly loved violinist. When you awake you find yourself "back to back in bed" with the violinist, who is unconscious. Because you are

11. Hart, pp. 66, 73.

the only person with the right blood type, you are the only person who can save his life. However, in order to do so you must remain plugged into him continuously for nine years. Thomson asserts that

> . . . the fact that for continued life that violinist needs the continued use of your kidneys does not establish that he has a right to be given the use of your kidneys. . . . if you do allow him to go on using your kidneys, this is a kindness on your part, and not something he can claim from you as his due.[12]

I agree with Thomson that to allow the violinist the use of your kidneys is an act of supererogation, indeed, an act of supererogation par excellence. But I also wish to assert that the violinist has a (prima facie) right to life and hence to the necessities of life and, in these particular circumstances, a (prima facie) right to the use of your kidneys. This is not to say, however, that you are obligated in the final, non-prima facie sense to give him the use of your kidneys. Rights, after all, even though perhaps the strongest sort of moral claims, are only prima facie. They can be overridden by other moral considerations and the obligations correlative to them (if any) can, under the appropriate circumstances, be excused. Thus, in the case of the violinist I hold there are prima facie grounds for coercion (coercing you to give him the use of your kidneys). Thomson thinks there to be no grounds for coercion in this case, nor even in such cases where no major sacrifice is required.

> Suppose you learn that what the violinist needs is not nine years of your life, but only one hour: all you need to do to save his life is to spend one hour in bed with him. Suppose also that letting him use your kidneys for that one hour would not affect your health in the slightest. Admittedly you were kidnapped. Admittedly you did not give anyone permission to plug him into you. Nevertheless it seems to me plain you ought to allow him the use of your kidneys for that hour—it would be indecent to refuse.[13]

12. Judith Jarvis Thomson, "A Defense of Abortion," *Philosophy & Public Affairs* 1, no. 1 (Fall 1971): 105, 112.
13. Thomson, p. 114.

This is an excellent example of how the term "ought" usually functions in our moral discourse. This sort of "ought" claim is not nearly as strong as a claim of right—the latter entails that coercion is justified, the former does not. If the violinist has a right to the use of a particular person's kidneys then we have a prime facie case for the legitimacy of force or the threat of force in making that person let the violinist use his kidneys. The claim that he "ought" to let the violinist use his kidneys, in the sense that his character will be morally contemptible if he doesn't, is certainly not as strong. Therefore, it is false that we can always describe situations where we are tempted to posit rights to well-being by means of speaking of obligations or the rightness or wrongness of acts.

Virtually anyone will agree that we haven't a (final or actual) obligation to give up nine years of our lives to benefit someone else no matter how great the benefit. But what if a person need only walk across a room and touch the violinist in order to save his life? Surely, in this case, we would be justified in forcing an obstinate or amoral person to do this one small thing. After all a human life is at stake! Thus, contrary to Hart and most other liberal theorists, there do exist situations in which, though no traditional rights to freedom are at stake, coercion is justified. It is these moral situations that make attractive the proposal to recognize rights to well-being.

This, perhaps, is not the only way to carve up moral discourse to account for these moral situations—we could speak in terms of coercible obligations or natural duties as do W. D. Ross and Rawls. But the recognition of rights to well-being and social contract rights is further supported by the fact that there are certain features or characteristics which all these various rights share and the fact that such a theory interlocks with certain other moral considerations and theories that support the acceptance of an expanded theory of rights.

III

Features common to the various types of rights mentioned at the beginning of this essay—autonomy rights, rights to well-being and social contract rights—provide the conceptual or linguistic basis for the recognition of rights to well-being and social contract rights. The first is the strength of rights—the fact that there is a conceptual link between rights and coercion such that coercion is justified to prevent or end the violation of rights. We have the strongest sort of grounds for grievance when the claims are denied, even grounds for extraordinary political action. The second is the connection of rights and gratitude—the fact that gratitude is not a fitting or appropriate reaction when our rights are respected by others. The acts which are required by claims of right are not supererogatory on the part of anyone. The third is the connection between rights and the concepts of equality and justice—the fact that rights serve as criteria by which to judge social, economic, and political arrangements. The fourth is the conceptual ties between rights and the concepts of human dignity and human worth.

In the linguistic dispute over whether or not to recognize rights to well-being and social contract rights as genuine rights—rights "in the full sense of the term"—I think we must take into consideration the features these various types of rights have in common as well as features which distinguish them (for example, some have correlative obligations and others don't). The fact that they have so many significant characteristics in common seems to weigh in favor of a linguistic decision to recognize rights to well-being as real or legitimate and to account for differences between types of rights by means of the concept of "family resemblance." This is probably not an earthshaking suggestion since the types of rights recognized in the more traditional accounts would no doubt receive the same sort of analysis. Think, for example, of the distinction Hart makes between general and specific rights and the distinction he should have made between general rights to non-interference and general rights to interference (for example, the right to stop a rape).

IV

Two theories which the expanded theory of human rights seems to support and be supported by are Vlastos' theory of human worth (and its relation to human rights) and theories of distributive justice (for example, that of Rawls).

It seems there exist certain important conceptual ties between rights and the concepts of human dignity and human worth, connections which seem to provide good theoretical or systematic reasons for us to recognize rights to well-being and social contract rights in addition to the more traditional variety of rights. Feinberg notes some of these connections:

> They [rights] are especially sturdy objects to "stand upon," a most useful sort of moral furniture. . . . This feature of rights is connected in a way with the customary rhetoric about what it is to be a human being. Having rights enables us to "stand up like men," to look others in the eye, and to feel in some fundamental way the equal of anyone. To think of oneself as the holder of rights is not to be unduly but properly proud, to have that minimal self-respect that is necessary to be worthy of the love and esteem of others. Indeed, respect for persons . . . may simply be respect for their rights, so that there cannot be the one without the other: and what is called "human dignity" may simply be the recognizable capacity to assert claims. To respect a person then, or to think of him as possessed of human dignity, simply *is* to think of him as a potential maker of claims.[14]

Gregory Vlastos derives a theory of human rights which recognizes both rights to freedom and rights to well-being from the concept of human worth. He points out that human worth, the intrinsic value we attribute to human beings regardless of their merit, is perhaps our most basic moral concept and the equal intrinsic value of all human beings perhaps our most basic moral principle. This concept underlies not only the concepts of justice and equality but also that of human rights. Vlastos points out that the two fundamental capacities of human beings are the capacity to experience and enjoy value in all its forms and the capacity to choose from among competing alternatives which values to pursue. From this and the principle of equal intrinsic worth Vlastos argues that "one man's well-being is as valuable as another's," that "one man's freedom is as valuable as another's," consequently that "one man's (prima facie) right to well-being is equal to that of any other," and that "one man's (prima facie) right to free-

14. Feinberg, "The Nature and Value of Rights," p. 252.

dom is equal to that of any other." From these two general rights, the argument goes, one can derive the specific rights of both varieties. From the equal right to well-being, Vlastos claims, we can derive specific social and economic rights such as: "the right to education, medical care, work under decent conditions, relief in periods of unemployment, leisure, housing, etc."[15]

My purpose is not to analyze this argument in detail but to point out that if the argument is sound we have excellent reason from a systematic point of view to accept the concept of rights to well-being and of social contract rights. (Note that Vlastos does not distinguish between basic rights to well-being and social contract rights. On my definition, the former are rights stemming directly from the concept of human worth and involve the guaranteed satisfaction of basic human needs; the latter are rights which arise out of considerations of distributive justice and may involve the satisfaction of "non-basic" needs or even wants as well as the satisfaction of basic needs.)

Someone like Hart may claim that Vlastos misuses the term "right" by speaking of rights other than rights having to do with the distribution or the limitation of freedom. The reply to such a claim is, in part, that if Vlastos can construct a normative theory which is in harmony with our considered moral judgments by adopting a more inclusive meaning of the term, this is excellent reason to do so.

V

Even if speaking of rights other than rights to freedom is conceptually legitimate and we have good systematic reasons to speak of such rights, it is by no means obvious what rights or kinds of rights we ought to recognize or what characteristics we should attribute to them. I should like to propose that we recognize both rights to well-being and social contract rights where the former are a subclass of the latter.

On my account, "rights to well-being" is not an all-inclusive category for any right to any benefit we may have (many of these will be social and economic rights which are social contract rights but not rights to well-being as I am using this last term). Rather, it is a cate-

15. Gregory Vlastos, "Justice and Equality," in *Human Rights*.

that they are overridden by other moral considerations. Consider a "crisis morality" situation: either we let Smith die a slow, agonizing death or every other living being in the entire universe will die a slow, agonizing death. In other cases, where no overriding moral considerations exist, we are *excused* from our obligations due to the fact that acting on them will require great personal sacrifice. This simply flows from the common-sense precept that morality does not require us to be martyrs. There is an area of legitimate self-interest within which we are not subject to moral dictates; within which, if we do act on our obligations the act is supererogatory. Rawls notes, for example, that "supererogatory acts are not required, though normally they would be were it not for the loss or risk involved for the agent himself."[16] From these considerations we can surmise the general principle that we are excused from our obligations if to act on them would involve substantial self-sacrifice or the risk of substantial self-sacrifice. Again there is a problem of the criteria of substantiality, but we are bound to agree on at least the paradigm cases.

To return for a moment to Thomson's example, I should like to assert that the violinist has a right to have his basic needs met and hence, in the circumstances, a right to the use of your kidneys. Being in a position to have a significant effect on the situation, you have a correlative obligation to meet his needs—to let him remain plugged into you for nine years. But I claim that you are excused from the obligation on grounds of substantial self-sacrifice. (Whether or not it was morally permissible for the violinist's friends and admirers to abduct you and plug you into the violinist without your permission is an altogether different question.)

VI

Now I should like to explicate the concept of "social contract rights." As I stated at the beginning of this essay, social contract rights are those rights which, as members of society, we can justly claim; they are the rights a just society, given its concrete conditions of production and so on, must guarantee us. These rights are derived by applying the basic normative principles which guarantee the institutional

16. John Rawls, *A Theory of Justice* (Cambridge, MA, 1971), p. 117.

structure of society to be just (those, for example, on Rawls' account, which would be chosen in the original position) to the concrete conditions of a particular society at a particular time.

J. G. Murphy characterizes social contract rights as follows:

> . . . Rights claims are *not* morally basic. Rather they are derivative from more general moral principles. "To have a right," Mill suggests, "is to have something which society ought to defend me in the possession of." The central idea here is that rights claims function, not to mark out some specially fine feature of persons, but rather to mark out which of all moral claims *ought to be enforced by the state, ought to be law.* On this view, a creature may be said to have a right to X if and only if it is morally reasonable, all things considered, to guarantee X to that creature as a matter of law.
>
> An individual should be understood as having a right to X if and only if a law guaranteeing X to the individual would be chosen by rational agents in the original position. This concept of a right I shall call a *Social Contract Right.*[17]

It is interesting that the former comment indicates agreement with Feinberg's analysis of rights—"To have a right is to have a claim against someone whose recognition as valid is called for by some set of governing rules or moral principles."[18] The latter comment indicates a divergence from Rawls' theory in that neither rights nor legal statutes (laws) are to be chosen in the original position on Rawls' account, but in the second and third stages of the decision-making process, respectively—in the constitutional convention and legislative stages, respectively. On this, I shall adhere to Rawls' theory.

It seems obvious that we shall demand that society recognize both traditional rights to freedom (rights connected with the concept of human autonomy) and basic rights to well-being, besides whatever other rights we shall demand; therefore I wish to distinguish between a broader and a narrower sense of social contract rights. The broader sense will designate all rights that society should recognize and

17. J. G. Murphy, "Rights and Borderline Cases," *Arizona Law Review* 19, no. 1 (1978): 232, 235.

18. Feinberg, "The Nature and Value of Rights," p. 257.

guarantee us (this includes autonomy rights and basic rights to well-being); the narrower sense will designate only those rights which we can justly demand of society over and above these two basic types of rights. Social contract rights in the narrow sense will include both social and economic rights, such as the right to an education and to civil liberties (the right to a fair trial).[19]

Social contract rights, in the narrow sense, are those rights which we have, not merely by virtue of being a person, but rather as a member of a particular society at a particular time. Using Hart's distinction between general and specific rights, we can say they are specific rights if we keep in mind that they need not arise from a particular voluntary action such as the act of promising.

The result of accepting the notion of social contract rights is an extension of rights to freedom and of rights to well-being. Many of our civil liberties must be construed as social contract rights. Though I may have the right to speak freely or to associate with whomever I like merely in virtue of being a person, surely I do not have a right to a fair trial or a right to vote outside of a set of social institutions, a set of cooperative social schemes. Property rights or, at least, rights to productive (as opposed to personal) property seem also to be social contract rights because there would be little sense in speaking of such rights outside of a cooperative social scheme.

Though I shall not attempt to defend this view at present or to trace out its consequences, I might note that much of liberal theory is predicated on the assumption that we possess property rights by virtue of merely being human and not by virtue of being members of a society. If property rights are social contract rights, they must derive from the basic moral principles which would govern the structure of a just society. Hence, they are not as strong as our basic autonomy rights or our basic rights to well-being and so are not inviolable or unalterable as libertarians, for example, assert. As Rawls notes, his theory is compatible with both private and public ownership of productive property and there is no a priori reason for choosing one over the other. A

19. Murphy carves up this realm of discourse differently. He prefers to speak of autonomy rights on the one hand and social contract rights on the other, where the latter category does not include the former.

decision on this issue is to be made in the second or third stages of the decision-making process, not in the original position, and is to be made in light of considerations of political economy and political sociology. If, for example, public ownership of productive property turns out to be more conducive to meeting the demands of the basic principles we choose to govern our social structure than private ownership does, then we shall choose a system of rights which does not include the right to own productive property.

Similarly, our rights to well-being would be extended into a realm of positive benefits which, at least potentially, go far beyoind the satisfaction of basic human needs. These particular social contract rights are often referred to as social and economic rights.

The problem remains of determining exactly what specific social and economic rights we have. This is a problem for rights to freedom also (without some sort of decision procedure, argument on these matters rapidly degenerates into mere tradings of intuitions). It is especially severe for social and economic rights because such rights are generally thought to evolve with the ability of society to meet the claims made on it by the population. For example, though it may seem plausible to attribute the right to regular holidays with pay to members of advanced industrial societies, given their great wealth, it seems absurd to attribute such a right to the members of the poorest third-world nations. Fortunately, a solution lies at hand. It has to do with the fact that such rights are intimately related to principles of distributive justice. S. I. Benn notes that such rights are

> . . . canons by which social, economic, and political arrangements can be criticized. Human rights, in short, are statements of basic needs or interests. They are politically significant as grounds of protest and justification for reforming policies. They differ from appeals to benevolence and charity in that they involve ideas like justice and equality.
>
> Human rights are the corollary, then, of the equally modern notion of social justice.[20]

20. S. I. Benn, "Rights," in *The Encyclopedia of Philosophy*, ed. Paul Edwards, 8 vols. (New York, 1976), 7: 198-199.

The solution to the specific problem of deciding what social and economic rights the members of a particular society have lies in specifying the relation between these rights and the principles of distributive justice.

My thesis is that we have a right to those benefits (goods, services and opportunities) which the principles of distributive justice dictate we should have, given the ability of our society to provide us with them—given its productive capacity and its population. (I shall not take up the issue of what principles of distributive justice ought to be accepted but I consider Rawls' maximin principle, or perhaps a hybrid principle which would incorporate Hart's bottom-floor principle into the maximin principle, as the most likely candidates.) On my account, all of our social contract rights would be decided upon at the constitutional convention stage of Rawls' schema. At this stage we decide upon ". . . the constitutional powers of government and the basic rights of citizens."[21]

In an advanced industrialized society such as that of the United States or the nations of Western Europe we shall presumably arrive at such rights as those mentioned in the United Nations Declaration of Human Rights—the right to free health care, free education, unemployment benefits, and periodic holidays with pay. In the poorer nations such as India, Sudan, and Bangladesh it is obvious, given the productive capacity of such societies, that no such rights exist (though on my account persons in these countries still have basic rights to well-being). Here I leave aside the objection of Marxists and other internationalists that the more advanced nations have a responsibility to help the less advanced solve their problems because they have helped to cause the problems as well. I also do not consider the objection that, since national boundaries are an arbitrary factor from a moral point of view, we have no right to calculate for social and economic rights in terms of nation-states but must make our calculations on the basis of the world community and the resources available to it. It is interesting to note that with all his concern with eliminating factors from our moral considerations which are arbitrary from a moral point of view, Rawls fails to even pose this question. In my

21. Rawls, *A Theory of Justice*, p. 197.

opinion this is a major failing for his theory. But even if we are convinced that national boundaries are arbitrary from a moral point of view, this does not vitiate the conclusions we have reached concerning social and economic rights. We simply make the calculations for the planet as a whole rather than for societies demarcated by national boundaries.

A view of human rights which recognizes social contract rights in the narrow sense solves several theoretical problems. First, it explains how it can be the case that "there is a continuous transformation, as society advances [toward greater abundance] of economic and social claims into civil and political rights" and thus it avoids "the anomaly of ascribing to all human beings now, even those in pre-industrial societies, such 'economic and social' rights as 'periodic holidays with pay.' "[22] Furthermore, it serves to elucidate the connection between such rights and the idea that we have a natural duty to support and promote just social institutions. The account of rights I have offered recognizes that social contract rights are founded on principles designed to judge the institutional structure of society. Therefore, the obligation to insure the observance of such rights does not fall on individuals as individuals but rather on individuals as members of a society. Individuals are not directly obligated to other individuals to make sure they receive the benefits they have a right to—they do not have to personally pay for as many children's educations as they are able if children have this social contract right but society is not just. Rather, we might say that individuals have an indirect obligation to other members of the society because of their natural duty to support and promote just social institutions; that is, institutions which, among other things, guarantee people their social and economic rights.

22. J.E.S. Fawcett as cited in Feinberg, "The Nature and Value of Rights," p. 254, and Feinberg, p. 255.

12

Deriving Welfare Rights From Libertarian Rights

ALLEN BUCHANAN

I

The aim of this essay is to examine and support the thesis that certain welfare rights can be derived from certain widely accepted libertarian rights.* The libertarian rights in question are (*1.*) the right to freedom of expression and (*2.*) the right to the benefits of the legal system. The right to freedom of expression is the right to communicate through various media and is not restricted to speech in the narrow sense. The right to the benefits of the legal system consists of a cluster of due process rights, the right to legal counsel, and the right to legal representation. Both the right to freedom of expression and the right to the benefits of the legal system are to be understood as *negative* rights—rights not to be interfered with in certain ways as one engages in certain activities. My right to freedom of expression, thus conceived as a negative right, is a right not to be interfered with by violence or the threat of violence, as I engage in certain communicative activities. As a negative right, my right to freedom of expression is *not* a right not to have my communicative activity limited in *any* way whatsoever. For example, if I somehow gain access to a broadcast microphone without paying for air-time, you, the owner of the network, may cut off the power. In such a case you would be interfering with my communicative activity, but not in a way which violates my right to freedom of expression. Similarly, my right to the benefits of the legal system is only a right against certain sorts of interferences —it is not itself a positive right to be provided with legal services.

The point of calling these negative rights "libertarian rights" is to emphasize that they are held to be genuine rights by libertarians. By "libertarians" I mean those who hold that the only morally justifiable state is one whose functions are limited to the enforcement of voluntary contracts, and to protecting citizens against bodily injury, theft, and fraud. Libertarians contend that any state which exceeds these minimal functions violates individuals' moral rights. According to libertarians such as Robert Nozick,[1] there are no welfare rights and any state which engages in welfare functions is illegitimate.

The libertarian view on rights of political participation is rather complex. Clearly, libertarians reject unlimited majority rule, since it would violate libertarian rights—for example, the right to property. But some variants of libertarian theory can include a right to run for office and to vote in elections to determine who shall be the officers of the minimal state. In what follows I will be concerned with the relation between (*1.*) the right to freedom of expression, (*2.*) the right to the benefits of the legal system, and (*3.*) the right of political participation, on the one hand, and welfare rights, on the other. Whether or not the right to political participation, like the other two rights, is a *libertarian* right is of little importance to my argument. For the sake of brevity I shall usually use the phrase "libertarian rights" to refer to all three, but the reader is invited to restrict its application to the right to freedom of expression and the right to legal benefits if he thinks this is fairer to the libertarian. My point in calling the right of political participation a libertarian right is to emphasize that it, too, is a negative right.

The point of saying that there are *rights* to freedom of expression, to legal benefits, and to political participation is complex. There are four basic elements in the concept of a right as I understand it here. First, a person who has a right to something has a *valid claim* to it—he is *entitled* to it. He may demand it as his due, rather than merely request it as something beneficial. Second, the fact that a person has a right to something implies a *corresponding obligation* on the part of others. Third, claims of right *take precedence over considerations of utility maximization.*[2] Fourth, rights are *enforceable*—coercion may be used to protect rights where other methods are inadequate.[3] The libertarian or minimal state theorist, as well as most of the rest of us, adds a further feature: It is the *state* which is the proper enforcer of the rights in question.

For purposes of my argument I make a further assumption: The coercively backed, state-enforced, negative rights in question are to be understood as *equal* rights. They accrue to all citizens (or at least to all competent adult citizens). The question of whether there are rights is distinct from the question of whether there are equal rights. I shall simply assume that there are equal rights to freedom of expression, to the benefits of the legal system, and to political participation, where these rights are understood to exemplify each of the features listed above. The question I shall attempt to answer can now be posed with greater precision: Granted that there are (equal) libertarian rights to freedom of expression, to the benefits of the legal system, and to political participation, where these are negative rights to be enforced by the state, are there also (equal) state-enforceable welfare rights?

Three more points must be added before the question can be fully specified. First, it is important to note that the libertarian rights are to be understood as *moral* rights, and that the question is whether they give rise to *moral* welfare rights. *Moral* rights are to be distinguished from *legal* rights, i.e., rights actually established in the positive law of a society. In this essay I am not concerned with the question of whether, granted that our legal system includes the libertarian rights, it follows that it also includes certain welfare rights. Second, I am not assuming that either the libertarian rights or the welfare rights to which they may give rise are that special sort of moral rights called *human rights*. By a "human right" I mean a moral right which accrues to all human beings simply by virtue of their being human, and hence which all human beings have regardless of the social, political, and economic circumstances in which they live. It is absurd to assume that every moral right is a human right. For example, even if there were a moral right, say, to periodic holidays with pay, or more generally, to income, this could not possibly be a human right, since not all human societies have reached a level of development at which it would even make sense to claim such rights. For one thing, not all human societies compensate labor through money. Similarly, it might be argued that the right to vote and to run for office could not be human rights since the very notion of such rights presupposes a rather complex background of social institutions not present in all human societies. Consequently, I shall make only the weaker assumptions that the libertarian rights are moral rights, and I shall argue that if there are such moral rights, there are also certain moral welfare rights.

One last term in our question requires clarification. What is meant by "*welfare* right"? A comprehensive definition may be hard to come by, but for now, illustration and rough characterization must suffice. The right to income support or the right to be provided with certain health care services or legal services are examples of welfare rights. In general, a welfare right is a right to be provided with cash or with certain material goods or services, either without charge or at a subsidized rate below their market value.

II

The importance of the thesis that welfare rights can be derived from libertarian rights now becomes apparent. Libertarians, by definition, believe that coercion may only be used to prevent or retaliate against coercion or fraud and to enforce contracts, and that consequently there are no welfare rights, though there are rights of free speech, legal benefits, and political participation. If it can be shown that welfare rights can be derived from rights which the libertarian himself recognizes, it will follow that the libertarian position is incoherent.

The attempt to derive welfare rights from libertarian rights is quite important, however, regardless of its implications for libertarianism. Whether they are libertarians or not, many who recognize the rights to free expression, to political participation, and to legal benefits reject welfare rights. The strategy of deriving welfare rights from libertarian rights, then, is a very powerful one: If it succeeds, it provides an indirect argument for welfare rights which should convince those who are unmoved by direct arguments. If successful, the derivation of welfare rights from libertarian rights has the virtue of establishing the controversial by appeal to the uncontroversial.

Further, if the indirect or derivative approach to the right to cash or goods or services succeeds, it calls into question the appropriateness of calling these rights *welfare* rights. For often a welfare right is taken to be simply a right that serves to secure or increase a person's welfare, where "welfare" is equated with the possession of material wealth. Libertarians sometimes encourage this interpretation by suggesting that welfare rights are advocated by those who view persons as passive consumers of utilities—utilities in the form of material goods and services. The libertarian then presents his defense of libertarian rights and his rejection of welfare rights as being grounded in an alternative conception of the person as a free agent. For the libertarian, increases in welfare—gains for the person as a consumer of utilities—cannot compensate for losses of freedom. It becomes tempting, then, to see the debate over the existence of welfare rights as a controversy rooted in two opposing conceptions of the person. Yet if welfare rights can be derived from libertarian rights, and if libertarian rights are rooted in the conception of the person as free, then this way of understanding the controversy over welfare rights is profoundly misleading.

III

I shall now explore one attempt to derive welfare rights from libertarian rights. It may be called the argument from fairness. The argument begins with a distinction between equal rights and equal effectiveness in the exercise of those rights.[4] Consider the right of political participation. Assume that all citizens equally possess the right to vote and to run for office, and that this right is impartially enforced by the state. Recall that this right is a coercively backed guarantee against certain sorts of interferences—interferences by violence or threat of violence. Yet even where each has an impartially enforced equal right of political participation there may be vast inequalities in the effectiveness with which different individuals can exercise their equal rights. Due to inequalities in wealth, in access to health care, and in educational opportunities, some persons are able to exercise their right of political participation much more effectively than others in pursuing their goals, whatever these goals happen to be.

Here is one example which nicely illustrates the divergence between equal rights and unequal effectiveness in their exercise for both the case of political participation rights and the right of freedom of expression. Suppose that a certain Mr. Jones is the commentator on a state-wide television news program in state *X*. For years Mr. Jones uses his unique position as a commentator to set out his political views. His success in becoming a Senator is due in large part to the fact that he was able to make his views widely known and to build up a large constituency years in advance of any official campaign. Even more interestingly, Jones happens to be the owner of the television station on whose news program he appears. Indeed, there is good reason to believe that Jones would not have been hired as commentator had he not been on such intimate terms with the owner. Mr. Smith, on the other hand, is an unemployed migrant worker who can't afford a television set, much less a television station. Both Jones and Smith have equal rights of political participation and freedom of expression. Yet there is an enormous inequality in the effectiveness with which the two can exercise their equal rights.

Differential access to mass media is only one of the more dramatic instances of gaping inequalities in the effectiveness of the exercise of equal rights to freedom of expression and political participation. Poor nutrition and lack of health care, compounded by the cultural deprivation and inferior public education prevalent in inner cities and many rural areas, produce millions of "citizens" who are illiterate, uninformed, and unable to communicate effectively their own interests.

Differences in wealth, educational opportunities, and access to health care also contribute to striking inequalities in the effectiveness of the equal right to the benefits of the legal system. The most cynical comment on these inequalities in the criminal law is the remark that "capital punishment" means you can avoid the punishment if you've got the capital. Leaving aside the role of poverty in the etiology of crime, there is strong evidence that poor persons who commit crimes are more likely to be prosecuted, if prosecuted are more likely to be convicted, and if convicted are more likely to get stiff sentences.[5] All of this is presumably due, at least in part, to the fact that the poor often suffer from severely restricted access to sound legal advice and able legal representation.

The disparity between equal rights and inequalities in the effectiveness with which they can be exercised is not, of course, restricted to the criminal law. In civil as well as criminal cases, those who are wealthier and better educated are better able to identify situations in which legal advice ought to be sought, better able to obtain sound legal advice, and better able to press their claims through the services of able legal representatives.

The argument from fairness can now be outlined. The system of libertarian rights has a crucial feature which the libertarian tends to overlook. The institutions which provide the libertarian rights constitute procedures by which individuals may pursue their goals and defend their interests and rights. But these procedures are inherently monopolistic: They impose severe limits on the ways and means by which an individual may pursue his goals and defend his rights and interests. The system of libertarian rights sharply restricts the ways in which a person may express his views, participate in the selection of political leaders and the resolution of public issues, and press his claims against others. The libertarian tends to view my possession of the equal rights in question strictly as a *benefit* for me. And, of course, coercively backed guarantees against violent interference with the freedoms in question are great benefits. But the price of these benefits is a system of rights which places me under serious liabilities. It is not simply that I have the *right*, for example, to protect my rights and interests through litigation: The system of legal rights precludes me from attempting to protect my rights and interests in certain other important ways. The state—even the minimal state—claims a monopoly upon enforceable adjudication, specifies the procedures through which such adjudication is to occur, and thereby puts me in an awesome condition of dependence upon these procedures.

A concrete example may be helpful. Suppose that I am a black activist. My right to free speech—if duly enforced by the authorities—enables me to pursue my goal of informing complacent liberals that the struggle for civil rights is not over. In exercising my right, however, I am required to recognize the same rights of others—including the Propaganda Minister of the Ku Klux Klan. The benefit of being able to express my views in safety comes at the price of a liability to suffer from the racial hatred which may be generated by others' exercise of this same right. The correlative of my enforced right is an enforced obligation to refrain from certain means of defending my rights and interests against attack. The system of equal rights precludes me from fighting racism in certain ways. If I have sufficient funds to secure access to effective media of communication, it may be reasonable for me to accept this liability and it may be fair for others to require me to accept it. But if illiteracy and poverty prevent me from being able to reply effectively to the Klan's racist propaganda, it may be neither reasonable nor fair. At least where certain extreme inequalities exist, compliance with the system of libertarian rights requires too much from some persons. They are unfairly expected to accept a system of procedures that significantly limits their resources for defending their rights and interests, without receiving the compensating benefits that others enjoy.

A libertarian such as Nozick might raise an important objection at this point. He would contend that the options precluded by the system of libertarian rights simply ought not to be counted as costs and that hence the question of whether they are adequately compensated for does not arise. It is true that the black activitist is precluded from using violence or threats to counteract the harmful effects of the Klan's racist propaganda. But the black activist cannot legitimately complain that he is barred from defending his rights and interests in *these* ways because his use of coercion would be morally wrong. The black activist cannot complain that he is unfairly prevented from doing that which he has no right to do.

Although this reply has a certain charming simplicity, it will not stand scrutiny. Even a libertarian like Nozick admits that prior to the establishment of the state as an effective protector of libertarian rights claiming a monopoly on the use of coercion, individuals have the moral right to protect themselves, through coercion if necessary. Consequently, the libertarian cannot block the argument from fairness by simply denying that the individual may count as costs the liabilities he incurs when the system of rights precludes him from defending himself in certain ways. The individual can be expected to relinquish his right to defend himself and forego those options only if the system of rights provides an effective set of procedures for defending his rights and interests. And the system of rights cannot perform this function where certain gross inequalities exist.

The libertarian might reply that all that fairness requires is that the loss of these options for self-defense actually be outweighed by the gain in security which the state-enforced system of libertarian rights provides. He would then contend that we are all much more secure and much better off under the minimal state than we would be were there no state. So no one can complain of unfairness, even if there are vast inequalities in the effectiveness with which different individuals can exercise their equal rights. It is true that a rich man can exercise his right to the benefits of the legal system much more effectively than a poor ghetto youth can. But even a poor ghetto youth is better off in a system that includes such a right than in one that does not. Hence, the libertarian concludes, it is not unreasonable or unfair to require the poor to accept the liabilities imposed by the system of rights.

This reply is flawed because it does not take the requirement of fairness seriously enough. The requirement of fairness might be satisfied if the only practicable alternatives were a Hobbesian state of nature or a system of unrestrained inequalities in the effectiveness of the exercise of libertarian rights. But unless the libertarian can show that these bleak alternatives are the only possibilities, fairness at least demands that we consider ways of insuring that the system of rights does not place unacceptable burdens on the poor.

The next task facing us is to see whether this sketch of the fairness argument can be developed into an argument for welfare rights. It is one thing to say that the argument supports the conclusion that certain inequalities violate a basic requirement of fairness. It is quite another to show that the argument generates a clearly formulable principle which specifies a determinate welfare right. It is yet a further step to ascertain what institutional arrangements would be needed for putting the welfare right into effect.

IV

It is tempting to conclude that the argument from fairness shows that all citizens must be able to exercise their equal libertarian rights with *equal effectiveness*. One could then argue that certain welfare arrangements are necessary to ensure equal effectiveness for the libertarian rights.

This temptation, however, must be resisted. One must not jump to the conclusion that if equal rights are desirable, then equality in the effectiveness of the exercise of rights is a reasonable goal. The argument from fairness at most makes a strong prima facie case for the conclusion that inequalities in effectiveness are unacceptable. This conclusion must be weighed against countervailing arguments which come to light as soon as we examine the goal of equal effectiveness.

The effectiveness with which an individual can exercise rights in the pursuit of his goals, or, more broadly, his conception of the good, depends upon many quite different factors. Some of these factors we have already noted: wealth, educational opportunities, and access to health care. But those who argue that equal rights require equal effectiveness in their exercise overlook the simple fact that there are other factors, including intelligence, motivation, personal qualities such as physical attractiveness and, most importantly, *the nature of one's goals*. Clearly, whether one can exercise one's right to free expression or one's right to political participation so as to achieve one's goals depends in part upon whether those goals are ambitious or modest, reasonable or unreasonable, popular or unpopular. Similarly, whether one can effectively exercise one's rights to the benefits of the legal system in the pursuit of one's ends will depend in part upon what one's ends are.

Once these other factors are recognized, it becomes clear that the demand for equal effectiveness in the exercise of rights cannot be satisfied by any welfare arrangements, no matter how radical. For even if radically egalitarian schemes for the redistribution of wealth were implemented, this would not suffice for achieving equal effectiveness, so long as individuals differ in motivation, intelligence, personal qualities, and goals. There are, unfortunately, measures which might be taken to equalize these other factors. Persons with superior motivation, intelligence, or personal qualities might be handicapped in various ways, and certain techniques of indoctrination and socialization might be used to produce homogeneity of goals.

Regardless of whether the goal of equal effectiveness is actually attainable, any serious attempt even to approximate it would require intolerable violations of individual freedom. Further, though I shall not belabor the point here, I suspect that any serious attempt to achieve *equal* effectiveness in the exercise of rights would require the abandonment of the commitment to equal rights. For example, the most effective way to insure that individuals with different goals and capacities can use their rights of political participation or their rights to legal benefits with equal effectiveness might be to accord them different rights. Those with superior capacities or more easily attainable goals would be accorded more restricted rights. If this suspicion is well founded, then the argument from equal rights to *equal* effectiveness undermines the commitment to equal rights on which it is based.

V

The argument of the preceding section shows that if a welfare right can be derived from the libertarian rights, it cannot be a right to whatever goods and services are required for equal effectiveness in the exercise of the libertarian rights. Is there a more plausible welfare rights principle which can be gotten from the fairness argument? John Rawls's Principle of Equality of Fair Opportunity presents a possibility worth exploring. This principle requires that persons with equal skill and motivation have equal chances of attaining social positions or offices, regardless of whether they are rich or poor, or come from families which occupy high or low social positions.[6]

The virtue of Rawls's principle is that it focuses on a particular goal—the attainment of a particular office or position—rather than upon the individual's goals or life plan in general. This particular restriction is not, of course, appropriate for addressing the *general* problem of inequalities in the effectiveness of the exercise of libertarian rights, because in many cases the individual is not attempting to attain any *office* or social *position* through the exercise of these rights. Yet the idea of restricting the notion of effectiveness may be crucial for deriving a welfare-rights principle which avoids the excesses of the principle of equal effectiveness discussed in the preceding section. That principle was unrestricted in the sense that it required that different individuals be able to exercise their equal rights with equal effectiveness in the pursuit of their goals in general, or more holistically, their life plans.

Examples will indicate how a restriction on the ideal of equal effectiveness might work. Suppose that Jones and Smith both desire to campaign for Congress on the platform of lowering property taxes—they are both one-issue candidates and they hold virtually identical positions on the same issue. Jones is extremely rich and well educated and is able to buy many hours of expensive media coverage to get his message across to the voters. Smith, on the other hand, is very poor, was forced to leave school at the age of fourteen to support his family, and is functionally illiterate. To conclude that equal rights of political participation are not by themselves adequate, one need not argue that Smith is unable to use his rights as effectively as Jones in the pursuit of his goals in general, whatever they happen to be. There is no need to ascertain the general goals or life plans of either Smith or Jones. We need only focus on a much more limited and manageable context of comparison. The pertinent question is whether it is fair that factors such as wealth and educational opportunities should be allowed to make such a tremendous difference in the chances which two individuals have for achieving *the same limited goal*—in this case, a successful campaign for Congress on the platform of property-tax cuts. We must ask whether, other things being equal, Jones would have a much greater prospect of winning this particular race on this particular platform if it were not for his great wealth and superior educational opportunities.

This way of approaching the issue of whether inequalities in the effectiveness of equal rights are unacceptable has two advantages over the approach which condemns all inequalities in the effectiveness with which different persons can use their rights to pursue their goals in general. First, it limits the goals with reference to which the question of effectiveness is raised. In the case at hand, we are concerned only with the very restricted goal of winning a certain election. We are not asked to gauge the effectiveness with which Jones can exercise his rights in the pursuit of his life plan and to compare this with the effectiveness with which Smith can pursue his life plan. Such ambitious comparisons are avoided by suitably restricting the scope of the notion of effective exercise. Second, we are asked to focus only on the role that certain factors, in this case wealth and educational opportunities, play in determining the effectiveness with which certain individuals can exercise their rights in the pursuit of the suitably restricted goal. We need not be concerned with every factor that may contribute to inequalities.

Similarly, to ascertain whether existing inequalities in the exercise of the right to legal benefits are unacceptable, we can again invoke a restricted notion of effectiveness and again consider actual and hypothetical cases. We may ask, for instance: other things being equal, would the defendant have been found guilty of this crime, on the basis of this evidence, if he had been able to buy the services of a skillful defense lawyer? If, on consideration of many such cases, we conclude that differences in wealth or educational opportunities or access to health care should not be allowed to make such a difference in the effectiveness with which different persons can use their rights in pursuing the same limited goals, then we can proceed to the problem of determining what sorts of institutional arrangements would be appropriate for remedying or at least ameliorating the situation. For example, the more extreme inequalities between persons such as Jones and Smith might be diminished by some combination of public campaign financing and programs for increasing educational opportunities for the poor. This way of proceeding is much less likely to commit us to the impalatable measures dictated by the much more demanding goal of ensuring that different individuals can exercise their equal rights with equal success in pursuing their life plans or goals in general, whatever they happen to be.

In the next section I will attempt a classification of the main institutional forms by which unacceptable inequalities in the effectiveness of libertarian rights might be reduced. Before exploring possible institutional arrangements, however, it would be helpful to get clearer about what exactly they are supposed to achieve. To do this, it will be helpful to review the argument so far. First, I distinguished between equal rights and inequalities in the effectiveness of the exercise of rights. Second, I argued that unrestrained inequalities in the effectiveness of the exercise of libertarian rights violate a basic requirement of fairness for institutional procedures. Third, I argued that this conclusion must be modified once it is realized that attempts to achieve (unrestricted) *equal* effectiveness would involve unacceptable restrictions on individual freedom. In the light of this third point, the fairness argument was viewed as an argument for the conclusion that inequalities in effectiveness are prima facie unfair, at least as far as they are due to differences in wealth, educational opportunities, and access to health care. Fourth, I suggested a much more restricted notion of equal effectiveness, along with a procedure for considering concrete cases of unequal effectiveness, as a way of making reasonable judgments about whether certain inequalities are in fact unacceptable.

I am not at all certain whether the argument thus far is capable of yielding any clear, crisp *principle* specifying welfare rights derivative upon libertarian rights. I am confident, however, that is has ruled out one attempt to specify the welfare right in question. A principle requiring that institutions be arranged so as to ensure that individuals can exercise their libertarian rights with equal effectiveness in pursuing their goals, whatever they may be, is wholly unacceptable.

The following principle seems to do a far better job of capturing the intuitive judgments about fairness which I appealed to in the concrete cases discussed above.

> Institutions are to be arranged so as to minimize significant differences in the effectiveness with which different individuals can exercise their libertarian rights in the pursuit of the same particular goals, insofar as these differences in effectiveness depend upon differences in wealth, educational opportunities, and access to health care.

Whether this principle or something like it turns out to be plausible can best be ascertained by considering some of the ways in which it might be implemented. Our intuitions about specific institutional arrangements may be clearer and firmer than our judgments about abstract principles.

VI

There are two main types of institutional arrangements for coping with the problem of inequalities in the effectiveness of the libertarian rights. The one may be called the *particularistic* approach, the other the *global* approach. The particularistic approach focuses on the particular phenomena in which inequalities in effectiveness are manifested. For example, public funds might be provided for political activities, for access to media, and for legal services, so as to diminish the influence of private wealth. A global approach, in contrast, would attempt to minimize inequalities in effectiveness by ensuring some minimum standard of living for all.

The distinction between global and particularistic approaches cuts across the familiar distinction between universal and needs-tested welfare programs. Public funding for political activities or for access to media might be provided to those who qualify for it by falling below some minimum income level, or a fixed sum of cash might be given to everyone, regardless of income level, in the manner of a "demogrant." Neither of these methods, however, would be effective by itself, since those with great wealth might still be at a great advantage. Measures for providing the wherewithal to the poor would presumably have to be combined with measures to limit the amounts that the rich may spend on political activities.

One advantage of the particularistic approach is that it allows us to target our efforts more closely. One disadvantage is that it seems incapable of getting at the root of some of the more extreme inequalities in the exercise of libertarian rights. Needs-tested or universal funding for political participation may be extremely helpful to poor persons who are sufficiently informed, educated, and motivated to use it. Such particularistic measures may prove ineffective, however, if significant numbers of the poor are so uneducated, uninformed, and habituated to political passivity that they are not likely to utilize the means for political participation even if they are available. Similarly, so long as large segments of the population are illiterate, malnourished, and impeded by the lack of adequate health care, it is very unlikely that they will be willing or able to take full advantage of free or subsidized legal services. The advantage of the global approach is that it attempts to improve a person's general condition up to a point at which his exercise of libertarian rights can be augmented by more particularistic measures. Presumably some combination of approaches would be most effective.

Both global and particularistic measures would qualify as programs providing welfare rights in the broad sense stated at the outset of this paper. Both types of arrangements would provide cash or material goods or services free of charge or at a subsidized rate, as a matter of enforced right. But if such rights are grounded on the considerations adduced in the fairness argument, it might be more appropriate to call them "citizenship rights" than "welfare rights."

VII

I have sketched an argument from the commitment to certain libertarian rights, via the idea that the system of libertarian rights must constitute a fair system of procedures, to a commitment to welfare rights. I have also discussed briefly the main types of arrangements by which those welfare rights might be provided. It is now time to consider very briefly one of the most basic objections which might be raised against any attempt to derive welfare rights from libertarian rights. In its simplest form, it is the libertarian objection that any significant welfare program aimed at minimizing the more extreme inequalities in the effectiveness of the rights of political participation, freedom of expression, and the benefits of the legal system would violate another basic right, the right to property.

The objection from an alleged right to property is not, of course, an objection only against welfare rights allegedly derived from the three libertarian rights discussed above. It is the standard libertarian objection against any sort of welfare right, derivative or nonderivative. As an objection against derivative welfare rights, however, it seems to me to be especially unconvincing. There are several difficulties which the libertarian must overcome if the objection is to have any force. First, the right to property must be specified as such a strong right that it can be seen to be incompatible with any significant redistributive measures aimed at minimizing the more extreme inequalities in the exercise of the other three libertarian rights. Clearly, not just any property right will be incompatible with such measures, since most, if not all, of these measures could be implemented through a system of taxation and transfers and since such a system is compatible with a wide range of stronger or weaker property rights. Contrary to Nozick and other libertarians, it is simply not obvious that all such taxation and transfer schemes are incompatible with stable and substantive property rights. Second, the libertarian's strong property right must not only be shown to be a genuine moral right; it must also be shown to be so basic that it overrides the plausible requirement that the other libertarian rights are to form a fair system of procedures.

Though I cannot pursue the point here, I believe that there is no defensible notion of a property right that is strong enough to block the derivation of welfare rights from libertarian rights. This is not to say, however, that considerations concerning the proper scope of a right to property will not play an important role in determining what measures are appropriate for minimizing inequalities in the effectiveness of the exercise of equal rights.

Notes

*I would like to thank Peter G. Brown, Norman Daniels, Gerald Dworkin, Conrad Johnson, Rolf Sartorius, and Paul Vernier for helpful suggestions on an earlier version of this paper.

1. Robert Nozick, *Anarchy, State, and Utopia* (New York: Basic Books, Inc., 1974), pp. 3–280.

2. This conception of a right as a claim which "trumps" considerations of utility (or welfare) is what Ronald Dworkin calls the strong conception of a right. *Taking Rights Seriously* (Cambridge, Mass.: Harvard University Press, 1977). Rawls advances essentially the same conception when he says that "Each person possesses an inviolability founded on justice that even the welfare of society as a whole cannot override." *A Theory of Justice* (Cambridge, Mass.: Harvard University Press, 1971), p. 3.

3. I am not assuming that every right may be coercively backed. Other sorts of sanctions—public opinion, peer pressure, etc.—may sometimes be appropriate where coercion is not. For the sake of my argument, I am assuming that the libertarian rights listed above may be backed by coercion where necessary.

4. Norman Daniels examines Rawls's related distinction between equal liberty and equal worth of liberty and argues that Rawls's concern with it indicates a serious flaw at the heart of his system. Daniels argues that if the parties to Rawls's hypothetical social contract would, as Rawls argues, choose greatest equal liberty, they would also choose equal worth of liberty. Daniels's argument differs from mine in that his does not rest on considerations of fairness and in that it is constructed as an ideal contractarian argument. Norman Daniels, "Equal Liberty and Equal Worth of Liberty," *Reading Rawls*, ed. Norman Daniels (New York: Basic Books, Inc., 1976).

5. For a provocative presentation of some of the relevant statistics, see R. Quinney, *Class, State, and Crime* (New York: David McKay Company, Inc., 1977), pp. 136–39.

6. Rawls, pp. 83–89.

14

Are There Welfare Rights?

A. I. MELDEN

In this essay I assume without argument at the outset that there are good moral reasons for instituting programs of public assistance for the needy. My concern here is with the claim that the needy have a moral right to that assistance, that this is a moral right that they have as human beings. For moral rights are quite special moral grounds for conduct—there are considerations other than rights that serve as moral grounds. But while I shall argue against the view that there is no human right *as such* to welfare support, the human rights that the needy have in common with all others are in fact relevant considerations that may be brought to bear upon the moral claim that they ought to receive welfare support.

Some Cautions

There are many things we ought to do, morally speaking, which involve no issue of rights. For example, we ought to act generously, but no one has any right to our generosity. Wherever possible, we ought to relieve those in pain, but it seems queer to say that, generally at least, those in pain have a right to the relief we may be able to provide—the fact that they are in pain is itself good and sufficient reason for the help we can provide. And if those who have transgressed against us have provided evidence of their remorse and determination not to repeat their offenses, we ought to forgive them. But do they have a right to our forgiveness? And, while it may be reprehensible when distributing candies to a group of urchins or pieces of pie to those seated at one's dining table, to do so in such a way that some get more than others and some get nothing at all, it will hardly do to assert that all such forms of maldistribution involve any deprivation of rights.

It is enough in such cases to say that one ought not to act in such ways. Why? Because of the unfairness involved. Indeed, what some have labeled "distributive justice," which calls for equity in the distribution of benefits and burdens—some distributions clearly being fairer and therefore better or more desirable than others—need involve no violation of any rights.

This last point, frequently overlooked, can be brought home by considering morally askew arrangements which fail to satisfy Rawls's difference principle. That principle, it will be recalled, states that social and economic inequalities are permissible only if they are to the advantage of the least advantaged members of our society.[1] For suppose—what clearly and sadly is untrue in the world in which we live—that no one in our society needs any income support in order to maintain a tolerable and decent existence, and that some individuals manage to accumulate, quite legally, great wealth without thereby adding in any way to the well-being of those less favored by fortune. For the Rawlsian-minded, at least, such a distribution would appear to be unfair—why should some prosper in ways that do not add to the well-being of others? Such an arrangement might well have an unfortunate tendency to create envy and jealousy. Besides, there is the Kantian point that if these high peaks in the fortunes of the favored few are associated with substantial deficiencies in moral virtue, it would be better if they had not occurred at all.[2] In any case, such a distribution of income or resources might well strike us as being less than the best.

Some might label such an arrangement "social injustice," the so-called injustice perpetrated by a fortune that is blind to moral merit and desert. But does it involve any infringement, deprivation, or violation of rights? Here some might say that the favored few have no right to the benefits they have received. But what does this mean? That rights have been violated in that clear and straightforward sense in which there is a violation of a right when someone, who has no right to do so, invades another's privacy? To say that the favored few have no right to the goods a morally blind nature has lavished upon them can only be a misleading way of saying that they do not deserve the goods they have acquired, that it would be better if either they had not acquired them or those with superior moral merit had been favored instead of them. It is only muddying the waters, in my view, to raise the issue of moral rights whenever maldistributions of benefits and burdens have occurred.

The point I have been making is that both philosophers and nonphilosophers have been much too inclined to engage in rights-talk in support of their moral views; this is especially clear in two such instances I want now to mention before going on to discuss the question of welfare rights. Animals obviously do feel pleasure and pain, at least those now being raised for human consumption; and we ought, surely, to avoid causing them pain when we hunt them, or maintain them in confined quarters, or ship them to slaughterhouses for butchering. But, not content with these undebatable claims, some have gone on to buttress them with the conclusion that animals enjoy rights just as human beings do, and that all of the various practices in which humans engage, from the eating of meat to those practices this encourages—the hunting, breeding, raising, and slaughtering of animals—violate animal rights.

Such a claim succeeds only in obscuring the need to make good a number of claims that stand in need of examination: that all of the practices mentioned above are and of necessity must be cruel to the animals destroyed for human consumption; that the raising of oysters, clams, and snails for human consumption is inherently cruel along with the gathering of snakes, locusts, grasshoppers, and bees now being consumed in certain parts of the world by human beings; that agriculture does not have any deleterious effect upon those animals in the fields, meadows, orchards, and surrounding territories who would intrude and devour the food being raised for human consumption; and, not by any means of minor importance, that cruelty and/or the killing of animals is a deprivation of moral rights. There is some reason for an inclination to ascribe moral rights to dolphins, whales, chimpanzees, gorillas, and family pets, but this is enormously distant from the conclusions urged by some vegetarians that we shun the eating of animals. Even less lacking in any rational support is the claim made by some who urge upon us a view that can be described only as frivolous, that we ought to protect and cleanse the environment in which we live on the ground that it—the environment that consists of such inorganic ingredients as earth, air, water, rocks, mountains—is the possessor of rights.

But enough of the need for arguments to offer rational support for this kind of environmentalist claim, and for a vegetarianism that starts with an appeal to our humane feelings about the imposition of cruelty on animals.[3] The question we need to ask is why in fact there is this temptation to appeal to moral rights without any apparent realization on the part of those who make such an appeal of the need to provide rational grounds for their conclusion. For of course we ought to avoid cruelty toward animals; surely the fact that something is cruel is good enough reason for eschewing it. And we ought to protect the environment and to take steps to cleanse it from the pollution human activities have produced—and for a variety of good and sufficient reasons.

But why has it been felt necessary to buttress such good/ought-talk by invoking the language of rights? The answer, I venture to suggest, is that our deepest moral feelings are evoked by the idea that there has been a violation of moral rights. This gives rise to the understandable temptation to evoke these feelings in order to buttress one's cause as strongly as possible. To succumb to this temptation in the two extreme cases I have just cited is to provide a way of saving oneself the necessity of doing what is far more difficult, namely, adducing considerations that serve as rational grounds for the cause one has endorsed. Perhaps we ought not to eat animals, but the case is not proven by citing the fact that cruelty toward animals is offensive. And in the case of environmentalism, it is ludicrous that any appeal to moral rights is felt to be necessary when there are in fact a number of supporting considerations that can be cited without too much difficulty, despite complications of cost and convenience.

It is not enough, therefore, to claim that there are moral rights. Considerations, at least of the sort Mill described in another context as being capable "of determining the intellect," are also needed; for the issue of whether any moral right is involved in any moral claim that is made is surely one that lies, as he put it, "within the cognizance of the rational faculty." Of course, I do not wish to assert or imply that the appeal to welfare rights in support of public assistance programs is or must be as farfetched as either of the last two cases I have mentioned in which moral rights have been alleged to obtain. I wish only to comment on the manifest excesses to which an uncritical appeal to moral rights *can* give rise in order to emphasize the point made earlier, that both philosophers and non-philosophers have been much too disposed to engage in rights-talk in cases in which the relevance of such talk is at best problematic. If it is claimed that there are welfare rights, discussion is needed to support the claim. Specifically, we need, first, to examine some of the distinctive features of our concept of a right, and second, to adduce considerations designed to show whether or not rights, thus understood, can reasonably be cited in justification of social or public programs of income support.[4]

The Distinctive Nature of Rights

Some philosophers have attempted to elucidate the concept of a moral right in terms of what it is that ought to be done. One such attempt is to be found in Chapter V of Mill's essay *Utilitarianism*, where he declares that "to have a right . . . is . . . to have something which society ought to defend me in the possession of." But what is it that one *has*, in the possession of which society ought to defend one? Surely not *that* to which one has the right, for one may have a right to something one will never gain, but, rather, the right that society ought to defend one in the possession of. A defender of Mill might retort that defending one's right means insuring that one will obtain *that* to which one has a right. Still, the tacit reference here to the right in this exegesis provides at least the appearance of circularity. In any case, persons have rights by virtue of the transactions in which they engage with one another or the relations in which they stand to one another, and it will hardly do to claim that they have these rights only if society ought to do whatever is needed in order to protect them.

Not every case of a broken promise that violates the right of the promisee, an untruthfulness that breaches the right that persons have to truthful declarations from others, or an unwarranted interference with the right one has to take a drink, or, minimally, to rub one's itching nose, would warrant invoking the protection of society. Individuals have rights sometimes by engaging in transactions with, or standing in relation to, other specific individuals, and sometimes, as in the case of the last two instances I have enumerated, simply as individuals who have the right, or liberty, to do certain things without any interference from others; but it would be excessively heavy-handed, at best, to call upon society with its social pressures and the penalties of the law for protection. Further, if society ought in point of moral fact, as Mill claims, to defend a person's possession of what he can earn in fair professional competition, because "society ought not to allow any other person to hinder him from endeavoring to earn in that manner as much as he can," surely this claim can only be based on the presumed right that persons have to earn what they can in fair competition.

Mill intends to avoid the logical circle by appealing at this point to the principle of utility—society ought not to allow persons to hinder others from earning what they can in what we describe as fair professional competition because this breaches the fundamental principle of morality specified by utilitarianism. But this is to invoke a philosophical doctrine I see no reason to accept and far too many reasons to reject. There is, of course, the legal right that persons have to engage in fair competition in the pursuit of their economic interests, but this legal right, established as it is by statute and judicial interpretation, is morally justifiable, in my opinion, because of the conception of a person embodied in our constitution as the possessor of certain rights which would be infringed by unfair competitive practices.

There are, however, more general points that can be made against any reductionist analysis of rights-talk in terms of ought-talk, the talk about what ought to be done. Why, for example, ought one to keep one's promise? Surely one good reason, insufficient as it may be in a special case, is that in doing so one would be meeting one's obligation. But to say that one ought to meet one's obligation is *not* to utter the complete triviality that one ought to do what one ought to do. It is rather to cite an obligation that one has *to a person*, in the present instance because of the promise given to him. The obligation to that person is the very same thing, viewed from the point of view of the person considering what is to be done, as the right the other person has against him; it is, as it is commonly put, the correlative of the right conferred by that paradigm of a right-conferring act, the making of a promise. One ought to keep one's promise because, in doing so, one will be according someone the right that person has against one. It is therefore the right (and its correlative obligation) that explains the ought, i.e., what ought to be done—not the other way around. The attempted reduction of rights-talk to ought-talk, in reversing the proper logical order, simply puts the cart before the horse.

The unsatisfactory character of Mill's definition of a right and the implausibility in general of the attempt to reduce rights-talk to ought-talk will be apparent as soon as we consider the conceptual complexity of the notion of a right. Rights, it has been pointed out, involve correlative obligations, in some cases to do (or to forebear from doing), as in the case of the rights created by promises; generally, these rights call for performances on the part of the promiser, although in special cases the obligation involved may be to abstain from performances, this being the subject of the promise-locutions. Some rights are mere liberties, as in the case of the right one has to smoke in the privacy of one's study, a right with respect to which no one else has any right to interference; here the correlative obligation is the obligation not to interfere.[5] And there are finer distinctions that can be and have been drawn.[6]

But this is only the beginning of the story that needs to be told. For rights may be acquired by entering into specific transactions with or relations to others, as in the case of those who receive promises from others and in the case of family members; and so, too, may they be forfeited by relevant circumstances, as in the case of a father who forfeits his paternal rights by failing to meet even the most elementary of his responsibilities. Some rights may be relinquished, and those who are bound by them are released from their obligations; although what sense can be ascribed to any talk of relinquishing one's right as a human being is another matter. And some rights may be waived without being relinquished or forfeited, as in the case of someone who waives the right he has acquired as the recipient of a promise, although the same caution about "waiving one's right as a human being" needs to be made, and for the same reason. But if there are those rights that can be called "special," because they arise in the special circumstances of human life, e.g., the occurrence of promises, the arrangements of family life, and even some of the forms of communication in which there is the right to truthfulness and the correlative obligation to be truthful, then there are rights that human beings have simply by virtue of their status as moral agents.[7]

Yet even this is not enough in order to indicate the scope of the conceptual ramifications of the concept of a moral right. For rights, special or human, may be infringed, justifiably or unjustifiably; and they may be exercised reasonably or unreasonably. Rights are not like bank drafts that are cashable on demand; that is to say, they may not be exercised, or accorded, regardless of any circumstances.[8] But even when an agent reasonably infringes the right of another, the agent is responsible to the person whose right has been infringed; that is to say, he is accountable to the latter and owes him an explanation, and if the infringement has caused him moral damage (as is the case when the right is a matter of importance to him as he pursues his interests), reparation, if possible, and even a sense of guilt for the damage for which he was responsible, are in order. And if the infringement is unjustified—that is to say, if the right has been violated—guilt has surely been incurred. The appropriate emotion here is not shame, for this may occur when, for example, one has been cowardly without in any way infringing upon the rights of others, and the remedy in the case of shame calls for something that only the person who feels the shame can provide, namely, remaking his character and having done so, hoping that the incident will be erased from his memory.

But in the case of the guilt suffered, and rightly so when the right of another agent has been violated, moral healing can be effected by the remorse suffered, the reparation paid, and the determination not to repeat the offense; these considerations should compel the victim of the offense to forgive the offender, thus restoring the trust that had existed before the offense had been committed, and thereby preparing the way for further good moral relations with him. But to forgive in this way is possible only for the person who has suffered the moral injury. As Locke put it, "He who has suffered the damage has a right to demand in his own name, and he alone can remit."[9] That is to say, the possessor of a right is endowed with a certain authority in his moral relations with others: to hold them to account as necessary and to forgive them when required. And as the possessor of the rights he has as a human being, he has sufficient authority to comport himself with a dignity apparent to others by the way in which he deals with them, be they high or low, in terms of moral equality with them, and prepared in ways they can observe from his demeanor that they must answer to him for any violation of his rights. Indeed, as the possessor of rights it is incumbent upon him, as circumstances warrant, to stand up and, by asserting his rights, display openly the dignity he has as the possessor of rights in common with everyone else.[10]

Space does not permit the full story that must be told in any adequate elucidation of the concept of a right—the possible rational grounds for waiving or even relinquishing certain of our rights, which serve also to justify infringing rights and, correlatively, refusing to meet one's obligations; the moral requirements or burdens imposed upon those who possess rights and those who are under the correlative obligations; the conceptual connections between rights and goods; the moral background or logical substratum of rights and obligations; and the rationale that operates in the way in which moral agents can reasonably weigh competing considerations of rights, obligations, and goods in arriving at their moral decisions. These are topics that cannot be discussed within the brief compass of a single paper, but I mention them here only in order to reinforce the points made earlier, that it is hopeless to attempt to reduce rights-talk to talk about what ought to be done, specifically, that the explanation offered by Mill of what a right is, notwithstanding the appeal it has had for some, is impossibly anemic.

The 'Basis' of Moral Rights

I turn now to the question of the 'basis' of moral rights. Here, as in some of the allegations that there are certain moral rights justifying certain sorts of conduct, there is a decided tendency among philosophers to offer views without adequate discussion or argument.

One frequently encountered ploy is to assert that individuals have moral rights by virtue of certain moral rules or principles. Unfortunately, the suggestion, coming as it does from a presumed analogy between moral and legal rights, is never explored. For if we ask, "What are the rules or principles in question?" it is difficult to see what possible candidates can do the trick. Our familiar moral precepts can hardly serve as the analogs of the statutes by which legal rights are established. For even if *one ought to keep one's promises* were a rule or principle that established the possession of the rights of promisees and the correlative obligations of promisers—which clearly it does not do[11]—it is too slender a reed to support the complex conceptual structure of our concept of a moral right. Nor would any principle that takes the form of a declaration that there are certain rights, as the Declaration of Independence, serve as the analog of the statutes, common law, and judicial pronouncements that have the force of law. For the declaration that there are certain rights is the *assertion* or *claim* that there are certain rights; but it does not itself *establish* the existence of these rights in the way in which statutes and judicial pronouncements do. Legal statutes, together with a body of common law and judicial interpretations, serve to explain not only the existence of legal rights, but also the complex implications such rights have in legal affairs; but there are no such moral rules or principles that do this trick for moral rights.

Why then do we ascribe moral rights as we do? The answer, I have argued elsewhere, lies in the conception of a person as a moral agent. For even Locke, who speaks of the laws of nature and reason that is that law, as he phrases it, when he attempts to explain the natural rights we have, appeals not to such laws but to considerations of quite a different nature: the allegedly self-evident claim that individuals have a right to their own persons and the further claim that by mixing their labor with what God has given them in common, they acquire rights to what they thereby obtain, by making them parts of their own persons.[12] There are, to be sure, serious difficulties in this account, but we would do well to follow Locke in abandoning any effort to employ the analogy with legal rights by claiming, as do some writers today, that there must be moral principles that explain the moral rights persons have.

We need, clearly, to distinguish between special and human rights. The former depend upon the latter and arise, as I have argued elsewhere, when there is a mutual understanding of the support that one person is to provide for the agency of another as the latter engages in the pursuit of interests that define the good or goods he seeks to achieve.[13] A promise is a formal device for establishing a special right, but there are other rights, e.g., the right to truthfulness and the complex distribution of rights, along with their correlative obligations, among the members of a family. In my view, what operates as a fundamental human right, without which none of these special rights can arise, is the right that human beings have to engage in the pursuit of their interests, interests defining goods that enable them to achieve lives worth living.

It is human rights and the claim that some sort of basis can be found for them with which I am now concerned. I shall put off, for the moment, the question of the extent and variety of such rights, and mention only one more claim concerning their basis. And once more, as in the case of the appeal to moral principles on the analogy of those principles or statutes by which legal rights are established, we find only the flat assertion without any of the argument and discussion needed to support the dictum. For it is widely thought and often said that moral rights—the rights that human beings as such possess—derive from the autonomy of human beings. I shall be brief at the risk of appearing dogmatic in dealing with this echo of Kantian thought.

By autonomy is intended, I believe, the ability of persons to choose and decide for themselves on the basis of reasons they can understand and invoke. But surely we ascribe rights to those unable or unwilling to decide for themselves: the pathetically submissive wife who accepts the choices and decisions made for her by a domineering husband, the slave who is content with a lot he has no role in fashioning, and the young child. And for most of us there is only more or less autonomy—those of us for whom orthodoxy, tradition, and the will of our parents and friends are a comfortable substitute for the disturbing insecurity threatened by any attempted self-criticism or departure from received opinion. And how much autonomy has the frightened patient who is told by his physician that he must freely give his assent to surgery—it is his right to decide whether or not to submit to the surgeon's knife—in order to remove a cancerous growth? And our autonomy varies with our moods and the medications we take.

We can go on and on in this way. Yet submissive wives, obedient slaves, patients trembling with fear in their physicans' offices, and you and I on our off-days and moments have rights as the human beings they and you and I are. Besides, by what logical hocus-pocus is it possible to squeeze the rich and complex structure of moral rights—a structure I was at pains to sketch earlier in this essay—out of a pallid rationality and the ability to bring it to bear in the decisions we make? For supposing we avoid circularity by stipulating that this rationality is not that reasonableness that is exhibited by persons who weigh rights and obligations, their own and those of others, in deciding how to conduct themselves, how can we derive rights from mere rationality?[14]

But enough of the moves designed to find some firm foundation for moral rights. For a right can be derived from nothing less than a right, e.g., the right to life from the right of agents to pursue their interests. And if we look to those features in human beings for a so-called basis for moral rights, nothing will do except what is manifest to the observer (not something hidden, for how else would it be possible for us unhesitatingly and reliably as we do to ascribe such rights to individuals)—specifically, those features that human beings exhibit when they proceed as responsible beings in meeting the normative requirements imposed upon them by their rights and those of others, or, when because of fault or necessity they do not meet those requirements, their responses to their own omissions and commissions: the explanations and excuses they offer to those who may hold them to account, the guilt and the remorse they suffer, and the remedies they recognize they are called upon to make, whatever it is possible for them to do so, for the moral injury for which they are responsible. In other words, what alone can be provided as an explanation of moral rights is not some basis or Cartesian foundation from which the possession of rights can be deduced, but only a more detailed description of those features of human beings relevant to the role that rights and obligations play in our common moral life. Explanations of rights can only take the form of more detailed descriptions of the ways in which to a greater or lesser degree and in the endlessly varied circumstances of human life rights play their role in our thought, feeling, and action.[15]

Welfare Rights—Arguments Pro and Con

I turn now to the question of whether or not there are moral welfare rights—the rights that individuals have to the income support, of some sort or another, needed to bridge the gap between whatever income, if any, they may have and that income level or its equivalent necessary for some minimal but acceptable level of well-being. I shall not attempt to discuss the complex and difficult questions involved in any attempt to specify such a level, or whether in fact it is possible to do so without taking into account such highly variable factors as cost of living, individual interests, aptitudes, and life-styles, age, state of health, and so on. But however that notion of an acceptable level may vary with relevant circumstances, we do have at least a rough conception of what a minimal standard of decent human life would be in specific cases. And however variable this conception and however difficult the problems of administering any program of welfare which attempts to take account of such variability, it is clear that many individuals are unable to muster enough income by their own efforts and need assistance from others in order to maintain decent conditions of life.

Since we can no longer accept the view that those unable to fend for themselves in tolerably decent ways have only themselves to blame, and that the assistance to be given them in order to improve their wretched lot is to take the form of charity, some programs of public assistance are clearly needed in order to provide these individuals with minimal but morally acceptable conditions of life. In recent years the claim that individuals have rights to the satisfaction of certain basic human needs has been implemented by legal and administrative measures designed to insure that these basic human needs are met. We do not question, I trust, that there are good and sufficient moral reasons for measures of this general sort; the only question we need to ask is what sort of moral reasons are in order. Are these moral reasons the welfare rights that individuals deficient in income levels possess?

If there are welfare rights, are these special rights that individuals have, as in the case of the rights of promisees, by viture of the transactions in which they engage with one another, or, as in the case of parents or children, by virtue of the relations in which they stand to one another? The answer would appear to be in the negative. For if there are rights of welfare recipients these would appear not to depend upon their relations to or transactions with others. Nor is there any mutual understanding of the support that others are to give them upon which the alleged welfare right depends; certainly welfare programs were instituted when no such understanding existed. It is, rather, the fact that individuals are presumably unable by their own efforts to satisfy their basic needs, and, accordingly that they are compelled to live below minimally acceptable standards of human decency. It would appear, therefore, that if there are welfare rights, these must be rights that they have as human beings.

But here we are faced with the prospect of adding one more to a large and growing list of putative human rights. If we look to what one writer has described as "the most complete of currently authoritative declarations of human rights, that passed by the Assembly of the United Nations in 1948,"[16] reaffirmed in recent days in the Helsinki agreement and in the public pronouncements of those deploring the trials of dissidents in Russia, we cannot fail to be impressed by the manner in which the list of such rights has grown since the days of Locke and Jefferson and by the change that has taken place since the days of Jeremy Bentham, for whom the doctrine of natural or human rights seemed to be "nonsense upon stilts."[17] The climate of opinion has indeed changed when not only philosophers but moralists and persons in government cite not only the rights to life, liberty, the pursuit of happiness, property, security, and resistance to oppression, but a wide variety of other alleged human rights, such as the rights to freedom of movement, to leave and to return to one's native land, to work without discrimination, to equal pay for equal work, etc., etc., including the right to rest, leisure, periodic holidays with pay, not to mention those rights in Article 25 of the *Universal Declaration of Human Rights* which call for a broad variety of social welfare programs.

I have no desire to denigrate an historically important document or to minimize the moral importance of the many things to which the title of "human right" is given in this document of the United Nations. But why not go on to add to these? Surely it would be mistreating human beings in factories not to permit them to leave their workbenches in order to answer the periodic calls of nature or to lay down their tools for coffee breaks. Shall we then say that workers in factories have, among their basic human rights, the rights to go to the toilet and to take midmorning or midafternoon coffee breaks?

There are those who may be undaunted by this apparently endless proliferation of human rights. And why not, since this seems to be in keeping with the currently fashionable talk about human rights at the highest levels of government? But the reply to this is not merely that we need to refrain from multiplying human rights beyond necessity, but that there are certain substantive considerations about the nature of human rights that tell against this proliferation.

For human rights, first, are fundamental in the sense that without them there could not be the variety of moral rights that depend for their existence upon the quite special circumstances within which individuals conduct their affairs with one another. The rights of the recipient of a promise, for example, arise with the mutual understanding of the support which a promiser is to provide for the agency of the promisee, but such a mutual understanding *by itself* is unable to generate any moral right the promisee has to the promised performance (or abstention); at best, the failure of the promiser to act in accordance with the mutual understanding that exists between promiser and promisee would be merely defeating the expectation of the latter, unless there is some right of the promisee that is breached with the breach of the mutual understanding created by the promised transaction. And, as I have argued elsewhere, this right that must exist independently of the promised transaction is the right that any agent has, as moral agent, to pursue his interests and thereby, it is hoped, to achieve the goods these define. For it is only on the assumption that there is such a right that the mutual understanding of the support the promiser is to provide the agency of the promisee, during the course of some line of conduct in which he intends to engage, can have this logical consequence, namely, that a failure to carry out the terms of that understanding and make good the assurance contained therein is to subvert the agency of the promisee in that line of conduct to which the promised action (or abstention) is essential, thereby doing him moral injury by failing to accord him his right.

So, too, with the relation between members of a family in which there is a characteristic distribution of rights and obligations that constitute the moral relations in which they stand to one another. The mutual understanding of the support each is to give to and receive from others serves to generate rights and obligations only if the members of the family have as a matter of human right the right to pursue their interests.[18] Throughout, therefore, this fundamental moral right of human beings is presupposed by the special rights they have against one another when the mutual understandings of the support they are to provide one another arise in the course of their transactions with and relations to one another.

Second, human rights are rights that persons have simply as human beings. They are rights they have in common without regard to the enormous differences in their circumstances or in their character, interests, or in any other features they exhibit as individuals. In respect of human rights, therefore, persons are on terms of equality.

Third, human rights are important and morally basic in that the recognition of their possession by individuals establishes that they are beings capable of entering into these special moral relations with other human beings, relations constituted by the special rights and obligations they have with respect to one another. To recognize others in this way is to recognize them as members of the moral community, as individuals with whom good moral relations are possible in principle, difficult as it may be in practice to achieve them. The alternative can be only to exclude them from the moral community, to regard them as beings devoid of rights whom we may treat kindly but against whom we need, as in the case of psychopaths, to adopt measures to protect them from the retaliation others may seek in response to the damage they may cause them, and to protect ourselves from the harm they are apt to do us. But for those to whom, unproblematically, we do ascribe human rights, there are moral requirements that stem from their rights; and I shall comment later on some of these in connection with social welfare programs.

We need at this point to examine whether the alleged human right of the needy to a minimal and decent level of income support exhibits the features of human rights I have enumerated, and, if not, what kind of moral grounds there are for such programs of income support.

First, how could one show that the alleged right to income support is basic or fundamental? Clearly, by showing that special moral rights, separately or collectively, imply the existence of such a right, that in the absence of such a right, there could not be the moral relations between individuals constituted by the rights that they have against one another. But it is wildly implausible to maintain, for example, that there could not be the right established by a promise, or the right of one member of a family with respect to another, without the right that any of these persons have to income support. For even if any of these persons were in need of the support required for them to enjoy a decent mode of life, with at least minimally adequate food, clothing, shelter, and other necessities, this would establish not that any of their rights could not exist without a right to income support, but something quite different, namely, that they could not enjoy such a life without receiving the required support.

The case is quite unlike that which obtains, for example, in the relation between the right persons have to pursue their interests and the right they have to life itself. For it is a truism that pursuing one's interest implies being alive, and it follows, accordingly, that if one has a right to the former, one will, necessarily, have a right to the latter. And the case is quite different from that of a paradigm case of a promise in which the promised performance is essential to an endeavor in which the promisee intends to engage, and in which there could not be any right he has to the promised action, unless he has a right as moral agent to engage in lines of conduct in which he pursues his interests and hopes to achieve his good.

The arguments for the alleged right to income support take quite a different form; they attempt to show, usually, the necessity of providing such support in order that the needy may achieve those goods that make life for them worthwhile and worthy of human beings. But this is far removed from the conclusion they seek to establish. In any case, it does not show that the alleged right is basic or fundamental in the required sense. For, unless one supplies the premise that individuals have a right to a decent form of life, the consideration that income support will enable certain individuals to achieve such a life simply does not establish that they have a right to the required support; we need to show not only that persons ought to enjoy lives worthy of human beings, but that they have a right to some of the things necessary for them to achieve this. And we need, further, to show that if any of them have a right as human beings to the income support needed in order to achieve such a life, that this right is basic or fundamental in the required sense.

I shall later consider one more argument for the view that the needy have a right to income support. But for the present I wish to turn to the second of the three features of human rights I mentioned earlier. Human rights, as we have seen, are invariant with respect to the circumstances and individual characteristics of human beings. They are, in addition, unalienable; that is to say, they cannot be waived or relinquished. And while an individual may cease to have the rights that human beings have in common, this is possible only if that being is transformed into something less than the human being he has been. By the same token, human rights cannot be acquired by any human being, for as a human being he already has them; there is nothing he can acquire in the form of human rights if he is already a human being with the features of a moral agent, just as there is nothing he can lose in the form of human rights as long as he remains the moral agent he is.

Now, the idea that persons have, among their human rights, the right to vacations with pay is incoherent, for this is a right that human beings have not in common with any other human beings but only as employees. Such a right, if indeed it is a moral right, can be acquired by becoming gainfully employed. But human rights are invariant with respect to the circumstances of human beings, and they can neither be acquired nor lost by human beings. In the same way, the doctrine that the needy have as their human right the right to income support, in order to bring them up to some satisfactory level of income that would provide them with certain goods essential to a minimally desirable form of human existence, would appear confused: this is a right that only the needy have, not those who are affluent. Further, such a right can be acquired by those who suffer severe economic losses that reduce their income below certain levels; and it can be lost by those who acquire the necessary income to enable them to escape from the deprivations they have previously suffered. It would appear, therefore, that whatever welfare rights may be, they cannot be human rights.

The reply to this argument is that welfare rights have been needlessly restricted to those who are in dire need, in the same way in which the right to vacations with pay *is* restricted to those who are employed. But why not formulate the doctrine of welfare rights so that what it asserts is that any human being has the right to a certain minimal level of well-being, whether or not in any given case supplementary support is necessary in order to bring the person to that level of well-being? If persons already enjoy that level of well-being by virtue of their own income, well and good—they have the morally desirable level of well-being and they need no help from any external source. It is only if they fall short of the required level of well-being that income support is needed in order to accord them the right to well-being they have as human beings. In short, whether or not they are in dire need, persons have as their human right the right to a certain minimal level of well-being. And this is a right they can neither acquire nor lose as long as their status as human beings remains unchanged.

Still, we need some argument to show that there is such a human right, for the mere fact that a certain level of well-being is morally desirable is hardly enough. Now, it has been argued by Henry Shue that there is a right to physical security that is basic on the ground that "no one can fully enjoy any right . . . if someone can credibly threaten him or her with murder, rape, beating, etc., when he or she tries to enjoy the alleged right. . . . No rights other than a right to physical security can in fact be enjoyed if a right to physical security is not protected."[19] And Shue goes on to argue that "subsistence, or minimal economic security . . . can also be shown to be as well justified for treatment as a socially basic right as physical security is—and for the same reasons."[20]

The argument is unlike the one stated previously which moves from the right to pursue one's interests to the right to life. For that argument proceeded on the basis of an entailment relation holding between the pursuit of one's interests and being alive. The present argument proceeds from the fact that there are certain basic human rights to the conclusion that there must be a right to minimal economic security, on the ground that otherwise there could be no *enjoyment* of these basic human rights. But the conclusion surely does not follow; for what is required in order that these human rights may be enjoyed is *not* that there be a *right* to this minimal economic security, but that there ought to be this minimal economic security. Otherwise an indefinitely large series of basic rights is threatened. For in the same way one could argue that in order to enjoy the right to minimal economic security there must be a basic right to the legislation by means of which alone it is possible to enjoy this right. And in order to enjoy the basic right to this legislation, there must be a basic right to institute proceedings to pass such legislation by means of which alone, etc., etc. And this is not only to launch a regress of basic or human rights, it is also to elevate to the status of human rights, rights that go beyond the nature of human beings as such since they relate to the structure of our political institutions.

But no such regress need be initiated. Granted the moral folly of ascribing rights to persons which admittedly they cannot possibly enjoy, what is required by the ascription of basic human rights to individuals is that there be the settings appropriate to those rights within which these may be enjoyed. Given then that there are such basic human rights, it follows not that there are basic rights to whatever is needed in order that these rights may be enjoyed, but, rather, that we ought to provide, by whatever means we can effectively and efficiently do so, the settings in which individuals may enjoy their rights as human beings, including the minimal economic security they need in order that they may go about their affairs, pursuing their interests and achieving the goods that make life worth living for them.

The situation here is by no means peculiar to human rights; it also holds true of special rights. For moral rights do not exist in vacuo, without regard to a setting appropriate to their exercise. For the moral rights established by the mutual understanding that exists between, e.g., a husband and wife, call for a setting appropriate to these rights; otherwise that moral understanding, in the case of a morally askew conception shared by a domineering husband and a submissive wife, of the roles they are to play with respect to each other, can only preserve the morally objectionable treatment by the husband of his wife, in which he is brutalized and she lives a life that is not worthy of a human being, however willingly she may accept it for herself. If we are to think of the moral rights of husband and wife as unproblematic, we must assume a setting that is appropriate for them, in which interests and capacities of both parties are allowed to develop and flourish in ways that enable the support that each is to provide the agency of the other, a support understood by both parties to be forthcoming, to contribute to making the lives they have joined worthy of them as the human beings they are.

And in the same way, if there are rights that persons have as human beings, a setting for their exercise and enjoyment is called for in which, among other things, there is a certain minimally acceptable level of economic security that will enable those capable of it to achieve their proper development in the societies in which they live, and thereby obtain for themselves the goods that make their lives worthy of the particular human beings they are.

The argument, therefore, that there is a fundamental right to a certain minimal level of income support, on the ground that without it no fundamental rights can be enjoyed, confuses two quite different matters: the fundamental rights we do in fact have and the conditions of their enjoyment, or, as I have put it, the settings within which such rights may be enjoyed. Granted that rights, fundamental or not, do not exist in vacuo, that they call for settings within which they may be exercised and enjoyed, and that, in the case of fundamental rights, there are moral requirements we must bear to ensure, as far as it is possible for us to do, that human beings live in the settings called for by such rights—granted all this, it simply does not follow that, by rejecting the claim that human beings have as one of their fundamental rights the right to an adequate level of income support, we are in effect reading the needy out of the moral community of persons. Our fundamental moral rights are enough to establish them as full-fledged members of the moral community without including among these a fundamental or human right to income support.

Conclusion

Are there fundamental or human rights to welfare? No. But there are serious moral requirements we must bear because of the settings called for by the fundamental rights of human beings, settings within which alone it is possible for persons to acquire and to pursue interests worthy of human beings so that their lives may be worthwhile. Hence it is *because* of the fundamental rights of persons—their human rights—that we must provide the needy with adequate levels of income support in order that it may be possible for them and for their children to live lives worthy of the human beings they are. And if we fail to do what we can in providing this assistance for those in dire need, our fault is no mere lack of generosity, kindness, or sympathy for those who encounter difficulty and need our assistance in order that they may succeed in their endeavors. Our failure to help is not an occasion for mere shame on our part; it is, rather, one that calls for a sense of guilt, because of our failure to contribute our assistance in providing them with a setting appropriate to the rights they have as human beings, just as was the case for those law-abiding or conforming individuals in Nazi Germany who went about their private affairs with the stench of burning human flesh in their nostrils or at the sight of Nazi bully-boys beating up defenseless Jews, as if these were matters that were none of their business.

The Founding Fathers of this nation, like John Locke before them, were wise in restricting the list of unalienable or natural rights to a very small number of items. For those who in recent years have expanded the catalog of natural or human rights were mindful, not of the *rights* which individual human beings have as individuals, but of the necessity of implementing such rights, given the radically altered social circumstances of human life in our contemporary society. Hence the talk of rights to travel freely from one community to another, to vacations with pay, and so on. For even if welfare rights are defined as rights to a certain minimal level of income support, the thinking here is in fact about a right that individuals are supposed to have as the beneficiaries of certain social services, which implies that this right, like the rights to paid vacations, to travel freely, and so on, are rights that individuals are alleged to have, not as the individuals they are because of their nature as human beings, but in virtue of their situations in the social circumstances in which they live.

This is not surprising, since the reason for claiming that there are such rights is the conviction, sound as it is, that unless some acceptable level of income support is assured to all who live in our present technologically developed and complicated social and political world, the rights that Locke and the Founding Fathers ascribed to human beings are likely to be, for many of us, empty moral possessions, as much so as the title of "Vice President in charge of . . ." that may be assigned to the most menial of employees. The motivation is clear, but the move is unnecessary, given the distinction I have drawn between rights and the requisite settings for their enjoyment. And the move may well prove to be counterproductive by fostering the suspicion, on the part of those who have any doubts at all that there are unalienable natural or human rights, that those of us who do talk about human rights are employing an inflated rhetoric that serves only to buttress our strong moral convictions.

Notes

1. John Rawls, *A Theory of Justice* (Cambridge, Mass.: Harvard University Press, 1971), p. 60.

2. See Kant's *Foundations of the Metaphysics of Morals*, at beginning of Sec. 1.

3. I shall not discuss those arguments for or claims made in support of vegetarianism based on quite different considerations: religious convictions about the sacred nature of all life or philosophical appeals to our kinship with fellow inhabitants on mother earth.

4. In this respect I fully endorse the view expressed by Paul Vernier in his chapter, "Rights to Welfare as an Issue in Income Support Policy," that advocates of moral rights should provide persuasive answers to these questions.

5. Cf. *Fundamental Legal Conceptions* (New Haven: Yale University Press, 1923).

6. For some of these, see H. L. A. Hart, "Are There Natural Rights?," *The Philosophical Review*, April 1955.

7. See my *Rights and Persons* for this and other claims made concerning the complex features of moral rights.

8. In this connection see my comments concerning the oft-repeated but mistaken claim (in no small measure fostered by Bentham's fierce and injudicious attack, in his *Anarchical Fallacies*, on the French Assembly's *Declaration of the Rights of Man and of Citizens*, an attack many have supposed must apply to Locke's views as well) that Locke held the absurd view that absolute rights may be exercised no matter what the circumstances may be, that they cannot be justifiably infringed. See in this connection my *Rights and Persons*, pp. 12–13.

9. *Second Treatise of Civil Government*, Ch. II.

10. See in this connection pp. 22–26 in my *Rights and Persons*. Dignity is not some esoteric attribute of a rationality invisible to the eye, as Kant thought, but manifest in the behavior of human beings in the public forum.

11. What this precept conveys is that the keeping of a promise is as such a reason for the relevant promise keeping act. It serves usually as a reminder to one who has promised that he or she does have a good moral reason, one that may be overridden (hence the familiar locution, "One ought to keep one's promises, but . . ."). But as it stands it offers no reason for why it is that it is a reason; that is to say, it does not itself cite any right as the underlying reason for the keeping of promises.

12. See my discussion of the issue of the alleged analogy between moral and legal rights in my *Rights and Persons*, pp. 227ff.

13. See my *Rights and Persons*, especially Chapters II and III in which I discuss a variety of rights, beginning with those established formally by means of promises.

14. Even if, with Kant, we were to concede that rational nature exists as an end in itself, and for *this* reason is worthy of our respect, how does *this* enable us to deduce the possession of moral rights, rights we ascribe not only to those whom, as we say, we do *not* respect because of their serious moral flaws, but also to those whom we do respect—not because of some abstract rationality that they have in common with scoundrels, but because of their manifest moral merit, in which the former are lacking?

15. It is not possible, because of lack of space, to do more than indicate the direction in which such explanations of rights must go. I have tried to provide a more detailed account in my *Rights and Persons*, pp. 199–206.

16. Cf. Gregory Vlastos in his essay, "Justice and Equality," published originally in *Social Justice*, ed. R. B. Brandt and reprinted with minor excisions and the addition of a concluding footnote in *Human Rights*, ed. A. I. Melden (Belmont, California: Wadsworth Publishing Co., 1970).

17. In *Anarchical Fallacies;* the selection in which this characterization occurs can be found in *Human Rights*, ed. A. I. Melden, pp. 28–39.

18. This is not the whole story, of course. Later, I shall remark upon one important feature of the logical substratum of rights, in addition to the point being made here that a human right is presupposed by the special rights that human beings have against each other.

19. In his paper, "Foundations for a Balanced U. S. Policy on Human Rights: The

Significance of Subsistence Rights," pp. 6–7. An expanded version will appear as Chapter 1 in Henry Shue, *Basic Rights: Subsistence, Affluence, and U.S. Foreign Policy* (Princeton: Princeton University Press, 1980).

20. *Ibid.*, p. 9.

A Libertarian Justification for a Welfare State

Libertarians today are deeply divided over whether a night watchman state can be morally justified. Some, like Robert Nozick, hold that a night watchman state would tend to arise by an invisible-hand process if people generally respected each other's Lockean rights.[1] Others, like Murray Rothbard, hold that even the free and informed consent of all the members of a society would not justify such a state.[2] Despite this disagreement, libertarians are strongly united in opposition to welfare rights and the welfare state. According to Nozick, "the state may not use its coercive apparatus for the purpose of getting some citizens to aid others."[3] For Rothbard, "the libertarian position calls for the complete abolition of governmental welfare and reliance on private charitable aid."[4] Here I argue that this libertarian opposition to welfare rights and a welfare state is ill-founded. Welfare rights can be given a libertarian justification, and once this is recognized, a libertarian argument for a welfare state, unlike libertarian arguments for the night watchman state, is both straightforward and compelling. I then show why my proposed justification for welfare rights and a welfare state is preferable to other attempts to get libertarians to acknowedge welfare rights and a welfare state.

Libertarians have defended their view in basically two different ways. Some libertarians, following Herbert Spenser, have 1) defined liberty as the absence of constraints, 2) taken a right to liberty to be the ultimate political ideal, and 3) derived all other rights from this right to liberty. Other libertarians, following John Locke, have 1) taken a set of rights, including, typically, a right to life or self-ownership and a right to property, to be the ultimate political ideal, 2) defined liberty as the absence of constraints in the exercise of these fundamental rights, and 3) derived all other rights, including a right to liberty, from these fundamental rights.

Each of these approaches has its difficulties. The principal difficulty with the first approach is that unless one arbitrarily restricts what is to count as an interference, conflicting liberties will abound, particularly in all areas of social life.[5] The principal difficulty with the second approach is that as long as a person's rights have not been violated, her liberty would not have been restricted either, even if she were kept in prison for the rest of her days.[6] I don't propose to try to decide between these two approaches. What I do want to show, however, is that on either approach welfare rights and a welfare state are morally required.

Spenserian Libertarianism

Thus suppose we were to adopt the view of those libertarians who take a right to liberty to be the ultimate political ideal. According to this view, liberty is usually defined as follows:

> *The Want Conception of Liberty:* Liberty is being unconstrained by other persons from doing what one wants.

This conception limits the scope of liberty in two ways. First, not all constraints whatever their source count as a restriction of liberty; the constraints must come from other persons. For example, people who are constrained by natural forces from getting to the top of Mount Everest do not lack liberty in this regard. Second, constraints that have their source in other persons, but that do not run counter to an individual's wants, constrain without restricting that individual's liberty. Thus, for people who do not want to hear Beethoven's Fifth Symphony, the fact that others have effectively proscribed its performance does not restrict their liberty, even though it does constrain what they are able to do.

Of course, libertarians may wish to argue that even such constraints can be seen to restrict a person's liberty once we take into account the fact that people normally want, or have a general desire, to be unconstrained by others. But other philosophers have thought that the possibility of such constraints points to a serious defect in this conception of liberty,[7] which can only be remedied by adopting the following broader conception of liberty:

> *The Ability Conception of Liberty:* Liberty is being unconstrained by other persons from doing what one is able to do.

Applying this conception to the above example, we find that people's liberty to hear Beethoven's Fifth Symphony would be restricted even if they did not want to hear it (and even if, perchance, they did not want to be unconstrained by others) since other people would still be constraining them from doing what they are able to do.

Moreover, it is important to note that being unconstrained from doing what one is unable to do does not constitute a liberty. Of course, some philosophers would object to this account, claiming, for example, that people might be free or have the liberty to run a four-minute mile even when they are unable to do so. However, if we allow that people can have the liberty to do what they are unable to do, then, presumably, they can also lack the liberty to do or be constrained from doing, what they are unable to do, which seems absurd.

One reason why philosophers have held that people can have the liberty to do what they are unable to do is that they believed that something of value is lost even when such a "liberty" is taken away.[8] F. A. Hayek suggests, for example, that penniless vagabonds who live precariously dependent on their own wits have more liberty than conscripted soldiers with all their security and relative comfort, despite the fact that the vagabonds lack the ability to derive much benefit from their liberty.[9] But although it is true that the vagabonds would lack the ability to derive much benefit from their liberty, it is also true that they would have the ability to exercise that liberty, however unsuccessfully, and it is this ability which is presupposed by the possession of any liberty whatsoever. Thus, in general, while it is possible to confuse having a liberty with having certain sorts of abilities (for example, having the liberty to run a four-minute mile with the ability to succeed in doing so), at the same time, it should be recognized that having a liberty does presuppose the ability to exercise that liberty in some fashion or other, however unsuccessfully. As a consequence, all liberties determined by the Want Conception of Liberty will turn out to be liberties according to the Ability Conception as well.

Of course, there will also be numerous liberties determined by the Ability Conception that are not liberties according to the Want Conception. For example, there will be highly talented students who do not want to pursue careers in philosophy, even though no one constrains them from doing so. Accordingly, the Ability Conception but not the Want Conception would view them as possessing a liberty. And even though such liberties are generally not as valuable as those liberties that are common to both conceptions, they still are of some value, even when the manipulation of people's wants is not at issue.

Yet even if we accept all the liberties specified by the Ability Conception, problems of interpretation still remain. The major problem in this regard concerns what is to count as a constraint. On the one hand, libertarians would like to limit constraints to positive acts (that is, acts of commission) that prevent people from doing what they are otherwise able to do. On the other hand, welfare liberals and socialists interpret constraints to include, in addition, negative acts (that is, acts of omission) that prevent people from doing what they are otherwise able to do. In fact, this is one way to understand the debate between defenders of "negative liberty" and defenders of "positive liberty." For defenders of negative liberty would seem to interpret constraints to include only positive acts of others that prevent people from doing what they otherwise are able to do, while defenders of positive liberty would seem to interpret constraints to include both positive and negative acts of others that prevent people from doing what they are otherwise able to do.[10]

Suppose we interpret constraints in the manner favored by libertarians to include only positive acts by others that prevent people from doing what they are otherwise able to do, and let us consider a typical conflict situation between the rich and the poor.

In this conflict situation, the rich, of course, have more than enough resources to satisfy their basic needs. By contrast, the poor lack the resources to meet their most basic nutritional needs even though they have tried all the means available to them that libertarians regard as legitimate for acquiring such resources. Under circumstances like these, libertarians usually maintain that the rich should have the liberty to use their resources to satisfy their luxury needs if they so wish. Libertarians recognize that this liberty might well be enjoyed at the expense of the satisfaction of the most basic nutritional needs of the poor. Libertarians just think that a right to liberty always has priority over other political ideals, and since they assume that the liberty of the poor is not at stake in such conflict situations, it is easy for them to conclude that the rich should not be required to sacrifice their liberty so that the basic nutritional needs of the poor may be met.

From a consideration of the liberties involved, libertarians claim to derive a number of more specific requirements, in particular, a right to life, a right to freedom of speech, press and assembly, and a right to property.

Here it is important to observe that the libertarian's right to life is not a right to receive from others the goods and resources necessary for preserving one's life; it is simply a right not to be killed unjustly. Correspondingly, the libertarian's right to property is not a right to receive from others the goods and resources necessary for one's welfare, but rather a right to acquire goods and resources either by initial acquisition or by voluntary agreement.

Rights such as these, libertarians claim, can at best support only a limited role for government. That role is simply to prevent and punish initial acts of coercion—the only wrongful actions for libertarians. And, as we noted before, libertarians are deeply divided over whether a government with even such a limited role, that is, a night watchman state, can be morally justified.

Of course, libertarians would allow that it would be nice of the rich to share their surplus resources with the poor. Nevertheless, according to libertarians, such acts of charity should not be coercively required, because the liberty of the poor is not thought to be at stake in such conflict situations.

In fact, however, the liberty of the poor is at stake in such conflict situations. What is at stake is the liberty of the poor to take from the surplus possessions of the rich what is necessary to satisfy their basic nutritional needs. When libertarians are brought to see that this is the case, they are genuinely surprised, for they had not previously seen the conflict between the rich and the poor as a conflict of liberties.[11]

When the conflict between the rich and the poor is viewed as a conflict of liberties, we can either say that the rich should have the liberty to use their surplus resources for luxury purposes, or we can say that the poor should have the liberty to take from the rich what they require to meet their basic nutritional needs. If we choose one liberty, we must reject the other. What needs to be determined, therefore, is which liberty is morally preferable: the liberty of the rich or the liberty of the poor.

I submit that the liberty of the poor, which is the liberty to take from the surplus resources of others what is required to meet one's basic nutritional needs, is morally preferable to the liberty of the rich, which is the liberty to use one's surplus resources for luxury purposes. To see that this is the case we need only appeal to one of the most fundamental principles of morality, one that is common to all political perspectives, namely, the "ought" implies "can" principle. According to this principle, people are not morally required to do what they lack the power to do or what would involve so great a sacrifice that it would be unreasonable to ask them to perform such an action.[12] For example, suppose I promised to attend a departmental meeting on Friday, but on Thursday I am involved in a serious car accident which puts me into a coma. Surely it is no longer the case that I ought to attend the meeting now that I lack the power to do so. Or suppose instead that on Thursday I develop a severe case of pneumonia for which I am hospitalized. Surely I could claim that I no longer ought to attend the meeting on the grounds that the risk to my health involved in attending is a sacrifice that it would be unreasonable to ask me to bear.

Now applying the "ought" implies "can" principle to the case at hand, it seems clear that the poor have it within their power to willingly relinquish such an important liberty as the liberty to take from the rich what they require to meet their basic nutritional needs. Nevertheless, it would be unreasonable to ask them to make so great a sacrifice. In the extreme case, it would involve asking the poor to sit back and starve to death. Of course, the poor may have no real alternative to relinquishing this liberty. To do anything else may involve worse consequences for themselves and their loved ones and may invite a painful death. Accordingly, we may expect that the poor would acquiesce, albeit unwillingly, to a political system that denied them the welfare rights supported by such a liberty, at the same time that we recognize that such a system imposed an unreasonable sacrifice upon the poor—a sacrifice that we could not morally blame the poor for trying to evade.[13] Analogously, we might expect that a woman whose life was threatened would submit to a rapist's demands, at the same time that we recognize the utter unreasonableness of those demands.

By contrast, it would not be unreasonable to ask the rich to sacrifice the liberty to meet some of their luxury needs so that the poor can have the liberty to meet their basic nutritional needs. Of course, we might expect that the rich for reasons of self-interest and past contribution might be disinclined to make such a sacrifice. We might even suppose that the past contribution of the rich provides a good reason for not sacrificing their liberty to use their surplus for luxury purposes. Yet, unlike the poor, the rich could not claim that relinquishing such a liberty involved so great a sacrifice that it would be unreasonable to ask them to make it; unlike the poor, the rich could be morally blameworthy for failing to make such a sacrifice.

Consequently, if we assume that however else we specify the requirements of morality, they cannot violate the "ought" implies "can" principle, it follows that, despite what libertarians claim, the right to liberty endorsed by libertarians actually favors the liberty of the poor over the liberty of the rich.

Yet couldn't libertarians object to this conclusion, claiming that it would be unreasonable to ask the rich to sacrifice the liberty to meet some of their luxury needs so that the poor could have the liberty to meet their basic nutritional needs? As I have pointed out, libertarians don't usually see the situation as a conflict of liberties, but suppose they did. How plausible would such an objection be? Not very plausible at all, I think.

Consider this: what are libertarians going to say about the poor? Isn't it clearly unreasonable to ask the poor to sacrifice the liberty to meet their basic nutritional needs so that the rich can have the liberty to meet their luxury needs? Isn't it clearly unreasonable to ask the poor to sit back and starve to death? If it is, then there is no resolution of this conflict that would be reasonable to ask both the rich and the poor to accept. But that would mean that the libertarian ideal of liberty cannot be a moral ideal that resolves conflicts of interest in ways that it would be reasonable to ask everyone affected to accept. Therefore, as long as libertarians think of themselves as putting forth such a moral ideal, they cannot allow that it would be unreasonable both to ask the rich to sacrifice the liberty to meet some of their luxury needs in order to benefit the poor and to ask the poor to sacrifice the liberty to meet their basic nutritional needs in order to benefit the rich. But I submit that if one of these requests is to be judged reasonable, then, by any neutral assessment, it must be the request that the rich sacrifice the liberty to meet some of their luxury needs so that the poor can have the liberty to meet their basic nutritional needs; there is no other plausible resolution, if libertarians intend to be putting forth a moral ideal that reasonably resolves conflicts of interest.

But might not libertarians hold that putting forth a moral ideal means no more than being willing to universalize one's fundamental commitments? Surely we have no difficulty imagining the rich willing to universalize their commitments to relatively strong property rights. Yet, at the same time, we have no difficulty imagining the poor and their advocates willing to universalize their commitments to relatively weak property rights. Consequently, if the libertarian's moral ideal is interpreted in this fashion, it would not be able to provide a basis for reasonably resolving conflicts of interest between the rich and the poor. But without such a basis for conflict resolution, how could societies flourish, as libertarians claim they would, under a minimal state or with no state at all?[14] Surely, in order for societies to flourish in this fashion, the libertarian ideal must resolve conflicts of interest in ways that it would be reasonable to ask everyone affected to accept. But, as we have seen, that requirement can only be satisfied if the rich sacrifice the liberty to meet some of their luxury needs so that the poor can have the liberty to meet their basic nutritional needs.

It should also be noted that this case for restricting the liberty of the rich depends upon the willingness of the poor to take advantage of whatever opportunities are available to them for satisfying their basic needs by engaging in mutually beneficial work, so that failure of the poor to take advantage of such opportunities would normally either cancel or at least significantly reduce the obligation of the rich to restrict their own liberty for the benefit of the poor.[15] In addition, the poor would be required to return the equivalent of any surplus possessions they have taken from the rich once they are able to do so and still satisfy their basic needs. Nor would the poor be required to keep the liberty to which they are entitled. They could give up part of it, or all of it, or risk losing it on the chance of gaining a greater share of liberties or other social goods.[16] Consequently, the case for restricting the liberty of the rich for the benefit of the poor is neither unconditional nor inalienable.

Even so, libertarians would have to be disconcerted about what turns out to be the practical upshot of taking a right to liberty to be the ultimate political ideal. For libertarians contend that their political ideal would support welfare rights only when constraints are "illegitimately" interpreted to include both positive and negative acts by others that prevent people from doing what they are otherwise able to do. By contrast, when constraints are interpreted to include only positive acts, libertarians contend, no such welfare rights can be justified.

Nevertheless, what the foregoing argument demonstrates is that this view is mistaken. For even when the interpretation of constraints favored by libertarians is employed, a moral assessment of the competing liberties still requires an allocation of liberties to the poor that will be generally sufficient to provide them with the goods and resources necessary for satisfying their basic nutritional needs.

One might think that once the rich realize that the poor should have the liberty not to be interfered with when taking from the surplus possessions of the rich what they require to satisfy their basic needs, it would be in the interest of the rich to stop producing any surplus whatsoever. Yet that would only be the case if first, the recognition of the rightful claims of the poor would exhaust the surplus of the rich and second, the poor would never be in a position to be obligated to repay what they appropriated from the rich. Fortunately for the poor both of these conditions are unlikely to obtain.

Of course, there will be cases where the poor fail to satisfy their basic nutritional needs, not because of any direct restriction of liberty on the part of the rich, but because the poor are in such dire need that they are unable even to attempt to take from the rich what they require to meet their basic nutritional needs. Accordingly, in such cases, the rich would not be performing any act of commission that prevents the poor from taking what they require. Yet, even in such cases, the rich would normally be performing acts of commission that prevent other persons from aiding the poor by taking from the surplus possessions of the rich. And when assessed from a moral point of view, restricting the liberty of these other persons would not be morally justified for the very same reason that restricting the liberty of the poor to meet their own basic nutritional needs would not be morally justified: it would not be reasonable to ask all of those affected to accept such a restriction of liberty.

Nevertheless, libertarians might respond that even supposing welfare rights could be morally justified on the basis of the liberty of the poor to take from the rich in order to meet their basic nutritional needs and the liberty of third parties to take from the rich in order to provide for the basic nutritional rights of the poor, the poor still would be better off without the enforcement of such rights.[17] For example, it might be argued that when people are not forced through taxation to support a system of welfare rights, they are both more productive, since they are able to keep more of what they produce, and more charitable, since they tend to give more freely to those in need when they are not forced to do so. As a result, so the argument goes, the poor would benefit more from the increased charity of a libertarian society than they would from the guaranteed minimum of a welfare state.

Yet, surely it is difficult to comprehend how the poor could be better off in a libertarian society, assuming, as seems likely, that they would experience a considerable loss of self-respect once they had ultimately to depend upon charity rather than a guaranteed minimum for the satisfaction of their basic needs. It is also difficult to comprehend how people who are so opposed to the enforcement of welfare rights would turn out to be so charitable to the poor in a libertarian society.

Moreover, in a libertarian society, the provision of welfare would involve an impossible coordination problem. For if the duty to provide welfare to the poor is at best supererogatory, as libertarians claim, then no one can legitimately force anyone who does not consent to provide such welfare. The will of the majority on this issue could not be legitimately imposed upon dissenters.[18] Assuming then that the provision of welfare requires coordinated action on a broad front, such coordination could not be achieved in a libertarian society because it would require a near unanimous agreement of all its members.[19]

Nevertheless, it might still be argued that the greater productivity of the more talented people in a libertarian society would provide increased employment opportunities that would benefit the poor more than a guaranteed minimum would in a welfare state. But this simply could not occur. For if the more talented members of a society provided sufficient employment opportunities to enable the poor to meet their basic needs then the conditions for invoking a right to a guaranteed minimum in a welfare state would not arise at least for those capable of working, since the poor are first required to take advantage of whatever employment opportunities are available to them before they can legitimately invoke such a right. Consequently, when sufficient employment opportunities obtain, there would be no practical difference between a libertarian society and a welfare state, since neither would justify invoking a right to a guaranteed minimum. Only when insufficient employment opportunities obtain, would there be a practical difference between a libertarian society and a welfare state, and then it would clearly benefit the poor to be able to invoke the right to a guaranteed minimum in a welfare state. Consequently, given the conditional nature of the right to a guaranteed minimum, and the practical possibility, and in most cases, the actuality of insufficient employment opportunities obtaining, there is no reason to think that the poor would be better off without the enforcement of welfare rights.

In brief, what this shows is that if a right to liberty is taken to be the ultimate political ideal, then, contrary to what libertarians claim, not only would a system of welfare rights be morally required, but also such a system would clearly benefit the poor.

Lockean Libertarianism

Yet suppose we were to adopt the view of those libertarians who do not take a right to liberty to be the ultimate political ideal. According to this view, liberty is defined as follows:

> *The Rights Conception of Liberty.* Liberty is being unconstrained by other persons from doing what one has a right to do.

The most important ultimate rights in terms of which liberty is specified are, according to this view, a right to life understood as a right not to be killed unjustly and a right to property understood as a right to acquire goods and resources either by initial acquisition or voluntary agreement. In order to evaluate this view, we must determine what are the practical implications of these rights.

Presumably, a right to life understood as a right not to be killed unjustly would not be violated by defensive measures designed to protect one's person from life-threatening attacks. Yet would this right be violated when the rich prevent the poor from taking what they require to satisfy their basic nutritional needs? Obviously, as a consequence of such preventive actions poor people sometimes do starve to death. Have the rich, then, in contributing to this result, killed the poor, or simply let them die; and, if they have killed the poor, have they done so unjustly?

Sometimes the rich, in preventing the poor from taking what they require to meet their basic nutritional needs, would not in fact be killing the poor, but only causing them to be physically or mentally debilitated. Yet since such preventive acts involve resisting the life-preserving activities of the poor, when the poor do die as a consequence of such acts, it seems clear that the rich would be killing the poor, whether intentionally or unintentionally.

Of course, libertarians would want to argue that such killing is simply a consequence of the legitimate exercise of property rights, and hence, not unjust. But to understand why libertarians are mistaken in this regard, let us appeal again to that fundamental principle of morality, the "ought" implies "can" principle. In this context, the principle can be used to assess two opposing accounts of property rights. According to the first account, a right to property is not conditional upon whether other persons have sufficient opportunities and resources to satisfy their basic needs. This view holds that the initial acquisition and voluntary agreement of some can leave others, through no fault of their own, dependent upon charity for the satisfaction of their most basic needs. By contrast, according to the second account, initial acquisition and voluntary agreement can confer title of property on all goods and resources except those surplus goods and resources of the rich that are required to satisfy the basic needs of those poor who through no fault of their own lack opportunities and resources to satisfy their own basic needs.

Clearly, only the first of these two accounts of property rights would generally justify the killing of the poor as a legitimate exercise of the property rights of the rich. Yet it would be unreasonable to ask the poor to accept anything other than some version of the second account of property rights. Moreover, according to the second account, it does not matter whether the poor would actually die or are only physically or mentally debilitated as a result of such acts of prevention. Either result would preclude property rights from arising. Of course, the poor may have no real alternative to acquiescing to a political system modeled after the first account of property rights, even though such a system imposes an unreasonable sacrifice upon them—a sacrifice that we could not blame them for trying to evade. At the same time, although the rich would be disinclined to do so, it would not be unreasonable to ask them to accept a political system modeled after the second account of property rights—the account favored by the poor.

Consequently, if we assume that however else we specify the requirements of morality, they cannot violate the "ought" implies "can" principle, it follows that, despite what libertarians claim, the right to life and the right to property endorsed by libertarians actually support a system of welfare rights.

Furthermore, how could one object to making property rights conditional upon whether others are able to meet their basic needs when it is generally recognized that what counts as a morally legitimate pursuit of one's own interests is conditional upon the effects that pursuit has on the interests of others? For property rights are a means for the pursuit of one's own interests. Consequently, if the pursuit of one's own interests depends for its moral legitimacy on the effects such a pursuit will have on the interests of others, then property rights, as a means to that pursuit, must be similarly dependent on the effects those rights will have on the interests of others.

Nevertheless, it might be objected that the welfare rights that have been established against the libertarian are not the same as the welfare rights endorsed by welfare liberals. We could mark this difference by referring to the welfare rights that have been established against the libertarian as "action welfare rights" and referring to the welfare rights endorsed by welfare liberals as both "action and recipient welfare rights." The significance of this difference is that a person's action welfare right can be violated only when other people through acts of commission interfere with a person's exercise of that right, whereas a person's action and recipient welfare right can be violated by such acts of commission and by acts of omission as well. However, this difference will have little practical import. For once libertarians come to recognize the legitimacy of action welfare rights, then in order not to be subject to the poor person's discretion in choosing when and how to exercise her action welfare right, libertarians will tend to favor two morally legitimate ways of preventing the exercise of such rights. First, libertarians can provide the poor with mutually beneficial job opportunities. Second, libertarians can institute adequate recipient welfare rights that would take precedence over the poor's action welfare rights. Accordingly, if libertarians adopt either or both of these ways of legitimately preventing the poor from exercising their action welfare rights, libertarians will end up endorsing the same sort of welfare institutions favored by welfare liberals.

Finally, once a system of welfare rights is seen to follow irrespective of whether one takes a right to liberty or rights to life and property as the ultimate political ideal, the justification for a welfare state become straightforward and compelling. For while it is at least conceivable that rights other than welfare rights could be adequately secured in a society without the enforcement agencies of a state, it is inconceivable that welfare rights themselves could be adequately secured without such enforcement agencies. Only a welfare state would be able to effectively solve the large-scale coordination problem necessitated by the provision of welfare. Consequently, once a system of welfare rights can be seen to have a libertarian justification, the argument for a welfare state hardly seems to need stating.[20]

Two Libertarian Objections

In addition to the objections to this libertarian justification for welfare rights and a welfare state that we have already considered, there are two related objections advanced by Murray Rothbard and Eric Mack, respectively, that merit consideration. Both Rothbard and Mack want to characterize severe conflict situations between the rich and the poor as lifeboat situations. Rothbard then seeks to deal with these situations by distinguishing between a "political ethics" which supports unconditional property rights even in the face of dire need and "a moral course of action" which may recommend the violation of such property rights.[21] By contrast, Mack seeks to deal with such situations by claiming that no one has any rights when such situations obtain; Mack thinks that in such situations all parties are at liberty to pursue their own interests.[22] Thus, although for different reasons, both Rothbard and Mack would object to our derivation of welfare rights from a consideration of severe conflict of interest situations between the rich and the poor.

Yet Mack avoids endorsing welfare rights in such situations only by giving up rights altogether, and so his account cannot provide a satisfactory resolution, even from a libertarian point of view.[23] On the other hand, while Rothbard distinguishes between a political ethics which supports unconditional property rights and a moral course of action which may recommend the satisfaction of basic needs, he still claims that in cases of conflict, it is always punishable and never excusable to follow a moral course of action. So Rothbard's alternative to following unconditional property rights seems to be a "moral course of action" in name only. In any case, he clearly has failed to deal with the strong moral challenge to unconditional property rights contained in the "ought" implies "can" principle.

Other Attempts to Derive Welfare Rights

Needless to say, there have been other attempts to get libertarians to acknowledge welfare rights. One such attempt seeks to determine the distribution of liberties and rights on the basis of what will least frustrate people's desires or what will minimize their disutility. Ernest Loevinsohn adopts this standard in arguing against the libertarian's opposition to welfare rights. Loevinsohn claims that when redistribution from the rich to the poor is justified,

> . . . the transfer of property brings about a decrease in the extent of the recipient's unsatisfied desires for items of property, and this decrease outweighs any increase in unsatisfied desires resulting from the transfer. So if the redistributive alternative is chosen then overall there will be less unsatisfied desire for items of property than on the non-redistributive alternative.[24]

But it is unlikely that libertarians would endorse this standard to arbitrate conflicts between the rich and the poor. Even when the standard is limited to acts of commission, as Loevinsohn proposes, libertarians could still object to its utilitarian character. By contrast, the "ought" implies "can" principle does not regard just any elimitable dissatisfaction as a basis for welfare rights: the dissatisfaction must constitute an unreasonably severe sacrifice for at least some members of a society before the "ought" implies "can" principle would support welfare rights. Consequently, while libertarians can reject a standard of minimizing disutility as begging the question against their view, they cannot similarly reject an appeal to the "ought" implies "can" principle.

Another attempt to get libertarians to acknowledge welfare rights seeks to deny the moral relevance of the commission/omission distinction on which libertarians standardly rely to support their commitment to an ideal of negative liberty over ideals of positive liberty. According to this view, any attempt to invest such a distinction with moral significance is doomed to failure because a similar causality underlies both types of actions.[25] In particular, this view holds that we are just as much a cause of a person's death when we kill as when we let die. From this, John Harris claims, it follows that "in whatever sense we are morally responsible for our positive actions, in the same sense we are morally responsible for our negative actions."[26] Hence, according to this view, there is little basis for the libertarian's prohibition of acts of commission but not of acts of omission when they both have the same consequences.

Yet while this view is correct in pointing out that there is a causal basis for moral responsibility in cases of acts of omission, the view is mistaken in identifying the standard causal role played by acts of omission with that played by acts of commission in the production of consequences for which people are morally responsible. For acts of omission causally contribute to the production of such consequences by failing to prevent a causal condition sufficient to produce those consequences, as in failing to save a person from drowning, while acts of commission causally contribute to the production of such consequences by creating a causal condition sufficient to produce those consequences, as in poisoning a person's food.[27] Thus, to take only the fact that both acts of omission and acts of commission contribute to such consequences to be morally relevant and to ignore the different ways in which both types of acts causally contribute to such consequences is to beg the question against libertarians who want to morally distinguish between these two types of acts. Consequently, only by proceeding as we have, and basing a justification of welfare rights on an interpretation of constraints of liberty (and violations of rights) that involves acts of commission for which people are morally responsible, can we avoid begging the question against the libertarian view.

Still another attempt to derive welfare rights from libertarian premises has been defended by Hillel Steiner.[28] Steiner's defense is directed primarily at Spenserian libertarians, and, hence, he appeals to a right to equal liberty as the ultimate political ideal. Steiner contends that such a right requires an unlimited right to the fruits of one's labor once natural resources have been justly distributed. Accordingly, he focuses on what would be a just distribution of such resources. Steiner claims that previous attempts to specify a just distribution of natural resources are flawed because they preclude historically later persons from exercising the same right of initial acquisition. To avoid this result, Steiner claims, we need to view society as a joint stock company which leases its assets to persons for a limited period of time, never to exceed a person's lifetime. On this view, each person can be seen as having an equal right that none of society's assets be disposed of without his or her consent, which is a right everyone could conceivably exercise.[29] Moreover, the effective exercise of such a right would be sufficient to ground welfare rights and a welfare state.

An obvious merit of Steiner's defense of welfare rights is that it forces libertarians to explain, on their view, how everyone is to exercise a right to equal liberty. Yet because Steiner renounces any attempt to assess liberties according to their value,[30] libertarians can still escape the welfare implications of his view. For libertarians can simply incorporate a right of acquisition within a more general right to property which allows property to be acquired either by initial acquisition or by voluntary agreement. Then libertarians could claim that this more general disjunctive right can equally be possessed and exercised by all, even though its exercise is compatible with the poor being unable to satisfy even their most basic nutritional needs while the rich have sufficient surplus resources to meet most of their luxury needs.

To avoid this consequence, we need to assess the value of liberties at least to the degree that we can reject distributions of "equal liberty" whose liberties are immensely valuable to some but of little value to others. Obviously one way to so assess the value of liberties is to appeal, as we have done, to the "ought" implies "can" principle. For it is only by evaluating the distribution of liberties (and rights) in some such fashion that we can adequately support welfare rights and a welfare state on a libertarian foundation.

Yet another attempt to derive welfare rights from a libertarian foundation begins with the libertarian's endorsement of various civil and political rights, like the rights of freedom of speech, press, assembly, due process and equality before the law. It is then argued that because the effective exercise of these rights requires adequate social and economic resources, libertarians should be committed to guaranteeing such resources to each and every person. Allen Buchanan, for example, has defended just such a provision of welfare on grounds of fairness.[31] Yet given the intimate connection between ideals of fairness and welfare rights, such a defense would appear to beg the question against the libertarian view.[32] Thus, a better approach would be to argue that libertarians should be committed to the provision of welfare necessary to secure an effective exercise of at least those civil and political rights, like due process and equality before the law, which relate to the imposition of significant burdens and penalties. For surely it would not be reasonable to ask people to accept the imposition of significant burdens and penalties unless they have been guaranteed an effective exercise of the rights of due process and equality before the law. Obviously this is again to appeal to the "ought" implies "can" principle. Nor can it be objected that the "ought" implies "can" principle is itself a standard of fairness since there are many impositions of burdens that although they accord with the principle are still unfair either because they are unequal or because they result from arbitrary procedures.

This argument, however, would not equally support the provision of welfare to secure the effective exercise of other civil and political rights, such as the rights of freedom of speech, press and assembly. For the exercise of these rights relates not so much to the imposition of burdens and penalties in society as the distribution of benefits. For this reason, the "ought" implies "can" principle is less likely to call for the provision of welfare with respect to civil and political rights of this sort.

In summary, it seems clear that none of the four alternative attempts to get libertarians to endorse welfare rights and a welfare state is preferable to the one defended in this essay. The first attempt by appealing to a utilitarian standard of minimizing dissatisfaction or disutility begs the question against the libertarian view. The second attempt does the same by ignoring the possible moral relevance of the different causal roles played by acts of commission and acts of omission in the production of consequences for which people are morally responsible. The third attempt fails because it disallows any assessment of liberties according to their value. The fourth attempt, when reconstructed so as not to appear to beg the question against the libertarian view, justifies a provision of welfare for the exercise of a subclass of the civil and political rights endorsed by libertarians only by appealing to some fundamental moral principle like the "ought" implies "can" principle. Hence, the approach taken in this paper of beginning with a right to liberty or, alternatively, a fundamental set of rights like the right to life and the right to property, and then appealing to the "ought" implies "can" principle appears to be the best way of providing a libertarian foundation for welfare rights and a welfare state.[33]

Notes

1. Robert Nozick, *Anarchy, State and Utopia* (New York: Basic Books, 1974), Part I.
2. Murray Rothbard, *The Ethics of Liberty* (Atlantic Highlands: Humanities Press, 1982), p. 230.
3. Nozick, *Anarchy, State and Utopia,* p. ix.
4. Murray Rothbard, *For a New Liberty* (New York: Collier Books, 1978), p. 148.
5. See, for example, James P. Sterba, "Neo-Libertarianism," *American Philosophical Quarterly* 15 (1978): 17–19; Ernest Loevinsohn, "Liberty and the Redistribution of Property," *Philosophy and Public Affairs* 6 (1977): 226–39; Zimmerman, "Coercive Wage Offers," *Philosophy and Public Affairs* 10 (1981): 121–45. To limit what is to count as coercive, Zimmerman claims that in order for P's offer to be coercive,

   > (I)t must be the case that P does more than merely prevent Q *from taking from* P resources necessary for securing Q's strongly preferred preproposal situation; P must prevent Q *from acting on his own* (or with the help of others) *to produce or procure* the strongly preferred preproposal situation.

   But this restriction seems arbitrary, and Zimmerman provides little justification for it. See David Zimmerman, "More on Coercive Wage Offers," *Philosophy and Public Affairs* 12 (1983): 67–68.
6. It might seem that this second approach could avoid this difficulty if a restriction of liberty is understood as the curtailment of one's prima facie rights. But in order to avoid the problem of a multitude of conflicting liberties, which plagues the first approach, the specification of prima facie rights must be such that they only can be overridden when one or more of them is violated. And this may involve too much precision for our notion of prima facie rights.

7. Isaiah Berlin, *Four Essays on Liberty* (New York: Oxford University Press, 1969), pp. XXXVIII–XL.
8. John Gray, "On Negative and Positive Liberty," *Political Studies* 29 (1980): 507–26.
9. F. A. Hayek, *The Constitution of Liberty* (Chicago: University of Chicago Press, 1960), p. 18.
10. On this point, see Maurice Cranston, *Freedom* (New York: Basic Books, 1953), pp. 52–53; C. B. Macpherson, *Democratic Theory* (Oxford: Oxford University Press, 1973), p. 95; Joel Feinberg, *Rights, Justice and the Bounds of Liberty* (Princeton, Princeton University Press, 1980), Chapter 1.
11. See John Hospers, *Libertarianism,* (Los Angeles: Nash Publishing Co., 1971), Chapter 7.
12. Alvin Goldman, *A Theory of Human Action* (Englewood Cliffs: Prentice Hall, 1970), pp. 208–15; William Frankena, "Obligation and Ability," in *Philosophical Analysis* edited by Max Black (Ithaca, Cornell University Press, 1950), pp. 157–75.

    Judging from some recent discussions of moral dilemmas by Bernard Williams and Ruth Marcus, one might think that the "ought" implies "can" principle would only be useful for illustrating moral conflicts rather than resolving them. (See Bernard Williams, *Problems of the Self* (Cambridge: Cambridge University Press, 1977), Chapters 11 and 12: Ruth Marcus, "Moral Dilemmas and Consistency" *The Journal of Philosophy* 80 (1980): 121–36. See also Terrance C. McConnell, "Moral Dilemmas and Consistency in Ethics," *Canadian Journal of Philosophy* 18 (1978): 269–87. But this is only true if one interprets the "can" in the principle to exclude only "what a person lacks the power to do." If one interprets the "can" to exclude in addition "what would involve so great a sacrifice that it would be unreasonable to ask the person to do it" then the principle can be used to resolve moral conflicts as well as state them. Nor would libertarians object to this broader interpretation of the "ought" implies "can" principle since they do not ground their claim to liberty on the existence of irresolvable moral conflicts.
13. See James P. Sterba, "Is There a Rationale for Punishment?" *The American Journal of Jurisprudence* 29 (1984): 29–44.
14. As further evidence, notice that those libertarians who justify a minimal state do so on the grounds that such a state would arise from reasonable disagreements concerning the application of libertarian rights. They do not justify the minimal state on the grounds that it would be needed to keep in submission large numbers of people who could not come to see the reasonableness of libertarian rights.

15. Obviously, the employment opportunities offered to the poor must be honorable and supportive of self-respect. To do otherwise would be to offer the poor the opportunity to meet some of their basic needs at the cost of denying some of their other basic needs.
16. The poor cannot, however, give up the liberty to which their children are entitled.
17. See John Hospers, "The Libertarian Manifesto," in James P. Sterba (ed.) *Morality in Practice*, (Belmont: Wadsworth Publishing Co., 1983), especially p. 26.
18. Sometimes advocates of libertarianism inconsistently contend that the duty to help others is supererogatory but that a majority of a society could justifiably enforce such a duty on everyone. See Theodore Benditt, "The Demands of Justice," in *Economic Justice*, edited by Diana Meyers and Kenneth Kipnis (forthcoming).
19. Sometimes advocates of libertarianism focus on the coordination problems that arise in welfare states concerning the provision of welfare and ignore the far more serious coordination problems that would arise in a night watchman state. See Burton Leiser, "Vagrancy, Loitering and Economic Justice," in *Economic Justice*.
20. Of course, someone might still want to object to welfare states on the grounds that they "force workers to sell their labor" (see G. A. Cohen, "The Structure of Proletarian Unfreedom," *Philosophy and Public Affairs* 12 (1982): 3–33 and subject workers to "coercive wage offers." (See Zimmerman, "Coercive Wage Offers.") But for a defense of at least one form of welfare state against such an objection, see James P. Sterba, "A Marxist Dilemma for Social Contract Theory," *American Philosophical Quarterly* 21 (1981): 51–59.
21. Rothbard, *The Ethics of Liberty*, pp. 149–53.
22. Eric Mack, "Individualism, Rights and the Open Society," *The Libertarian Reader* (Totowa, Rowman and Littlefield, 1982), pp. 9–11.
23. On this point, see Rothbard, *The Ethics of Liberty*, pp. 151–53.
24. Loevinsohn, "Liberty and the Redistribution of Property," p. 234.
25. John Harris, *Violence and Responsibility* (Boston: Routledge & Kegan Paul, 1980), p. 58.
26. John Harris, "The Marxist Conception of Violence," *Philosophy and Public Affairs* 3 (1974): 211.
27. Of course, sometimes a person who performs an act of omission which contributes to the production of consequences for which the person is responsible may do so as part of a larger act of commission which is a sufficient causal condition for the production of those consequences. And sometimes a person who performs an act of commission which contributes to the production of consequences for which the person is

responsible does so as part of a larger act of omission which simply fails to prevent those consequences. On this point see O. H. Green "Killing and Letting Die," *American Philosophical Quarterly* 20 (1980): 195–204; Raziel Abelson, "To Do or Let Happen," *American Philosophical Quarterly* 22 (1982): 219–27.

28. Hillel Steiner, "Individual Liberty," *Proceeding of the Aristotelian Society* 75 (1974–5): 33–50; "The Structure of a Set of Compossible Rights," *Journal of Philosophy* 74 (1977): 761–75; "The Natural Right to the Means of Production," *Philosophical Quarterly* 27 (1977): 41–49; "Slavery, Socialism and Private Property," *Property, Nomos XXII,* edited by Roland Pennock and John Chapman (New York, New York University Press, 1980), pp. 244–66.
29. Steiner, "Slavery, Socialism and Private Property," p. 259.
30. Ibid., pp. 245–46.
31. Allen Buchanan, "Deriving Welfare Rights from Libertarian Rights," in *Income Support,* edited by Peter Brown and others (Totowa, Rowman and Littlefield, 1981).
32. Of course, libertarians do need to provide some account of an ideal of fairness, but a well-grounded critique of libertarianism should not begin with such an ideal whose interpretation is widely contested. I made this mistake in "Neo Libertarianism." But see the expanded version in *Justice: Alternative Political Perspectives,* edited by James P. Sterba (Belmont: Wadsworth Publishing Co., 1979), especially pp. 185–86.
33. I wish to thank Neil Delaney, Alan Fuchs, John Hospers, Eric Mack, Jeff Paul along with the participants at the First Fulbright Anglo-American Colloquium held at St. Andrews University, especially Jim Fishkin, Jeff McMahan and Tom Donaldson, for their helpful comments on an earlier version of this paper. Financial assistance in writing the paper was provided by a Ludwig von Mises Fellowship.

James P. Sterba
Department of Philosophy
University of Notre Dame

RAYMOND PLANT

3

NEEDS, AGENCY, AND WELFARE RIGHTS

A fully developed theory of rights has to provide an account of at least four things:

1. The agent to whom the rights are ascribed.
2. The features of the agent that justify the ascription of such rights.
3. The nature of the objects, resources, states of affairs, processes, or forbearances to which the rights are rights.
4. The range of individuals or institutions who have the duties or obligations that correspond to the rights of other agents: that is, who or what has the duty to respect, implement, or satisfy the rights that individuals have.

Following Gewirth (1982, 3) we might put these features into the following formula: **A** has a right to **X** against **B** in virtue of **Y.**

So we have to give an account of the agent, **A;** what it is about the nature of **A** that grants the right, **Y;** the nature of the right asserted, **X;** and against whom it is asserted, **B.** Can a theory of welfare as a basic right satisfy the various elements of this formula in a cogent and coherent manner? I shall argue that it can, basing the justification of the right on an account of the needs of a rational agent. However, as we shall see, such a view also challenges some generally accepted assumptions about the scope of the responsibilities and obligations that accompany rights. My strategy in this chapter will be to consider ways in which arguments in relation to the four features mentioned in Gewirth's formula are deployed in relation to rights such as life or liberty, and then to try to show that there are corresponding and equally cogent arguments in the case of the rights to welfare.

Two elements (at least) of Gewirth's formula are interdependent—the account of the agent to whom rights are ascribed and the characteristics in virtue of which they are ascribed (i.e., features **A** and **Y** in the formula). Clearly these cannot be wholly separated because the features in terms of which rights are justified will have a clear bearing upon the identity of the agents to whom they are ascribed.

What might such features be? In answering this question it is, I believe, possible to apply two formal constraints upon any potential answer. First, if certain features of existence are potential grounds for basic rights, then these features must be universal. That is to say, if they are to underpin a theory of universal rights, then those features of life in virtue of which such rights are held must themselves be universal. By "universal" here I mean not specific to culture, religion, or ethnic origin.

The second constraint is moral relevance. Because the attribution of rights specifies a range of claims and duties that rights bearers can hold against one another, these rights presuppose some moral sensibility, an ability to claim rights and to recognize duties as binding in the light of rights. As rights specify a sphere of moral relationships, those features of life that are held to ground rights must be morally relevant. Hence, although it might be a distinctive feature of human beings that they possess ear lobes, this could not be a ground for the ascription of rights because, however biologically distinctive this feature is, it is not morally relevant! Given these two constraints, we can say that any account in virtue of what **X**'s rights are will have to be both universal and morally relevant.

The criterion of moral relevance here can be taken in two ways. It could mean that a proposed criterion is part of a particular substantive morality, or it could mean that it is a presupposition of any possible morality. It is fairly clear that a theory of universal rights could be compatible with the former view only if this particular substantive morality could objectively and rationally be grounded so that other individuals accepting other moral outlooks would have to accept *it* as rational and fundamental. However, the history of moral thought since Plato does not give us any grounds for optimism for believing that such a foundational and acceptable moral theory could be arrived at. The diversity of values is so great that if the ground for ascribing rights to individuals could be derived only from a particular substantive moral code, then, although such a view of rights might be cogent and authoritative *within* that morality, its authority would extend only as far as the general authority of that morality. Thus, to provide the grounds for a general or universal theory of rights we must look at the other possibility. Instead of looking to a *particular* moral code or outlook, we should rather look at the question of whether, given the facts of moral diversity, there are still any universal features of human life that appear to be necessary presuppositions or conditions for morality, whatever such moralities may turn out to be. If there are any such features, then they would be universal and, as presuppositions of morality, necessarily morally relevant.

This basically Kantian way of posing the problem seeks a transcendental deduction of the grounds of rights by reflecting upon the necessary preconditions of morality. Kant, of course, argued that such preconditions were to be understood in terms of rational, autonomous agency and the ability to formulate rules of universal scope (Kant, 1974). These features of existence would be very difficult to deny in terms of moral relevance in the sense that any moral code is presumably going to invoke ideas of ought and ought not, right and wrong, good and bad—all notions that presuppose a capacity for choice between alternatives, at least as they are envisaged *within* that morality. We might argue with Kant that rational agency could be seen to be a necessary condition of any moral code inasmuch as any such a code will prescribe ends to be followed and alternatives to be avoided, and these presuppose a capacity for agency. This does not mean that agency would of itself have to be rated highly or at all within the moral code in question; only that, recognized or not, it is implicitly assumed in the very notion of moral conduct.

On this view the capacity for rational agency might be regarded as both a universal and necessary condition for morality and therefore a possible foundation for a theory of rights. What sense of rights could the idea of rational agency or autonomy ground? One answer is: rights to forbearances of various sorts. If we emphasize autonomy as the basis of rights, then it seems an easy thing to move to the Nozickian position that the central way of protecting human inviolability is through a set of rights that impose constraints upon the possible range of interferences by others (Nozick, 1974). In other words, rights are to be understood negatively as requiring the absence of interference, coercion, assault, killing, and so on.

This view would, of course, exclude the idea that agency could act as a ground for welfare rights understood as the positive right to resources rather than as the negative view of liberty. If agency and autonomy are universal, necessary features of a morality that could act as a basis for rights, then on a negative view of liberty, freedom and autonomy are diminished only by intentional coercion. My freedom to choose and to act is constrained only if there is an identifiable individual who is intentionally coercing me. A negative account of rights could then cope with these sorts of infringements of autonomy because such rights demand forbearance from coercion and interference of all sorts. However, on this view, freedom and autonomy require not resources and opportunities but merely the absence of coercion. This kind of autonomy can ground a negative view of rights; that is, it is in virtue of their possession of autonomy that individuals should be protected by a set of rights against coercion and interference. However, it cannot ground a more positive view of rights as rights to resources, just because on the negative view of liberty the absence of resources is not a restriction of freedom. The only restrictions on freedom arise from the intentional coercive actions of other agents.

This negative view of the requirements of autonomy is based upon the following considerations. It is argued that there must be a clear distinction drawn between freedom and ability in the sense that there is a wide range of things I am unable to do that it would be absurd to regard as infringements of my liberty. These inabilities may be of all sorts:

1. Logical inabilities: I cannot draw a picture of a mountain without a valley.
2. Physical impossibilities: I cannot as a male bear a child.
3. Inabilities arising from my own nature and character: I am unable to become a creative mathematician.
4. Episodic inabilities: I cannot ride my bicycle uphill today—the wind is too strong.
5. Inabilities arising from my own earlier choices, which have affected my present circumstances: I am now unable to become a Roman Catholic priest; I am unable to run in a marathon.
6. Inabilities arising from circumstances that are not alterable by human action: An irreparable lesion in the spinal cord may limit physical activity.

There are, no doubt, many other forms of inability that could be categorized in different ways, but in each of these cases the limitations on my power are not caused by intentional coercion; and although in each case my abilities may be limited, my freedom is not. I am free to do these things; I am unable to do them. This point is made very clearly by Hayek in *The Constitution of Liberty:* "We presuppose a human agent if we say that we have been coerced. . . . Coercion implies both the threat of inflicting harm and the intention thereby to bring about certain conduct" (1960, 9).

Given this definition of coercion, autonomy does not require resources; on the contrary it requires the absence of intentional restraint and coercion. Autonomy is thus to be protected by negative rights and not by guaranteed rights to resources.

There is a subsidiary argument here, turning upon the intentional nature of coercion. Economic markets in particular are not to be seen as coercive in their outcomes for the worst-off members of society. The poverty that an individual may experience as the result of the operation of a free market is not, on this view, to be construed as a limitation of liberty and autonomy. The reason for this is a conjunction of the points made above. First, the possession of resources, powers, and opportunities is distinct from liberty, which is freedom from coercion; second, the outcomes of markets are an unintended and unforeseen result of individual decisions to buy and sell, taken on all sorts of different grounds. Hence, poverty is not caused by intentional action and is not a restriction of liberty. Sir Keith Joseph and Jonathan Sumption, in their book entitled *Equality* (1979), have clearly seen the point at stake here. In a chapter devoted to arguing that poverty is not unfreedom, they argue that the contrary view—that it is a limitation on liberty—would require coercive action on the part of the state to remove poverty in order to secure liberty as a basic right. Accepting the arguments stated above, they reject this approach.

Hence, on this view, although agency, autonomy, and liberty are universal and necessary preconditions for any moral code, they do not imply any welfare rights. The demand for autonomy is the demand to be left alone, requiring a right to forebearance rather than rights to welfare. However, there are arguments that can weaken the force of this position.

The first is the idea, which John Rawls has developed, of the worth or value of liberty. For if freedom is the absence of intentional coercion, we must surely be able to explain what the worth of liberty is to an individual. Why do we want to be free from coercion? The answer must surely be that if we are free from coercion we shall be able to do more of what we want to do. In this sense the idea of ability, of being enabled to do more things, enters into the justification of liberty because it contributes to the worth of liberty. So if we are interested in the worth and value of liberty to an individual person, we must also be concerned with what the individual is able to do. This would be the basis for saying that the value of liberty, as an effective power to act, requires resources. Thus, the value of liberty requires not just rights against intentional coercion but also rights to those resources, which would secure the same value of liberty for each individual considered as a moral equal. If the power to do something is central to why we find liberty valuable, and if we believe in an equal right to liberty, there is no clear reason why this should be defined only as an equal basic liberty to be free from coercion, as opposed to an equal right to those basic resources that are necessary for individual agency and that will secure an equal basic value of liberty between individuals.

These points about the interrelationship between liberty and ability or power are also reflected in our ordinary language distinctions. For example, if one is freed from a clear, direct intentional coercion, (e.g., the removal of handcuffs), we could say that this removal enabled one to do certain things (if one chooses) that one was not able to do before. On the other hand, to place such coercion on someone is to render one unable to do what one was able to do before. There are therefore great dangers in arguing that to be free is to be protected by rights against coercion, but that one's ability and power need not be protected at all by rights.

However, not all inabilities should be seen as a restriction of freedom. If they are, then it would absurdly follow that the state could protect my liberty only if it could secure my omnipotence, because any restriction on my ability or power would be a limitation on my freedom. If we wish to provide a defense of positive freedom and the positive welfare rights that would flow from this, we will have to try to define a class of basic goods that are necessary conditions of agency, as such, and should therefore be protected in terms of rights, and distinguish between these goods and all the other goods that a particular agent might desire.

The attempt to define a class of basic goods of agency is important in another way, too. Many critics of positive liberty have objected to it because it moralizes the concept. I am free only if I am able to do certain things and these things are sanctioned by a specific moral code. This definition is held to be illiberal and potentially totalitarian. If we can identify in a morally neutral way a set of basic goods of agency, then both objections to positive freedom, at least in this restricted form, would fail.

This strategy has two advantages. First, it would meet the Hayekian objection that the positive libertarian cannot distinguish between freedom and omnipotence; it would also be more logically coherent with a theory of rights because it would be concerned with whether there are any basic goods of agency, autonomy, and liberty, irrespective of the particular culture within which an individual might live and the individual conceptions of the good life that individuals might be enabled to attain within that culture. In this sense, attempting to identify the basic goods that would be required by agency would meet the universalistic requirement implicit in a theory of rights.

One way of putting the point, and one that might make it sound less abstract, would be to argue in terms of needs, or basic needs. The issue can be put thus: Are there any needs basic to agency that can be defined independently of the specific needs that an individual may have in a particular culture or morality? If there are such needs, they would then define the set of basic rights that would reflect such needs.

The needs of agency will plausibly include, first of all, physical survival in the platitudinous sense that an agent is unable to exercise agency without physical integrity and survival. But there is more to the physical needs of agency than mere survival; agency must also include some element of a worthwhile life or physical well-being, because it is very difficult to imagine how a life of rational agency could ever be pursued if the whole effort of a person's life is devoted to securing the bare minimum to survive. In this sense, to secure the capacity for agency for individuals will require not just restrictions on coercion defined by negative rights but also positive rights to those resources that will contribute to both survival and well-being. Hence, food, shelter, and health care of a sort relevant to and effective in a particular society would constitute basic goods of agency. However, the capacity of agency will also require other kinds of basic goods such as education, which, in the terms relevant to a particular society, will be needed to sustain a capacity for agency, choice, and effective functioning.

The rights to freedom secured by rights to these sorts of resources is not a freedom to do any specific thing but, rather, a general set of conditions that will enable the individual to go on to the sorts of things she or he wants to do. Basic needs have to be satisfied in order to do anything at all; nonbasic needs are for those goods an individual needs to fulfill one's particular plan of life in *one person's* particular circumstances. Rights have to do with the first type of need but not with the latter. The first are universally and morally relevant; the latter are morally relevant but not universal.

So, if the ideas of agency, autonomy, and freedom are basic to morality, then they could underpin a set of rights that would be both negative rights to freedom from coercion, but also to those positive resources that are necessary conditions of acting in a purposeful way at all. These conditions would ground a positive theory of rights. At the same time it would answer the Hayekian objection that there would be no difference between freedom and omnipotence. The difference would be in terms of defining a set of necessary basic goods for liberty, rather than the optimal set of goods required for a particular free action.

This kind of argument can, I believe, provide a basis for thinking about the coherence of positive rights, and it answers the first point of the formula with which I began. It will also give us a way of characterizing those who are bearers of rights—namely, those who are capable of rational agency, or at least have the capacity for such agency.

However, when we move to other parts of the formula, the idea of positive rights to welfare runs up against a number of severe difficulties that will have to be countered before a conception of welfare rights can be regarded as morally defensible. If we concentrate attention first of all on what individuals have a right to (the **X** in Gewirth's formula quoted at the beginning of this chapter), then it is clear that problems arise. On a negative view of rights, what the individual has a right to is a form of forebearance on the part of others—a right to their abstaining from action. So the right to life is the right *not* to be killed, and the right to freedom of speech is the right *not* to be interfered with (unless, in exercising my right, I am interfering with another's right). Because these rights are therefore rights that certain things *not* be done, they are, so it is argued, costless and not subject to scarcity. Welfare rights, however, as rights to resources, always imply costs and scarcity. This, it is sometimes argued, entails a theoretical difference between negative and positive rights. More important, these considerations give rise to issues of practicability. Because negative rights are asserted to forebearances, they are costless and always practicable, whereas welfare rights always involve costs and may not be practicable. How can a theory of human rights consistently endorse a set of rights that may not be practicable, because the resources to meet them in particular society may be too great? Charles Fried poses the problem as follows:

> A positive right is a claim to something—a share in a material good, or some particular good such as the attentions of a lawyer or doctor, or perhaps a claim to a result like health or enlightenment—while a negative right is a right that something not be done to one, that some particular imposition be withheld. Positive rights are inevitably assigned to scarce goods and consequently scarcity implies a limit to the claim. Negative rights, however, the rights not to be interfered with in forbidden ways, do not appear to have such natural, such inevitable limitations. If I am left alone, the commodity I obtain does not appear of its nature to be a scarce or limited one. How can we run out of people not harming each other, not lying to each other, leaving each other alone? (1978, 110)

On this view, there is a major difference between the kinds of things to which rights are asserted as between negative rights and positive or welfare rights. The critic of welfare rights will also argue that these considerations actually strike at the heart of the rationale of rights. If positive rights are always rights to scarce resources, then, by definition, such rights cannot be realized at the same level simultaneously by all right holders. If scarcity prevents an equal realization of this right, then there will have to be a rationing procedure to determine whose rights are to be realized to which resources in a set of given circumstances. The critic will argue that these decisions will typically be made on consequentialist or utilitarian grounds (Glover, 1977), whereas the whole thrust and rationale of rights-based theories is against consequentialist and utilitarian considerations—that there are ways of dealing with people that are wrong irrespective of the calculation of consequences. However, the very fact of scarcity plunges us into consequentialist considerations. Take, for example, the right to life as construed as a right to resources rather than as the negative right not to be killed. If circumstances arose in which there is only one life-saving resource with two persons having a right to it, then assuming there are no overriding clinical reasons for giving that resource to one rather than to the other, the distribution of the resource will be based upon consequentialist arguments such as a cost-benefit analysis or whatever. In that sense, the positive right to life cannot be assigned or respected without getting into utilitarian calculation. However, if the right to life is the negative one of not killing, then, so it is argued, the failure to give a life-saving resource to **A** does not, on **A**'s death, mean that **A** has been killed. Rather, it will be said that he or she died of, for example, kidney failure, not as the intentional result of the failure to provide dialysis. Hence, negative rights to the nonperformance of actions imply no scarcity, and so enable us to steer clear of utilitarian calculation.

These are very cogent points, and any theory of positive rights has to confront them. There are two basic issues here: the extent to which negative rights can be regarded as costless and the problems of acts and omissions in relation to forbearance. The first of these is easier to deal with than the second.

There is a common initial objection to the point that Charles Fried makes—namely, that negative rights are not costless because the appropriate amount of forbearance may not be present. Thus, protecting negative rights will require legislation, sanctions, police, law courts, and prisons, and these are not costless. In this sense, in the world as it is, the decision of how far to go in the legal protection and enforcement of negative rights may well involve utilitarian calculation. However, the critic of welfare rights could still argue that there is a logical or conceptual difference in the sense that we could imagine a world—for example, a community of saints—in which there was always the degree of forbearance required to secure negative rights in a costless and unconstrained way, whereas even in such a world positive rights are rights to resources and will still involve utilitarian calculation. In such a possible world, therefore, we can see the logical difference between positive and negative rights, even though in the world in which we live the differences are less obvious in practice.

However, this is a difficult thesis to sustain, not just because of its counterfactual basis but also because a very similar counterfactual is open to the defender of welfare rights. One can envisage a possible world without material scarcity, and in such a world securing the rights to welfare goods would be costless. In other words, both counterfactuals are about scarcity. The first imagines a world in which there is no scarcity in those forms of human motivation that underpin forbearance; the latter imagines a world in which there is no material scarcity. Both are equally logically possible, but neither throws much light on the nature of rights. Indeed, one would be inclined to say that in a community of saints, as in a world without material scarcity, rights would be irrelevant. What would be the point of insisting upon rights in such a world? Thus, rights have a place in a world where there is scarcity both of motivation and resources; moreover, if a theory of rights is of any point and purpose in life, it has to be capable of making sense in the world as we know it, marked as that world is by scarcity.

That said, it still remains the case that, as both negative and positive rights are asserted against a background of scarcity of both motivation and material goods, there may have to be procedures for dealing with priorities to claims to rights. If these are not to be dealt with on a consequentialist/utilitarian basis, which might undermine ideas of rights, then a rights-based theory must be able to produce a decision procedure and a way of prioritizing rights claims that will avoid utilitarian calculation. This is a very difficult theoretical issue, but it is one that affects negative as much as positive rights, if my arguments in the previous paragraph are accepted as cogent. If the rights in question are supposed to be absolute, then one cannot choose one right over another on consequentialist or utilitarian grounds. However, the assumption that these rights are absolute seems unrealistic. If all rights involve costs, there may have to be choices made among them. But if they are thought of as only prima facie rights that can be overridden by consequentialist calculations, then in what sense are they rights at all? Jonathan Glover in *Causing Death and Saving Lives* has argued this point: "A doctrine of absolute rights goes further than this and excludes the possibility of ever justifying killing by its consequences. But the claim that we have only a prima facie right to life does not exclude this possibility" (1977, 83).

So, is there a decision procedure within rights theory that could avoid the collapse of absolute rights into prima facie rights and these into utilitarianism? I certainly cannot construct such a procedure here, but in any event it would have to satisfy two criteria. It would first have to be developed out of a further elaboration of the grounds in virtue of which rights are ascribed in the first place. In terms of the theory offered here, this would be a development of the theory of needs and agency. If these needs can be ascribed in greater detail than I have attempted in this chapter, then they could perhaps be put in order of priority in terms of the urgency of their satisfaction. Thus, for example, the need for survival would come before that of well-being and autonomy. However, there are difficult issues beyond this; but without confronting these, both negative and positive rights run the risk of collapsing into utilitarianism.

The other strategy is to claim that rights can only be overridden by other rights:

> A theory of *prima facie* human rights could be to the effect that only rights, and never other values or consequences, can override rights. Such a *prima facie* rights theory would have no affinities at all with utilitarianism other than having a maximising calculus. However, it would be a calculus about maximising satisfactions of rights and only that. Such a theory could be one in terms of a hierarchy of rights, such that, solely by reference to the rights involved and their place in the hierarchy, we could determine what rights were absolute. (McCloskey, 1984, 132)

Clearly such a hierarchical theory would have to develop its hierarchical structure from reflection upon, for example, the theory of needs on which rights are based, perhaps combining such reflection on needs with a contractual model of justice. In this sense, a theory of rights can only be a *part* of a theory of justice. It is necessary to elaborate the decision procedure for prioritizing rights claims in a way that seeks to avoid a collapse into utilitarianism.

There is a further difference between the nature of the rights in negative and positive rights claims—a difference that is often used by critics of welfare rights to assert that there is a categorical difference between the two sorts of rights. It is argued that the sorts of resources to which positive rights are asserted are vague and indefinite so that it is difficult to specify the corresponding duty with any precision. In the case of negative rights, the duty is clear and precise—it is abstinence from action, interference, killing, and so on. In the case of welfare rights, these rights are asserted to physical well-being, education, and so forth. If there is a corresponding duty to satisfy these rights, based as they are upon an account of the needs of a rational agent, then it is very unclear how extensive this duty is. Any attempt to define the duty with more precision will be arbitrary. For example, if we take the right to life on the negative view, it is the right not to be killed and this duty is plain and categorical; whereas if the right to life is taken to imply a right to the means to life, then it is much less clear how far this duty extends. Do I have a right to all those medical interventions and technologies that will keep me alive? If not, then the cutoff point will be arbitrary, probably based upon utilitarian calculation; it will also be inconsistent with the general theory of rights in question. This point is often made with reference to the idea of needs, which, as I have argued, provides us with the basic criteria in terms of which rights are ascribed.

The argument here is twofold. First of all, there is a claim that needs are insatiable and that they are essentially culturally relative, so that in the light of these two considerations it is impossible for a theory of needs to provide a basis for a clear duty corresponding to the rights claimed on the basis of such supposed needs. These features of needs, which yield such unclear duties, mean that institutions and authorities seeking to satisfy such needs will be forced to act in an arbitrary and discretionary way just because a theory of needs cannot provide us with a watertight account of corresponding duties (Gray, 1984). Such arbitrariness and unpredictability in relation to rights makes a nonsense of the whole idea of rights. Insofar as needs are culturally relative and relative to subcultures within a society, similar problems of corresponding duties will arise. Gray argues this thesis as follows:

> The objectivity of basic needs is equally delusive. Needs can be given no plausible cross cultural content but instead are seen to vary across different moral traditions. . . . One of the chief functions of the contemporary ideology of social justice may be, as Hayek intimates, to generate an illusion of moral agreement whereas there are in fact profound divergencies of values. (Gray, 1983, 182)

This latter point can perhaps be answered first. The argument is that there is some objectivity of basic needs as a ground for rights. This objective content will be generated by arguing not about what are the necessary conditions for pursuing a view of the good as seen within this, that, or the other moral code but, rather, by arguing that there are certain basic needs that will have to be fulfilled if *any* conception of the good is to be pursued. These needs will be both negative and positive; that is, freedoms from intentional coercion and interference are necessary for agency, but so also are certain resources such as physical well-being and education. Now it may well be that what is thought to be appropriate in the way of resources to provide well-being and education may vary from society to society, but nevertheless the right to some standard in these cases provides a benchmark against which to assess the social responsibilities of government. It has to be accepted, however, that the exact content of these responsibilities in terms of the possession of goods and services cannot be settled in advance by reflection on the conceptual structure of the rights involved. However, although this is a concession to the critic, how serious is it? Does it mark a difference between positive rights to resources and negative rights?

If we accept the argument deployed earlier, that in the world as we know it, negative rights cannot just be based upon noncoerced forbearance but will have to involve positive protection by government in the way of police, courts, prisons, and so on, then it becomes very unclear that the concession does mark a difference. The degree of protection that may be required to secure negative rights cannot be excogitated from the nature of the rights in question any more than it can in the case of welfare rights. These are matters for policy and politics; but, nevertheless, a right such as the right to privacy does not lose its force as a benchmark against which to assess governments any more than does a right to welfare. But the extent of the institutional provision to protect a right of privacy is a contingent matter, not a conceptual one, and, furthermore, one that, like medical needs, will change with technological advances. Computers and information technology pose a range of threats to privacy that could not have been foreseen two or three decades ago, and the degree of protection needed to secure such rights will therefore vary with technological advance. Very similar kinds of arguments can be made about the nature of political and legal rights, assuming, as I argued earlier, that such rights do require institutional forms of provision. Such forms will then be a matter of political negotiation and cannot just be "read off" the nature of the rights in question.

This point can be resisted only if we were to take a purist view of negative rights, that they do not in fact require, as I have suggested they do, a positive form of protection by government. This point is argued in the following way by Charles Fried:

> My right to freedom of speech is not a right to be heard, much less a right to have my views broadcast and applauded. If my right implied these things, then certainly it would be equivalent to a positive right, and would run up against the limits of scarcity. . . . But what if others would deprive me of my freedom of speech—a hostile mob for instance? Surely it is the case that in asking for protection against the mob I make an affirmative claim upon the scarce resources of the community. But this objection misses the point too, for the fact that I have a right to freedom of speech against the government does not mean that I have a right that the government protect any exercise of that right. (Fried, 1978, 120–122)

Fried goes on to argue that this type of argument, which he is here criticizing, neglects the distinction between what is done to a person and what is allowed to happen. This point is crucial and, as we shall see, has salience not only for the object of the right in Gewirth's formula but also for forming a coherent idea of against whom a right is asserted.

The point at stake in Fried's argument is that a negative right can be wholly satisfied by forbearance. The right to life is satisfied by my not being killed, the right to privacy by not having my mail tampered with, the right to freedom of speech by not interfering with my exercise. The forbearance in question is a duty that is always capable of being discharged. Thus Trammel argues as follows:

> It is an empirical fact that in most cases it is possible for a person not to inflict serious physical injury on another person. It is also an empirical fact that in no case is it possible to aid everyone who needs help. The positive duty to love one's neighbour or help those in need sets a maximum ethic which would never let us rest except to gather strength to resume the battle. But it is a rare case when we must really exert ourselves to keep away from killing a person. (1980, 168)

To extend rights to resources and aid extends our responsibilities in an irrational way and makes the duties connected with rights difficult to characterize and thus to discharge.

Clearly part of the answer to these claims rests upon what has gone before—namely, that a theory of rights based upon needs is bound to imply that even so-called negative rights are going to imply the commitment of resources; and therefore the sharp distinction made by Fried and Trammel cannot be maintained. However, the more serious criticism of this view is about the definiteness of the duties of negative rights based upon the idea that we have a very clear idea of forbearance and omission and the responsibilities connected with these. Yet, particularly in the case of not killing, this can be doubted, and in doubting this we shall be forced to look briefly at the ethical issues of killing and letting die. The assumption of the argument is that there is a categorical moral distinction between the two, that the former involves the infringement of rights whereas the latter does not, and that responsibility in the former case is clear and unequivocal, and in the latter case vague and extensive. However, there are a number of reasons for coming to doubt the view that there is a simple moral distinction at stake here. The issues are very complex, but there is no clear distinction and the assumption about acts and omissions upon which it rests are not sufficient to account for a difference in the rights at stake in each case. If killing and allowing to die are, in certain circumstances, morally equivalent, then these acts and omissions cannot be correlated with rights in terms of forbearance and the provision of resources, because the failure to provide resources for life could then be regarded as morally equivalent to killing and thus an infringement of the right to life.

A more general way of putting the point is this: If the fundamental duty implied by a negative right is the duty not to harm, then this may well imply positive duties because the failure to act (to forbear) can itself produce harm and, indeed, a degree of harm that is morally equivalent to the intentional infliction of harm. Certainly John Stuart Mill held this view when he argued in the *Essay on Liberty* that "a person may cause evil to others not only by his actions but by his inaction and that in either case he is justly accountable to them for the injury" (1910, 74). If this argument is accepted, then it is difficult to maintain the idea that infringing a right is always an intentional action and that the right can always be respected by the appropriate form of forbearance.

One way in which critics of positive rights attack this idea is by arguing that harm can be caused only by omission, if there is an antecedent duty toward the person or if the omission is performed by an agent who has some special responsibility toward the individual in question. Consider, for example, a contractual relationship between **X** and **Y** such that if **X** omits an action, she or he may say that **Y** has been harmed. Thus if a doctor has assumed responsibility for the care of a patient and then fails to fulfill that obligation, we can say that his or her inaction has caused harm. Similarly, if a parent neglects a child, this inaction causes harm because there is an antecedent obligation to aid and care for one's children. In an example used by Gewirth, in *Reason and Morality*, he discusses the case of a signalman whose failure to pull a lever causes the train to crash and thus harms those involved (1978, 222). However, although it may be true in these cases that inaction causes harm and so violates the rights of the people concerned, this is only because there is an antecedent duty based upon contract (in the case of the doctor), a conventionally accepted set of expectations (in the case of the parent), or a rule book (in the case of the signalman). In these cases the individual who fails to act stands in a special relationship of duty with the person harmed, and it is in this case that we can say that the inaction or the forbearance causes harm. Unless there is an antecedent basis for a duty that creates a corresponding right to benefit from the performance of such a duty, there can be no basis for accepting the rights in question.

This argument turns upon two considerations. The first is whether omissions can cause harm only if there is a specific contractual or quasi-contractual relationship between individuals; the second is whether the theorist of positive rights has a cogent argument for saying that there is an antecedent duty to meet the needs of people more generally. If so, which people and how generally?

The first question raises a deep problem not only in political theory but also in the philosophy of science because the issue is about negative causal responsibility—namely, that a failure to act causes harm. This way of putting the point should alert us to the potential weakness in the critic's position. If **X**, in failing to act, is negatively causally responsible for the harm that befalls **Y**, then presumably, as with all cases of causation, this will depend upon the state of the world. Yet how can **X**'s *moral* relationship with **Y**, which for the critic is crucial, make a difference to the sequence of causation? The critic is prepared to say that in certain circumstances in which **X** and **Y** stand in a moral relationship, **X**'s inaction may cause harm to **Y**; however, assuming that **X** does not stand in such a moral relationship to **Z**, the same failure to act does not cause harm. If this is so, then we have to be prepared to argue that a conventional relationship, of the sort that a contractual relationship is, may make a categorical difference to whether **X** causes harm to **Y**.

Take the following example. In the first instance the parent, at no possible personal risk, fails to rescue his or her child from drowning in shallow water. In this case, we would have to say that the failure to act caused harm and that the parent infringed the rights of the child because, given the moral relationship in question, the child had a right to expect protection in both the positive and the negative sense from its parent. In the second case, imagine that a total stranger failed to save a child in similar circumstances knowing that he or she is the only person in a position to save the child. This failure to save the child would not be said to have caused it harm because there is no antecedent relationship between the child and the potential rescuer. Saving the child would be a meritorious act, but failing to save the child would not mean that one is responsible for the harm that befalls it. In each case the child ends up dead as the result of two forms of inaction. But what is not clear, and what is vital to the critic's case, is how the issue of the moral relationship or the lack of it between the parties concerned makes any difference to the causal circumstances. These are obviously very large issues, but I doubt whether a theory of antecedent moral obligation can enable us to draw the distinctions required in the categorical way assumed by distinction between negative and positive rights in the way the critic takes to be central. If, as Jan Narveson argues (criticizing Gewirth), the signalman's "inaction is a cause because there is an antecedent basis for the positive duty" (1973, 99), *we need to have a theory about how obligations can make a difference to causation.*

The second crucial question is whether the positive rights theorist can in fact provide a basis for the obligation to aid. The negative rights theorist will argue that we have a positive duty to aid only when we stand in a specific moral, contractual, or professional relationship with another individual and that we cannot generalize from these to other cases. So if the positive rights argument is to go through, we need antecedent grounds for the obligation to aid others even when we do not stand in such a self-assumed relationship with them. Part of the argument to be deployed by the positive rights theorist here will be in terms of needs and the resource preconditions of rational agency. However, the critic of positive rights can still argue that this argument is insufficient. We still need arguments on which my supposed obligation to meet needs of others as a right can be based. It may be true that rational agency requires these needs to be satisfied, but that does not of itself yield a right to the resources of others. Why should I pay attention to the needs of others even though I recognize them? What moral force, if any, do needs have, and how do they relate to the claim that they can serve as the basis of rights?

This argument is central, but complex. I have tried to deal with it elsewhere (Plant et al., 1981) in relation to Kant's views on the subject, but let me make an attempt of my own in this context. Any rights-based theory, whether positive or negative, is going to have at its center some basic idea of human dignity and worth, and this idea has to be defended by argument before it can provide a secure basis for a philosophical theory of rights. The most obvious defense of it is to be found in the Kantian idea of moral capacity noted earlier—the capacity to form a view of the good and to follow it. If moral capacity is the basis of human respect and the dignity of persons, then we have to ask what such respect requires from us. On Nozick's view it requires negative rights because anything more would itself interfere with the autonomy of persons. But I have defended the view that morally illegitimate harm can be caused by inaction as well as by interference, and that argument alone should weaken Nozick's case. However, there are additional points to make. The first is that respect for persons requires us to respect not their particular view of the good but, rather, the capacity of a person to pursue such a good—namely, the capacity for agency. As I have already argued, this capacity requires resources as well as forebearance. We cannot both respect a person's moral capacity and be indifferent to whether he or she has the means on which the realization of that capacity depends. This means that respect requires that the person be provided not with the specific means to meet specific goals but, rather, with the basic goods of agency that are required for the pursuit of any good at all.

We have to turn now to the final aspect of Gewirth's formula—namely, the person, persons, or institutions against whom or which the right is claimed. On the face of it, if human rights are generally universal, then they should be held equally as claims against every other person. In the case of the negative interpretation of rights, it is argued, sense can be made of this requirement. The reasoning here is parallel to the cases discussed earlier—that forbearance and abstaining from action is sufficient to satisfy negative rights. So, insofar as I am not actively killing, assaulting, and interfering with the rights of others, I am respecting their rights. If we take the case of an individual who is destitute, insofar as I did not intentionally cause her or his poverty I can respect her or his right merely by abstaining from action, and this is as true for a destitute member of my own society as it is for any other society. Hence, the idea of each having a duty to respect the rights of all other right holders individually is capable of fulfillment on this basis. However, it is not at all clear against whom social and economic rights are claimed. It would seem clear that although I have a strict duty to respect the negative rights of all other individuals simultaneously, and given the nature of those rights, this can be done in a costless way; nevertheless, no single person can have a duty to fulfill the economic and social rights of other persons. As Narveson says: "One could work twenty-four hours a day at the relief of suffering and could impoverish oneself contributing to charity, but it is felt that to require one to do this would be going rather too far" (1973, 235).

Although I have a general moral duty not to harm and interfere with the lives of others, and although others have a right to claim such forbearance from me, I cannot have a general and strict moral obligation to provide resources to relieve the suffering of all who suffer, and they in turn have no right to my resources for such relief.

If this is so, then it would seem that welfare could not be a right just because the right could not be claimed against any particular person; no particular individual could be blamed for the nonfulfillment of the right, and no specific individual would be responsible for any claim to compensation falling due as the result of the failure to implement that right. It would seem that, again, it would be best to see welfare as a matter of humanity, generosity, altruism, and therefore an imperfect duty, to which there would be no corresponding right.

It might be thought that the answer to this argument would be that the right to welfare is a right to be claimed not against individuals but, rather, against society as a whole, or more specifically the government, and this is in part the answer that Narveson gives in his interesting utilitarian discussion of this question. However, this still does not go quite as far as the welfare right theorist wants to go. As Narveson himself says (1973, 275), this move would still make the right in question an imperfect one. If we go back to Mill's distinction—that an imperfect duty is one that is directed against no particular person—the case we are now considering is closely parallel (1910, 305). The right to welfare would become a right against no one in particular and thus, by parity of reasoning, would be an imperfect right. In the same way as no specific right corresponds to an imperfect duty, so an imperfect right could not imply a specific duty on the part of anyone. To be forced into this position would be just about the same as having to recognize that there is no right to welfare.

However, it is possible, following the lead of Narveson, to take matters further than this. Consider what Narveson says:

> But a duty has to be someone's duty. It can't just be no one's in particular. Consequently the thing to do is to make it everyone's duty to do something, even if that "something" is a matter of seeing that someone else does it. Those who are put on the business end, such as the police, medical people, firemen, etc., should, of course, be compensated for going to the trouble of performing these activities. The simplest solution is simply to make these professions supportable by the public. (1973, 235–236)

If this is accepted, and I think that there are good reasons for accepting it, then the strict or perfect duty of individuals would be not the personal provision of resources to deprived individuals but, rather, the support of institutions, welfare agencies, social workers, and so on, that attempt to meet social needs. As a strict duty such support could then be required by government through taxation to support the meeting of social needs. In this way we could still see the welfare state in terms of rights and duties rather than in terms of institutionalized altruism. To see the human right to welfare as implying a duty to support government welfare measures would be equivalent to seeing due process of law as a human right. A specific individual has the duty not to provide such due process but, rather, to see that the procedures of due process are in fact carried out. The perfect duties corresponding to the rights of welfare are not, then, the personal provision of resources and services to individuals but the duty to support governments and institutions that are organized to meet such needs. Hence my argument has been that if there are rights at all, then there are positive as well as negative rights, and that a positive theory of rights can be developed in such a way as to satisfy the cogent demands of Alan Gewirth's formula. Clearly the moral basis on which rights of any sort are grounded needs further elaboration. Nevertheless, it is a consequence of the argument deployed in this chapter that the case for negative and positive rights stands or falls together.

REFERENCES

Fried, Charles (1978). *Right and Wrong.* Cambridge, Mass.: Harvard University Press.

Gewirth, Alan (1978). *Reason and Morality.* Chicago: University of Chicago Press.

——— (1982). *Human Rights.* Chicago: University of Chicago Press.

Glover, Jonathan (1977). *Causing Death and Saving Lives.* Harmondsworth, England: Penguin.

Gray, John (1983). "Classical Liberalism, Positional Goods and the Politicization of Poverty." In Adrian Ellis and Krishan Kumar, eds., *Dilemmas of Liberal Democracies.* London: Tavistock.

——— (1984). *Hayek on Liberty.* Oxford: Basil Blackwell.

Hayek, Friedrich A. (1960). *The Constitution of Liberty.* London: Routledge and Kegan Paul.

Joseph, Keith, and J. Sumption (1979). *Equality.* London: J. Murray.

Kant, Immanuel (1974). *Groundwork to the Metaphysics of Morals.* H.J. Paton, trans. London: Hutchinson.

McCloskey, H.J. (1984). "Respect for Moral Rights Versus Maximising Good." In R. Frey, ed., *Utility and Rights.* Oxford: Basil Blackwell.

Mill, John Stuart (1910). *Essays on Liberty.* London: J.M. Dent.

Narveson, J. (1973). *Morality and Utility.* Baltimore: Johns Hopkins University Press.

Nozick, Robert (1974). *Anarchy, State, and Utopia.* Oxford: Basil Blackwell.

Plant, Raymond, H. Lesser, and P. Taylor-Gooby (1981). *Political Philosophy and Social Welfare.* London: Routledge and Kegan Paul.

Trammel, R. (1980). "Saving Life and Taking Life." In B. Steinbeck, ed., *Killing and Letting Die.* New York: Prentice-Hall.

THE RIGHT TO AN ADEQUATE STANDARD OF LIVING: JUSTICE, AUTONOMY, AND THE BASIC NEEDS*

By David Copp

Article 25 of the Universal Declaration of Human Rights reads as follows: "Everyone has the right to a standard of living adequate for the health and well-being of himself and of his family, including food, clothing, housing and medical care and necessary social services."[1] I shall refer to the right postulated here as "the right to an adequate standard of living" or "The Right."

My goal in this essay is to stimulate interest in the idea that there is such a right, an idea that I find quite plausible. I shall argue that The Right is best viewed as a conditional right against the state, a right to be enabled to meet one's basic needs, provided that one's society is in favorable circumstances. Since a just state would satisfy the rights that people have against it, I claim that satisfying The Right is a requirement of social justice. Of course, there are other considerations of morality and justice than this right alone, and significant economic questions would have to be resolved in order to decide how best to implement The Right. Also, The Right is conditional and qualified in ways that mean, for example, that a society could succeed in meeting it without thereby successfully eliminating all remnants of poverty. Nevertheless, in order for everyone to be enabled to meet his basic needs, I believe there would have to be a massive redirection of economic resources, even in many of the most wealthy societies.

The thesis that there is a right to an adequate standard of living appears to be a minority view in contemporary political philosophy. Libertarians would claim, of course, that there is no such right; they recognize only

* This paper was presented to the Social Philosophy and Policy Center conference "Economic Rights" in San Diego, California, October 11-14, 1990. I would like to thank all the participants for their helpful comments. I also received very useful comments and suggestions from Carl Cranor, David Dolinko, John Fischer, Jean Hampton, Craig Ihara, Steve Munzer, Mark Ravizza, and the editors of this volume, and I want to express my appreciation to all of them.

[1] I assume that those who drafted the Declaration were following the rule according to which the pronoun "he" and its cognates are read as gender-neutral when the context permits. I follow the same rule in the present paper to conform to this volume's style guidelines. The Universal Declaration was adopted on December 10, 1948, by the General Assembly of the United Nations. It is reprinted, for example, in A. I. Melden, *Human Rights* (Belmont: Wadsworth, 1970), pp. 143-49.

minimal entitlements, such as rights to noninterference. And they would object that, in certain circumstances, The Right would license redistributive schemes under which a state would transfer resources from better-off to worse-off members of society, to enable the latter to meet their basic needs.[2] Egalitarians and liberals would presumably agree that redistributive schemes can sometimes be justified, but familiar liberal and egalitarian principles do not imply a right to an adequate standard of living. For example, according to Rawls's difference principle, justice requires the distribution of "primary goods" in society, such as income and wealth, to work to the advantage of the worst-off "sector" or "representative person." Yet, unlike The Right, the difference principle would not entitle specific disadvantaged individuals in wealthy societies to complain of injustice on the basis that they have not been enabled to meet their basic needs.[3] The claim that there is The Right implies that considerations of justice can sometimes entitle an individual to complain about his standard of living in a way that would not be the case if justice required merely that a given pattern be maintained in the distribution of goods among social classes or groups.[4]

I shall attempt to provide a careful formulation of The Right and to connect it to central ideas in moral and political philosophy. I shall begin by examining the concept of a right, in order to explain what is at stake in speaking of a right to an adequate standard of living. I shall explain why The Right is best regarded as a right against the state. I shall then attempt to explain the notion of an "adequate standard of living," by invoking the idea of basic human needs. I will explain basic needs as, roughly, requirements of rational autonomy. Finally, I will suggest various strategies that might be attempted in order to ground The Right. Of course, there are limits to what I can do in this paper: I cannot attempt to answer all the likely objections, nor to provide a fully developed theory to support the claim that there is The Right, nor to explain fully how I would assess the relative importance of The Right in a developed moral and political theory.

Nor shall I pay attention to the problem of how best to implement The Right. I take it that if The Right exists, then the state ought to provide economic and social institutions that enable each person to achieve an adequate standard of living. But we would have to resolve some difficult

[2] Robert Nozick expresses a libertarian view in his *Anarchy, State, and Utopia* (New York: Basic Books, 1974).

[3] John Rawls, *A Theory of Justice* (Cambridge: Harvard University Press, 1971), pp. 7, 64–65.

[4] A Rawlsian might propose that if there is a group of people who do not enjoy an adequate standard of living, such a group should be regarded as the worst-off group in society for purposes of applying the difference principle. But the principle still would not license the members of this group to complain that they personally were being treated unjustly. They could complain, at best, like anyone else, of injustice in the basic structure of the society.

empirical issues in order to support more specific claims about its implementation. Some would argue that an unregulated market economy would be best. In the real world, though, I believe a market economy would have to be regulated and supplemented for a variety of reasons, including the need for a safety net—comprising such things as a guaranteed minimum income, a universal health care insurance scheme, and an unemployment and disability insurance scheme—to ensure that those with special needs are cared for. Yet regulations and supplementary programs would have to be designed carefully to minimize negative effects on incentives and self-respect. Given the need for self-respect, and given that dependency tends to undermine self-respect, it would certainly be advisable in implementing The Right to create an institutional environment in which as many people as possible are enabled to meet their needs through gainful and worthwhile work.[5] I shall not have much more to say about implementing The Right.

I. Autonomy-Protecting and Welfare-Enhancing Rights

In this section, I will explain what I take to be the difference between the claim that there is a *right* against the state to be enabled to enjoy an adequate standard of living and the claim that the state has a corresponding duty (or that an ideal state would have a corresponding goal). I will attempt to explain why I hold that there is such a right, but nothing in my argument turns on my use of the term 'right'. The claim I wish to defend can be expressed as a thesis to the effect that the state has a duty, although it is a duty with a special status. I will postpone until the next section the question of why it is plausible to think that The Right is held against the state rather than against individual people.

I think that the right to an adequate standard of living would entail an obligation of the state, but not vice versa. Hence, if there is a right against the state to an adequate standard of living, then a state has the duty—and an ideal state would have the goal—to ensure that its members are enabled to enjoy an adequate standard of living. (At least, as I will explain, a state would have this duty and goal if it were in favorable circumstances.) But the converse claims do not hold. Many goals of an ideal state would not be mandated by an obligation; those goals would lack the special urgency of the goal of respecting individual rights. And a right against the state is not simply a duty owed by the state, for it has a special status.

The special status of rights has been thought to have three aspects. First, rights have priority over the ordinary goals and duties of the state

[5] Self-respect is in this way an important "mediating concept" in Gregory Kavka's argument that the handicapped have a right to work. See his "Disability and the Right to Work" in this volume.

and over the goal of promoting the general welfare. Rights can only be overridden in the interest of a goal or duty of special urgency.[6] Second, rights can be claimed as their due by the people who possess them. Right-holders are wronged if their rights are abridged.[7] Third, a person who claims something to which he has a right does not thereby demean himself or undermine his grounds for self-respect or self-esteem. On the contrary, a person with proper self-respect and self-esteem would claim the things to which he had a right, unless he had a good reason not to do so.[8]

I believe the idea that rights have this threefold special status makes it more plausible to claim that there is The Right than to claim merely that states (in favorable circumstances) have the duty that is entailed by The Right. People have to meet their basic needs in order to be successful in most of their endeavors. I will argue that people must have the ability to meet their basic needs in order to be fully autonomous. These are reasons to think that a state ought to give high priority to enabling people to meet their basic needs. Many people, including people with special needs, require help at certain times in their lives. Because of this, it is important to view the grounds of self-respect and self-esteem as secure against the need to seek help. Now, if citizens have The Right, then (in favorable circumstances) a citizen has been wronged if he has not been enabled to enjoy an adequate standard of living, and he is entitled to demand assistance in meeting his needs without this in any way undermining the grounds of his self-respect. Of course, people may sometimes feel that their self-respect is undermined if they need to ask the state for help. Nevertheless, the idea that there is The Right implies that people are *entitled* to ask for help and that asking for help is no *reason* to feel less worthy. For these reasons, it seems more plausible to hold there is The Right than to hold that a state (in favorable circumstances) merely has the duty—which is entailed by The Right—to enable people to meet their basic needs.

Some would argue to the contrary, however, that even if the state ought to enable people to meet their needs, the state does not have a duty

[6] See Ronald Dworkin, *Taking Rights Seriously* (Cambridge: Harvard University Press, 1977), pp. xi, 91-92, 188-92. See also Richard Wasserstrom, "Rights, Human Rights, and Racial Discrimination," ed. David Lyons, *Rights* (Belmont: Wadsworth Publishing Company, 1977), pp. 46-57.

[7] See David Lyons's introduction to ed. Lyons, *Rights*, pp. 1-4. Joel Feinberg uses the idea of a claim in explaining the idea of a right in his "The Nature and Value of Rights," ed. Lyons, *Rights*, pp. 78-91, at pp. 84-85. Wasserstrom speaks of rights as entitlements in his "Rights, Human Rights, and Racial Discrimination," p. 48.

[8] Feinberg relates respect for rights to respect for persons in his "The Nature and Value of Rights," p. 87. See also Thomas E. Hill, Jr., "Servility and Self-Respect," *Rights*, pp. 111-24. Steve Munzer suggested the importance of self-esteem. See also David Sachs, "How to Distinguish Self-Respect from Self-Esteem," *Philosophy and Public Affairs*, vol. 10 (1981), pp. 346-60.

to do so, or does not have a duty with this special status. The arguments I have in mind depend on a loose distinction between putative rights against the state that are or would be "autonomy-protecting," in that observing them would consist in protecting citizens against interferences with their autonomy, and putative rights against the state that are or would be "welfare-promoting," in that observing them would consist in promoting the good of citizens in other respects. The arguments are intended to show that there are no welfare-promoting rights. The Universal Declaration postulated both kinds of right. It proposed civil and political rights that protect basic liberties, due process of law, and so on, such as the right not to be subjected to torture (article 5), the right to "equal protection before the law" (article 7), and the right not to be subjected to arbitrary arrest or detention (article 9). Rights such as these would typically be classified as autonomy-protecting. The Declaration also postulated economic, social, and cultural rights, concerning such things as basic needs, health care, and the like, which would typically be classified as welfare-promoting. Examples are the right to a minimum level of education (article 26) and the right to an adequate standard of living (article 25).

Why might it seem that "welfare-promoting" duties, unlike "autonomy-protecting" duties, would lack the special status of rights? L. W. Sumner thinks we would be reluctant to claim that failures to ensure the enjoyment of putative welfare rights "would necessarily constitute an injustice," and he points out that governments in all but the wealthiest nations often have excuses for failures in this area. He says that "rights in this second category may lack the conceptual connections with the notions of obligation and justice" which are characteristic of rights in the narrow sense. "Rights in the narrow sense formulate urgent or insistent demands precisely because they constrain the pursuit of social goals." But, he concludes, the so-called economic, social, and cultural rights are best understood as "ideals or objectives for societies" rather than as requirements of justice in the treatment of individuals. The use of the language of rights to formulate social goals of this sort marks a kind of "conceptual drift."[9]

There appear to be three objections here. Welfare-promoting rights demand nontrivial resources for their fulfillment, and sufficient resources are not always available. Hence, first, a state that fails to give some of its citizens the opportunity to enjoy an adequate standard of living has not by that very fact failed to meet a requirement of justice. Second, it may not even have done anything wrong. Sumner appears to think that only the autonomy-protecting rights can plausibly be thought to have the urgency that is distinctive of rights, for only they can be respected regardless of material circumstances. Third, although an ideal state might have

[9] L. W. Sumner, *The Moral Foundation of Rights* (Oxford: Oxford University Press, 1987), pp. 16–17.

the goal of giving everyone the opportunity to enjoy an adequate standard of living, rights are not merely goals: they are constraints on the pursuit of social goals. Sumner says that to preserve the special urgency of rights, "we must construct a concept of a right" which conforms to "the root idea that the function of rights is to serve as one kind of constraint on the pursuit of social goals."[10]

The last objection can be laid aside, for there is no special difficulty in viewing welfare-promoting rights as setting constraints on the pursuit of social goals. The distinction between a social goal and a constraint on social goals is not sharp. Rights define required social goals, even though such goals have a priority that makes it sensible to speak of them as setting required constraints on the pursuit of more ordinary goals. For example, if there is a right not to be subjected to arbitrary arrest, then an ideal society would aim to ensure an absence of arbitrary arrests. But the priority of achieving this goal would "constrain" the pursuit of other social goals. Similarly, if there is a right to an adequate standard of living, then an ideal society would aim to ensure that its citizens are enabled to enjoy an adequate standard of living. But the priority of this goal would constrain the pursuit of other social goals. Both the "welfare-promoting" right to an adequate standard of living, and the "autonomy-protecting" right to be free from arbitrary arrest, could in this way be described as defining both a required goal and a required constraint on the pursuit of other social goals.

The first and second objections can be treated together. An adequate standard of living cannot be provided to everyone in all circumstances. In a poor society, people may not have been wronged even if they have not had the opportunity to enjoy an adequate standard of living. Yet this does not show that there is no such thing as The Right. What it shows is that if The Right exists, it is conditional on favorable circumstances. It is the right of every person to an adequate standard of living *if* his society is wealthy enough to provide an adequate living standard to every member.

This right is not unique in being conditional on favorable circumstances. In fact, all of the rights in the Universal Declaration, whether "welfare-promoting" or "autonomy-protecting," are best understood to be conditional on circumstances. They would have few implications, for example, in pre-state societies, such as aboriginal hunting and gathering societies. Many of the rights presuppose the existence of a legal system. This is obviously true of the civil liberties, such as the right to a fair trial (article 11), but it is also true of the right to own property (article 17). The Declaration glosses "the right to freedom of opinion and expression" as

[10] *Ibid.*, p. 47. Robert Nozick distinguished between goals and side constraints and argued that rights should be taken as constraints. But he allowed that rights could be treated as goals in a kind of "utilitarianism of rights." He thought it would be a moral mistake to view rights this way, not a conceptual mistake. See his *Anarchy, State, and Utopia*, pp. 28–33.

including the right "to seek, receive and impart information and ideas through any media" (article 19), which would be of little import outside a relatively advanced economy. And the right to education is intended as the right to a formal education, including the general availability of "technical and professional" education (article 26), which obviously could not be fully implemented in a primitive or a poverty-stricken society.

The rights listed in the Declaration are conditional on circumstances. Moreover, very few of them could be implemented without state action involving the expenditure of resources. The civil liberties could not be implemented without the creation of effective judicial and policing agencies. A legal system does not recognize the right to own property unless it includes a fabric of enabling legislation and protective criminal legislation. Even the right not to be subject to arbitrary arrest or detention (article 9), which may seem the paradigm of an autonomy-protecting right, cannot be implemented in a modern society unless there is a set of legal restrictions on arrest and a set of institutions capable of enforcing the restrictions. Hence, although the right to an adequate standard of living could not be implemented without state action in a relatively prosperous society, it is not unique in these respects.[11]

An additional argument against the idea that there are welfare-promoting rights depends on the so-called "choice theory" of rights.[12] The choice theory offers an explanation of the idea that rights correspond to duties that are *owed to* the right-holder. For example, if someone has a right not to be interfered with in certain ways, then some other agents have duties not to interfere with him in the prohibited ways, and they owe these duties *to him*. According to the "choice theory," this means that he has *control* over the relevant duties of these other agents. He has the power to waive the duty, for example, or to demand its performance.[13] In this way, rights are essentially connected to the autonomy of agents.

[11] There are many other examples from among the rights affirmed in the Universal Declaration. The following presuppose at least the existence of a functioning legal system and the commitment of resources sufficient for their enforcement or implementation: the right not to be subjected to torture (article 5); the right to "equal protection before the law" (article 7); "the right to freedom of movement and residence" (article 13); "the right to a nationality" (article 15); "the right to marry and to found a family" (article 16); "the right to freedom of thought, conscience and religion" (article 18); the right "not to be held in slavery or servitude" (article 4). And consider the "right to be presumed innocent until proved guilty according to law in a public trial at which [one] has had all the guarantees necessary for [one's] defence" (article 11). This is largely a procedural due-process right, but it entails that accused persons have a right to certain affirmative guarantees, including presumably the right to counsel, which would be a right to share in a scarce resource. Similarly, "the right to the protection of the law" against interference with "privacy, family, home or correspondence" (article 12) is a right not to be interfered with combined with a right to affirmative protection on the part of the state. Consider finally "the right to take part in the government of [one's] country, directly or through freely chosen representatives" (article 21).

[12] The argument is sketched by Jeremy Waldron in his introduction to ed. Waldron, *Theories of Rights* (Oxford: Oxford University Press, 1984), p. 11.

[13] See *ibid.*, p. 9; Sumner, *The Moral Foundation of Rights*, pp. 42–46; H. L. A. Hart, *Essays on Bentham* (Oxford: Oxford University Press, 1982), ch. 7.

And, it may therefore seem, rights function to protect our freedom to choose. Sumner suggests that the choice theory about the "owing-to" relation may generalize to the view that rights are "protected choices": in virtue of having a right, a person has "the freedom to choose among a set of options," where his freedom is "protected by a set of duties imposed on others."[14] Unfortunately, while this conception fits autonomy-protecting rights such as the right to free speech, it would appear to rule out welfare-promoting rights such as the right to an adequate standard of living. For this right demands that people have access to resources, not simply that they be provided with an area of free choice.

Yet the argument is invalid. The choice theory is an account of the owing-to relation. It does not entail the view that all rights are autonomy-protecting rights; it simply entails that whatever a given right protects or ensures, the right-bearer has the power to demand or to waive its performance. It would therefore be possible to combine the choice theory with the view that there are welfare-promoting rights.

In any event, the choice theory is not plausible if it is taken to imply that all rights can be waived. For there are many rights that it is plausible to say cannot be waived, such as the right not to be tortured and the right not to be assaulted.[15] It is a controversial moral issue, moreover, whether it is possible to waive the right not to be enslaved. It therefore is not a conceptual truth that all rights can be waived, and the choice theory is implausible if it is taken to imply that this is a conceptual truth. Perhaps the right to an adequate standard of living cannot be waived. But if it cannot be, it is not unique in this respect.

Moreover, many so-called welfare-promoting rights promote the autonomy of agents. For example, the right to free education would presumably be justified on the basis that its effective implementation would secure for every person the opportunity to acquire the minimum knowledge and psychological and social skills required to live a self-determining life. And, as I shall argue, the right to an adequate standard of living would be justified on the basis that its effective recognition would give every citizen the opportunity to be free from the requirement to satisfy his basic needs, and it would thereby enhance his freedom to choose the kind of life he would prefer.[16]

In summary, I assume that the thesis that there is The Right is roughly equivalent to the claim that states (in favorable conditions) have a duty to enable every citizen to meet his basic needs, and that this duty has the threefold special status discussed before.

[14] Sumner, *The Moral Foundation of Rights*, p. 46.

[15] As Hart realized, for example, in proposing the account. See his *Essays on Bentham*, ch. 7. See also Waldron in *Theories of Rights*, p. 9, n. 21.

[16] I discuss the reason-giving force of needs in my "Reason and Needs," a paper I presented to the Bowling Green State University Conference "Value, Welfare, and Morality"

II. Rights against the State

The idea of a right against the state raises metaphysical as well as normative issues that go well beyond the scope of this paper. I have addressed some of these issues in other places, but here I shall restrict myself to normative problems that are specific to the alleged right to an adequate standard of living. I shall leave aside such larger issues as the following. What is a state? What distinguishes a state from a society? Is it possible for a collective entity, such as a state, to have an obligation?[17] If I am correct, the right to an adequate standard of living, and most of the rights listed in the Universal Declaration, are much more plausible if viewed as rights against the state than if viewed as rights against specific individuals.

In order to explain this, let me introduce yet another objection to the idea of welfare-promoting rights—an objection Rodney Peffer has called "the problem of near-innumerable positive obligations."[18] If rights (of the kind at issue in this discussion) entail correlative obligations of the sort standardly assumed, and if there is The Right, then a person with The Right holds it against some other agent or agents who *ipso facto* have a corresponding obligation which they owe to him. Since it seems there is no one in particular against whom The Right would be held to the exclusion of other people, The Right would have to be held against every other person. Every other person would have an obligation to ensure that a person with The Right is enabled to enjoy an adequate standard of living. Hence, if everyone has The Right, then everyone has an obligation to enable every other person to enjoy an adequate standard of living. This may seem quite implausible.

One response to this objection, of course, would be simply to accept the consequences that everyone has a duty toward every other person to enable him to enjoy an adequate standard of living. Perhaps The Right is a conditional right which obligates each of us to provide assistance to others, but only to the extent that we are able. It is indeed common to recognize a charitable duty to provide assistance, but it is common to hold that charity is not owed to anyone as a matter of right. This first response

---

on April 20-22, 1990. The present essay presents some modifications in my ideas about needs.

[17] I have addressed some of these issues in the following papers: "Collective Actions and Secondary Actions," *American Philosophical Quarterly*, vol. 16, no. 3 (July 1979), pp. 177–86; "Hobbes on Artificial Persons and Collective Actions," *The Philosophical Review*, vol. 89, no. 4 (October 1980), pp. 579–606; "Do Nations Have the Right of Self-Determination?", ed. Stanley G. French, *Philosophers Look at Canadian Confederation* (Montreal: Canadian Philosophical Association, 1979), pp. 71–95; "What Collectives Are: Agency, Individualism and Legal Theory," *Dialogue*, vol. 23, no. 2 (June 1984), pp. 249–69; "The Concept of Society," *Dialogue*, forthcoming.

[18] See Rodney Peffer, "A Defense of Rights to Well-Being," *Philosophy and Public Affairs*, vol. 8 (1978), pp. 65–87, at p. 71.

seems therefore to depart from common sense, for it requires treating duties that would commonly be regarded as duties of charity as though they have the stringency and status of duties that correspond to and derive from the rights of others. A second response to the objection, which is favored by Peffer, would be to deny the correlativity of rights and duties.[19] But while I would not want to defend the doctrine of correlativity in its full generality, I do think that the right to an adequate standard of living, and similar rights that can ground legitimate claims, are best thought to correspond to obligations. I believe that possession of The Right entitles a person to demand to be enabled to meet his basic needs, at least when his society is in favorable circumstances, as I shall explain. He is entitled to make this demand in the sense that his right corresponds to an obligation that the state has toward him.

The most natural reply to the problem of innumerable obligations is to hold that the right to an adequate standard of living and similar rights are rights against the state. Why do I think this is the natural response? First, it allows us to maintain that The Right implies a duty on the part of some other agent, but it does not require us to maintain that this duty is, like charity, incumbent on everyone indifferently. Second, the state and its agent, the government, are the only agencies with the ability to address the large-scale economic and social issues that would typically have to be dealt with in order to satisfy The Right in situations where some people have not been enabled to enjoy an adequate standard of living. Third, there are many rights that seem best construed as rights against the state, including many that are listed in the Universal Declaration. Examples include the civil liberties and the right to an education. For although the idea that there is a right to an education might be invoked to explain the view that parents have a duty to provide their children with an education, no person other than a parent or someone who has similar special responsibility for a child has the duty to provide that child with an education. And a person who believes in the right to an education will typically believe that the state has a duty to provide education for its citizens, provided it is in a position to do so. The right to an adequate standard of living is similar in this respect to the right to an education. Finally, the intent of the Universal Declaration was surely that the rights listed in it are rights against the state.[20]

[19] *Ibid.*

[20] The Universal Declaration called on "all peoples and all nations" to promote "respect" for the rights listed in the Universal Declaration and, "by teaching and education" and "progressive measures," to secure their "universal and effective recognition and observance." Effective recognition would amount to different things in different cases. For example, no one country would be considered obligated by the proposed right to a nationality to permit unconditional immigration and citizenship to anyone who asked for it (article 15). And no one country could ensure by itself the putative right "to seek, receive and impart information . . . regardless of frontiers" (article 19). But in the other cases, each country would be considered obligated under the Declaration to initiate measures to secure the observance of the rights within its borders in whatever way would be appropriate and effective.

It is beyond the scope of this paper to discuss at any length the respective moral statuses of the society, state, and government. I propose viewing the government as the agent of the state, which is in turn the agent of the society. That is, in effect, the responsibility rests with the society to organize itself by engaging some party as its agent and then charging the agent with the responsibility to discharge its duties—and, in particular, to fulfill the right of its members to an adequate standard of living. A state is at least one kind of entity that can result from the appropriate organization of society, and the government is the agent of the state. It may seem, then, that it would be better to describe The Right as a right of the citizen against his society as a whole. But since a society could not act effectively to satisfy The Right unless it were organized into a state or some similar entity, I prefer saying The Right is held against the state. Government action would be necessary in order to secure effective recognition of The Right, but governments come and go while the responsibility to satisfy the right remains with the state.

It is beyond the scope of this paper to consider global justice. But if there is a global society, then my view implies that that society ought to organize itself so that it is able to meet the right of all people to be enabled to enjoy an adequate standard of living. I do not know what form of global organization would be best, but I have discussed elsewhere the conditions under which it would be appropriate to speak of there being a global society.[21]

III. The Right to an Adequate Standard of Living

I have claimed that The Right is or would be a conditional right against the state. Pending further qualifications, it can be formulated as the right of each citizen to be enabled to enjoy an adequate standard of living, provided that the society is capable of providing an adequate standard for all. This is still quite an abstract formulation, and there are details that need to be explored. I suspect that many of the questions that arise cannot be resolved by arguments from first principles.[22] Nevertheless, in this section I will work toward a more concrete formulation by invoking arguments based in considerations about justice. I will leave the problem of explaining what is meant by the adequacy of a standard of living until the next section, and I will not attempt to provide a deep argument for The Right until the final two sections.

[21] See my "The Concept of Society."

[22] My suspicion should not occasion concern or surprise. We are accustomed to dealing with abstract formulations of rights. We speak, for instance, of the right to freedom of speech, but there is room for a great deal of controversy even among people who agree on an abstract formulation of this right. There are political issues here, as well as jurisprudential and philosophical issues, and it is doubtful that all of them can be resolved by arguments from philosophical first principles.

A. Justice does not require the state to force people to have any given standard of living or quality of life. For example, we require a nutritious diet for our health, but The Right does not imply that the state must ensure that everyone has a nutritious diet. It does imply that the state must ensure the availability of a food supply sufficient to enable everyone to have a nutritious diet. But no injustice can be laid at the door of the state if, in the midst of a plentiful supply, some people opt for an unhealthful diet, assuming they can properly be held responsible for their choice. Again, The Right does not imply that the state must invariably compensate people for losses they incur as a result of their own voluntary choices, assuming again that they can properly be held responsible for their own choices. The foolish and the improvident must be given the opportunity to achieve an adequate standard of living, but if they squander the opportunity, and if they can properly be held responsible for their own choices, they cannot complain that their Right has been violated. Accordingly, I shall say The Right requires the state to *enable* everyone to bring it about that he enjoys an adequate standard of living. I do not, however, know how to specify what "enabling" amounts to in this context in a sufficiently general way to cover all imaginable cases.[23]

Consider the following simplified example. Suppose that a given stock of resources is provided to a person by the state, a stock that is sufficient to enable him to enjoy an adequate standard of living. But suppose that, as an adult, he gambles away these resources while fully aware of what he is risking. And suppose that he is not able to recoup his loss, so that he finds himself living in poverty. He clearly can ask for charity, and morality may give him additional grounds for argument. Perhaps, for example, he can stand on egalitarian considerations and argue that there is injustice in a situation in which he is in poverty while others are living well. If he is a parent, perhaps he could invoke the right of his children to an adequate standard of living, and their need for parenting, in an argument that he ought to be given further help by the state. But he could hardly justifiably complain of being treated unjustly simply on the ground that the situation resulting from his gambling is one in which he cannot achieve an adequate standard of living.

[23] Suppose a society introduces a lottery in which the prize is a fund of resources sufficient to guarantee an adequate standard of living. Only one person in the society can win the prize, but everyone is given a ticket. There is a sense in which everyone is enabled by this system to achieve an adequate standard of living, but not a relevant sense, for it is not possible in this system for every person to enjoy an adequate standard. The losers can all complain of having been treated unjustly (assuming the society is in favorable circumstances). Even the winner can complain of having been treated unjustly, for it is only by chance that he enjoys an adequate standard of living. To have the opportunity in the relevant sense implies being in a position to bring it about that one enjoys an adequate standard of living, and no one under the lottery system has the power to bring this about. A society in favorable circumstances must enable every citizen to achieve an adequate standard of living in the sense that it must both provide each person with the opportunity to enjoy an adequate standard of living and also make it possible that every person enjoys an adequate standard of living (subject to the qualifications mentioned in the text).

There is a need to qualify my formulation of The Right in a way that I will explain here but not mention again. The Right requires that each person be enabled to achieve a standard of living *as nearly* adequate to his basic needs as is possible, given the existing technology and the facts of the case. A person with a terminal illness cannot be enabled to regain his health and well-being, but this obviously does not show that he has been wronged by the state. A paraplegic cannot be enabled to walk, but he can be given a wheelchair which would enable him to move about. This may be sufficient to satisfy his claim under The Right.

B. The right to an adequate standard of living is conditional on favorable circumstances. There are two kinds of cases to be distinguished.

Consider, first, a society in favorable circumstances: a society that is wealthy enough or otherwise well-enough placed that there is a "feasible" and "morally realizable" future state of affairs in which every citizen enjoys an adequate standard of living. It should be clear enough what is meant here, although there are nontrivial complications. The idea is that in favorable circumstances, a state has policy options at its disposal that would actually bring about a situation in which each person would have the opportunity to enjoy an adequate standard of living; each person would have an adequate standard if he used the available opportunities, and if everyone used the available opportunities everyone would have an adequate standard. Further, the state could implement these options without violating any moral constraint of equal or higher priority than The Right. I have not yet discussed the relative moral priority of The Right, and I shall have little enough to say about it. But a society would not be in favorable circumstances for these purposes if, for example, it would have to invade and conquer a weaker neighboring state and deprive that state's citizens of their rights in order to achieve an acceptable standard of living for its own people. Nor would a society be in favorable circumstances if it would have to resort to murderous means of population control in order to reduce the demands on it sufficiently to be in a position to provide its citizens with an adequate standard of living.

In summary, if a society is wealthy enough or otherwise well-enough placed that there is a feasible and morally realizable future state of affairs in which every citizen enjoys an adequate standard of living, then The Right requires the state to bring about or maintain a state of affairs in which every individual is well enough placed to make it the case, if he so chooses, that he enjoys an adequate standard of living. If a citizen has dependents within his family, he must be well enough placed to bring it about that they too enjoy an adequate standard of living.

Now consider a poor society—a society that is *not* in favorable circumstances. A person who belongs to such a society, and who has not been enabled to enjoy an adequate standard of living, could not properly complain of unjust treatment on that basis alone. Yet if there is The Right, then he has the property, whatever it is, that grounds possession of The Right—the property in virtue of which the society *would* have a duty to enable him to enjoy an adequate standard of living *if* it were in favorable circumstances. Everyone has this property. Because of this, The Right presumably should be taken to imply that a poor society has both of the following duties. First, it ought to strive for the capability of providing something as close as possible to an adequate standard of living for all of its members as soon as it can. Second, subject to this longer-term goal, it ought to enable as many as it can to come as close as possible to an adequate standard of living while treating each of its members fairly. Call this second duty the fall-back duty.

It is not entirely clear how best to interpret the fall-back duty.[24] On one interpretation, it is a duty to ensure substantive equality. It implies that a poor state ought to enable each person to come as close as possible to an adequate standard of living, given the constraint that each person is to be enabled to enjoy approximately the same standard of living as everyone else. In circumstances of extreme poverty, however, a requirement of substantive equality could lead to everyone's living a life that no one would view as worth living. On another interpretation, the fall-back duty requires only what could be called procedural equality. It requires a poor state to give each person an equal chance of being enabled to reach an adequate standard of living, and to enable as many as possible to reach an adequate standard, while doing as well as possible for the remaining people given the remaining resources. On this interpretation, The Right would at least give every person a chance of being enabled to live a life worth living. Hence, in very bad circumstances, the procedural interpretation will seem more plausible than the substantive. But in circumstances where substantive equality would give everyone a life he would himself view as worth living, the substantive interpretation may seem more plausible than the procedural, since the latter might leave some people with a life no one would regard as worth living. I will have to set these difficulties to one side, for there are additional possible interpretations of the fall-back duty, and the existence of people with extraordinarily costly needs leads to further complications.

C. There are people with needs that could only be met with a very large investment of resources. Some are dying; even so, though, their lives can be prolonged and made more comfortable, if only at tremendous cost. Some of the severely ill and disabled can have their needs met, but only given a large expenditure of resources. If there are great numbers of needy people in these categories, the costs of meeting their needs can be significant in relation to the other expenditures of government. And with advances in medical technology, the numbers of people in these categories and the costs of treatment will presumably increase.

Would a state be required by The Right to enable the very needy to meet their basic needs even if, in order to do so, it would have to reduce

[24] Jean Hampton and the editor of this volume helped me to see different interpretations of the duty.

to bare adequacy the standard of living of everyone else? If it would *not* be required to do so, then the duties of a state under The Right must be limited by what I shall call a "stop-loss provision." A stop-loss provision would specify that a state is not obligated to exceed a defined relative cost in order to enable any given person to enjoy an adequate standard of living. Hence, a state—even a state in favorable circumstances—might fail to enable some very needy people to enjoy an adequate standard of living without thereby abridging their rights.

The problem, however, is to explain what can justify treating extraordinarily costly needs differently from more ordinary needs. Why should we suppose, for example, that The Right implies that the state has a duty to ensure that routine medical needs are met but not that all medical needs are met that can be met? And where is the line between the routine and the costly? A principled solution to this problem would derive a stop-loss provision directly from the underlying rationale of The Right. But the interest in autonomy and rational agency, which I think grounds The Right, does not lose its urgency when a person comes to have extraordinary needs.

It seems to me that the rationale underlying The Right would permit a state to limit benefits to the very needy in order to protect the ability of the better off to meet their own basic needs, but not otherwise. If institutions could be created and funded that would enable the very needy to meet their needs without compromising the ability of the better off to meet their needs, then The Right would require the state to create the institutions. But in circumstances in which the state could not enable the very needy to meet their needs without putting the ability of other people to meet their needs at risk, the interest of the very needy in being able to meet their needs would be balanced by the interest of the remaining citizens in continuing to be able to meet their needs. In these conditions, it is arguable that the underlying rationale of The Right would permit limiting the expenditure of resources to help the very needy. If so, then the fall-back duty must be understood to prohibit reducing anyone's standard of living to the point that he is not able to meet his basic needs.

Of course, there are other moral considerations that are relevant to the evaluation of social institutions; in some cases, they will come into conflict with The Right or override it. Accordingly, there may be moral considerations which justify abridging The Right of people with extraordinarily costly needs when doing so is necessary to prevent the reduction of everyone else's standard of living to bare adequacy. This means that recognizing The Right does not necessarily commit one to holding that state expenditures to enable people to meet their costly needs cannot be limited until everyone else has had his living standard reduced to mere adequacy. But, considered by itself, The Right would mean this.

The problem of extraordinarily costly needs afflicts many theories of social justice. In order to bring about equality, for example, whether it be equality of welfare, equality in the opportunity for welfare, equality of resources, or equality of meeting needs, it may be necessary to worsen the situation of the better off to the point that they do not enjoy even an adequate standard of living.[25] John Rawls's difference principle implies that social and economic inequalities are justified only if they work to the advantage of the worst-off class in society. This means that inequalities in the "primary goods" of income and wealth, power and authority, and the "social bases of self-respect" are justified only if they improve the position (in respect of these primary goods) of a representative member of the class in society that is worst off (in respect of these same primary goods).[26] But the difference principle only takes into account people's command over primary goods; it does not take into account their standards of living. And greater command over primary goods does not necessarily mean a better standard of living: you may have fifty percent more income than I, but if you must spend ninety percent of your income to buy the drugs you need to stay alive while I am in perfect health, I am able to enjoy the better standard of living. Since the difference principle does not consider standards of living as such, it could mandate reducing the expectations of the better off to the point that some or all of them are no longer able to enjoy an adequate standard of living. And it could mandate improving the situation of the worst off beyond the point at which they are enabled to enjoy merely an adequate standard.[27] On the other hand, the difference principle does not guarantee that the result of the process of transferring primary goods to the disadvantaged will be that they are enabled to enjoy an adequate standard. Given their needs and handicaps, they may remain unable to enjoy an adequate standard of living even if the difference principle is satisfied.[28] It is quite possible, moreover, that a situation in which the people with extraordinarily costly needs *were* enabled to enjoy an adequate standard of living would be in violation of the difference principle. For, even if their standard of living

[25] Richard J. Arneson, "Liberalism, Distributive Subjectivism, and Equal Opportunity for Welfare," *Philosophy and Public Affairs*, vol. 19 (1990), pp. 158–94. Ronald Dworkin, "What is Equality? Part 1: Equality of Welfare" and "What is Equality? Part 2: Equality of Resources," *Philosophy and Public Affairs*, vol. 10 (1981), pp. 185–246 and pp. 283–345. David Braybrooke, *Meeting Needs* (Princeton: Princeton University Press, 1987), pp. 143-50, 293–301.

[26] John Rawls, *A Theory of Justice*. I should mention that Rawls intends to set aside the problem of costly needs as a "difficult complication." He claims only to deal with "the fundamental case" of a society in which "no one suffers from unusual needs" and "all citizens are fully cooperating members . . . over the course of a complete life." It is nevertheless worth pointing out the implications of the difference principle for cases in which there are people with costly needs. See John Rawls, "Kantian Constructivism in Moral Theory: The Dewey Lectures 1980," *The Journal of Philosophy*, vol. 77 (1980), p. 546.

[27] Virginia Held makes essentially the same point in her *Rights and Goods: Justifying Social Action* (New York: The Free Press, 1984), p. 187.

[28] Amartya Sen discusses "variable conversion rates of primary goods into achievements" in his "Justice: Means versus Freedoms," *Philosophy and Public Affairs*, vol. 19 (1990), pp. 118. The issue here is variable conversion rates of primary goods into the satisfaction of needs. On this issue, see also Amartya Sen, *The Standard of Living*, ed. Geoffrey Hawthorn (Cambridge: Cambridge University Press, 1987), p. 18.

remained low, their greater command over primary goods would not necessarily work to the advantage of those in the society with less in the way of primary goods.

The right to an adequate standard of living, as I conceive of it, does at least impose two cut-off points on the process of transferring resources from the better off to the worse off. First, it does not require worsening the situation of the better off to the point that they do not enjoy an adequate standard of living. Second, it does not require any further redistribution once the extraordinarily needy have been provided with the opportunity to enjoy an adequate standard of living. Of course, other moral considerations might require further changes.

A more detailed account would have to say much more about the relative weight of The Right by comparison with other moral considerations. But a theory of rights and of justice would be required before anything very deep could be said. The Right is not a complete account of distributive justice. At the very least, other rights against the state would have to be recognized in a complete theory. And there are, of course, other moral considerations beside justice, including, for example, the consequentialist consideration that redistribution might undermine economic productivity. Rights have an urgency and a special status which includes a priority over the ordinary goals of the state, such as economic efficiency. But this does not mean that competing rights, or a sufficiently important combination of goals, cannot override or limit a right.

D. The Universal Declaration counts The Right as a human right, and it may seem that an adequate defense of it would have to show it to be a human right. On my account, however, The Right is a right against the state, and it is conditional in the sense that the duties it imposes on the state are conditional on the state's circumstances. It would seem to follow that people have The Right only if they are citizens of states and only if they are fortunate enough to live in relatively prosperous societies. This may suggest that The Right is not a human right.

But nothing in my argument turns on whether The Right is considered a human right. We have already seen that many other rights that are postulated by the Universal Declaration are rights held against the state, and many of them are conditional on favorable circumstances. The Right is not unique in these respects. Moreover, my account permits us to say that people "as such" have the right to an adequate standard of living, for it implies that everyone is such that, if he lived in a state, the state would owe him the relevant conditional duty. But nothing turns on whether we choose to speak in this manner.

IV. Adequacy of a Standard of Living

The Universal Declaration is concerned with the adequacy of a person's standard of living to the person's "health and well-being." I shall define the boundary between adequate and inadequate standards of living in terms of *basic needs*. I will have to explain what I mean by a basic need, of course, but I think it would be reasonable to interpret The Right as the right of each person to be enabled to meet his needs for health and well-being. And since, as I shall argue in the next section, there is no reason to give favored treatment to some of a person's basic needs while ignoring others, it is reasonable to generalize the idea. I therefore understand The Right as the right to be enabled to meet one's basic needs.[29]

There is vagueness in the notion of a basic need, and my account therefore leaves vagueness in the boundary between adequate and inadequate standards of living. And this means it leaves vagueness in my specification of The Right. But the best we can hope for is a rough indication of what adequacy amounts to. We cannot expect a precise boundary.

There is a difference between the merit of a claim to additional resources made by a person with an expensive and unfilled *taste* and the merit of a claim made by a person with an expensive and unfilled *need*. The idea that there is a right to be enabled to meet one's basic needs can explain this difference. For example, a lover of fine champagne who cannot afford to satisfy his desire has no ground for complaint on that score, even if he is not in any way responsible for the fact that he has the desire. Assuming that he does not require the champagne in order to meet his basic needs, he cannot expect resources to be transferred to him to enable him to indulge his desire. But a person with a respiratory disability who cannot afford a supply of bottled oxygen may have a valid complaint against his society; if we have a basic need for an appropriate amount of oxygen, and if he requires bottled oxygen in order to supply his body with the necessary amount, then he requires a supply of bottled oxygen in order to meet his basic needs. Hence, if he has The Right, and if his society is in favorable circumstances, then his right has been abridged.[30] People with addictions present an intermediate case. If their addiction prevents them from meeting their basic needs, they have a basis for complaint under The Right. They ought to be given access to the substance they require or treatment for their addiction. On the other hand, those who became addicted due to simple foolishness and who are responsible for their own foolishness (if there are any in this category) may be viewed as having squandered their entitlements under The Right, and they may have to depend on charity for additional help.

My proposal to relate the adequacy of a standard of living to the meet-

[29] Virginia Held proposes a similar reading of the right in her *Rights and Goods*, pp. 184–85.

[30] Richard Arneson denies that it is possible to justify "discriminating in the treatment of physical handicaps and other expensive preferences." See his "Liberalism, Distributive Subjectivism, and Equal Opportunity for Welfare," p. 194. I claim that the fact that handicaps are deprivations of what we need is what justifies treating them differently from unfulfilled preferences.

ing of basic needs meshes with the conception of the standard of living advocated by Amartya Sen, who explains the standard of living as a matter of so-called "functionings" and "capabilities."[31]

One might think that a person's standard of living is measured by the degree to which he is happy or has pleasure or the degree to which his desires are satisfied. But, as Sen points out, a person who is "poor, exploited, overworked and ill, but who has been made satisfied with his lot by social conditioning" is hardly doing well "just because he is happy and satisfied." Nor would we view his situation differently if we were informed that he has fulfilled his desires.[32] We would think his desires must also be due to social conditioning. Nor would we think better of his life if we were told that he would not have any different desires even if he considered his life calmly, clearly, and with full information, without making any errors of reasoning. We would think that the conditioning must have been especially effective.[33] When we think of a person's standard of living, we think of a more objective measure of his life than one defined in terms of his own psychological states.

A more objective measure could be defined in terms of possession of commodities or resources. Sen quotes A. C. Pigou's characterization of a minimum standard: "The minimum includes some defined quantity and quality of house accommodation, of medical care, of education, of food, of leisure, of the apparatus of sanitary convenience and safety where work is carried on, and so on."[34] However, to follow Sen's reasoning, one person may have more income than another and succeed in buying and consuming more food, but if he "has a higher metabolic rate and some parasitic disease" he may be more "undernourished and debilitated." If so, then he would have a lower standard of living on any reasonable account. In general, variations in psychological, social, medical, climatic, and other factors mean that a given commodity bundle can be associated with quite different standards of living.[35] Sen concludes that "the focus has to be on what life we lead and on what we can or cannot

[31] See Amartya Sen, *The Standard of Living*.

[32] *Ibid.*, pp. 8, 11. Sen comments on p. 11: "The battered slave, the broken unemployed, the hopeless destitute, the tamed housewife, may have the courage to desire little, but the fulfillment of those disciplined desires is not a sign of great success."

[33] Richard Arneson proposes to answer Sen's objection by invoking hypothetical desires. He also proposes to invoke considerations about the conditions under which desires are formed to avoid the worry about conditioning. But I submit we already know enough about a person who is "poor, exploited, overworked and ill" to know that he does not have a standard of living adequate for his health and well-being. We do not have to inquire into the conditions under which his desires were formed. See Arneson's "Liberalism, Distributive Subjectivism, and Equal Opportunity for Welfare," pp. 163, 167–70.

[34] Sen, *The Standard of Living*, p. 14, quoting A. C. Pigou, *The Economics of Welfare* (London: Macmillan, 1952), p. 759.

[35] *Ibid.*, pp. 15–16.

do, can or cannot be." He calls the various living conditions we can or cannot achieve our "functionings" and our ability to achieve them our "capabilities."[36]

In order to give content to the right to an adequate standard of living, however, we obviously need to decide which "functionings" a person would have to have the "capability" of achieving in order to enjoy an adequate standard of living. Unfortunately, Sen's account does not provide or suggest a natural way of deciding on the adequacy of a given standard of living. Still, in Sen's terminology, one "functioning" is a living condition in which our basic needs are satisfied and one "capability" is the ability to achieve such a condition, or the ability to satisfy our basic needs. My proposal is that the ability to satisfy basic needs is a nonarbitrary and theoretically defensible criterion of the minimal adequacy of a standard of living. The basic thing about food intake is that it be sufficient for one's nourishment, for that is what one needs. And the basic thing about housing is that it be usable in a way that satisfies one's needs for shelter, a sanitary means of waste disposal, and so on. Hence, while Sen's proposal is plausible, the required minimum quantity and quality of the various commodities and resources Pigou mentions is surely at least a quantity and quality sufficient to satisfy basic needs.

In the next section, I briefly explain the concept of a basic need and relate our basic needs to our autonomy and rationality. In the concluding section, I propose that the right to an adequate standard of living is grounded in our interest in satisfying our basic needs, which is in turn grounded in our interest in our autonomy and rationality. Unfortunately, I will be able to do little more than suggest the line of reasoning that I find plausible and that I would like to develop. The details will have to await another opportunity.

V. Basic Human Needs

There are things that a person needs in order to achieve a goal or to satisfy a desire and that he would not otherwise need. Needs of this sort I shall call "occasional needs," since they are occasioned by goals or desires. Hence, if I want to speak with a friend, I may need to make a telephone call, but if I had no other goal or desire that I could advance with a phone call, I would not need to make one. The matters of basic need, however, are things a person requires regardless of his goals or desires. For example, each person needs a nutritious diet. There is, then, a distinction between basic needs and occasional needs.[37]

[36] *Ibid.*, p. 16.

[37] There are discussions of the distinction in many places. For a particularly good discussion, see Garrett Thomson, *Needs* (London: Routledge and Kegan Paul, 1987), pp. 1–10. Occasional needs could also be called "instrumental needs," but this term may be misleading, since basic needs are also instrumental to achieving one's goals.

Of course, in order to meet one's basic needs, one requires other things, and these are needed in their own right as "forms of provision" for the basic needs.[38] Hence, medical care may be required by someone in order to meet his basic need to preserve his body intact, and specific foods are needed for a nutritious diet. There is a distinction between the basic needs and the forms of provision. Every human needs a nutritious diet, but differences in metabolism, sex, climate, health, and so on contribute to differences in what kinds and amounts of food a person must have in order to meet his need for a nutritious diet. And everyone needs a sense of self-respect, but different things are required in different cultures and circumstances in order to sustain a sense of self-respect. There are also relevant differences between people due to differences in their psychologies. Every human has basic needs that are the same at some level of description as those of every other human, even though the forms of provision needed may vary from person to person and circumstance to circumstance, depending on a variety of factors, including culture.[39]

There is obviously a distinction between a preference and a basic need. I need a nutritious diet regardless of what kind of diet I prefer. And although I prefer chocolate ice cream to vanilla, I do not need ice cream at all.[40]

There is also a distinction between basic needs and all-purpose resources, such as Rawls's primary goods.[41] Primary goods would be instrumental to virtually any goal, and they are also usually required by us if we are to meet our basic needs. But they are not themselves matters of basic need. I do not have a basic need for income and wealth, for example, and ascetics may not have any need at all for income or wealth. Matters of basic need, of course, are required in order to achieve many of our goals, and so they are also usually needed instrumentally, but they are

[38] The term comes from David Braybrooke, *Meeting Needs* (Princeton: Princeton University Press, 1987).

[39] There are complications that would need to be addressed in a full treatment of the issue. Suppose, for example, that the culture of one's society views a kind of housing as contemptible, although housing of this kind would be adequate to satisfy anyone's need for shelter. If so, housing of this kind might be inadequate to sustain a sense of self-respect, and so a case could be made for enabling everyone to have better or different housing than is strictly needed to provide adequate shelter. But differences in psychology can lead to unwelcome complications. Suppose, for example, that a person's self-esteem comes to depend on his having much fancier housing than most other people. He should not be viewed as having an entitlement to the fancier housing. For, assuming that there are other routes to self-esteem, he should be expected to look for another route, and his case should not be assimilated to a case of costly needs.

[40] Richard Arneson says, however, "The conviction that mere preferences are analytically distinguishable from true human needs may prove to be illusory." See Arneson, "Liberalism, Distributive Subjectivism, and Equal Opportunity for Welfare," p. 191. The distinction is discussed by several authors, including Braybrooke, *Meeting Needs*; David Wiggins, "Claims of Need," in his *Needs, Values, Truth* (Oxford: Basil Blackwell, 1987), pp. 1-57; Garrett Thomson, *Needs*, pp. 98–107.

[41] John Rawls, *A Theory of Justice*, pp. 62, 90–95.

needed independently of our goals and regardless of our circumstances. We do not need to know anything about your goals, desires, or circumstances in order to know that you need a nutritious diet.

Any credible analysis of the concept of a basic need would imply that most or all of the following are either basic needs or forms of provision for a basic need: the need for nutritious food and clean water, the need to excrete, the need otherwise to preserve the body intact, the need for periodic rest and relaxation (which I presume to include periodic sleep and some form of recreation), the need for companionship, the need for education, the need for social acceptance and recognition, the need for self-respect and self-esteem, and the need to be free from harassment.[42] This list is perhaps redundant or incomplete, but it can help to orient our thinking.

I should perhaps remind the reader that I am proposing a right to be *enabled* to meet one's basic needs; I am not proposing a right to be *provided* with what one needs. Hence, for example, although the state can hardly *provide* people with self-respect, companionship, and social acceptance and recognition, it may be able to design institutions that enhance the ability of people to meet these psychological and social needs. For example, a state could create a national medical insurance scheme that would provide a person with an entitlement to psychological counseling when his psychological or social needs are not being met and there is evidence that therapy would enhance his ability to meet those needs. But a state clearly could not ensure that people are able to meet needs of these kinds. The Right must therefore be qualified; it entitles people to call on their society to enable them to meet their basic needs, but only insofar as the nature of the case makes it possible for the society to enable them to do so.

There seems to be a conceptual connection between the basic needs and the avoidance of harm; if a thing is a matter of basic need for a person, then, the idea is that the person requires it in some quantity and in some form in order to avoid harm. David Wiggins suggests that deprivation of a matter of basic need would constitute a harm or create a probability of harm, given the "laws of nature, unalterable and invariable environmental facts, or facts about human constitution."[43] Garrett Thomson suggests that a person needs something only if the thing is "practically necessary" for the person, in the sense that his "life will be blighted or seriously harmed without it."[44] There may be something that a person needs in this sense as a "form of provision" for a matter of basic need, which is not itself a matter of basic need. For example, as we

[42] The list is adapted from David Braybrooke, *Meeting Needs*, p. 36.

[43] David Wiggins, "Claims of Need," p. 15, also p. 10. See also Joel Feinberg, *Social Philosophy* (Englewood Cliffs: Prentice-Hall, 1973), p. 111; D. W. Stampe, "Need," *Australasian Journal of Philosophy*, vol. 66 (1988), p. 135.

[44] Garrett Thomson, *Needs*, p. 8.

saw in Section III, a person may have a disability that makes it very costly to meet his basic needs. He may have a respiratory disability in virtue of which he requires a supply of bottled oxygen. But a supply of bottled oxygen is not itself a matter of basic need, even though some people require a supply of bottled oxygen in order to meet their basic needs. Matters of basic need are things anyone would require in some quantity and in some form in order to avoid a blighted or harmed life.[45]

This account is vague, but it is perhaps as much as we can expect from the concept of a basic human need. We require, however, an account of what is meant by a blighted or harmed life in order to unify and provide a theoretical justification for the list of matters of basic need. David Braybrooke has suggested that, in brief, basic needs are things that are "essential to living or to functioning normally." More fully, basic needs are things that, at some time in the course of the life of every member of the population, are "[presumptively] indispensable to mind or body in performing [without derangement] the tasks assigned [them] under a combination of basic social roles, namely, the roles of parent, householder, worker and citizen."[46] Presumably, the idea here is not that a person is inevitably leading a blighted life if he is not performing some combination of these basic social roles. It is rather that a person's life is blighted if he does not have the things needed to perform in this combination of roles. We do not want to be committed to the claim that a person who has freely chosen the life of an ascetic, and who is living alone on a mountain in the desert, must be living a harmed and blighted life. But if he had the choice of what kind of life to live, and if he made it freely, then he must have had available to him the necessities of a more standard life. A person may not *choose* to live such a life, but if he is *unable* to choose it and take it up because he is deprived of one of the necessities, then his life is blighted. Perhaps, then, Braybrooke's account would be more plausible if he were to say that the basic needs are things that are required in order to have the opportunity both to choose and to live a standard life.

If a person's life would be blighted if he were unable to choose and live a standard life, it would also be blighted if he were unable to choose and live anything *but* a standard life. Hence, there is the more general point that a person's life is blighted if he is not able to choose how to live his

[45] I do not believe it is a conceptual truth that a person has a right not to be harmed. But even if this is a conceptual truth, it would not follow from the line I am exploring in the text that a person has a right not to be deprived of a matter of basic need. For the argument in the text suggests that it is a conceptual truth that deprivation of a matter of basic need creates a risk of harm, but to create a risk of harm is not necessarily to cause a harm. More important, the right against the state to be enabled to meet one's basic needs would not follow from the right not to be harmed, even if depriving a person of a matter of basic need invariably caused harm. For a state that *fails to enable* a person to meet his needs has not necessarily *deprived* the person of a matter of basic need.

[46] Braybrooke, *Meeting Needs*, pp. 31, 48.

life and to implement his choice—if he is not able to form his own values and evaluate his life in relation to them and to choose a life that suits them and live it. Now the inability to form values, or to evaluate one's life in terms of one's values, or to choose how to live one's life, or to implement such a choice seems to mark a degradation of one's autonomy or rationality. Hence, I shall say, a person with inabilities of these kinds is falling short of full "autonomy" or "rationality." Using this terminology, then, I suggest that the kind of harm relevant to understanding the basic needs would consist in being deprived of the things that are indispensable to one's acquiring and preserving over one's life the status of autonomous rational agent. I propose, therefore, that the basic needs are the things that, at some time in the course of life, are indispensable in some form and quantity to a rational and autonomous life for a human, given the "laws of nature, unalterable and invariable environmental facts, or facts about human constitution."

I cannot fill in all the details of this account of the basic needs here, and there are details I have not yet worked out. The first idea is that of a rational and autonomous agent. At a minimum, such an agent has a set of values that are his own, in some important sense that needs to be explained, and he has the capability of forming new values, evaluating his values, and pursuing his values. Autonomy and rationality are obviously matters of degree, but I think that any person who falls short in one of these respects is suffering a loss—and the more he falls short, the greater the loss. To some degree, he is suffering a harm. The second idea is that anything that qualifies as a basic need is something essential to one's status as a rational and autonomous agent; namely, it is essential either for maintaining the capability of pursuing one's values or for ensuring that one develops values of one's own and continues to have the capacity to develop and evaluate them.[47] Clearly, however, the idea that certain things are "essential" to rational autonomy needs to be explained. And it is important to preserve the distinction between matters of basic need, such as a nutritious diet, and the things required to meet these needs, such as forms of provision. There are details to work out.

The most important test of my account of the basic needs is whether it can account for the items on the above list of matters of need. It is a commonplace that people who lack the basic necessities of life have limited options. They are at risk of exploitation and have no choice but to devote their attention to these basic needs.[48] I hope it is clear, therefore, that my account supports the claim that people need food, water, shelter, sanitation, health care, and the like. Both physical and psychological integrity are obvious requirements of rationality and autonomy. Without self-respect and self-esteem, one would be incapable of genuine choice.

[47] I developed this idea in somewhat more detail in "Reason and Needs."
[48] Virginia Held stresses this point in *Rights and Goods*, pp. 184–87.

Without companionship and social acceptance and recognition, one would lack the assurance needed for genuine choice. And without education in one form or another, one would lack the needed information and skills to make genuine choices. To be sure, the notion of a "genuine" choice is vague and needs further explanation. And these remarks need to be qualified to take into account the fact that the details of what any given individual requires, in order to provide for the basic needs, depend on one's specific biological, psychological, and social circumstances.

There are many remaining questions that I cannot address in this paper, but I will discuss two problematic examples.[49] First, although we want to say that there is a need for a nutritious diet, it seems false that a person's rationality or autonomy must inevitably be undermined by an inadequate diet. A sufficiently horrible diet would undermine a person's health, but a person does not need to be in the best possible physical condition in order to be autonomous and rational. This much ought to be conceded, but the claim that people need a nutritious diet should not be taken to imply that any departure from ideal nutrition counts as a harm. The idea is rather that a generally nutritious diet is needed over one's lifetime, a diet that is good enough to maintain one's health. Different people in different stages of life and in different states of health will be affected in different ways by their diet. Second, some people may be able to meet the conditions of autonomous rationality without any formal education and with only the most minimal companionship, but we still view education and companionship as matters of basic need. There are at least two ways to deal with this worry. On the one hand, we could insist that everyone needs education and companionship, and explain the relevant differences between individuals as differences in what they require in order to achieve what they basically need rather than as differences in what they basically need. On the other hand, we could seek a more abstract description of the underlying matters of basic need and describe companionship and education (and perhaps certain other items on the list) as things typically required in order to meet the basic needs. We could even claim that rationality and autonomy are the most fundamental matters of basic need, and that the items on the list, such as rest and relaxation, are typically required in order to satisfy these basic needs. For present purposes, I do not need to decide among these strategies. We can live with the remaining looseness in my account provided that it seems at least plausible in outline.

I claimed that the right to an adequate standard of living should be understood to be the right to be enabled by one's society to meet one's basic needs, provided one's society is in favorable circumstances. I do not see any reason of principle to give favored treatment to certain of a person's basic needs. The Universal Declaration formulated The Right as the

[49] Mark Ravizza and Richard Arneson urged me to confront these worries.

right to a standard of living adequate for health and well-being, but I do not think that health and well-being are deserving of special protection. For if I am correct, every need is a requirement of rational autonomy and is as important on this count as every other. It is true, however, that there are limits to what a society can do to enable people to meet their needs. Hence, as I said before, The Right is the right to be enabled by one's society to meet one's basic needs insofar as it is possible in the nature of the case for the society to do so. I will not mention this qualification again.

VI. Arguments from Rational Autonomy

In order to show that there is The Right, I would have to show that the state has a qualified and conditional duty to enable people to meet their needs, a duty with the special status I sketched above. I shall outline some arguments, but I do not claim that they eliminate all possible grounds of disagreement. There are two main problems that I face.

The deepest problem is methodological. There are many different strategies that are currently in use to support normative claims in ethics and politics. The familiar ones include, for example, Rawlsian contractarian strategies, Hobbesian rational choice or contractarian strategies, utilitarian strategies, Kantian strategies, and so on. In my view, no one of these strategies is sufficiently defended, entrenched, or understood to permit ignoring the others. It is as if scientists lacked any shared understanding of how evidence is to be appraised. I will attempt to show that The Right can be defended by means of a variety of argumentative strategies in order to show that it has broad appeal.[50]

The second problem is that each of the arguments rests on questionable and undefended premises. This is unavoidable, of course. There is, moreover, no reason to expect deductive arguments in this field; there is no reason to demand a moral geometry when a moral science would suffice.

Consider, first, Rawls's argument from the "original position."[51] The people in society who are best off with respect to their command over

[50] I will not attempt to explore Hobbesian contractarian arguments, but Gregory Kavka uses a form of Hobbesian argument to argue for the right of disabled persons to work, which may perhaps be viewed as a corollary of The Right, in "Disability and the Right to Work." It should be noted, however, that Kavka's conception of the constraints on such arguments differs significantly from the conceptions of other contractarians, such as Jan Narveson and David Gauthier. See Narveson's *The Libertarian Idea* (Philadelphia: Temple University Press, 1989), and David Gauthier, *Morals by Agreement* (Oxford: Oxford University Press, 1986). I discuss what I take to be fundamental problems with Hobbesian arguments of the sort used by Gauthier in my "Contractarianism and Moral Skepticism," ed. Peter Vallentyne, *Contractarianism and Rational Choice: Essays on Gauthier* (Cambridge: Cambridge University Press, 1990).

[51] John Rawls, *A Theory of Justice*. Rawls's argument has been widely criticized in the literature. Here, for the sake of argument, I do not question his basic assumptions except (mainly) the assumption that the parties to the original position would be concerned with

Rawlsian primary goods could have some extraordinarily costly medical needs and a poor standard of living as a result. And if their greater command over primary goods did not work to the advantage of those in the society with less in the way of primary goods, the situation would be in violation of the difference principle. It would be in violation of the principle, moreover, even if those with the costly needs counted as among the worst-off people on the basis of their standard of living, and even if the standard of living of those with command over less income were relatively high. In this situation, the difference principle would count the distribution of primary goods as unjust even though redistribution from the better off in primary goods to the worst off in primary goods would be redistribution from the worst off in standard of living to the better off in standard of living. It is reasonable to claim that if people in Rawls's original position realized that this is a possibility, they would choose on Rawlsian grounds to recognize a right to be enabled to meet one's basic needs, and they would give it priority over the difference principle. They would not want the difference principle to be taken to require redistribution unless redistribution would leave intact people's ability to meet their basic needs.[52]

The remaining arguments exploit the connection I have suggested between the standard of living, basic needs, and rational autonomy. I argued that a person is able to enjoy an adequate standard of living, in that he is able to meet his basic needs, roughly when he is capable of living a life as a rational agent, making choices that determine his own way of life on the basis of values that he has formed autonomously, and doing so with sufficient information and appreciation of options that the choices promote his actual values.

Many moral views, including Kantian and Aristotelian views, suggest that a good society would foster the rational agency of its members. On my account, fostering this would involve promoting a situation in which each member is able to meet his basic needs. Kantians and Aristotelians can see enabling people to meet their basic needs as a way for a society to promote the rational agency of each person, and utilitarians can see it as a way for a society to promote the welfare of its members. Hence, each of these theories supports the claim that a good society would enable its members to meet their basic needs.

---

their command over the primary goods of income, wealth, power, authority, and self-respect. I claim they would be reasonable to be concerned about their ability to meet their basic needs.

[52] This argument depends crucially, however, on the claim that those in the original position would choose on the basis of the "maximin" choice rule, which is of course controversial. Rawls explains and gives the rationale for maximin in *A Theory of Justice*, pp. 152ff. Kavka's Rawlsian and Hobbesian contractarian arguments assume that the contractors are risk-averse and would at least tend to insure against worst outcomes. See his "Disability and the Right to Work."

There is reason, moreover, to think that society has a duty to bring this about. For if meeting one's basic needs is necessary to avoid harm, then any theory that implies a duty to help people avoid harm would imply a duty to help people meet their basic needs. And since one particularly important kind of harm threatened by failure to meet one's basic needs is damage to one's rational autonomy, any theory that implies a duty to promote the rational autonomy of others as well as of oneself would imply a duty to help people to meet their basic needs. Certain forms of consequentialism and certain interpretations of Kantianism would presumably imply such duties, although I cannot here explore the details.

Now, in order effectively to promote people's ability to meet their basic needs, it seems that a society would have to be efficiently organized; in the modern world, the state is the typical form of organization. Given this, and given that the state is the agent of the society as a whole, then if the society has the duty to bring it about that its members are enabled to meet their basic needs, the state has this duty.

This is not yet an argument for the claim that individuals have a *right*. One plausible theory of rights holds that a person has a right when the protection of an interest of his is the ground for the duties and obligations of others. Rights are requirements generated by individual interests of a special urgency.[53] If I am correct, the duty of the state to assure its citizens the ability to meet their basic needs is grounded in the interest of each person to secure and promote his autonomy and rational agency. This is an interest of special urgency according to virtually any moral view. Hence, the interest theory of rights supports the claim that citizens have a right against the state to be enabled to meet their basic needs.

If there is a right to an adequate standard of living, then the duty of the state to enable people to meet their basic needs has the special status I discussed before. First, when there is conflict between the goal of enabling people to meet their basic needs and the more ordinary goals of the state—such as the goal of promoting economic efficiency or the goal of promoting the general welfare—the state ought to give priority to enabling people to meet their needs, except in extraordinary circumstances. Second, citizens can claim as their due that the state should enable them to meet their basic needs. Third, there is a link between claiming one's Right and one's self-respect. A full argument to support these claims is beyond the scope of this paper. Yet it is reasonable to claim that the goal of respecting the autonomy of the citizen ought to have priority over the goal of promoting the general welfare or economic efficiency. The ground of other rights against the state, such as the rights of free speech and free-

[53] This view is sketched by Waldron in ed. Waldron, *Theories of Rights*, pp. 9–10, 12–14. Waldron credits the theory to D. N. MacCormick, "Rights in Legislation," ed. P. M. S. Hacker and J. Raz, *Law, Morality and Society: Essays in Honour of H. L. A. Hart* (Oxford: Oxford University Press, 1977), pp. 192ff.

dom of association, is surely at least in part that they protect the citizen's autonomy from the encroachment of government. If so, then recognizing rights of this kind, and recognizing them for this reason, commits one to regarding the goal of not abridging the autonomy of the citizen as having a higher priority than the goal of promoting the general welfare, except perhaps in extraordinary circumstances. The reason for giving priority to this goal is presumably the value accorded to autonomy. It is a small additional step to claim that, except in extraordinary circumstances, the state ought to give priority to enabling the citizen to preserve and promote his rational autonomy. On my account, this means the state ought to give priority to enabling each citizen to meet his basic needs. Now if the state ought to give priority to this goal, it would seem that each citizen has a ground for complaint if he is unable to meet his basic needs, assuming favorable conditions and assuming that the state can do more than it has already done to assist him. And he is not forced to ask for charity or to view assistance to him as requiring his gratitude. Hence, a citizen who demanded the assistance of the state in meeting his basic needs would not thereby be demeaned in any way.[54] I conclude, then, that a good case can be made in favor of a right against the state to be enabled to meet one's basic needs.

It may be useful to mention the obvious libertarian objections to my argument here. Libertarians would agree with me about the value of individual autonomy. They would insist, however, that the rights of individual citizens not to have their autonomy abridged would be violated by transfer programs designed to enforce transfers of income or wealth from the better off in society to the less well off. Robert Nozick claims, for example, that taxes designed to effect transfers from the better off in society to the less well off are akin to forced labor.[55]

I agree that if there are rights not to have one's autonomy abridged, these rights may have priority over the right to an adequate standard of living. For the latter boils down to a right to be enabled to meet the conditions required to achieve and maintain one's rational autonomy. It may be that, in cases of conflict, the duty of government not to encroach on people's autonomy would override its duty to promote the conditions of people's autonomy.

This concession does not amount to accepting the libertarians' objection, however. For I do not agree that taxation of the better off, to enforce transfers from the better off to the less well off, must inevitably violate the

[54] He might *feel* demeaned, of course, because of his psychology. But if there is The Right, then a (normative) judgment that he is less worthy, or that he has demeaned himself, would not be warranted. As I said before, in designing institutions to implement The Right, the state ought to take into account the likely psychological effects of various institutions and aim to enhance people's self-respect, since people have a need for self-respect.

[55] Robert Nozick, *Anarchy, State, and Utopia*, pp. 167–74. I cannot attempt to deal fully with Nozick's objection here.

rights of the better off. The considerations that argue in favor of a duty of the state to enable its citizens to meet their basic needs would also argue in favor of a duty of each citizen to enable everyone else to meet their basic needs if each citizen had the resources of a state. I assume, for example, that every agent ought to respect the autonomy of every person and that this is why the state ought to respect the autonomy of its citizens. Now, as I said before, I do not think that everyone has a right against every other ordinary citizen to be enabled to meet his basic needs. The state has a special responsibility for the condition of the society as a whole. And the state is typically the only agent capable of promoting the economic and social conditions required to enable the citizens to meet their basic needs. Ordinary citizens are ordinarily poorly placed to do anything of more than a piecemeal nature. For these reasons, the state has a special responsibility to enable citizens to meet their needs, and an ordinary citizen lacks any such special responsibility—at least with respect to most of his fellow citizens. Hence, an ordinary citizen is typically not in a position to make a justified claim against another ordinary citizen; he does not have a right against every other citizen, to be enabled to meet his needs. Yet this explanation of why The Right is a right against the state is compatible with the claim I now wish to make: that ordinary citizens have a duty to assist the state in discharging its duty by contributing to programs intended to enable every citizen to meet his basic needs.

The state cannot discharge its duties without the support of individual members of society, and the state is the agent of the society, which is an aggregate of its members. I would argue on this basis that, at least in ordinary cases, if a state has a moral duty, its citizens have a duty to support it in discharging that duty. This means the state would not have to rely on voluntary contributions. It would need only to ask people to do their duty, and it would not inevitably be violating their rights if it required them to do their duty. If I am correct, then, there is a duty to pay one's share of the cost of programs designed to fulfill the government's responsibility to enable people to meet their basic needs. And to require people to pay their share is hardly akin to "forced labor." Perhaps it is true that the government is not entitled to enforce transfers from the rich to the poor once the point has been achieved that the worst off are enabled to meet their basic needs. My claim is simply that in favorable circumstances, the better off have a duty to pay their share *until* the point is reached that the worst off are enabled to meet their basic needs.

Moreover, the libertarian defense of minimal government is built on a foundation of assumed rationality and autonomy. For example, Nozick assumes that individuals in the "state of nature" are sufficiently rational and autonomous to decide fundamental questions about their lives. They are able to decide freely and rationally to band together into "mutual-protection associations" rather than to stand on their own, for instance.[56] If I am correct, the libertarian's assumption that individuals are fully rational and autonomous involves the implicit assumption that they are able to meet their basic needs. Hence, I would say, the libertarian defense of minimal government presumes that The Right will not be abridged by the emergence of the minimal state, and it presumes that everyone in the minimal state will enjoy an adequate standard of living. This means that the existence of The Right is moot in the imaginary circumstances of the emergence of Nozick's minimal state.

VII. Conclusion

I have claimed that the right to an adequate standard of living amounts to a right against the state to be enabled to meet one's basic needs, insofar as it is possible for the state to be of assistance and provided that one's society is in favorable circumstances. I attempted to defend this thesis on the basis of a theory that takes the basic needs to be things that are needed in order to achieve and maintain one's status as an autonomous and rational agent. I have not attempted to respond to all of the objections that are to be anticipated. To do so, I would need to embed my argument in a complete moral and political theory or examine in detail the case that would be made by the opponents. I must leave these tasks for other occasions or other authors.

People ought to be able to develop their talents fully and to enjoy happy and thriving lives; it may therefore seem quite modest only to demand that they be enabled to meet their basic needs. Moreover, given the inequalities between poor and wealthy societies, it is arguable that citizens of poorer societies have claims against wealthier ones; it does not seem adequate only to consider the claims they have against their own societies. Yet the richest societies do not even assure the ability of their own citizens to meet their basic needs. So there is surely some value in arguing that justice requires that they do this.

Philosophy, University of California, Davis

[56] *Ibid.*, ch. 2.

TARA SMITH

ON DERIVING RIGHTS TO GOODS FROM RIGHTS TO FREEDOM

ABSTRACT. This paper examines a particular type of argument often employed to defend welfare rights. This argument contends that welfare rights are a necessary supplement to liberty rights because rights to freedom become hollow when their bearers are not able to take advantage of their freedom. Rights to be provided with certain goods are thus a natural outgrowth of a genuine concern to protect freedom.

I argue that this reasoning suffers from two fatal flaws. First, it rests on an erroneous notion of what it is to have a right, neglecting the fact that the exact source of a person's inability to exercise a right is crucial to determining whether that right is being respected. Second, the argument equivocates as to the "freedom" that rights are intended to protect, sometimes confusing freedom with ability, sometimes confusing not being free with not having other desired things, and sometimes confusing what a person is able to do with what a person is entitled to do.

Amid many rights that have gained greater attention in recent years, one type that has enjoyed particular prominence has been welfare rights. These are alleged rights to be provided by others with certain concrete goods.[1] Whether such rights are justified, and what their justification is, however, remain controversial. Here, I wish to examine one of the stronger arguments offered on behalf of welfare rights. I will contend that this argument, despite its superficial appeal, suffers from two fatal flaws: it rests on an erroneous notion of what it means to possess a right, and it equivocates as to the kind of freedom that rights are intended to protect.

I will dub the argument in question the "precondition argument"

[1] Among those who accept some form of welfare rights are Martin Golding, Alan Gewirth, Carl Wellman, Rodney Peffer, Theodore Benditt, Diana Meyers, William Aiken, James Nickel, Hugo Bedau, Jeffrie Murphy, Charles Fried, H.J. McCloskey, D.D. Raphael, and Frank Michaelman.

Law and Philosophy 11: 217–234, 1992.

(PCA), because it asserts that welfare rights are a necessary precondition for respecting the freedom which rights have traditionally been thought to defend. According to the PCA, welfare rights are founded upon rights to freedom. That is, rather than appealing to separate grounds to justify welfare rights, this argument maintains that the very same grounds that support rights to freedom also support rights to goods. One would be inconsistent in accepting liberty rights while rejecting welfare rights.[2]

This is a striking thesis. It is one thing for a Marxist, for instance, based on a completely alternative perspective, to defend welfare rights; it is another to be told that liberty rights proponents themselves must embrace welfare rights out of fidelity to their own principles. If successful, the PCA means that the welfare rights advocate is not pushing radically novel views, but is actually the truest, most consistent defender of liberty rights.

Before elaborating on the PCA, we should establish terminology. "Liberty rights" are entitlements to freedom of action, claims protecting the rightholder from others' interference with her actions. "Welfare rights", by contrast, are entitlements to goods, such as money, food, health care, or education. Welfare rights entitle their bearers to goods other than those that they have earned or contracted for (such as a paycheck), however. Loosely, welfare rights are entitlements to goods that a person possesses in virtue of nothing more than her need for the goods.[3]

---

[2] The proponents of this type of argument include Henry Shue, *Basic Rights* (Princeton: Princeton University Press, 1980); James Sterba, 'A Libertarian Justification of a Welfare State', *Social Theory & Practice* **11** (1985): 285–306; Allen Buchanan, 'Deriving Welfare Rights from Libertarian Rights', in Peter Brown et. al. (eds.), *Income Support*, (Totowa: Rowman & Littlefield, 1981); and Hillel Steiner, 'The Natural Right to the Means of Production', *Philosophical Quarterly* **27** (1977): 41–49. The "PCA" is a generic label I apply to these authors' common brand of argument, but I am not claiming that each author is guilty of all of the particular errors I shall discuss.

[3] Welfare rights thus differ from property rights, though they may share certain features in common. This account of liberty and welfare rights borrows somewhat from Martin Golding, 'The Primacy of Welfare Rights', *Social Philosophy &*

I. THE "PRECONDITION" CASE FOR WELFARE RIGHTS

The PCA revolves around a simple but powerful claim: without welfare rights, all other rights are rendered worthless. Liberty rights become hollow when their bearers are not in a position to take advantage of their liberties. If a person is not assured, by rights, of the minimal ingredients of subsistence, her possession of liberty rights is useless. Having rights without having the means necessary to utilize those rights does a person no good. It is little comfort to the poor to be reminded that their freedom is intact; without food, their freedom is of negligible value. The aim of the entire practice of rights is to allow people to be able to enjoy life, and to lead their lives as they wish. When people do not know where their next meal is coming from, the proposal is, they are not free. Unless we recognize welfare rights alongside liberty rights, we might as well not recognize liberty rights.[4]

This reasoning rests on two suppositions: 1) certain goods are necessary in order for people to be able to make use of their liberty rights; and 2) people have rights to those things which are necessary for the enjoyment of their liberty rights. Henry Shue explicitly identifies this second assumption: "If everyone has a right to y, and the enjoyment of x is necessary for the enjoyment of y, then everyone also has a right to x."[5]

Shue explains, "People should be able to enjoy, or exercise, their other rights". It is morally inadequate merely to "have" rights when the rightholder is unable to make any use of the substance of her rights. "The infant and the aged do not need to be assaulted in order to be deprived of health, life, or the capacity to enjoy active rights.

Policy **1** (1984): 119–36. The exact meaning of welfare rights is itself a matter of some contention. See Carl Wellman, 'Bibliographic Essay – Welfare Rights', in Kenneth Kipnis & Diana T. Meyers, (eds.) *Economic Justice*, Totowa: Rowman & Allanheld, 1985) 229–45.

[4] Shue acknowledges that the original motivation for his work was "anger at the lofty-sounding, but cheap and empty, promises of liberty in the absence of the essentials for people's actually exercising the promised liberty", p. ix.

[5] Shue, p. 32.

The classic liberal's main prescription for the good life – do not interfere with thy neighbor – is the only poison they need."[6]

Allen Buchanan agrees that welfare rights emerge from a concern for the "effectiveness" of rights. While he does not hold that all rights must have equal effectiveness, he does maintain that significant inequalities in rights' effectiveness would violate basic requirements of fairness.[7]

According to the PCA, to whatever extent a concern for human well-being underwrites the recognition of any rights, that concern simultaneously provides grounds for the recognition of welfare rights. Without such rights, we would defeat our original purposes in affirming liberty rights.

Thus, it is urged, welfare rights are not different in kind from liberty rights. Welfare rights are not a new breed whose time has come. Rather, the PCA offers a reinterpretation of the proper meaning and implications of all rights. Welfare rights do not require a unique, independent justification; they are simply logical outgrowths of liberty rights.

II. WHAT RIGHTS ARE

Rights are claims that individuals are entitled to press in virtue of a particular moral principle: the principle that governs freedom of action in social contexts. Rights are inviolable claims which protect a person's freedom of choice and action against certain obstructions which other persons may impose. As such, rights do not simply express aspirations. Rather, rights are entitlements, expressing certain ways that people may not treat one another. To attribute a right to a person is not merely to observe how desirable it would be if she were to have the object of that right; it is to assert that she is wronged if she is denied it.[8]

---

[6] Shue pp. 20, 19. See also pages 16, 27.

[7] Buchanan, pp. 239–43.

[8] H. J. McCloskey is the author of the "entitlement" interpretation of rights, in 'Rights', *Philosophical Quarterly* **15** (1965): 115–27. Joel Feinberg's reading of

The freedom that rights protect is not freedom from unfortunate circumstances, human biology, or accidents of nature. Rights shield freedom only from other persons' potential intrusions.[9] Consequently, to provide their protective service to rightsbearers, rights will always entail obligations for others (even if the obligations are merely to refrain from interfering with the rightholder's freedom). These obligations are the muscle by which rights accomplish their work. Similarly, all rights are bounded by others' rights. A rightholder's protected freedom extends only so far as another person's protected freedom. If these boundaries were not recognized, the point of rights would be defeated. Without obligations to respect the perimeters around others' protected freedom, we would be allowing the very actions which rights are designed to guard against.[10]

---

rights as an especially firm brand of "valid claims" seems equally satisfactory, and not much different from the entitlement conception. See Feinberg, 'The Nature & Value of Rights', *Rights, Justice, & the Bounds of Liberty* (Princeton: Princeton University Press, 1980).

Since the PCA itself acknowledges that rights are intended to protect freedom, we need not address possible controversy about that. Indeed, the very phrase "liberty rights" is a relatively recent development; in the past, rights' service to liberty was understood and undisputed, so we had no need to distinguish types of rights according to their different supposed objects.

[9] A complete theory of rights, of course, must explain precisely which actions of others it is that freedom protects a person from. For our purposes, it should be helpful simply to observe that, as Isaiah Berlin notes, "mere incapacity to attain a goal is not lack of political freedom". 'Two Concepts of Liberty', *Four Essays on Liberty* (New York: Oxford University Press, 1969), p. 122. A person is free in the sense used here if no other person constrains her second order action of choosing among the actions that are possible to her. But one's inability to solve problems in multivariable calculus, for instance, does not represent any lack of this sort of freedom. This characterization is taken from David Kelley, 'Life, Liberty and Property', *Social Philosophy & Policy* **1** (1984): 110. For a systematic discussion of different meanings of freedom, also see Richard E. Flathman, *The Philosophy and Politics of Freedom* (Chicago: University of Chicago Press, 1987).

[10] The kinds of rights we are concerned with correspond to "claim-rights" in the famous Hohfeldian classification. Wesley Hohfeld, *Fundamental Legal Conceptions* (New Haven: Yale University Press, 1919). Shue acknowledges this on pp. 177–78, notes 3 and 4. I shall use "duties" and "obligations" interchangeably.

It is crucial to realize that an account of rights supplies just one component of a complete moral theory. Rights govern the issue of a person's legitimate freedom of action, but disputes about freedom do not exhaust the field of moral questions. To attribute a right to a person is to make a claim about what she should be free to do, but that is not identical with a claim as to what she morally, "all things considered", ought, or is permitted, to do. To say that Baker should be free to x (has a right to x) is not morally to endorse her doing x; it is to state that others would wrong her if they attempted to prevent her from doing x. But the overall moral propriety of her doing x is a distinct, further question.[11]

III. WHAT IT IS TO HAVE A RIGHT

According to the PCA, in order truly to possess a right, one must be able to enjoy it. If a person is not in a position to make use of her right, she cannot fairly be said to have it.

To determine whether this conception of possessing rights is correct, we must sort out the different relationships that may obtain between a rightholder and her right. I suggest the following taxonomy: to "have" a right is simply to be in possession of it; it is to be entitled to assert the "final claim" that a right is. To "exercise" a right, though, is actually to invoke it, to make use of it. When one does so, this may or may not result in the ends that the rightholder desires. A person may exercise her right of free speech on behalf of some candidate without successfully achieving her aim: the candidate's election. She may exercise her right to invest money without achieving what she seeks in doing so: making more money. What exercising one's right does guarantee is that others are morally bound not to interfere with one's actions.[12]

---

[11] Thus taking rights seriously should not be mistaken for taking only rights seriously. Jeremy Waldron provides a clear discussion of the domain of rights in 'The Right to Do Wrong', *Ethics* **92** (1981): 21–39, and 'Galton on Rights', *Ethics* **93** (1983): 325–27.

[12] No moral principle could guarantee what people's behavior will actually be, of course.

We can also identify a third possible relationship: a rightholder "capitalizes" on her right when she exercises it effectively, meaning "successfully for her intended purposes". In other words, a person capitalizes on a right when she exercises it and, by doing so, she attains the ends that she desires.[13]

Now recall the PCA. Is it true that a person's having a right must incorporate her being able to exercise that right?

We should imagine what would actually be required to fulfill rights, on this interpretation. Many factors determine a person's "abilities": intelligence, natural aptitudes, looks, and education, among other things. Some are within one's control, some are not. If Baker's right to x entails her right to whatever is needed in order for her to be able to exercise her right to x, then Baker will sometimes be entitled to goods such as money, food, or training. Moreover, notice that often, in order for a person to be able to exercise a right, certain other conducive conditions, beyond her control or apparent authority, must obtain. What determines a person's ability to exercise a right is not only what she herself does and does not possess; surrounding circumstances may also affect her options. Seemingly, Baker is only able to exercise her right to buy beer if stores sell beer and are open for business when she wants it; she is only able to exercise her right to make her living as a cobbler if sufficient demand can sustain such work.

A problem arises when we realize that sometimes, these requisite conditions won't be met. Surrounding circumstances are not always conducive to the fulfillment of all of people's desires. Given that a rightholder is unable to exercise her right in a particular desired way when all the necessary ingredients are not conveniently in place, the PCA would have us conclude that her rights are not being respected,

[13] This is not to suggest that rights are only valuable when they are "capitalized" upon. Indeed, rights need not even be "exercised" in order to serve their purpose. The right to be left alone does not require special invocation in order to entail that others are obligated to refrain from interference with the rightholder. I am not deliberately "exercising" my rights most hours of every day, yet they do protect me from others' potential intrusions. Often, it only makes sense to invoke a right or to call attention to one's possession of it in the face of some perceived threat. But the failure to exercise a right (let alone capitalize on it) does not indicate the right's worthlessness.

or that she does not really possess the right in question. This seems an unduly demanding rendering of what it is to have a right.

It is one thing to claim that given certain conditions, a person is free to respond in a variety of ways. It is another to hold that a person is entitled to have certain conditions obtain (e.g., that there be liquor stores, sufficient demand to keep a cobbler in business, and so on).[14]

In fact, I suspect that the view that inability to exercise a right constitutes failure to possess it acquires plausibility because of a misleading shorthand we have adopted in talking about rights. We often speak of rights to do specified things such as "the right to buy beer", or "the right to be a cobbler". Yet these are not actually separate, self-sufficient rights. A person does not possess thousands of rights, reflecting all the different activities she may engage in. Rather, the specific rights we speak of are simply so many particular applications of the general right (roughly) to lead one's life as one pleases. We do not hold, in addition to that right, the right to buy beer, the right to work as a cobbler, etc. Speaking of these as though they were independent "rights" usually presents no difficulties, though it may support the mistaken notion that "a right that a person cannot exercise is a right that she hasn't got". We must realize that strictly, when a person exercises the "right to buy beer/be a cobbler/attend a certain school", she is not "exercising" distinct rights; she is utilizing her general right to freedom of action for these particular purposes. These "rights" are only so many different applications of that general right to freedom.[15]

Consequently, when a person is not in a position to do something that she'd like to do (e.g., buy beer, because it isn't available), her right to freedom is not thwarted. It is the ability to use her freedom in a particular way that is frustrated. But a right to freedom does not

[14] Inasmuch as a government assumes the specific responsibility of protecting citizens' rights, it will bear more extensive obligations toward rights than an average citizen will. This does not demonstrate, however, that rights in and of themselves entail such weighty obligations.

[15] For convenience, I shall continue to use this shorthand, but it is, strictly, inaccurate.

promise unlimited abilities to use one's freedom to satisfy all of one's desires.

If having rights did require the eternal and uninterrupted existence of conditions in which one could exercise her rights so as to fulfil any desire she might have, then rights would give people entitlements to have the rest of the world be exactly as they'd like it to be, supplying the desired products, schools, jobs, etc. Only in this way could a rightholder be assured that she could always exercise her rights to suit whatever preferences she had. But such a view would reverse the basic work that rights perform: rather than protecting freedoms, rights would handcuff people to one another's desires. Instead of the recognition of rights liberating people to lead their lives as they wish, each person would have to clear all of her personal plans against others' wishes, so as to assure that her activities would not prevent others from using their rights to attain whatever ends they might have.[16]

One needn't possess extraordinary insight to foresee that under such a policy, people's freedom would be considerably reduced. Indeed, the domain over which a person enjoyed sovereign control would shrink so much that it would no longer be appropriate to refer to what one's rights protected as freedom. If a person must obtain permission to do what she wishes, then she is not sovereign over her actions. The leeway one experiences at the end of a leash should not be mistaken for freedom.[17]

---

[16] One might suspect that this is an exaggeration. Once a system of protected freedoms is in place, an individual's rights will extend only as far as others' rights. Thus one might reason that not all personal plans will require others' approval; only those which would encroach on others' rights will. The PCA, however, advances claims concerning what character this "system of protected freedoms" should have. My point here is that if this system assumes the shape that PCA advocates urge – if recognition of rights requires all that the PCA suggests – then a person will require permission for her activities in the way described.

[17] Ironically, Shue himself seems to recognize this when he writes that "to enjoy something only at the discretion of someone else, especially someone powerful enough to deprive you of it at will, is precisely *not* to enjoy a *right* to it", p. 78 (emphasis his).

Under certain circumstances, a person will not be able to make use of a right in the ways that she, at other times, is able to use it. (When demand cannot sustain it, one will not be able to exercise her general right to freedom by making a living as a cobbler.) This does not mean that her right is erased or fraudulent, however. It is not a prerequisite of a right's authenticity that conditions conducive to every conceivable exercise of that right always obtain. To think that it is, is to enlarge rights' role, and to view rights as protections not merely against others' interference, but against disappointment. Such a view would represent a fundamental misunderstanding of the purpose of rights.[18]

Granted, what many welfare rights advocates are primarily concerned with is the fulfillment of basic needs, not the indulgence of a rightholder's every wish. Yet what the PCA fails to realize is that in assessing whether one has a right when she is unable to exercise it, we must look to the reason for her inability. Only some such reasons will be morally objectionable, and only some will constitute infringements of rights.[19]

It is perfectly true that no one can deliver on the full potential of her rights if she lacks the essentials for a healthy, active life. And it is certainly desirable that people be able to "cash in" on their rights in various ways – rights are meant to be useful to people. Yet its being desirable that people taste many fruits of their rights does not entail that they have further rights to those fruits themselves. The PCA runs together two distinct issues.

An inability to exercise a right does not constitute a failure to have

---

[18] Rights' purpose, again, is to protect a person against others' interference with one's freedom, but rights do not promise all good things which their bearers may seek. Thus rights do not insulate us from all the effects of what other people may do (or not do).

[19] Sometimes, no doubt, public acknowledgment of rights is hollow. Some nations' constitutions affirm rights which are a sham. Promising a right to free expression which, if actually exercised, will result in arrest and imprisonment is clearly a disingenuous commitment to rights. But such cases must not be confused with those in which an individual rightholder's own inability or circumstances prevent her from exercising some of her rights which would, if exercised, be respected.

it. A person may have many rights, but only be able to exercise some of them. This does not nullify those which she cannot now exercise. Recognizing that she has these rights means that morally, she is entitled to exercise them, if and when she is able and so inclined. A right to pursue x means a right to pursue x if one is able and chooses to. But it does not include the claim that one is, or must be, able to pursue x.

Baker's right to travel, for example, may be as genuine as many other people's right to travel, but finances will place different people in stronger and weaker positions to exercise that right. Yet even if she never makes use of it in her entire life, Baker possesses that right; others would wrong her if they deliberately thwarted her attempts to take a trip.[20]

A PCA advocate might insist that there is no material difference between two people, one of whom never travels due to lack of funds, and one of whom never travels because she is not recognized as having the right to travel. The bottom line is: both stay at home. Yet what this perspective overlooks is that not having the means to exercise a particular right is morally different from not having the right itself. It is the difference between having a certain freedom and not having it. This difference is attested to by simply imagining that these two people suddenly inherited millions. That money could make a difference to the person who has the right to travel, but not to the person who does not, illustrates that having a right without the means to exercise it is not empty. A poor person who has the right to travel is always free to take whatever modest trip she can afford; the unfree person may not go anywhere, even if she becomes richer than Midas.[21]

---

[20] Laryngitis does not erase Baker's right to free speech; ignorance of quantum mechanics does not erase her right to read what she chooses; atheism does not cancel her right to practice the religion of her choice. These conditions simply limit her means of utilizing these rights, or the exercises of these rights that can be fruitful for her. But lacking the means of exercising or capitalizing on a right cannot be equated with lacking the right.

[21] The protection which a right offers might be likened to the protection that a security guard offers. If a threat or attack arises, the guard acts to resist the

IV. UNABLE OR UNFREE?

All of this notwithstanding, one might still believe that, at least in some cases, the inability to exercise one's rights in certain ways does amount to a lack of freedom. We can imagine situations in which a destitute person is quite capable of taking what she needs from another (e.g., of grabbing a sandwich out of another person's plate). The obstacle is that certain "rules" prohibit her from doing so. (If she does take the sandwich, she stands to suffer legal penalties.) The point is, it is not an ability that she lacks; the "rules" render her not free to do something which she is perfectly capable of doing. Thus freedom and ability are not as neatly distinguishable as I have maintained. It is not always apparent whether a person is "unfree" or "unable" to do something. My insistence that people without welfare rights lack an ability rather than a freedom is therefore not well-founded.[22]

This objection is useful because it requires us to sharpen our conception of the freedom that rights protect. Clearly, there's something that the imagined poor person wants and hasn't got. Does her not being "allowed" simply to seize it reveal that she is not free?

In one sense, the answer is yes. For according to the "rules", the destitute person is not free to take another person's property; she can do so only at the price of legal prosecution. Notice, though, that in this sense, the "comfortable" person is equally unfree, because she may not seize the poor person's coat. She would be liable to prosecution if she did that. In fact, no one is free to seize another's property (regardless of relative financial positions). Laws against theft make all the people under their jurisdiction "unfree" in this sense.

What this realization alerts us to is that this sense of freedom is not the appropriate one to use when trying to determine which rights

---

"invasion". That a guard is not continuously engaged in such resistance does not mean that the guard is not doing her job, or is useless. Similarly, that a right is not ceaselessly warding off would-be trespassers does not mean that it is useless. The right stands ready to deliver its protective services under appropriate circumstances.

[22] Jeremy Waldron first suggested this example to me, though it was offered in a somewhat different context.

people have, or what respect for rights requires. The concept of rights relies on a distinction between two types of actions, those that a person is allowed to take and those that a person is not entitled to take. To appreciate the significance of this, it may be helpful, strictly as a heuristic device, to suppose a further distinction between two types of freedom: "generic" and "rightful".

By "generic freedom", suppose that we mean simply a person's ability to perform various actions. Generic freedom refers to possession of the wherewithal – physical, intellectual, emotional, what-have-you – to do various things. No moral assessment is involved in attributing this kind of freedom to someone. A person has the generic freedom to do anything that she is capable of doing, however immoral some of these actions may be. Right now, I have the generic freedom equally to continue writing or to walk into the library across the hall and take books with the intention of never returning them. Because I am capable of doing these things, I am free to do them in this "generic" sense.

Assume that "rightful freedom", on the other hand, means the freedom that a person is entitled to exercise, or the freedom that others are morally bound to respect.[23] Rightful freedom protects all those activities that a person may take that others are obligated to refrain from interfering with. I am not free in this "rightful" sense to steal books from the library, though I am free to steal the books in the broader generic sense.[24]

---

[23] Acting within one's rightful freedom does not guarantee that one's action is morally permissible. Because rights do not address an action's overall moral propriety, but govern only the issue of freedom of action, acting within one's rights means that one's action is morally permissible from the perspective of other people's rights. When one has rightful freedom to do x, that means that doing x does not infringe on anyone else's rights. But this leaves open the question of whether it is, overall, a morally permissible action. Freedom vis-á-vis other persons' entitlements does not immunize one's action from all possible moral blame.

[24] One may be tempted to suppose that rightful freedom is a subset of a person's generic freedom, since rightful freedom protects those actions that a person is capable of taking which she is also titled to take. The relationship between the

Against this background, it should be easier to see that rights protect only certain (namely, rightful) freedom. The freedom the imagined poor person lacks is not a freedom that she is entitled to; her "unfreedom" is not a morally objectionable unfreedom (at least, an independent case would have to be made that it is). She lacks the same freedom that all people lack under a system of rights.

One might object that this response begs the question. I may appear to be stipulating which freedoms people are entitled to. Yet how to distinguish rightful from generic freedom, and how to determine which freedom rights protect, are precisely what is in dispute.

This charge cannot stand, however. While these are legitimate questions which a full-fledged theory of rights must address, they are not the subject at issue between defenders of liberty rights and advocates of the PCA. PCA proponents who would offer the sandwich example maintain that any restriction on a person's freedom eradicates her freedom. That is the claim that I am denying by reference to the rightful-generic distinction.

At this stage, one might suppose that my response simply misses the point. The PCA concerns what freedom itself requires, not which freedoms are permissible. Whether we are talking about "generic" or "rightful" freedom, a lack of freedom is a lack of freedom; that is all the PCA requires, seemingly, to press its case that without welfare rights, liberty rights become useless.

In fact, though, one must distinguish between these two types of freedom when discussing rights.[25] If individuals had legitimate grounds for resisting any constriction of their generic freedom (as the PCA

---

two kinds of freedom is not that simple, however, for a person may be entitled to do things which she is not actually capable of doing. She may have the rightful freedom to swim though she lacks the generic freedom to do so (she does not know how). Thus rightful freedom may apply to actions that are not contained within a person's generic freedom. I am grateful to a reader for this journal for pointing this out.

[25] The more accurate claim is that one must distinguish between two classes of actions, those that are and those that are not entitled to protection. I shall elaborate on this below.

defense above implies), then we could recognize no rights, and no one could enjoy protection from rights. The duties imposed by any rights would be impermissible curtailments of those duty-bearers' freedom.

Rights perform their protective function through the obligations they impose. That is, rights protect people *by placing restrictions on our generic freedom*. In defining rights in section II, we observed that rights entail obligations on others to respect the rights recognized. The freedom which one's own rights protect is bounded by the obligation one has to honor others' rights. This alone indicates that rights do not promise completely unfettered freedom. Rights do not protect all of the actions that a person is capable of taking. It is a straightforward consequence of rights imposing duties (which rights must do, in order to provide protection) that people will be "unfree" in certain ways. To complain about the duties correlative to rights as restraints upon one's freedom is thus to misunderstand the function of rights and the ways that rights must operate in order to perform that function. If we reject the duties correlative to rights because they limit freedom, we are in fact rejecting rights, since rights collapse without correlative duties. The distinction between generic and rightful freedom is thus essential to the concept of rights.[26]

To use the sandwich example to insist that the destitute are unfree and that rights to freedom are consequently hollow without rights to certain goods is to neglect this distinction. It is to rely on the mistaken assumption that all unfreedom is wrongful unfreedom which cries out for remedy.

The claim that the poor are unfree succeeds only if one equivocates on the meaning of freedom, using it first to represent generic freedom, and later to refer to rightful freedom. The "rules" do curtail a poor person's generic freedom by imposing penalties on her for taking certain actions. But observations about generic freedom cannot by themselves yield conclusions about rightful freedom. That a person's generic freedom is restricted does not show that her rightful freedom

[26] Rights are not intended to institute or preserve anarchy. Moreover, it is worth reiterating that denial of the relevance of the rightful-generic freedom distinction entails that rich and poor alike are unfree.

is infringed or artificial. In fact, the poor person is not unfree in the relevant sense (i.e., in the sense of freedom that rights purport to safeguard). Her actions and possessions are entitled to the same respect from others as are anyone else's. The restriction of a person's generic freedom is no embarrassment to rights; it is the very means by which rights accomplish their work.

We are now in a position to understand a final clarification. In truth, acceptance of rights does not rely on our recognizing two different "kinds" of freedom. What I have called "generic freedom" is not actually freedom at all. Freedom is neither an ability nor a set of activities that a person is capable of engaging in. Freedom protects certain abilities or activities. Better yet, freedom is a condition, marked by the absence of the relevant types of impediments, in which (given the satisfaction of other conditions) a person may use her abilities to engage in certain activities.[27]

The "freedom" allegedly deprived the would-be sandwich snatcher corresponds to what I have called "generic freedom". This actually refers to a person's capacity to perform certain actions, however. This capacity is not entitled to unhindered exercise. As I suggested above, we are not entitled to perform all of the actions that we are capable of performing. This is the point that many advocates of the PCA (in particular, those who maintain that the poor are unfree for reasons exposed by this example) fail to appreciate. The crucial distinction that acceptance of rights relies on is that originally suggested: between actions that a person is entitled to take and those which she is not. Only by conflating the two could one conclude that a poor person is unfree because she is not allowed to steal.[28]

---

[27] Rights protect a person's ability to choose her own actions from one particular type of obstacle (others' use or threat of force). But to guard against this is neither to guard against all possible impediments to the exercise of that ability, nor to ensure the effective exercise of that ability.

[28] All of the pivotal claims about freedom in the preceding discussion could be reinterpreted in light of this realization about actions, and the case would stand.

It is a further implication of this realization that respect for rights does not demand some sort of sacrifice, as references to a "loss" of a person's "generic

CONCLUSION

The PCA contends that without welfare rights, liberty rights become hollow. We can only respect the freedom that people are entitled to if we assure people the ability to make use of their freedom. Welfare rights, by guaranteeing people minimal necessities, provide that assurance.

I have resisted this reasoning. I have tried to demonstrate that the PCA stands on an inflated notion of what it means to have a right, and that it equivocates as to the type of freedom that rights protect. In order to make its case convincing, the PCA must treat freedom as something else, more than freedom. It conceives of rights as having broader aspirations than they actually do, and confuses not being free with not having other desired things.

To insist that people are not free when or because they have not achieved a certain level of well-being suggests that one's objective is not protecting freedom, but insuring certain states of affairs. In terms of net outcomes, it is undeniable that some people's freedom "buys them less stuff". This discloses a defect in the authenticity of their liberty rights, however, only if one assumes that outcomes provide the proper test of whether a person's rights have been respected. That assumption is completely at odds with a commitment to rights. Because rights protect individuals' freedom, respecting rights leaves undetermined the results that people's actual exercises of freedom will bring about. If one wishes to maintain that certain outcomes are absolutely intolerable, or that others simply must be realized, one is surely free to pursue that line of argument. We must recognize, though, that that position is an alternative to acceptance of rights, rather than a supplement to it.

In sum, respecting freedom does not require the provision of certain goods, so this "necessary precondition" defense of welfare rights

---

freedom" may have suggested. Recognition of rights entails that persons will not be permitted to do certain things which, it is thought, they are not entitled to do. To be restricted in this way is not to suffer a loss, as a person cannot lose what was not hers in the first place.

fails. More generally, I suspect that the true alternative to recognizing only liberty rights is not to usher in other types of rights beside them; it is to deny that we have any rights at all. The choice we face is not about which of various "species" of rights to accept, but between acknowledging only liberty rights, and giving up rights all together. But that's a thought to be pursued on another occasion.[29]

Dept. of Philosophy,
University of Texas at Austin,
Austin, TX 78712,
U.S.A.

[29] I am grateful to several people for very helpful criticisms of earlier versions of this paper, most notably: Susan Wolf, Richard Flathman, Jeremy Waldron, Carl Wellman, and colleagues at the University of Texas. Special thanks to the Institute for Humane Studies for sponsoring a workshop discussion of an earlier draft, and to all the participants in that discussion.

PETER SINGER

Famine, Affluence, and Morality

As I write this, in November 1971, people are dying in East Bengal from lack of food, shelter, and medical care. The suffering and death that are occurring there now are not inevitable, not unavoidable in any fatalistic sense of the term. Constant poverty, a cyclone, and a civil war have turned at least nine million people into destitute refugees; nevertheless, it is not beyond the capacity of the richer nations to give enough assistance to reduce any further suffering to very small proportions. The decisions and actions of human beings can prevent this kind of suffering. Unfortunately, human beings have not made the necessary decisions. At the individual level, people have, with very few exceptions, not responded to the situation in any significant way. Generally speaking, people have not given large sums to relief funds; they have not written to their parliamentary representatives demanding increased government assistance; they have not demonstrated in the streets, held symbolic fasts, or done anything else directed toward providing the refugees with the means to satisfy their essential needs. At the government level, no government has given the sort of massive aid that would enable the refugees to survive for more than a few days. Britain, for instance, has given rather more than most countries. It has, to date, given £14,750,000. For comparative purposes, Britain's share of the nonrecoverable development costs of the Anglo-French Concorde project is already in excess of £275,000,000, and on present estimates will reach £440,000,000. The implication is that the British government values a supersonic transport more than thirty times as highly as it values the lives of the nine million refugees. Australia is another country which, on a per capita basis, is well up in the "aid to Bengal" table. Australia's aid, however, amounts to less than one-twelfth of the cost of Sydney's new opera house. The total amount given, from all sources, now stands at about £65,000,000. The estimated cost of keeping the refugees alive for one year is £464,000,000. Most of the refugees have now been in the camps for more than six months. The World Bank has said that India needs a minimum of £300,000,000 in assistance from other countries before the end of the year. It seems obvious that assistance on this scale will not be forthcoming. India will be forced to choose between letting the refugees starve or diverting funds from her own development program, which will mean that more of her own people will starve in the future.[1]

These are the essential facts about the present situation in Bengal. So far as it concerns us here, there is nothing unique about this situation except its magnitude. The Bengal emergency is just the latest and most acute of a series of major emergencies in various parts of the world, arising both from natural and from man-made causes. There are also many parts of the world in which people die from malnutrition and lack of food independent of any special emergency. I take Bengal as my example only because it is the present concern, and because the size of the problem has ensured that it has been given adequate publicity. Neither individuals nor governments can claim to be unaware of what is happening there.

What are the moral implications of a situation like this? In what follows, I shall argue that the way people in relatively affluent countries react to a situation like that in Bengal cannot be justified; indeed, the whole way we look at moral issues—our moral conceptual scheme—needs to be altered, and with it, the way of life that has come to be taken for granted in our society.

In arguing for this conclusion I will not, of course, claim to be morally neutral. I shall, however, try to argue for the moral position

1. There was also a third possibility: that India would go to war to enable the refugees to return to their lands. Since I wrote this paper, India has taken this way out. The situation is no longer that described above, but this does not affect my argument, as the next paragraph indicates.

that I take, so that anyone who accepts certain assumptions, to be made explicit, will, I hope, accept my conclusion.

I begin with the assumption that suffering and death from lack of food, shelter, and medical care are bad. I think most people will agree about this, although one may reach the same view by different routes. I shall not argue for this view. People can hold all sorts of eccentric positions, and perhaps from some of them it would not follow that death by starvation is in itself bad. It is difficult, perhaps impossible, to refute such positions, and so for brevity I will henceforth take this assumption as accepted. Those who disagree need read no further.

My next point is this: if it is in our power to prevent something bad from happening, without thereby sacrificing anything of comparable moral importance, we ought, morally, to do it. By "without sacrificing anything of comparable moral importance" I mean without causing anything else comparably bad to happen, or doing something that is wrong in itself, or failing to promote some moral good, comparable in significance to the bad thing that we can prevent. This principle seems almost as uncontroversial as the last one. It requires us only to prevent what is bad, and not to promote what is good, and it requires this of us only when we can do it without sacrificing anything that is, from the moral point of view, comparably important. I could even, as far as the application of my argument to the Bengal emergency is concerned, qualify the point so as to make it: if it is in our power to prevent something very bad from happening, without thereby sacrificing anything morally significant, we ought, morally, to do it. An application of this principle would be as follows: if I am walking past a shallow pond and see a child drowning in it, I ought to wade in and pull the child out. This will mean getting my clothes muddy, but this is insignificant, while the death of the child would presumably be a very bad thing.

The uncontroversial appearance of the principle just stated is deceptive. If it were acted upon, even in its qualified form, our lives, our society, and our world would be fundamentally changed. For the principle takes, firstly, no account of proximity or distance. It makes no moral difference whether the person I can help is a neighbor's child ten yards from me or a Bengali whose name I shall never know, ten thousand miles away. Secondly, the principle makes no distinction between cases in which I am the only person who could possibly do anything and cases in which I am just one among millions in the same position.

I do not think I need to say much in defense of the refusal to take proximity and distance into account. The fact that a person is physically near to us, so that we have personal contact with him, may make it more likely that we *shall* assist him, but this does not show that we *ought* to help him rather than another who happens to be further away. If we accept any principle of impartiality, universalizability, equality, or whatever, we cannot discriminate against someone merely because he is far away from us (or we are far away from him). Admittedly, it is possible that we are in a better position to judge what needs to be done to help a person near to us than one far away, and perhaps also to provide the assistance we judge to be necessary. If this were the case, it would be a reason for helping those near to us first. This may once have been a justification for being more concerned with the poor in one's own town than with famine victims in India. Unfortunately for those who like to keep their moral responsibilities limited, instant communication and swift transportation have changed the situation. From the moral point of view, the development of the world into a "global village" has made an important, though still unrecognized, difference to our moral situation. Expert observers and supervisors, sent out by famine relief organizations or permanently stationed in famine-prone areas, can direct our aid to a refugee in Bengal almost as effectively as we could get it to someone in our own block. There would seem, therefore, to be no possible justification for discriminating on geographical grounds.

There may be a greater need to defend the second implication of my principle—that the fact that there are millions of other people in the same position, in respect to the Bengali refugees, as I am, does not make the situation significantly different from a situation in which I am the only person who can prevent something very bad from occurring. Again, of course, I admit that there is a psychological difference between the cases; one feels less guilty about doing nothing if one can point to others, similarly placed, who have also done nothing. Yet this can make no real difference to our moral obligations.[2] Should I consider that I am less obliged to pull the drowning child out of the pond if on looking around I see other people, no further away than I am, who have also noticed the child but are doing nothing? One has only to ask this question to see the absurdity of the view that numbers lessen obligation. It is a view that is an ideal excuse for inactivity; unfortunately most of the major evils—poverty, overpopulation, pollution—are problems in which everyone is almost equally involved.

The view that numbers do make a difference can be made plausible if stated in this way: if everyone in circumstances like mine gave £5 to the Bengal Relief Fund, there would be enough to provide food, shelter, and medical care for the refugees; there is no reason why I should give more than anyone else in the same circumstances as I am; therefore I have no obligation to give more than £5. Each premise in this argument is true, and the argument looks sound. It may convince us, unless we notice that it is based on a hypothetical premise, although the conclusion is not stated hypothetically. The argument would be sound if the conclusion were: if everyone in circumstances like mine were to give £5, I would have no obligation to give more than £5. If the conclusion were so stated, however, it would be obvious that the argument has no bearing on a situation in which it is not the case that everyone else gives £5. This, of course, is the actual situation. It is more or less certain that not everyone in circumstances like mine will give £5. So there will not be enough to provide the needed food, shelter, and medical care. Therefore by giving more than £5 I will prevent more suffering than I would if I gave just £5.

It might be thought that this argument has an absurd consequence. Since the situation appears to be that very few people are likely to give

2. In view of the special sense philosophers often give to the term, I should say that I use "obligation" simply as the abstract noun derived from "ought," so that "I have an obligation to" means no more, and no less, than "I ought to." This usage is in accordance with the definition of "ought" given by the *Shorter Oxford English Dictionary*: "the general verb to express duty or obligation." I do not think any issue of substance hangs on the way the term is used; sentences in which I use "obligation" could all be rewritten, although somewhat clumsily, as sentences in which a clause containing "ought" replaces the term "obligation."

substantial amounts, it follows that I and everyone else in similar circumstances ought to give as much as possible, that is, at least up to the point at which by giving more one would begin to cause serious suffering for oneself and one's dependents—perhaps even beyond this point to the point of marginal utility, at which by giving more one would cause oneself and one's dependents as much suffering as one would prevent in Bengal. If everyone does this, however, there will be more than can be used for the benefit of the refugees, and some of the sacrifice will have been unnecessary. Thus, if everyone does what he ought to do, the result will not be as good as it would be if everyone did a little less than he ought to do, or if only some do all that they ought to do.

The paradox here arises only if we assume that the actions in question—sending money to the relief funds—are performed more or less simultaneously, and are also unexpected. For if it is to be expected that everyone is going to contribute something, then clearly each is not obliged to give as much as he would have been obliged to had others not been giving too. And if everyone is not acting more or less simultaneously, then those giving later will know how much more is needed, and will have no obligation to give more than is necessary to reach this amount. To say this is not to deny the principle that people in the same circumstances have the same obligations, but to point out that the fact that others have given, or may be expected to give, is a relevant circumstance: those giving after it has become known that many others are giving and those giving before are not in the same circumstances. So the seemingly absurd consequence of the principle I have put forward can occur only if people are in error about the actual circumstances—that is, if they think they are giving when others are not, but in fact they are giving when others are. The result of everyone doing what he really ought to do cannot be worse than the result of everyone doing less than he ought to do, although the result of everyone doing what he reasonably believes he ought to do could be.

If my argument so far has been sound, neither our distance from a preventable evil nor the number of other people who, in respect to that evil, are in the same situation as we are, lessens our obligation to mitigate or prevent that evil. I shall therefore take as established the principle I asserted earlier. As I have already said, I need to assert it only in its qualified form: if it is in our power to prevent something very bad from happening, without thereby sacrificing anything else morally significant, we ought, morally, to do it.

The outcome of this argument is that our traditional moral categories are upset. The traditional distinction between duty and charity cannot be drawn, or at least, not in the place we normally draw it. Giving money to the Bengal Relief Fund is regarded as an act of charity in our society. The bodies which collect money are known as "charities." These organizations see themselves in this way—if you send them a check, you will be thanked for your "generosity." Because giving money is regarded as an act of charity, it is not thought that there is anything wrong with not giving. The charitable man may be praised, but the man who is not charitable is not condemned. People do not feel in any way ashamed or guilty about spending money on new clothes or a new car instead of giving it to famine relief. (Indeed, the alternative does not occur to them.) This way of looking at the matter cannot be justified. When we buy new clothes not to keep ourselves warm but to look "well-dressed" we are not providing for any important need. We would not be sacrificing anything significant if we were to continue to wear our old clothes, and give the money to famine relief. By doing so, we would be preventing another person from starving. It follows from what I have said earlier that we ought to give money away, rather than spend it on clothes which we do not need to keep us warm. To do so is not charitable, or generous. Nor is it the kind of act which philosophers and theologians have called "supererogatory"—an act which it would be good to do, but not wrong not to do. On the contrary, we ought to give the money away, and it is wrong not to do so.

I am not maintaining that there are no acts which are charitable, or that there are no acts which it would be good to do but not wrong not to do. It may be possible to redraw the distinction between duty and charity in some other place. All I am arguing here is that the present way of drawing the distinction, which makes it an act of charity for a man living at the level of affluence which most people in the "developed nations" enjoy to give money to save someone else from starvation, cannot be supported. It is beyond the scope of my argument to consider whether the distinction should be redrawn or abolished altogether. There would be many other possible ways of drawing the distinction–for instance, one might decide that it is good to make other people as happy as possible, but not wrong not to do so.

Despite the limited nature of the revision in our moral conceptual scheme which I am proposing, the revision would, given the extent of both affluence and famine in the world today, have radical implications. These implications may lead to further objections, distinct from those I have already considered. I shall discuss two of these.

One objection to the position I have taken might be simply that it is too drastic a revision of our moral scheme. People do not ordinarily judge in the way I have suggested they should. Most people reserve their moral condemnation for those who violate some moral norm, such as the norm against taking another person's property. They do not condemn those who indulge in luxury instead of giving to famine relief. But given that I did not set out to present a morally neutral description of the way people make moral judgments, the way people do in fact judge has nothing to do with the validity of my conclusion. My conclusion follows from the principle which I advanced earlier, and unless that principle is rejected, or the arguments shown to be unsound, I think the conclusion must stand, however strange it appears.

It might, nevertheless, be interesting to consider why our society, and most other societies, do judge differently from the way I have suggested they should. In a well-known article, J. O. Urmson suggests that the imperatives of duty, which tell us what we must do, as distinct from what it would be good to do but not wrong not to do, function so as to prohibit behavior that is intolerable if men are to live together in society.[3] This may explain the origin and continued existence of the present division between acts of duty and acts of charity. Moral attitudes are shaped by the needs of society, and no doubt society needs people who will observe the rules that make social existence tolerable. From the point of view of a particular society, it is

3. J. O. Urmson, "Saints and Heroes," in *Essays in Moral Philosophy*, ed. Abraham I. Melden (Seattle and London, 1958), p. 214. For a related but significantly different view see also Henry Sidgwick, *The Methods of Ethics*, 7th edn. (London, 1907), pp. 220-221, 492-493.

essential to prevent violations of norms against killing, stealing, and so on. It is quite inessential, however, to help people outside one's own society.

If this is an explanation of our common distinction between duty and supererogation, however, it is not a justification of it. The moral point of view requires us to look beyond the interests of our own society. Previously, as I have already mentioned, this may hardly have been feasible, but it is quite feasible now. From the moral point of view, the prevention of the starvation of millions of people outside our society must be considered at least as pressing as the upholding of property norms within our society.

It has been argued by some writers, among them Sidgwick and Urmson, that we need to have a basic moral code which is not too far beyond the capacities of the ordinary man, for otherwise there will be a general breakdown of compliance with the moral code. Crudely stated, this argument suggests that if we tell people that they ought to refrain from murder and give everything they do not really need to famine relief, they will do neither, whereas if we tell them that they ought to refrain from murder and that it is good to give to famine relief but not wrong not to do so, they will at least refrain from murder. The issue here is: Where should we drawn the line between conduct that is required and conduct that is good although not required, so as to get the best possible result? This would seem to be an empirical question, although a very difficult one. One objection to the Sidgwick-Urmson line of argument is that it takes insufficient account of the effect that moral standards can have on the decisions we make. Given a society in which a wealthy man who gives five percent of his income to famine relief is regarded as most generous, it is not surprising that a proposal that we all ought to give away half our incomes will be thought to be absurdly unrealistic. In a society which held that no man should have more than enough while others have less than they need, such a proposal might seem narrow-minded. What it is possible for a man to do and what he is likely to do are both, I think, very greatly influenced by what people around him are doing and expecting him to do. In any case, the possibility that by spreading the idea that we ought to be doing very much more than we are to relieve famine we shall bring about a general breakdown of moral behavior seems remote. If the stakes are an end to widespread starvation, it is worth the risk. Finally, it should be emphasized that these considerations are relevant only to the issue of what we should require from others, and not to what we ourselves ought to do.

The second objection to my attack on the present distinction between duty and charity is one which has from time to time been made against utilitarianism. It follows from some forms of utilitarian theory that we all ought, morally, to be working full time to increase the balance of happiness over misery. The position I have taken here would not lead to this conclusion in all circumstances, for if there were no bad occurrences that we could prevent without sacrificing something of comparable moral importance, my argument would have no application. Given the present conditions in many parts of the world, however, it does follow from my argument that we ought, morally, to be working full time to relieve great suffering of the sort that occurs as a result of famine or other disasters. Of course, mitigating circumstances can be adduced—for instance, that if we wear ourselves out through overwork, we shall be less effective than we would otherwise have been. Nevertheless, when all considerations of this sort have been taken into account, the conclusion remains: we ought to be preventing as much suffering as we can without sacrificing something else of comparable moral importance. This conclusion is one which we may be reluctant to face. I cannot see, though, why it should be regarded as a criticism of the position for which I have argued, rather than a criticism of our ordinary standards of behavior. Since most people are self-interested to some degree, very few of us are likely to do everything that we ought to do. It would, however, hardly be honest to take this as evidence that it is not the case that we ought to do it.

It may still be thought that my conclusions are so wildly out of line with what everyone else thinks and has always thought that there must be something wrong with the argument somewhere. In order to show that my conclusions, while certainly contrary to contemporary Western moral standards, would not have seemed so extraordinary at other times and in other places, I would like to quote a passage from a writer not normally thought of as a way-out radical, Thomas Aquinas.

> Now, according to the natural order instituted by divine providence, material goods are provided for the satisfaction of human needs. Therefore the division and appropriation of property, which proceeds from human law, must not hinder the satisfaction of man's necessity from such goods. Equally, whatever a man has in superabundance is owed, of natural right, to the poor for their sustenance. So Ambrosius says, and it is also to be found in the *Decretum Gratiani*: "The bread which you withhold belongs to the hungry; the clothing you shut away, to the naked; and the money you bury in the earth is the redemption and freedom of the penniless."[4]

I now want to consider a number of points, more practical than philosophical, which are relevant to the application of the moral conclusion we have reached. These points challenge not the idea that we ought to be doing all we can to prevent starvation, but the idea that giving away a great deal of money is the best means to this end.

It is sometimes said that overseas aid should be a government responsibility, and that therefore one ought not to give to privately run charities. Giving privately, it is said, allows the government and the noncontributing members of society to escape their responsibilities.

This argument seems to assume that the more people there are who give to privately organized famine relief funds, the less likely it is that the government will take over full responsibility for such aid. This assumption is unsupported, and does not strike me as at all plausible. The opposite view—that if no one gives voluntarily, a government will assume that its citizens are uninterested in famine relief and would not wish to be forced into giving aid—seems more plausible. In any case, unless there were a definite probability that by refusing to give one would be helping to bring about massive government assistance, people who do refuse to make voluntary contributions are refusing to prevent a certain amount of suffering without being able to point to any tangible beneficial consequence of their refusal. So the onus of showing how their refusal will bring about government action is on those who refuse to give.

4. *Summa Theologica*, II-II, Question 66, Article 7, in *Aquinas, Selected Political Writings*, ed. A. P. d'Entreves, trans. J. G. Dawson (Oxford, 1948), p. 171.

I do not, of course, want to dispute the contention that governments of affluent nations should be giving many times the amount of genuine, no-strings-attached aid that they are giving now. I agree, too, that giving privately is not enough, and that we ought to be campaigning actively for entirely new standards for both public and private contributions to famine relief. Indeed, I would sympathize with someone who thought that campaigning was more important than giving oneself, although I doubt whether preaching what one does not practice would be very effective. Unfortunately, for many people the idea that "it's the government's responsibility" is a reason for not giving which does not appear to entail any political action either.

Another, more serious reason for not giving to famine relief funds is that until there is effective population control, relieving famine merely postpones starvation. If we save the Bengal refugees now, others, perhaps the children of these refugees, will face starvation in a few years' time. In support of this, one may cite the now well-known facts about the population explosion and the relatively limited scope for expanded production.

This point, like the previous one, is an argument against relieving suffering that is happening now, because of a belief about what might happen in the future; it is unlike the previous point in that very good evidence can be adduced in support of this belief about the future. I will not go into the evidence here. I accept that the earth cannot support indefinitely a population rising at the present rate. This certainly poses a problem for anyone who thinks it important to prevent famine. Again, however, one could accept the argument without drawing the conclusion that it absolves one from any obligation to do anything to prevent famine. The conclusion that should be drawn is that the best means of preventing famine, in the long run, is population control. It would then follow from the position reached earlier that one ought to be doing all one can to promote population control (unless one held that all forms of population control were wrong in themselves, or would have significantly bad consequences). Since there are organizations working specifically for population control, one would then support them rather than more orthodox methods of preventing famine.

A third point raised by the conclusion reached earlier relates to the question of just how much we all ought to be giving away. One possibility, which has already been mentioned, is that we ought to give until we reach the level of marginal utility—that is, the level at which, by giving more, I would cause as much suffering to myself or my dependents as I would relieve by my gift. This would mean, of course, that one would reduce oneself to very near the material circumstances of a Bengali refugee. It will be recalled that earlier I put forward both a strong and a moderate version of the principle of preventing bad occurrences. The strong version, which required us to prevent bad things from happening unless in doing so we would be sacrificing something of comparable moral significance, does seem to require reducing ourselves to the level of marginal utility. I should also say that the strong version seems to me to be the correct one. I proposed the more moderate version—that we should prevent bad occurrences unless, to do so, we had to sacrifice something morally significant—only in order to show that even on this surely undeniable principle a great change in our way of life is required. On the more moderate principle, it may not follow that we ought to reduce ourselves to the level of marginal utility, for one might hold that to reduce oneself and one's family to this level is to cause something significantly bad to happen. Whether this is so I shall not discuss, since, as I have said, I can see no good reason for holding the moderate version of the principle rather than the strong version. Even if we accepted the principle only in its moderate form, however, it should be clear that we would have to give away enough to ensure that the consumer society, dependent as it is on people spending on trivia rather than giving to famine relief, would slow down and perhaps disappear entirely. There are several reasons why this would be desirable in itself. The value and necessity of economic growth are now being questioned not only by conservationists, but by economists as well.[5] There is no doubt, too, that the consumer society has had a distorting effect on the goals and purposes of its members. Yet looking at the matter purely from the point of view of overseas aid, there must be a limit to the extent to which we should deliberately slow down our economy; for it might be the case that if we gave away, say, forty percent of our Gross National Product, we would slow down the economy so much that in absolute

5. See, for instance, John Kenneth Galbraith, *The New Industrial State* (Boston, 1967); and E. J. Mishan, *The Costs of Economic Growth* (London, 1967).

terms we would be giving less than if we gave twenty-five percent of the much larger GNP that we would have if we limited our contribution to this smaller percentage.

I mention this only as an indication of the sort of factor that one would have to take into account in working out an ideal. Since Western societies generally consider one percent of the GNP an acceptable level for overseas aid, the matter is entirely academic. Nor does it affect the question of how much an individual should give in a society in which very few are giving substantial amounts.

It is sometimes said, though less often now than it used to be, that philosophers have no special role to play in public affairs, since most public issues depend primarily on an assessment of facts. On questions of fact, it is said, philosophers as such have no special expertise, and so it has been possible to engage in philosophy without committing oneself to any position on major public issues. No doubt there are some issues of social policy and foreign policy about which it can truly be said that a really expert assessment of the facts is required before taking sides or acting, but the issue of famine is surely not one of these. The facts about the existence of suffering are beyond dispute. Nor, I think, is it disputed that we can do something about it, either through orthodox methods of famine relief or through population control or both. This is therefore an issue on which philosophers are competent to take a position. The issue is one which faces everyone who has more money than he needs to support himself and his dependents, or who is in a position to take some sort of political action. These categories must include practically every teacher and student of philosophy in the universities of the Western world. If philosophy is to deal with matters that are relevant to both teachers and students, this is an issue that philosophers should discuss.

Discussion, though, is not enough. What is the point of relating philosophy to public (and personal) affairs if we do not take our conclusions seriously? In this instance, taking our conclusion seriously means acting upon it. The philosopher will not find it any easier than anyone else to alter his attitudes and way of life to the extent that, if I am right, is involved in doing everything that we ought to be doing.

At the very least, though, one can make a start. The philosopher who does so will have to sacrifice some of the benefits of the consumer society, but he can find compensation in the satisfaction of a way of life in which theory and practice, if not yet in harmony, are at least coming together.

Vulnerabilities and Responsibilities: An Ethical Defense of the Welfare State

ROBERT E. GOODIN
University of Essex

We all acknowledge strong special responsibilities towards families, friends, clients, and compatriots. The moral basis of these responsibilities is traditionally analyzed in terms of self-assumed obligations. That analysis substantially restricts their scope, because we voluntarily commit ourselves to only a limited range of people. In this article I argue that it is the beneficiary's vulnerability rather than any voluntary commitment as such on the part of the benefactor that generates these special responsibilities. This analysis provides an argument for broader notions of responsibility, because there are many more agents vulnerable to us (individually or collectively) than to whom we have made commitments, in any sense. The welfare state is one particularly apt way of discharging at least some of these further responsibilities. Unlike more individualized responses, the welfare state can satisfy the criteria of a morally acceptable dependency relationship.

The aim of this article is to broaden our sense of social responsibility. It is first and foremost an argument in favor of state welfare services. The basic strategy is to try to put them morally on a par with the services we render—and which we firmly believe we *should* render—to family and friends. The method of discharging these other responsibilities differs but, I will argue, their moral basis is the same. A parallel argument, which here I have space only to sketch baldly, generates analogous international and intergenerational responsibilities and responsibilities for protecting animals and natural environments. Thus this approach promises to provide a unified analysis of a great many of our moral responsibilities.

The argument employs the method of the "reflective equilibrium," in which the goal is to bring our general moral principles and our "settled intuitions" about what is right and wrong in any particular case into line with one another, striving all the while for coherence within our set of general principles and for concordance between those principles and our various other "background theories" (Daniels, 1979; Rawls, 1971, sections 4 and 9).

In such a procedure, we must always be prepared to reject some of the moral duties and responsibilities that untutored intuition lays upon us. By the same token, the reflective equilibrium can also carry us well beyond ordinary moral instincts by showing us that we have moral duties and responsibilities that intuitively we might deny having. This is the side of the reflective equilibrium that interests me here.

The moral theory that best explains those intuitions that we do have will, typically, also commit us to moral judgments about what we should do in situations that are strictly analogous but about which we have no strong intuitions. By showing us what lies hidden within our ordinary moral sentiments, the reflective equilibrium can thus drive us to acknowledge commitments we would preanalytically have shunned.

Special Responsibilities

My argument starts from what I take to be one of our firmest moral intuitions, one that we would be loath to sacrifice in this process of reflective equilibrium. That is the intuition that we have especially strong responsibilities toward our families, friends, clients, and compatriots. Charity, we seem strongly to believe, not only does but *should* begin at home. Our primary responsibilities are toward those who stand in some special relationship to us. Strangers get, and are ordin-

Received: February 14, 1984
Revision received: October 5, 1984
Accepted for publication: December 19, 1984

This essay draws on work done while I was attached to the Social Justice Project at the Australian National University (Goodin, 1985a). Earlier versions were read there and at the Universities of Auckland, Otago, Canterbury, Melbourne, and Essex. I am grateful for comments, then and later, from Annette Baier, Brian Barry, Stanley Benn, Ted Benton, Derek Browne, Tom Campbell, Jim Fishkin, Jim Flynn, Diane Gibson, John Kleinig, David Miller, David Novitz, Onora O'Neill, Carole Pateman, Philip Pettit, Val (Routley) Plumwood, Wojciech Sadurski, Marian Sawer, Christine Swanton, Richard (Routley) Sylvan, David Tucker, Patricia Tulloch, Jeremy Waldron, Hugh Ward, and this *Review*'s anonymous referees.

arily thought to deserve, only what (if anything) is left over.

An example from Bernard Williams effectively evokes this intuition. Suppose you were in a fiery air crash and able to pull out only one other victim before the entire plane exploded. On one side of you is a distinguished surgeon, black bag at hand, who could save the lives of several other passengers thrown clear of the airplane when it went down. On the other side is your son. It would, according to the intuition Williams shares with so many others, be morally reprehensible for you to save the surgeon in preference to your own son.[1]

Now, of course, such favoritism would be perfectly understandable from any number of perspectives. Both psychologically and sociologically, it is easy to see why our affections should extend principally to those "of our own kind" rather than to the unknown strangers the surgeon might save. Sociobiologists would point out that saving your son increases the chances of your own genes surviving in the next generation. There is no shortage of adequate explanations for why you would, in fact, favor your own flesh and blood. The question is whether morally you should.

A long tradition in moral theory says firmly you should not. Indeed, any universalistic theory—be it Kantian or utilitarian—would take just that stand. But that, say many philosophers and even more laypersons, is precisely what is wrong with all universalistic ethics. Sir David Ross (1930, p. 21) insists that "the essential defect of the . . . utilitarian theory is that it ignores . . . the highly personal character of duty"; he is outraged that, for example, act-utilitarians are incapable of distinguishing between my giving $10 to my benefactor and my giving the same sum to someone who needs it just as badly but "to whom I stand in no special relation." In a continuing stream of articles, Williams (1973, p. 110; 1981) has been arguing for the moral importance of respecting people, which entails among other things respecting their "projects," including their special commitments to their families and friends. For Parfit (1984, p. 95), "common-sense morality largely consists" in "special obligations" owed to "the people to whom we stand in certain relations—such as our children, parents, pupils, patients, members of our own trade union, or those whom we represent." Or, for a final example, a central theme in Walzer's (1983, p. 31) *Spheres of Justice* is that, "The idea of distributive justice presupposes a bounded world, a community within which distributions take place, a group of people committed to dividing, exchanging and sharing, first of all, among themselves."

Our firm moral intuitions go further still. Not only do we feel that we have these special duties to family and friends, alongside our other, more general moral duties. We also feel that "carrying out these obligations has priority over helping strangers," as Parfit (1984, p. 95) goes on to say. Perhaps those special obligations are not quite strong enough to override negative duties not to harm others. It would be thought wrong for us to commit murder, even if that were necessary for us to feed our own children. But apparently those special duties are quite strong enough to override any duties we might have to render positive assistance to others in general. In *Bleak House*, Dickens ridicules Mrs. Jellyby's "telescopic philanthropy," that is, her tendency to aid distant Africans while neglecting her own family. No doubt most of us are intuitively inclined to say that it is right to satisfy our own children before giving food to needy neighbors. The consequence of acting on such intuitions, however, is that our duties to those with whom we enjoy some special relationship ride roughshod over our duties to help others at large. That, obviously, is an outcome that any theory of social justice, or even of simple humanity, would dearly hope to avoid.

In what follows, I shall *not* be arguing that we lack any such responsibilities toward family and friends. Neither shall I be denying the strength of such claims. What I shall be arguing is that there is *nothing special* about those responsibilities. There are many others with precisely the same basis—and, depending on circumstances, perhaps even the same strength—as those responsibilities that we have always regarded as particularly binding. The upshot of this argument, if it is successful, is that we are not justified in our present practice of serving one set of claimants systematically to the exclusion of the other.

Alternative Bases of Special Responsibilities

The theory ordinarily offered to account for the moral importance of these intuitively appealing special responsibilities deals in terms of self-assumed obligations. That analysis figures most famously in H.L.A. Hart's classic essay, "Are There Any Natural Rights?" which first introduced the concepts of special rights and duties into modern moral philosophy. "I think it is true of all special duties," Hart (1955, p. 185) wrote,

[1]This is just updating and inverting Godwin's (1793, bk. 2, chap. 2) infamous example of being forced to choose between saving your mother or some greater public benefactor (Archibishop Fenelon) from a house fire. William's air crash example is related by Hare (1981, p. 138), who is highly critical of the conclusions reached by Williams there and elsewhere (Williams, 1981, pp. 17-18). See similarly Gorovitz (1977), Blum (1980), Oldenquist (1982), and Winkler (1982).

"that they arise from previous voluntary acts." Hart's own discussion is characteristically cagey, abounding with qualifications, exceptions, and ambiguities. His general principle, however, has passed into the philosophical conventional wisdom pretty well shorn of equivocation. Thomson (1971, p. 65), for example, asserts quite baldly, "Surely we do not have any . . . 'special responsibility' for a person unless we have assumed it, explicitly or implicitly" (see similarly Rawls, 1958, p. 158).

The great appeal of the model of self-assumed obligations is that it explains so neatly what is "special" about our special rights, duties, obligations, and responsibilities. Special obligations are distinguished from general ones in two ways. First, whereas everyone has the same general duties, special obligations vary from person to person: I have special responsibilities that you do not. Second, whereas general duties are owed to everyone equally, special obligations are owed to specific others: I have different responsibilities to different people. The analysis of special obligations as self-assumed obligations accounts for both features beautifully. According to that analysis, I have some obligations that others do not because I have assumed them and others have not; my obligations vary because I have assumed obligations with respect to some people but not others.

The paradigm case of a special obligation is, for Hart (1955, pp. 183-184) as for all advocates of this model, a promissory or contractual obligation. A promissor, through a voluntary act of will, imposes upon himself an obligation that is peculiarly his own, not shared by the world at large, and his obligation is owed to a specific individual, the promisee, rather than to the world at large. Various other special responsibilities—of businessmen to their customers and employees (Atiyah, 1979), of professionals to their clients (Fried, 1974, p. 78), of all of us to our families (Hart, 1958, p. 104) and friends (Montaigne, 1580/1958, p. 137)—are, within this model, seen as more-or-less attenuated instances of this same basic promissory pattern.

Perhaps the most important practical consequence of analyzing special responsibilities as self-assumed obligations is to reinforce our intuitions about their restricted scope. After all, most of us voluntarily assume responsibility in any way whatsoever for only a very limited number of people. On this account, we have no special responsibilities (but only, at most, much weaker general responsibilities) that have not been voluntarily self-assumed.

The model I want to counterpose to that traditional one traces our special responsibilities to the peculiar vulnerabilities of specific others to our actions and choices. It is their vulnerability, not our promises or any other voluntary act of will on our part, that imposes upon us special responsibilities with respect to them. The promissory obligations that figure so centrally in the traditional account are, on this analysis, just a special case of vulnerability. If I promised and others are depending on me in consequence, then I am obliged to do as I promised—not because I promised, but merely because they are depending on (i.e., are vulnerable to) me.[2]

Whereas the paradigm of self-assumed special obligations is the promise or contract, the paradigm for the vulnerability model is family responsibilities. Hart (1955, p. 187) himself admits the difficulty of assimilating these rights and duties to his model of self-assumed obligations. And well he should. You do not enter into families voluntarily. You do not ask to be born; you do not choose your parents or siblings. In the first instance, anyway, you make them no promises and extract none from them.

Even areas of family life that appear on first brush to be contractual turn out not to be completely so. The standard "marriage contract," for example, deviates crucially from the legal ideal of a contract. The authors of the *Second Restatement of the Law of Contracts* are at pains to emphasize that fact: "Although marriage is sometimes loosely referred to as a 'contract,' the marital relationship has not been regarded by the common law as contractual in the usual sense" because "many terms of the relationship are seen as largely fixed by the state and beyond the power of the parties to modify" (Braucher & Farnsworth, 1981, sec. 90; see further Pateman, 1981). Even if marriage partners were to write their own contract, there would be certain duties (such as the duty of support) that would be regarded legally as "essential features" of the marital relationship and which the two parties involved would be legally unable to alter, even by mutual consent. That, of course, violates a fundamental precept of contracting.[3]

To see how completely ill-suited a model built

[2]Hence, I basically have no obligation to keep a promise when the promisee is not depending on me in any way to do so. The only reason I then would is that everyone in society depends on the maintenance of the institution of promising, which is vulnerable to being undermined (however slightly) by my breach. That fact explains why the courts award damages, but only nominal ones, in cases where one party suffers no loss from the other's breach of contract. See Braucher and Farnsworth (1981, sec. 346) and, more generally, Atiyah (1979), Gilmore (1974), and Kronman (1981).

[3]Champions of the voluntaristic model might reply that the parties have at least voluntarily assumed their roles and the concomitant (albeit unalterable) duties.

around contractual or quasi-contractual notions of reciprocity is to the analysis of family responsibilities, consider just two of its more absurd conclusions. First, on that account, a child who lived at home until age 21 would have incurred a debt to his parents 16.6% greater than that of his sister, who left home at 18. But surely the children's obligations to aid their ill and aged mother depend merely on her present needs and their relative capacities to meet them, and not on their past performances. It would be absurd to suggest that the son who remained at home longer should pay 16% more, even though he is now earning 50% less than his sister. (If it really were a case of debt, notice, it would not be absurd: our business obligations are invariant with respect to our capacities to meet them, at least until we declare bankruptcy.) Second, it would be equally absurd to suggest that the debt children owe their parents might at some point be fully repaid, and the children relieved of any further obligation to help parents, however ill they may be. Once contractual debts have been met, any special relationship between creditor and debtor dissolves. The two parties then stand in exactly the same relationship as before the debt was incurred. That is simply not how families or friendships work. A favor and a return-favor do not cancel each other out and dissolve the relationship; instead, they strengthen it (English, 1979, p. 345; Heath, 1976, pp. 59-60).[4]

What most fundamentally underlies the reciprocal duties of family life—of spouses to one another, of parents to their children, of children to their aged parents—is the vulnerability of those parties to one another. The protracted dependency of the human infant is, biologists tell us, one of the most striking features of the species. Much vulnerability is material in nature. Wageless members of the family depend on the wage-earner(s) to bring home the bacon; children depend upon their parents to feed, clothe, and shelter them; in the absence of adequate collective provision, ill or infirm parents are often dependent upon their children for care of a very material sort.[5] But we must not focus exclusively upon these material forms of vulnerability. Much of the vulnerability, in family life and friendships more generally, is of an emotional sort. That fact provides a crucial link in the argument explaining why the material support in question has to come from the particular person it does (for example, the parent, child), instead of some unrelated other who might be in an objectively better position to provide it.[6]

One way to demonstrate the superiority of the vulnerability model would be to survey systematically those "special relationships" that we so readily acknowledge. Among the cases that might be discussed, in addition to the family responsibilities just mentioned, are the special responsibilities of businessmen for the safety of their employees and customers, of professionals (especially doctors and lawyers) for their clients, of friends to one another, and of beneficiaries to their benefactors. The aim would be to show that the vulnerability model can offer a plausible account of all features of all these special responsibilities, whereas the model of self-assumed obligations can at best account for only a few features of a few of them. Such a case-by-case demonstration is, however, beyond the bounds of the present essay and is conducted elsewhere (Goodin, 1985a, chap. 4) instead.

The best quick demonstration of the superiority of the vulnerability model is this. Imagine someone who is utterly helpless. The model of self-assumed

---

Although that may explain why marriage partners have special responsibilities, no such voluntaristic analysis can explain what they are; for that, a separate account must be given. The vulnerability model, in contrast, provides a unified account of both the fact and the content of those duties.

[4]Where families and friendships are concerned, reciprocal favors create bonds transcending the simple sort of trust that underlies long-standing commercial relationships, which amounts to little more than "trust to honor your debts and to keep your word" (Hardin, 1982; Macneil, 1980).

[5]I treat these as "social facts" which should, at least provisionally, be taken as given. In these and many other cases, people end up being vulnerable to certain particular individuals merely because society happens to assign those particular people responsibility for caring for them (for example, parents for children). The only reason that this social allocation of responsibility matters morally is, I would argue, because of the vulnerability and dependency that it engenders. If it is regarded as your job, and no one else will do it if you do not (and if furthermore it is a job that really ought be done by someone), then there is a strong argument for you to do it. That is not to say that it should be your job, or that you (or we) should not try to get someone else to accept responsibility for doing it. It is merely to say that until and unless they do, you should keep on performing it. This is a topic to which I return in discussing collective responsibilities.

[6]Thus, although the courts are committed to doing whatever is in "the best interests of the child," children are not removed from marginally less suitable natural parents whenever marginally more suitable foster parents can be found, and the reason given (the risk of "separation trauma") points, just as my argument here suggests it should, to the emotional vulnerabilities of the child. See Mnookin (1973) and, more generally, Parfit (1984, p. 96) and Blum (1980, p. 56).

obligations says you have only such responsibilities with respect to that person as you voluntarily assume. You might agree to do all sorts of nice things for that person. It would be terribly kind of you to do so, and of course once you have assumed responsibilities it would be obligatory at that point for you to discharge them. But, within this model, you are initially under absolutely no obligations to agree to do all (or any) of those favors. You are morally at liberty to press your bargaining advantage to the hilt, and to exploit mercilessly the other's weakness. You can, and morally you *may*, force that person to agree to arrangements that are highly inequitable, to say the least. For examples, if any are needed, reflect upon the classic cases of "unconscionable contracts": peddling useless drugs to desperately ill patients at inflated prices, or charging $1000 for a hamburger when you find yourself enjoying a monopoly on food at some disaster site.

Now, according to the model of self-assumed obligations, parties in strong bargaining positions like these would be violating none of their moral responsibilities by pressing their advantage to the hilt. The vulnerability model, in contrast, regards it as the height of immorality for them to exploit the other's weakness in this way. The same thing that would enable the stronger to drive a hard bargain with (and, within the model of self-assumed obligations, to evade altogether any responsibility for) the weaker would, within the vulnerability model, impose a heavy responsibility upon the stronger to look after the weaker. In such cases, the implications of the two models diverge clearly. And surely our considered moral judgments, backed up by all our "background theories," side with the vulnerability model on this score. As Green (1881, p. 372) remarked, "There is no clearer ordinance of that supreme reason, often dark to us, which governs the course of man's affairs, than that no body of men should . . . be able to strengthen itself at the cost of the other's weakness."

Protecting the Vulnerable

In spelling out the details of this vulnerability model of special responsibilities, I shall confine myself to three general remarks. The first concerns definitions of key terms: vulnerability, dependency, and responsibility. I use "vulnerability" and "dependency" interchangeably to refer to the following situation: *A* is vulnerable to *B* if and only if *B*'s actions and choices have a great impact on *A*'s interests. Here I equate "interests" with "welfare," following Barry (1965, p. 176; see also Reeve & Ware, 1983) in reading "*x* is in *A*'s interests" to mean "*x* increases *A*'s opportunities to get what *A* wants." Protecting the vulnerable is thus morally desirable because, *ceteris paribus*, it is morally desirable that people's interests and welfare should be furthered.[7]

Central to the concepts of "vulnerability" and "dependency" is the fact that they are relational. You are always vulnerable *to* or dependent *upon* some individual or group of individuals who have it within their power to help or to harm you in some respect(s). This relational character of the concepts is an enormous help in deciding where to settle responsibility for rendering assistance. If vulnerability gives rise to moral claims, then those moral claims must be principally against those agents to whose actions and choices one is vulnerable. Thus, this might be characterized as a "directed needs" model. Saying merely that "*A* is in need" leaves unspecified who should be responsible for meeting those needs. Saying that "*A* is vulnerable to *B*" provides a ready answer to that question.

Vulnerabilities are also relative. *A* would be more vulnerable to *B* than to *C* if *B*'s actions and choices make a greater impact on *A*'s interests than do *C*'s actions and choices. Those to whom one is relatively more vulnerable have relatively greater responsibilities. Anyone to whom *A* is uniquely vulnerable (no one else will help if that person does not) has the greatest responsibilities of all.

Although primary responsibility falls to whomsoever is in the best (or, in the limiting case, the unique) position to protect the vulnerable, that does not relieve others of responsibility altogether. Those who could help, albeit not as well as those with primary responsibility, retain a residual responsibility to do so should the others default, and they also have a continuing responsibility to monitor the situation to see whether or not their

[7]My principle is more catholic than it might appear. Although the definition of "interests" is recognizably liberal, the slippage between what people want and what is objectively best suited to satisfying their desires allows substantial scope for Marxian notions of false consciousness to operate. Similarly, although my principle is welfare-consequentialistic in form, deontologists can embrace it just so long as the *ceteris paribus* clause is understood to include their cherished rights-based constraints on action. Notice also that my principle treats acts and omissions symmetrically. Glover (1977, p. 94), Goodin (1982b, pp. 14-15), and Bennett (1983) show that, once other morally relevant correlates are factored out, not helping when you could have done so is morally indistinguishable from causing harm when you could have avoided doing so. That argument applies with particular force to bearers of standard special responsibilities (e.g., bodyguards and firemen), and would by extension apply equally forcefully to all vulnerability-based responsibilities that I have here argued are analogous.

assistance is in fact required (Feinberg, 1970, p. 244).[8]

Let us consider next the definition of responsibility. There are various forms, among them: causal responsibility (you produced this result); moral responsibility (you are to blame for it); and task responsibility (it's your job). Often we slide carelessly from one sense to another. To employ a pun that has frequently been mistaken for an argument, it is commonly said that those who are responsible should be made responsible. That is to say, (task) responsibility should be settled on those who are (causally) responsible. If *A*'s actions have caused some unfortunate situation, then according to this rule it should be *A*'s job to correct it. Most especially, if *A* got himself into a jam, it should be *A*'s responsibility to get himself out of it.

My argument is that task responsibility and causal responsibility are separable, logically, and should often be separated in practice. On my analysis, how *A* got into his present state is irrelevant. All that matters now is who is best able to get him out.[9] Sometimes—maybe even typically, for all I know—the person causally responsible for producing a state of affairs will be best able to reverse it. If so, then the pun will point us in the right direction. But in a great many cases, the agent best able to get a person out of a jam might well be someone other than the agent who got that person into it. Then, I would argue, task responsibility should be settled upon the former, even though that agent is in no way causally responsible. When the wake from a passing speedboat capsizes my sailboat, it must be the responsibility of other nearby sailors rather than the long-gone speeder to pull me out of the water.

That rule might, admittedly, tend to encourage improvident behavior. People could always rely on others to clean up their messes or get them out of jams they got themselves into. But providing appropriate counters to those perverse incentives is a practical rather than a moral matter. Incentives, as Rawls (1971, sec. 48) and Feinberg (1970, p. 94) rightly emphasize, are nothing more than socially necessary bribes; they do not necessarily have anything at all to do with moral deserts. On this nonmoralized view of incentives, encouraging people to get others out of bad situations is, in principle, just as important as discouraging those people from getting themselves into those situations in the first place. Where the emphasis should fall, in any particular instance, is simply a technical optimization exercise: we should just choose the most cost-effective method, or combination of methods, for avoiding suffering all around. This typically leads us to assign responsibility largely (and, on some analyses, almost exclusively) to people who were in no way causally responsible for the situations they are now being asked to remedy.[10] Furthermore, there are in any case clear limits on the use of incentives. They must be effective in accomplishing their desired goal; they must be no larger than strictly necessary to do so; and they must be no more costly than the goal itself is worth. All this combines to suggest that incentive considerations will not lead us to deviate often or largely from the course of action recommended by my principle of protecting the vulnerable.

The separate question of moral deserts remains.[11] It presents itself as a counterargument to my vulnerability model in two respects. One argument concerns those who find themselves in

[8]Notice an important asymmetry. When those with primary responsibility have acted, those with subsidiary responsibilities are relieved of any obligation to do so. But when those with subsidiary responsibility have, owing to the inability or especially the unwillingness of those with primary responsibility, been forced to act in their stead, that in no way relieves the latter of their obligations or excuses their defaulting.

[9]This saves my principle from the counterintuitive consequence that we have stronger responsibilities for protecting the rich than the poor, because, *ceteris paribus*, people are more vulnerable, the more they have to lose. But of course the more you have to lose, the better able you are to protect yourself from loss: the rich can protect themselves; it is the poor who need our help.

[10]The incentive problem posed here is discussed more fully by economists concerned with allocating the costs of accidents between those whose negligence created a dangerous situation, on the one hand, and those with the "last clear chance" to avoid the accident, on the other. Wittman (1981) has shown that the optimal incentives there require us to impose the bulk of the charges on the latter party rather than the former one. This is consistent with my suggestion that task responsibility should be predominantly forward-looking (who can remedy the situation?) rather than backward-looking (who caused the situation?).

[11]As a kind of hybrid between the incentive and desert arguments, there is a third proposition, which holds that it is our moral responsibility to protect the long-term interests of the profligate poor (or their or our successors, who would otherwise have to pay their bills) by creating appropriate incentives in the present to encourage them to do what they (or their or our successors) will at some future time wish they had done. But the same limits apply to this argument as the earlier incentive argument: it justifies incentives only insofar as they are necessary, effective, and entail less overall harm than benefit to the interests they are designed to protect. Thus, if the arguments of footnote 19 below are correct, the issue will simply not arise. Even if it does, this duty to be "cruel to be kind in the long term" might be counterbalanced by our duty not to be cruel in the short term.

difficulty through their own improvidence: some would say that they had it coming, that is, they deserve whatever they got and it would actually be *wrong* for anyone to help them out of their difficulty. The other argument concerns those who have done nothing to cause another's distress but are (perhaps uniquely) in a position to help relieve it: some would insist that they have done nothing to deserve this burden, and that it would be wrong to impose it on them although of course it would be terribly nice of them if they chose to assume it.[12]

Both claims, however, extend the notion of "deserts" beyond its proper bounds. Take the second counterargument first. Incurring a duty or a responsibility is not necessarily, nor even characteristically, something that you deserve. More often than not, it is something that just happens to you. When walking along a deserted beach, you see a child floundering in shallow water. Nothing in your background or character suggests that you deserve to bear the burden of effecting the rescue. It would, however, be absurd to say that you are therefore morally at liberty to leave the child to drown.

The notion of "deserts" is ordinarily equally out of place in the first counterargument as well. By and large, the improvident should be regarded as foolhardy people whose recklessness is to be discouraged through appropriate disincentives, not as evil people whose wickedness deserves to be punished. In dealing with people in precarious situations, questions of fault, blame, and desert are simply out of place. When two victims of a traffic accident are brought into the hospital emergency room with similar injuries, surely they should be treated with equal care and attention, even though one caused the accident while the other was its innocent victim. The need, dependency, or vulnerability of the victims, not their deserts, is what dictates physicians' responsibilities (Goodin, in press).

The third and final general point about my vulnerability model is that the "agents" to whom these responsibilities fall might be either individuals or collectivities. Consider the problem of famine relief. Millions of people are starving daily. But realistically what could I do to help? There are millions of them and only one of me. In such cases it may make little sense to hold anyone individually responsible; maybe, in my terms, those in need are just not very vulnerable to any single other individual.

Such invulnerability would, on my argument, relieve us individually of any responsibility for helping with famine relief efforts. Excuses of that sort, however, typically serve merely to get us out of the fire and into the frying pan (Austin, 1956). The price of letting individuals off the hook in that way is to put collectivities there in their place. The starving people of the world certainly *are* vulnerable to the actions and choices of those of us in rich nations, taken collectively. Hence we collectively have heavy responsibilities in respect of them.

Collective responsibilities are laid, in the first instance, upon the group as a whole to organize and to implement a scheme of coordinated action to protect the vulnerable agent or agents' interests. But these group responsibilities ultimately devolve onto individuals constituting the group. Each member of the group is responsible, so far as that person is able consistently with that person's other moral responsibilities: 1) to see to it that the group organizes a scheme of coordinated action that protects the vulnerable agent or agents' interests as well as it can; and 2) to discharge fully and effectively the responsibilities allocated to him or her under any such scheme that might be organized, just so long as it protects the vulnerable agent or agents' interests better than no scheme at all would protect them.[13]

In many ways, making something a collective responsibility only complicates things. In one important respect, however, it simplifies them. Making something a collective rather than an individual responsibility removes any objection to the social enforcement of that responsibility. Individuals have many moral duties which, for one reason or another, we think society ought not compel them to discharge. Where the duty is a collective one from the outset, however, collective action is clearly appropriate. Then the collectivity

[12]The most famous counterexample of this sort is Thomson's (1971, p. 48) of a dying violinist, who can survive only if plugged into your circulatory system. My principle does indeed require you to give the violinist's interests serious consideration; but they may of course be outweighed by the other responsibilities, including responsibilities to yourself, on which you would have to default to save the violinist's life. In this way my principle can wriggle out of Thomson's counterexample. Here it is to the credit of my theory that it requires some squirming: they simply answer, "It's my body, and that's that," surely makes far too short work of what truly is a terrible moral dilemma.

[13]Philosophers (McKinsey, 1981) tend to recognize the latter duty but not the former; for more details see Goodin (1985a, chap. 5). There is obviously some scope for trading off these two duties for one another, with political action designed to alter the scheme being preferred to cooperation under the scheme whenever it is likely to be sufficiently effective in instituting a scheme that is sufficiently better at promoting the vulnerable agent or agents' interests sufficiently quickly to justify the short-term damage to those interests.

is fully justified in compelling each of its constituent parts to play its full, appointed role in discharging those obligations, duties, and responsibilities.

Broader Implications

The aim of this essay is to demonstrate that we have a broader range of social responsibilities than we traditionally acknowledge. What I hope to establish here is essentially a point of principle. The practicalities—how best to discharge these broader responsibilities—largely remain as open questions, although at the end of this essay I shall offer reasons for believing that the welfare state is a good way of discharging at least some of them.

The argument for broader responsibilities goes like this. We all acknowledge strong responsibilities toward our own families, friends, and certain others. Once we start examining the sources of those responsibilities, we discover there is nothing "special" about them. It is the vulnerability of the others, rather than any voluntary act of will on our part, that generates those responsibilities. There are many more people vulnerable to us, individually or especially collectively, than stand in any of the standard "special relationships" to us. If my analysis of the true basis of those standard responsibilities is correct, then we have strictly analogous (and, potentially, equally strong) responsibilities toward all those others as well. Aid to vulnerable strangers is thereby justified on the same basis as aid rendered to our own parents or children.

To see what all is at stake in this argument, its ramifications must be sketched, however briefly and unsatisfactorily. First and foremost, notice that state welfare services are essentially mechanisms whereby we attempt collectively to protect vulnerable members of our own society. They may or may not be the best mechanisms available for so doing, and I shall return to that issue presently. But for now, just note that the welfare state, as a device for protecting the vulnerable, can claim at least *prima facie* moral justifiability on my principle.

The vulnerability model, in its collective form, might also underwrite far stronger international obligations than are ordinarily acknowledged (Singer, 1972). People in very poor countries are enormously vulnerable to the actions and choices of people in very rich ones. Again, how we might best go about discharging these responsibilities is an open question and turns heavily upon various matters of empirical fact. It seems very likely, however, that the responsibility imposed on the rich will turn out to be a collective rather than an individual one.[14]

Yet another potential application concerns our obligations to future generations. Intergenerational transfers, especially spanning several generations, are singularly one-way affairs. We can do whatever we like to our distant successors without fear of retaliation. Future generations are enormously vulnerable to the actions and choices of present people, both individually and especially collectively. The things we destroy or use up will be unavailable for them to enjoy. Their extraordinary vulnerability to our actions and choices seems to be the best basis for assigning strong responsibilities to present generations to provide for the further future.

Finally, this model might entail responsibilities to protect animals and natural environments. "Dumb animals," delicate coral reefs, and ecosystems more generally have proven enormously vulnerable to the actions and choices of human agents, both individually and especially collectively. Whether or not that gives rise to any responsibilities on our part to protect them depends on whether this constitutes "vulnerability" in the relevant sense. Earlier, "vulnerability" was defined in terms of the impact of our actions and choices on the *interests* of those who are affected. The question thus becomes one of whether animals and other nonhuman entities can have genuine interests. This is not the place to enter into that debate.[15] It is enough to say that if (and insofar as) we see sentient creatures, ecosystems, or the natural environments upon which they depend as having "interests" at all, then their vulnerabil-

[14]Glover (1975) points out that, although none of us acting alone could eliminate world poverty, virtually any of us acting entirely alone could lift at least several starving Asians out of poverty. The essential flaw with individualistic programs such as "adopt-a-child," though, is that they work on a child-by-child basis; consequently they can end up doing as much harm as good, both for the putative beneficiaries and for those around them. To be sure our well-intentioned gifts have the desired effects, they must be set in the context of some reasonably comprehensive and well-integrated scheme for restructuring the recipient community as a whole. That requires a kind of coordination well beyond anything isolated donors—or even relatively large-scale voluntary charities—could reasonably hope to accomplish. Nozick (1974, pp. 266-267) makes just such a case for organized collective action.

[15]Feinberg (1980, pp. 159-206) persuasively argues that animals, at least, do have interests and hence interest-based claims; and since Routley and Routley (1979) are right to insist that the burden of proof must fall upon anyone who proposes to treat different agents' interests differently, animals' interests must at least presumptively enjoy the same status as our own.

ity will once again generate *prime facie* responsibilities on our part to protect them.

Of course, we will have to balance off one set of responsibilities against others. How much should we allocate to our collective responsibilities for social welfare, as against our private responsibilities for the well-being of our families and friends? How much to foreign assistance, as against domestic social services? How much to future generations, as against present people? How much to the protection of animals and environments, as against humans?

Some might regard these responsibilities as utterly incommensurable and therefore deny that any such balancing can ever be done. Recall Sartre's example of "the young man who is torn between remaining with his ailing mother and going off to join the Resistance. Sartre's point is that there is no way of adjudicating between these two strong claims on his moral allegiance through reason. . . ." But, as Taylor (1976, pp. 290-291) goes on to say, if there really were no bases for comparing the claims of kin and country, then the moral dilemma itself would disappear: the son should just "throw himself" one way or the other, as Buridan's ass in choosing between two equally good haystacks; since neither choice would be right or wrong, there would be no point agonizing over the choice. But that cannot be a correct analysis. We may find it hard to say which is the right choice, but we are quite confident that, whatever else, it is rightly to be regarded as a hard choice. That fact is conclusive evidence that the responsibilities cannot really be incommensurable, after all.

Here I suggest that the notion of "vulnerability," cashed out in terms of the notion of "interests," can not only account for the force of these dilemmas but can also help us resolve them. The dilemmas arise because discharging our responsibilities with respect to some of those who are vulnerable to us entails defaulting on our responsibilities with respect to some others who are also similarly vulnerable to us. Which we should favor depends, I suggest, upon the relative vulnerability of each agent. We must determine 1) how strongly that agent's interests would be affected by our alternative actions and choices, and 2) whether or not that agent would be able to find other sources of assistance or protection should we fail to provide it.[16]

On balance, it seems likely that those relatively near to us in space and in time probably will be rather more vulnerable to us in these ways. Hence my argument is saved from the traditional *reductio* of requiring us to give everything we have to starving Asians, or always to be saving everything for the ever-receding infinity of future generations, or to have our own lives and projects constantly interrupted to serve others. My argument would seem to allow—indeed, to require—us to show *some* bias toward our own kind, however defined. But that bias must not be absolute. The vulnerability of others—be they needy fellow-citizens, foreigners, heirs or hares—to our actions and choices may well be sufficiently large, and how we (and perhaps we alone) can help sufficiently clear, to require us to give their interests some substantial weight in reckoning our own responsibilities. Charity may indeed begin at home, but morally it must not stop there.

Reducing Immoral Vulnerabilities

Up to this point, my argument has taken vulnerabilities and dependencies as given. I have argued that, if people are vulnerable to us, then it is our responsibility to protect them. Sometimes, however, it might be even better to try to eliminate the conditions making them vulnerable and dependent. A few of these conditions may be naturally fixed, inevitable and immutable. But most vulnerabilities will turn out to have been created, shaped, or sustained at least in part through certain social arrangements (Titmuss, 1958). In some respects, this is true of even those dependencies that would seem at first brush to be the most natural, such as those connected with childhood (Marks, 1975; Skolnick, 1975) or old age (Walker, 1980; 1982).

It is obviously immoral to hold people in an unnecessarily dependent status against their will. Moral theories built around notions of free choice, self-respect, or autonomy all yield that same conclusion. But in some cases people willingly do—and it seems morally and prudentially desirable that they should—render themselves vulnerable to a variety of other people for a variety of purposes. In personal relationships, love can plausibly be analyzed as putting yourself in one another's power. "A world in which no one had power over another, and in which no one was vulnerable, a world in which people could be moved to action by force or reason alone, would be a world without love, an inhuman world"

[16]We also need to decide how to weight one agent's interests relative to another's. Where human beings are concerned, I am firmly inclined to weight everyone's interests equally (Goodin, 1975). I am just as firmly inclined to weight future generations' interests the same as our own (Goodin, 1982a). But where animals or inanimate objects are concerned, I am far less certain what the appropriate weighting should be.

(Wilson, 1978, p. 315). In commercial relations, interdependence is the essence of trade and hence of all mutually profitable business ventures. Similarly in politics, interdependence forms the basis of. all kinds of alliances and coalitions (Baldwin, 1980). Objectionable though we might find the particulars of any specific arrangement, there is surely nothing wrong with exchanges or alliances as such merely because they engender vulnerabilities of this sort.

Our moral theories must, then, allow for vulnerabilities, some of which are inevitable and some of which are self-selected. Yet at the same time we must recognize that such relationships are subject to abuse, and we must insist upon certain conditions to guard against that kind of abuse. The standard proposal is that, insofar as vulnerabilities or dependencies are within our power to create or alter or eliminate, they should be reciprocal or mutual. The real objection, various commentators observe, is not to dependency as such. It is instead to *unilateral* dependency, to *asymmetrical* power relations. That asymmetry is what creates opportunities for the strong to exploit the weak. Were each party equally dependent upon the other, there need be no fear of such behavior (Wilson, 1978, p. 315; see similarly Held, 1974; Pateman, 1981; Thompson, 1825; and Wollstonecraft, 1792).[17]

It is, however, wildly unrealistic to demand that dependencies or vulnerabilities be completely symmetrical, that is, that each depend on the other in exactly the same measure. That condition is satisfied in virtually no trading relation, in virtually no alliance, and probably in very few personal relationships. Neither is complete symmetry strictly necessary for a morally acceptable dependency relationship. There are, in fact, two acceptable alternatives.

The first is described by a pair of conditions. One is interdependency: each party must get something out of the relationship; or, alternatively, each must stand to lose something if it were terminated. The other condition is that neither party is so heavily dependent upon the other that the dependent party would cease to meet basic needs were the relationship terminated (Baldwin, 1980; Shue, 1980). The latter condition could be waived in cases of perfectly symmetrical vulnerabilities but becomes increasingly important the greater the asymmetry.[18]

The second alternative would permit monopoly suppliers of needed resources to exist. What it would crucially demand is merely that they have no discretionary control over the disposition of those resources. *B*, who needs the resource, would still be dependent upon *A*, the monopoly supplier of that resource. But *A* cannot *exploit B*'s dependency unless *A* can withhold the resource at will. And it is exploitable dependencies which we find morally most offensive.

An Application: The Welfare State

The *raison d'etre* of the welfare state clearly is to discharge in part the responsibility I have here been discussing, namely, to protect vulnerable members of society. The early British initiatives—old-age pensions, health and unemployment insurance, minimum wage policies, and the like—were all aimed explicitly at "protecting the weakest and most vulnerable elements in society, such as the aged poor, the unemployed workman, the sweated worker" (Robson, 1976, p. 21). The subsequent history of the welfare state has similarly consisted in the increasing recognition of and response to "states of dependency" (Titmuss, 1958, pp. 42-43). Contemporary arguments for the expansion of the welfare state are all likewise couched in terms of dependency and vulnerability (van Lennep, 1981, p. 9; Australian Royal Commission on Human Relationships, 1977, vol. 1, p. 63).

Assuming my earlier arguments have proven persuasive, it is clear that we have a strong moral responsibility to protect those who are vulnerable to our actions and choices. The only remaining question is whether the welfare state is the best way of doing so. Of course, any particular welfare state may fail for reasons peculiar unto itself. It is important, therefore, to separate out and concentrate on what is generic to the welfare state as such.

For purposes of this discussion, I shall assume the defining features of the welfare state—and the features that must therefore be justified in any defense of it—are as follows. The welfare state necessarily entails *compulsory, collective provision for certain basic needs as a matter of right.* Welfare state provision is said to be compulsory and collective to distinguish it from private, voluntary charity; as distinct from more thoroughgoing egalitarian regimes, it provides only for people's basic needs; and as distinct from

[17]"Symmetry" must be subjectively defined: what one party gains from the relationship (or would lose were it terminated) must occupy as important a role in that party's overall life plan as what the other party gains or would lose plays in that other's.

[18]Symmetrical dependencies, even very great ones, admit of no abuse. If each party depends equally upon the other for the satisfaction of basic needs, then neither could exploit the other through a credible threat to terminate the relationship.

the old Poor Law, the welfare state allows beneficiaries to claim their entitlements as a matter of right.

The principal challenge facing any defense of the welfare state must surely be to show why protecting these vulnerable people should be a collective rather than an individual responsibility. There are basically two individualistic options available here. The first focuses upon the responsibilities of needy individuals themselves, while the second focuses upon the responsibilities of their families and friends.

Certainly it is true that people are even more vulnerable in even more ways to their own actions and choices than they are to those of the collectivity. For that reason, they should indeed bear primary responsibility for attending to their own needs. The state's responsibility is in the nature of a secondary, back-up responsibility, activated only when those with primary responsibility have failed to discharge it. Why they have failed, I have argued, is morally irrelevant: my analysis of responsibilities is, recall, forward-looking (asking only "Who is best able to help now?") rather than backward-looking (asking "Who is to blame for this situation?").[19] All that matters is that these individuals are now at risk of failing to have their most basic needs satisfied. That in itself is quite enough to activate secondary responsibility on the part of others to protect them.

The second individualistic option is to admit any need for someone to bear second responsibilities in such a case, but to lodge those responsibilities with some other private individuals rather than with the state. Specifically, this approach suggests that if people are unable to provide for themselves, it should be left to their families and friends to do so. That, curiously, is what "self-reliance" has come to mean in contemporary social policy debates (Goodin, 1985b). No doubt families and friends do, on my account, have strong moral responsibilities to provide assistance in such situations, and at its best, this system is no doubt preferable to state provision: material assistance from families and friends might betoken a deeper affection, in a way that state assistance necessarily cannot. The question is not whether families and friends should help out those in need. It is instead whether those in need should be forced to rely upon their families and friends for such support.

At this point, there is a strong case to be made for welfare-state provision as a kind of back-up to the back-up. An important part of this case is brutally empirical. One of the primary obstacles to an effective system of family responsibility for needy members is that needy people are ordinarily found in needy families, who are in no position to make any great sacrifices (Goodin, 1985b; Steiner, 1981, p. 114). There is also a principled objection to such policies, however, which would prove decisive even if these empirical facts were otherwise.

This principled objection harks back to the standards of an acceptable dependency relationship laid down above. Dependency might be acceptable if: 1) it were symmetrical; or 2) basic needs were not at stake; or 3) no one were to enjoy discretionary control over needed resources. *Ex hypothesi,* we are here discussing an asymmetrical relationship where the subordinate's basic needs are indeed at stake.

The only thing that could make such a relationship morally acceptable would be for the agent upon whom the subordinate depends not to have discretionary control over those needed resources. Where that agent is a person's family or friends, that condition cannot possibly be met: family and friends must inevitably enjoy discretionary control over resources that are, in the final analysis, still their own. Where the subordinate is dependent instead upon the state, however, it is possible to vest that person with a legal entitlement to assistance. Once such laws have been enacted, state officials (unlike families, friends, or private charities) lack any discretion in deciding whether or not to honor claims of needy petitioners (Goodin, 1985b; Smith, 1949, 1955; Titmuss, 1971).[20] The welfare state, defined as an institution which meets people's basic needs as a matter of right, is therefore a morally necessary adjunct

[19]Backward-looking considerations are relevant only insofar as, through incentive effects, they might have future consequences. But there is a substantial body of evidence suggesting that the poor tend to be poor planners and hence are largely impervious to incentives whether these are positive (e.g., incentives to slack off work when guaranteed a minimal income) or negative (e.g., incentives to avoid hazardous jobs); see Danziger, Haveman, and Plotnick (1981), Viscusi (1979), and Goodin (1985b). It is perfectly reasonable that the poor should be unresponsive to incentives: marginalist calculations are a costly business, and the poor have more pressing demands on their time and attention. Given that, however, restricting welfare benefits would probably amount to no more than bringing a gratuitous disincentive to bear on a group that is largely impervious to incentives of any kind.

[20]Discretion disappears only after such laws have been enacted; state officials are left with discretionary control over what laws they enact. But it is the exploitation of dependencies that worries us, and it is in the administration rather than in the enactment of welfare policies that the greatest danger (although certainly not the exclusive one) of such exploitation arises.

to other more individualistic responses to the problems of vulnerability and dependency in our larger community.

References

Atiyah, P. S. *The rise and fall of freedom of contract.* Oxford: Clarendon Press, 1979.

Austin, J. L. A plea for excuses. *Proceedings of the Aristotelian Society,* 1956, *57,* 1-30.

Australia, Royal Commission on Human Relationships. *Final report.* Canberra: Australian Government Publishing Service, 1977.

Baldwin, D. A. Interdependence and power: a conceptual analysis. *International Organization,* 1980, *34,* 471-506.

Barry, B. *Political argument.* London: Routledge & Kegan Paul, 1965.

Bennett, J. Positive and negative relevance. *American Philosophical Quarterly,* 1983, *20,* 185-194.

Blum, L. A. *Friendship, altruism and morality.* London: Routledge & Kegan Paul, 1980.

Braucher, R., & Farnsworth, E. A. *Restatement (second) of the law of contracts.* St. Paul, Minn.: American Law Institute, 1981.

Daniels, N. Wide reflective equilibrium and theory acceptance in ethics. *Journal of Philosophy,* 1979, *76,* 256-282.

Danziger, S., Haveman, R., & Plotnick, R. How income transfer programs affect work, savings and income distribution. *Journal of Economic Literature,* 1981, *19,* 975-1028.

English, J. What do grown children owe their parents? In O. O'Neill & W. Ruddick (Eds.), *Having children.* New York: Oxford University Press, 1979.

Feinberg, J. *Doing and deserving.* Princeton, N.J.: Princeton University Press, 1970.

Feinberg, J. *Rights, justice and the bounds of liberty.* Princeton, N.J.: Princeton University Press, 1980.

Fried, C. *Medical experimentation.* New York: American Elsevier, 1974.

Gilmore, G. *The death of contract.* Columbus: Ohio State University Press, 1974.

Glover, J. It makes no difference whether or not I do it. *Proceedings of the Aristotelian Society (Supplement),* 1975, *49,* 171-190.

Glover, J. *Causing death and saving lives.* Harmondsworth, Mddx.: Penguin, 1977.

Godwin, W. *Enquiry concerning political justice.* London: G. G. J. & J. Robinson, 1793.

Goodin, R. E. How to determine who should get what. *Ethics,* 1975, *85,* 310-321.

Goodin, R. E. Discounting discounting. *Journal of Public Policy,* 1982a, *2,* 53-72.

Goodin, R. E. *Political theory and public policy.* Chicago: University of Chicago Press, 1982b.

Goodin, R. E. *Protecting the vulnerable: A re-analysis of our social responsibilities.* Chicago: University of Chicago Press, 1985a.

Goodin, R. E. Negating positive desert claims. *Political Theory,* in press.

Goodin, R. E. Self-reliance versus the welfare state. *Journal of Social Policy,* 1985b, *14,* 25-47.

Gorovitz, S. Bigotry, loyalty and malnutrition. In P. Brown & H. Shue (Eds.), *Food Policy.* New York: Free Press, 1977.

Hardin, R. Exchange theory on strategic bases. *Social Science Information,* 1982, *21,* 251-272.

Hare, R. M. *Moral thinking.* Oxford: Clarendon Press, 1981.

Hart, H. L. A. Are there any natural rights? *Philosophical Review,* 1955, *64,* 175-191.

Hart, H. L. A. Legal and moral obligation. In A. I. Melden (Ed.), *Essays in moral philosophy.* Seattle: University of Washington Press, 1958.

Heath, A. *Rational choice and social exchange.* Cambridge: Cambridge University Press, 1976.

Held, V. Marx, sex and the transformation of society. *Philosophical Forum,* 1974, *5,* 168-183.

Kronman, A. T. A new champion for the will theory. *Yale Law Journal,* 1981, *91,* 404-423.

Macneil, I. R. *The new social contract.* New Haven, Conn.: Yale University Press, 1980.

Marks, F. R. Detours on the road to maturity. *Law and Contemporary Problems,* 1975, *39* (Summer), 78-92.

McKinsey, M. Obligations to the starving. *Nous,* 1981, *15,* 309-323.

Mnookin, R. H. Foster care—in whose best interests? *Harvard Educational Review,* 1973, *43,* 599-638.

Montaigne, M. Of friendship. In D. M. Frame (Trans.), *The complete essays of Montaigne.* Stanford, Calif.: Stanford University Press, 1958 (originally published 1580).

Nozick, R. *Anarchy, state and utopia.* Oxford: Blackwell, 1974.

Oldenquist, A. Loyalties. *Journal of Philosophy,* 1982, *79,* 173-193.

Parfit, D. *Reasons and persons.* Oxford: Clarendon Press, 1984.

Pateman, C. The shame of the marriage contract. Mimeo, University of Sydney, 1981.

Rawls, J. Justice as fairness. *Philosophical Review,* 1958, *67,* 164-194.

Rawls, J. *A theory of justice.* Cambridge, Mass.: Harvard University Press, 1971.

Reeve, A., & Ware, A. Interests in political theory. *British Journal of Political Science,* 1983, *13,* 379-400.

Robson, W. A. *Welfare state and welfare society.* London: Allen & Unwin, 1976.

Ross, W. D. *The right and the good.* Oxford: Clarendon Press, 1930.

Routley, R., & Routley, V. Against the inevitability of human chauvinism. In K. Goodpaster & K. Sayre (Eds.), *Ethics and problems of the twenty-first century.* Notre Dame, Ind.: Notre Dame University Press, 1979.

Shue, H. *Basic rights.* Princeton, N.J.: Princeton University Press, 1980.

Singer, P. Famine, affluence and morality. *Philosophy and Public Affairs,* 1972, *1,* 229-243.

Skolnick, A. The limits of childhood. *Law and Contemporary Problems,* 1975, *39* (Summer), 38-77.

Smith, A. D. Public assistance as a social obligation. *Harvard Law Review,* 1949, *63,* 266-288.

Smith, A. D. *The right to life.* Chapel Hill: University of North Carolina Press, 1955.

Steiner, G. Y. *The futility of family policy.* Washington, D.C.: Brookings Institution, 1981.

Taylor, C. Responsibility for self. In A. O. Rorty (Ed.), *The identities of persons.* Berkeley: University of California Press, 1976.

Thompson, W. *Appeal of one half of the human race.* London: Longman, 1825.

Thompson, J. J. A defense of abortion. *Philosophy and Public Affairs,* 1971, *1,* 47-66.

Titmuss, R. M. The social division of welfare. In R. M. Titmuss, *Essays on "the welfare state."* London: Allen & Unwin, 1958.

Titmuss, R. M. Welfare "rights," law and discretion. *Political Quarterly,* 1971, *42,* 113-132.

van Lennep, E. Opening address. In *The Welfare state in crisis.* Paris: Organisation for Economic Co-operation and Development, 1981.

Viscusi, W. K. *Employment hazards.* Cambridge, Mass.: Harvard University Press, 1979.

Walker, A. The social creation of poverty and dependence in old age. *Journal of Social Policy,* 1980, *9,* 49-75.

Walker, A. Dependency in old age. *Social Policy and Administration,* 1982, *16,* 115-135.

Walzer, M. *Spheres of justice.* New York: Basic Books 1983.

Williams, B. A critique of utilitarianism. In J. J. C Smart & B. Williams, *Utilitarianism, for anc against.* Cambridge: Cambridge University Press 1973.

Williams, B. *Moral luck.* Cambridge: Cambridge Uni versity Press, 1981.

Wilson, J. R. S. In one another's power. *Ethics,* 1978 *88,* 299-315.

Winkler, E. R. Utilitarian idealism and personal rela tions. *Canadian Journal of Philosophy,* 1982, *12,* 265-286.

Wittman, D. Optimal pricing of sequential inputs: las clear chance, mitigation of damages and related doc trines in the law. *Journal of Legal Studies,* 1981, *10* 65-91.

Wollstonecraft, M. *A vindication of the rights o women* (2nd ed.). London: J. Johnson, 1792.

CHARITY, FAMILY AID, AND WELFARE RIGHTS

James W. Nickel

Early in his first term, President Reagan made a number of statements advocating private charity as a partial replacement for the expensive welfare programs he wanted to prune or eliminate. For example:

> I have a distinct feeling . . . that we have drifted, as a people, too far away from the voluntarism that so characterized our country for so many years. And we have, in a sense, abdicated and turned over to government things that used to be functions of the community and neighborhood. And now with what we're doing here in our economic plan, there is a great need to return to that.[1]

One reason why Reagan's idea of substituting private charity for welfare programs is attractive to many people is that it combines an emphasis on the shortcomings of welfare programs with praise of the generosity that one finds in voluntary giving. Reagan suggested that private charity systems are preferable to systems of welfare rights because they allow the giver to benefit from acting on charity and compassion; because they "recapture the spirit of generosity that suffocates under heavy taxation and bureaucratic redtape"; because they have lower overhead costs; and because they encourage self-help more than welfare systems: "one of the things that government has done with its good intentions is to violate the old rule that you can give a hungry man a fish and he'll be hungry tomorrow, or you can teach him to fish and he'll never be hungry again."[2]

The emphasis on private charity as a replacement for welfare rights did not survive the second year of the Reagan administration; the probable explanation of this is that it became apparent—and was eventually admitted by the White House—that there was no chance whatever that private giving could in fact replace welfare programs. Nevertheless, this idea continues to be attractive to some people, particularly libertarians, and hence some reflection on "private" alternatives to the welfare state is worthwhile. In this paper I focus on two such alternatives: private charity and duties on families to aid their members. I will try to show that the limitations of these systems—which were the ones we mainly relied on before we had a welfare state—provide good reasons for the transition to a tax-supported system of aid to the needy.

The Traditional System

Reagan's vision of the good society sees it as having sturdy, energetic, and productive people who take care of themselves within a free legal and economic structure. The means of doing this, he suggests, are self-help and voluntary aid. Self-help means that most people will provide for their own needs through work, saving, and private insurance. There are, of course, people who cannot provide for themselves because of illness, age, bad luck, or oppressive economic conditions, and this is where voluntary aid is needed. Both individuals and organized charities can provide such aid through voluntary contributions.

Self-help and voluntary aid were certainly key features of the American social system prior to the emergence of the welfare state (and, of course, are still key features today). But this description of the elements of the traditional system of support for the needy leaves out one key component, namely duties on families to provide for members who are unable to provide for themselves. During infancy, childhood, illness, and old age, all of us are likely to require assistance from others. The traditional way of providing this assistance was to impose duties on families to support and care for their members during these periods. We still use this approach for children; parents have moral and legal duties to provide them with support. But the welfare state has partially relieved families of the duty to provide their members with care during illness and support during disability and old age.

Reflection on these matters makes it apparent that the main historical alternative to the welfare state was not private charity; it was, rather, a system that placed duties to aid on families. And these duties were often very burdensome. Charitable giving never replaced these duties of families; its role in this area was mainly to aid people without families or whose families were unwilling or unable to help them. Charity has never borne more than a small part of social welfare costs; it was families that traditionally bore the bulk of these costs. Thus, if one really wanted to eliminate or severely prune the welfare state, one would have to advocate something less popular than a greater role for private charity. One would have to advocate a greater role for morally and legally backed duties of family aid.

The Nature and Limitations of Charity Systems

A. *The Nature of Charity.* To understand the difference between charitable aid and aid in response to welfare rights, think of a continuum with rights to aid correlated with duties to give at one end, and pure gifts totally unconnected with duties or responsibilities at the other.

Right to Aid		No claim; pure gift
x	---	x
Duties to give		Full discretion about giving

Charity need not involve any duties at all; in some cases it is simply a natural human response, based on sympathy or compassion, to people in need. In this kind of case, there is full discretion about giving; nothing is mandatory. But we don't view all charitable aid as being at the extreme right of this continuum; we recognize duties of charity that require us to make donations of a certain size but leave us discretion as to whom to give to, what to give, and when. For example, we may recognize the duty to tithe, or the duty to assist our neighbors when they are in need. But such duties of charity allow considerable discretion as to the time and manner of their discharge. They are not duties *to* specific parties and hence don't generate rights.

Aid in response to rights, on the other hand, is largely nondiscretionary. If the right holder chooses to exercise his or her right to aid, the addressee of the right has little choice about whether and what he or she will give. Compare, for example, the situation of the victim in the Parable of the Good Samaritan with the situation he would have been in today as a holder of welfare rights in a first-world welfare state. In the parable, the victim had been robbed and beaten and needed help, and a number of people ignored his needs (they exercised their discretion as to which parties to help). Finally, a Samaritan voluntarily aided the victim by binding his wounds, taking him to a hotel where he could recover, and paying his bill in advance. Today the victim could have called out for one of the passersby to call an ambulance, knowing that an ambulance crew is obligated to come, and that the government health service, or universal health insurance, will cover the ambulance and hospital costs. Removing most aspects of the giver's discretion about whether and when to give aid is essential to the transition from a system of charity to a system of rights.

B. *Informal Charity Systems.* Instances of informal charity systems include giving to a panhandler or helping out a neighbor. It may be in these sorts of giving that the values of charity identified above are best expressed. It is somewhat misleading to call these activities a "system," since they are not very systematic. As informal activities, they have few established procedures.

But the defects of informal charity systems as sources of aid to the needy are obvious. First, they are small in scale; their capacities are limited. There may be too few donors for the needs present. Second, coverage for those in need is likely to be spotty, uncomprehensive. This may be because no donor is within call or because the donors that are within call have used their discretion and given to other, perhaps more distant, causes. This spottiness was noted by John Stuart Mill. He remarked that "Charity almost always does too much or too little: it lavishes its bounty in one place, and leaves people to starve in another."[3] Third, many people will not belong to groups that will help them. Derelicts may be driven from town. The discretion to give or withhold may allow givers to restrict their help to those that they approve of, thus making destitution the penalty for immorality or having the wrong religious beliefs. And fourth, the help provided may be incompetent; we want an ambulance, not a Good Samaritan with a donkey.

C. *Formal Charity Systems.* To overcome these limitations, we have developed formal or bureaucratic charities. In a formal charity system, hired and voluntary workers encourage giving, collect funds, budget those funds, and distribute part of them to target groups. This yields a relationship with three parties; there is now a person in the middle between the donor and the recipient. The most important aspect of this, I think, is that collection (paying) is separated from disbursement (serving).

The advantages of large charitable organizations are that giving can be increased through formal solicitation, much larger projects can be undertaken, and the spottiness of informal charity systems can be partially eliminated. The absence of donors during a given season can be prevented by budgeting. The absence of donors in a location can be prevented by seeking out members of the target group wherever they are.

But formal charity systems also have substantial disadvantages. First, because the gift relationship is divided into collection and disbursement, some of the value that informal aid has for the donor is lost. Writing a check usually isn't as expressive of love or solidarity as delivering food. Second, the overhead of organized charities is often high. When many people need help, large bureaucratic organizations are inevitable. And there is little reason to think that private bureaucracies will be more efficient than public ones. Further, since giving is discretionary, the costs of raising money are likely to be much higher than they are when one can rely on an income tax system.

Leaving education aside, early government efforts in the welfare area included pensions for former soldiers, military hospitals, famine relief, and poor houses and poor farms to provide aid to indigents who were not assisted by private charities. When most of the burden of support for those unable to support themselves was borne by families and community groups, government programs could be small and relatively inexpensive. This illustrates a general feature of welfare systems, namely that how expensive they are will depend in part on how many of those eligible decide to forgo benefits because reliance on private sources promises a better quantity or quality of service.

Income support programs today include Social Security, welfare and Aid to Families with Dependent Children, food stamps, housing subsidies, and unemployment compensation programs. These are among the "entitlement" programs that consume much of our nonmilitary federal spending, and their costs are fairly high. Social spending includes not only these costs but also expenditures for health care and education.

Systems of welfare rights have the capacity to deal with millions of people, to provide a regular and reliable supply, and to eliminate spottiness, i.e., to offer services to every person who meets the need requirements. In order to match these capacities – given the numbers of people who now rely on public assistance – organized charities would have to become immensely larger and more bureaucratic, and their fund-raising efforts would need to twist the arms of hundreds of millions of people. Since arm-twisting is an expensive way of raising money, overhead costs would be enormous.

The cost of public assistance programs is in the hundreds of billions, and hence the idea that these programs could be adequately replaced by private donations is preposterous – as the Reagan administration now admits.

Duties of Families

As we saw earlier, the real alternative to income support systems is family support, not charitable giving. Prior to 1930, Americans who were unable to support themselves usually had to rely on their families for support; welfare and charity systems mainly served those who did not have families to support them.

The burdens involved in caring for the sick, disabled, retarded, and elderly are often severe ones involving both money and time. Food and medical bills have to be paid, and personal care must be provided. For example, meeting duties of this sort may involve contributing thousands of dollars to an aged parent's medical bills or rest home care, staying home every day for many years to care for a severely retarded child, or sharing one's home and food with an unemployed, disabled, or aged family member. To get most people to bear burdens of this size, substantial social or legal pressure is necessary – and many societies have created systems to generate and apply such pressure. But even with such pressure available, these burdens are extremely difficult for many families to bear and simply impossible for some. Thus the traditional system has severe disadvantages in regard to the size of burdens it imposes on some families and the spottiness of the coverage it provides.

A system of family aid is a simple form of insurance system since it spreads the costs of caring for people during infancy, illness, disability, and old age over a group of people – albeit a small one – and hence makes it more likely that burdens can be borne and that care will be available. But given the severity of the burdens involved in caring for the disabled, sick, retarded, and aged, systems of insurance that spread these costs over larger groups will be attractive.

Insurance systems can be viewed either as mechanisms for self-help (means whereby a prudent person provides in advance for situations in which he will be unable to help himself) or for meeting duties of family aid (where a family purchases a health insurance plan for a member to ensure that it alone will not have to bear that member's medical expenses). If insurance is obtained by a family as a matter of forward-looking self-help, then it will be like saving in that it spreads the costs over time.

Insurance systems are similar to systems of state-supported welfare rights in that their benefits can be claimed as matters of rights and that the insurer is obligated to provide for all members who qualify for benefits. But they differ from welfare rights in the spottiness of their coverage. This spottiness is not merely a matter of the failure of some people to be foresightful enough to take out insurance when it was available; it is rather often a matter of insurance not being generally available or of families being unable to afford the premiums. Affordability is particularly a factor if we think of the ability of many working people to pay the premiums on a retirement annuity that would provide adequate support in old age.

As this suggests, important rationales for the welfare state include easing the burdens on families in caring for members that are unemployed, sick or disabled, and overcoming the inherent spottiness of the family-aid system by using the state to provide an insurance system that is affordable and that provides coverage for all. The system of welfare rights allowed many families to escape crushing burdens of support, and made coverage available to many who were unable to afford private insurance.

Systems of social insurance benefited not only the needy but also middle-class families who would otherwise have had to bear heavy duties of support. They made family finances more predictable and freed many women from the task of home care of the ill or aged. But it also made close ties with one's family less essential, and fifty years of this sort of system have resulted in looser family ties. In many cases today, family ties are not strong enough to resume the burden of caring for the unemployed, disabled, and aged.

This means that the family-aid system is much less viable today and that it would be very difficult to go back to it. Some conservatives might wish to drive Americans back into tighter family ties by removing the alternatives, but I doubt that the causal connection will work in reverse. Other changes that have occurred in American society also make such a reversal unlikely. First, the women's movement has encouraged many women to pursue their own careers, and the result is that far fewer women are willing to stay home and care for the disabled, sick, and aged. This is work that mothers and grandmothers have traditionally done, but we now think it unfair to expect women to bear this burden. Second, many families need the income that two wage-earners provide, and thus many families would find it extremely difficult or impossible to assign one of these parties to unpaid full-time home care.

Conclusion

I have tried to make three main points in this paper. The first is that the main alternative to welfare rights is not a system of private charity but rather a system of duties on families to aid their members when those members are in need. When we see that this, and not private charity, is the alternative, we escape from a false contrast between duty on the welfare rights side and discretion on the side of the alternative; we rather have duties, and burdensome ones at that, on both sides. The second point is that when we compare welfare rights to their main alternative, we see that their ability to spread widely the heavy costs of caring for people in need gives them important advantages: they avoid spottiness and they avoid imposing ruinous burdens on unlucky families. The third point is that social changes have made the system of family aid less feasible than it once was; it would be extremely difficult to return to it as the main means of providing for those unable to support and care for themselves.

University of Colorado–Boulder

Notes

1. President Reagan made these remarks at a breakfast meeting with representatives from the private sector engaged in volunteer work, 21 September 1981. See also the *New York Times*, 25 October 1981.
2. See note 1, above.
3. John Stuart Mill, *Principles of Political Economy*, Book V, Chapter xi, paragraph 14.

MORAL DUTY AND THE WELFARE STATE

JEFFREY OBLER
University of North Carolina at Chapel Hill

AID to Families with Dependent Children, Food Stamps, and Medicaid are among the programs in the American welfare system that are intended primarily to help the poor. These programs have been most adversely affected by President Reagan's efforts to control social spending.[1] They have been so vulnerable, in part, because the poor who benefit from them do not form a large enough voting bloc to protect their interests. Such programs ultimately must rely on the support of the more affluent who are not, and probably will never be, welfare recipients. And this support faded in the late 1970s when middle- and upper-income voters became frightened by inflation and economic uncertainty. If one wants to protect welfare from further erosion, such voters must be convinced to act contrary to their short-term, material self-interest by supporting welfare programs for which they must pay but from which they receive no direct benefits. How is this to be done? There seem to be three available strategies.

The first plays on bourgeois fears, pointing out that without welfare the poor would be disruptive, committing crimes against property and persons and engaging in violent protests. Welfare, according to this view, mollifies the poor, silencing their opposition to a social order dominated by the bourgeoisie. This is called the "social control" strategy (Piven and Cloward 1971; O'Connor 1973: 162-68).

The second strategy appeals to bourgeois compassion, seeking to promote among the more prosperous a concern for the well-being of poor strangers. It then attempts to demonstrate to those who do care that public assistance is the most efficient way for them to transfer their funds to the poor. This is the "state charity" strategy.[2]

The third strategy reminds the more affluent that they have a moral duty to help the poor. To ignore the needy, this strategy says, is morally wrong. The fairest and most practical way to carry out this duty is to allow the state, acting on behalf of the non-poor, to assume the duty to aid those in need. This is the "moral duty" strategy (Tinder 1979). This strategy differs from the state charity strategy inasmuch as it assumes that state aid to the poor is morally required, and failure to provide such aid is morally wrong. It considers state welfare as analogous to the duty of parents to care for their small children. For the state charity strategy, on the other hand,

[1] As of fiscal 1982, spending for AFDC, Food Stamps, and Medicaid were, respectively, 13 percent, 13 percent, and 5.9 percent less than if Reagan's budget cuts had not been introduced. These figures were drawn from the Congressional Budget Office by the Urban Institute and reported by Nicholas Lemann (1984).

[2] The state charity strategy is derived from economists' efforts to demonstrate that public redistribution of income can take place without violating the criterion of Pareto optimality (Hochman and Rodgers 1969). For a critical view of this position see Morris Silver (1980).

state welfare is desirable but not morally imperative, similar in this sense to private American efforts to alleviate suffering in, say, Ethiopia.

It is the moral duty strategy that is the subject of this study. My thesis is that it is not likely to succeed because the moral and political arguments on which it is based are incompatible with how most Americans view morality and politics. More precisely, I hypothesize that most Americans (1) believe that they have at best a supererogatory duty to provide poor strangers the kind of help most welfare programs offer, and (2) have little incentive to make a "contract" to provide poor relief.

Even if most Americans reject the arguments on which the moral duty strategy rests, it does not mean that these arguments are wrong. These people may be morally misguided. Thus one might justifiably contend that the American government does have a duty to help the poor regardless of what most Americans believe. I have no quarrel with this view. Yet people's moral beliefs, while not necessarily valid, may be politically relevant. Thus to defend welfare as a state duty when few affluent Americans recognize this duty is politically inexpedient. A moral position must be widely accepted if it is to have an enduring effect on political choices. J. O. Urmson (1969: 69) appreciates the limitations of a moral code that requires too much from ordinary people:

> In the only sense of "ideal" that is of importance in action, it is part of the ideal that the moral code should actually help to contribute to human well-being, and a moral code that would work only for angels (for whom in any case it would be unnecessary) would be a far from ideal moral code for human beings.

True, one need not be an angel to endorse the government's duty to help strangers; yet such help, in the view of most Americans, may be beyond the call of duty. If so, then those concerned about the well-being of the poor would be well-advised to adopt an alternative justification for public assistance.

One might further object that I am mistaken about the moral convictions of affluent Americans who, contrary to my claim, do recognize the government's duty to aid the indigent. This is, of course, an empirical question, and I have no intention to offer opinion data to support my position. (Such data are hard to find.) Much opinion data, however, does suggest that my position is plausible: when a national sample was asked in 1978 whether they believed that the government should guarantee people jobs and a decent standard of living or allow people to fend for themselves, 56 percent more respondents earning more than $25,000 per year chose the latter over the former (Miller et al. 1980: 189), and in an August 1981 Gallup Poll (Gallup Report 1981: 40) only 23 percent of the respondents in the same income group believed that the Reagan administration was treating welfare recipients unfairly. Instead, I hope to show that my position is plausible by revealing that the arguments in favor of a state duty to help the poor are, on close inspection, contrary to current moral intuitions.

Nevertheless, the moral duty strategy is usually preferred by those who are most sympathetic to social welfare. They favor it, however, not because they believe it is the best way to win support; in fact, they are not particularly preoccupied with how this strategy affects those who must pay for welfare. Instead, they choose it because it is the only one consistent with their moral conception of the welfare state. This conception, which focuses on those who receive rather than those who provide welfare, rests on the premise that the poor have a right to help, and it is this right that, more than anything else, makes public assistance preferable to private charity. In establishing the right to receive, public assistance, according to this view, preserves the dignity and self-respect of the poor while providing them with regular and adequate aid. By minimizing the poor's subservience to those who give help, it also reduces the stigma and humiliation that often accompany dependence. Charity, on the other hand, grants no rights and offers only spasmodic help for which the poor can only hope but never expect or demand. Charity, this view claims, accentuates the subordination of the poor, further eroding their already tarnished self-esteem (Raphael 1981: 75-76).

If, as many welfare advocates profess, the well-being of the poor requires that they have a right to help, then someone must have the duty to give help. The social control and state charity strategies impose no such duties; the former instructs the bourgeoisis to manipulate the poor while the latter encourages them to pity the poor. Thus neither is acceptable. This leaves only the moral duty strategy.

Moral Duty

The distinction between inclination and duty as motivations for giving has its philosophical origins in Kantian ethics. Although admirable, giving inspired by inclination — compassion, sympathy — has, for Kant, no intrinsic moral worth (Kant 1949: 144-45). Sympathy and compassion are particular and subjective, they come and go and vary from one person and time to another. They, therefore, cannot serve as the basis of moral rules that must be universal and objective, applying impartially to all persons. Actions based on feelings cannot bind all persons, since not everyone can be expected or commanded to feel the same way. If charity were prompted solely by inclinations, then a person without the appropriate sentiments would not have an inclination or a reason to be beneficent. And since there is no way to compel this person to acquire such sentiments, charity can neither be universally commanded nor morally required.

Reason and not inclination, Kant says, is the source of moral action. Reason makes moral behavior possible, directing the will to act out of duty to practical moral laws. These laws have intrinsic moral value: they are universal and objective. They must be respected and followed for their own sake and not to satisfy any inclination or to achieve a particular end. Kant claims that we have a duty of beneficence because to neglect the poor is to violate these practical moral laws. This duty extends to everyone, even the most callous and heartless. In fact, Kant is especially impressed when such misanthropes assist the poor, for it then becomes apparent that this assistance is offered out of duty and not inclination, giving the action a uniquely uncontaminated moral quality.

Kant dramatically spells out this position in the following passage from the *Groundwork:*

> To be beneficent when we can is a duty; besides this, there are many minds so sympathetically constituted that without any other motive of vanity or self-interest, they find a pleasure in spreading joy about them and can take delight in the satisfaction of others so far as it is their own work. But I maintain that in such a case, however proper, however amiable an action of this kind may be, it nevertheless has no true moral worth, but is on a level with other inclinations. . . . For the maxim lacks the moral ingredient that such actions be done *out of duty*, not from inclination. Put the case another way and suppose that the mind of a philanthropist were clouded by sorrow of his own, extinguishing all sympathy with the lots of others, and while he still has the power to benefit others in distress he is not touched by their trouble because he is absorbed with his own; suppose that he now tears himself out of this deadening insensibility, and performs the action without any inclination for it, but simply from duty, only then has his action genuine moral worth. (145-46)

For Kant, then, duty transcends feelings so even the most drastically unfavorable change in the benefactor's mood does not absolve him from helping the poor.

Kantian morality requires a denial of personal self-interest as well as indifference to the consequences of actions. Accordingly, cost-benefit considerations would be for Kant irrelevant. We have a duty to assist the needy, Kant says, not because of the benefits of our charity but because reason requires us to help. Kant says that if one were to will the maxim "it is permissible to neglect the needy" as a universal law, one would be willing neglect of oneself when one needed assistance. Kant says that this contradiction should be appreciated by rational beings who, even if they firmly believe that they would never actually require help, understand that indifference to the poor can never be willed as a universal law and therefore cannot be a moral act. Kantian morality, demanding an unwavering commitment to pure rationality, is not in harmony with American mass political behavior which, as demonstrated by abundant empirical evidence, is shaped to a considerable extent by self-interest. One need not cast any doubt on the intrinsic worth of the Kantian ethic to recognize that it is not likely to serve as the basis for political choice among most Americans. Beyond this, the welfare state poses a dilemma for Kant; he stresses that the duty to give alms, like other duties, must be carried out by autonomous, rational beings who will their actions in accordance with universal laws. Yet by making coercive income transfers, the welfare state precludes autonomous choices and thereby makes genuine moral actions problematic. True, one can delegate one's duty to the state; but this would still deny a moral choice to all those who would choose not to act morally.

How one seeks to elicit generosity depends on whether it is inclination or duty that induces beneficence. If the former, then one must set out to regulate feelings, stimulating and sustaining those sentiments that are most likely to induce giving. This is the tack followed by most private charities, which, unable to assume that anyone has a duty to support their cause, must attract donations by evoking among would-be donors sufficient sympathy and concern. Intricate moral arguments, unlikely to stir emotions, are eschewed in favor of simple, direct, dramatic appeals, highlighting likable, innocent victims of disease and poverty. When successful, these appeals prompt people to give in order to satisfy their preference to help those for whom they have compassion. Charities cannot take this compassion for granted; if unattended, it will atrophy, drying up donations. Thus it is essential for charities to repeat their appeals year after year, rekindling the appropriate feelings among prospective donors.

For the moral duty strategy, such continuous manipulation of feelings is not necessary. Duty supersedes feelings. One has a duty of beneficence no matter how one feels; it hinges not on compassion, sympathy, empathy, pity or any other feeling. Once the duty is accepted, further persuasion is superfluous. Thus the moral duty strategy entails only one step: to convince people that they have an obligation to help poor strangers.

So clear to Kant, this distinction between inclination and duty fades as one ponders the complexities of actual moral and political choices. Rarely is one or the other the sole motivation for a given choice, the two so subtly enmeshed that any effort to disentangle them would baffle even the most adept social investigator. Yet, the distinction is useful. Moral appeals and judgments are often based on either inclinations/feelings or duty depending on the kind of action considered. We insist, for example, that fathers, separated from their families, have a duty to support their dependent children even if they feel no love or compassion for them. We expect, on the other hand, that most Americans would offer to help the starving children of Ethiopia *only* if they felt sympathy for them. Those who, unmoved by the famine victims, do not help are not judged culpable in the same way as are fathers who neglect their children.

There is, however, no agreement over whether state welfare is a duty or an act of sympathy. Leaders of the Democratic party are ambivalent. They do not deny the role compassion plays in prompting Americans to help each other. But they also believe that it would be an injustice for the government to ignore the poor and that the government's responsibility for the poor is not unlike parental duty. As suggested by their rhetoric, then, state welfare is required by justice. Lyndon Johnson meant by justice that "in a land of great wealth, families *must* not live in hopeless poverty. In a land rich in harvest, children just *must* not live in hopeless poverty" (*Vital Speeches* 1965: 190, emphasis added). For Johnson, any choice other than helping the poor and feeding the hungry is wrong. Jimmy Carter told Americans, ". . . to follow the admonition of the Old Testament, 'Defend the poor and fatherless; give justice to the afflicted and needy' " (Ibid. 1980: 709). The theme of parental duty underlined Governor Mario Cuomo's much acclaimed keynote address to the 1984 Democratic National Convention. Cuomo envisioned government as a family. And while the family embodies not only mutual duties but also intimate affection and sympathy, it is clear that Cuomo had the former in mind when he said that "the fundamental idea" that best describes what a "proper government should be'' is ''the idea of the family. Mutuality. The sharing of benefits and burdens for the good of all'' (Ibid. 1984: 647).

For many years Ronald Reagan, along with other conservative Republicans, spoke out against welfare programs which, they claimed, wasted taxpayers' money and, even worse, mired welfare recipients in a cycle of destructive dependency. Yet President Reagan has not and will not abolish welfare programs for the truly needy. What, then, is his moral justification for state welfare? It is *not* that the state has a duty to aid the poor. In defending his welfare policies, Reagan rarely if ever refers to justice, duties, or rights. Instead, his justification is couched in terms of love, sympathy, compassion, and generosity. He sees the American people as naturally compassionate and generous and he sees government welfare as a mere expression of this compassion and generosity. Here are two examples of Reagan's approach to welfare: ''How can we love our country and not love our countrymen? And loving them reach out a hand when they fall, heal them when they're sick and provide opportunity to make them self-sufficient so they will be equal in fact and not just in theory: (Ibid. 1981: 259), or ''At the same time, with our independence goes a generosity of spirit more evident here than in almost in any other part of the world. Recognizing the equality of all men and women, we are able and willing to lift the weak, cradle those who hurt, and nurture the bonds that tie us together one nation under God''[3] (Ibid. 1984: 646).

This shift to the state charity strategy has been simple and effortless. True, liberal intellectuals have complained that the shift jeopardizes the poor's dignity and security. But most Americans seem indifferent. And this is not surprising, for few were ever wedded to the idea that the state has a duty to aid the needy. Why not? For one thing, welfare advocates have not been eager to proselytize, apparently believing that this duty was widely accepted, having been inculcated through the moral education that takes place in families, churches, and schools. But Reagan's success proved them wrong. Others have made the effort to instill this idea of state duty through three moral arguments. First, people have a natural duty to help others. Second, people have a contractual obligation to help others. Third, people have a duty to guarantee the right to welfare. In the following pages, I will critically assess each argument.

The Natural Duty to Provide Welfare

As human beings, we have certain natural duties toward one another independent of any special relations — family, citizenship — that might connect us. Among these natural duties, is the duty to help others in trouble (Rawls 1971: 114-17). Daniel Lyons argues that subsumed under this natural duty is the duty to provide welfare to poor strangers (Lyons 1969: 92-96). This duty, he says, is required by the general ''human right to benefi-

[3] In his 1985 State of the Union Address, President Reagan said, ''New freedom in our lives has planted the rich seeds for future success: . . . For an America of compassion that opens its heart for those who cry out for help.'' *New York Times*, February 7, 1985, p. 13.

cence'' that exists when recipients' benefits clearly exceed donors' costs. He seeks to lend credence to his argument by showing that the human right to beneficence is consistent with the way gratitude is normally expressed. When people gain much from others' slight sacrifices, only perfunctory thanks is required, for the recipients are entitled to the help. This is the case, he says, when ''. . . Abel without cost could throw Bill a rope to save him from certain drowning. . . .'' Here routine thanks is enough; indeed''. . . if Bill crawled out to throw himself wetly at Abel's feet, dedicating his rescued life to his savior's services, Abel would be more alarmed than gratified'' (p. 94). But when benefits are not greater than costs, genuine thanks is called for, indicating the absence of a right to beneficence.

Further consideration of the norms of gratitude reveals to Lyons an exception to his proposition: there are, he says, sacrifices that no one should be morally required to make even if the benefits realized surpass the costs. If Abel risks his life by plunging into a raging river to save a larger, hysterical Bill from certain drowning, perfunctory thanks would surely not do, and Abel could rightfully expect genuine, profuse gratitude, suggesting that Bill does not have a right to be saved. But this is inconsistent with Lyon's basic proposition, for the benefit, rescue from certain drowning, is still greater than the cost, the risk of drowning. Lyons resolves this apparent contradiction by stating that a right to beneficence exists only if the would-be helper can be subject to others' blame for not offering help: there must be someone to reproach for not fulfilling his/her duty. Abel is not blameworthy, so Lyons says, because it would be too much to ask him to risk his life to save Bill's, and, therefore, in this case, Bill has no right to be rescued (p. 95).

How does welfare fit into Lyons' scheme? Does it impose on taxpayers unacceptable sacrifices? Is it more akin to Abel saving Bill by ''throwing a rope'' or ''plunging into a raging river?'' Lyons has no doubt about the answers: he claims that the poor have a right to welfare payments because the transferred funds aid them more than they harm their benefactors. For these payments, the poor, consistent with his proposition, owe the rich no more than perfunctory thanks, if that, and the rich could be blamed for refusing to help the poor (p. 96). Yet a closer look at this issue suggests that Lyons has not established a right to welfare payments.

For Lyons, rights to beneficence are revealed by how people express their appreciation for others' *voluntary* help. Neither Bill, rescued when Abel throws him a rope, nor a welfare client is required to offer more than routine thanks. This does not necessarily mean, however, that they both have a right to beneficence. Abel, not legally required to act, throws Bill a rope because he recognizes Bill's moral right to help and the moral duty this right imposes on him. This moral right to beneficence is affirmed by the understanding that Bill owes no real gratitude and that Abel would have been morally delinquent, though not legally responsible, if he had not tried to save Bill. Abel has little in common with rich taxpayers who do not necessarily accept others' moral right to beneficence when they make welfare payments; they may just as likely consider these payments as a legal obligation the neglect of which is an act of civil disobedience. They do not expect gratitude because these payments are not expressions of generosity but a legal requirement; their duty is to obey the law rather than to assure others' right to beneficence. For their part, the poor are not inclined to thank the rich for doing what they are legally required to do. In the case of welfare payments, then, the absence of gratitude signifies the presence of a legal right (a point that can be made without recourse to moral argument) but says nothing about whether this legal right conforms to a moral right to beneficence.

Whether the poor have a moral right to aid, then, would be determined by considering whether gratitude and blame are typical reactions to *voluntary* welfare. Let us look at some cases: (1) parents of a critically ill child cannot afford life-saving surgery, and (2) an unemployed man may lose his house because he is unable to keep up with his mortgage payments. (The first is analogous to Lyons' examples inasmuch as it is a life-threatening situation while the second, though not life-threatening, entails difficulties not unlike those often addressed by welfare programs.) Suppose a rich stranger, hearing of these troubles, offers to pay for the surgery and to make the mortgage payments until the unemployed man finds another job. Suppose further that this generosity would inflict on the benefactor no financial hardship. How would Lyons judge these cases? Would he claim that the parents and the unemployed man have a right to help which the rich stranger has a duty to provide? Yes, if he considers only his basic proposition, for, after all, given diminishing marginal utility, the assistance benefits the recipients far more than it costs the donor. Yet, contrary to Lyons' expectations, the assistance would demand an outpouring of real gratitude, and if the rich stranger would ignore these peoples' plight, he would not be vilified. This generosity resembles "plunging into the raging river" more than "throwing a rope." Applying Lyons' criteria, the rich stranger is not morally required to help, a position that, I believe, conforms closely to conventional American morality. Hence, Lyons' argument is not likely to persuade many Americans that they have a moral duty to help poor strangers.

Lyons might complain that my criticism is unfair since Abel and the rich stranger find themselves in such different positions. Abel, after all, is the only person who can save Bill. But there are countless other wealthy people besides the rich stranger who could assist the victims I've described. He is entitled to gratitude, then, for taking the initiative to do what others chose not to do. Gratitude is called for, Lyons might explain, not because no one has a duty to provide relief to strangers but rather because it is so difficult to determine who has this duty.

Jan Narveson (1967) appreciates this practical dilemma. He believes that people have a right to have their suffering relieved, a right that would surely subsume attempts to mitigate poverty through welfare payments. Yet he is reluctant to impose on private individuals the duty to guarantee this right. His reluctance rests on practical concerns. It is, he says, so difficult to define limits to such help. "One could work twenty-four hours per day at the relief of suffering and could impoverish oneself contributing to charity, but it is felt that to require one to do this would be going rather too far" (p. 231). Moreover, the burden of relieving suffering may, as a result of arbitrary circumstances (e.g., Jones happens to be in the neighborhood when misfortune strikes Smith) fall haphazardly, and therefore, unfairly on the shoulders of some while others are not called on to do anything. Now if sufferers have a right to help, but no particular person has a strict duty to help them, where does the duty rest? It is, Narveson replies, a duty of "society," by which he means that ". . . every member of the society has a duty to play some part in seeing to it that somebody performs the action in question" (p. 235). The "somebody," Narveson says, must be the government, for only it, acting on behalf of society, can assure the right to have one's suffering relieved. Private charities will simply not do; "If a duty is genuinely a duty of society, then it is contradictory to say that it should be left up to individuals consciences to be done . . ." (p. 237). Yes, some private individuals may take the initiative to help others, but it would be unfair to rely solely on their efforts. Narveson explains why:

> People who relieve suffering hardly ever do it because they enjoy it; they do it because their conscience tells them that they should. But if their consciences are correct, then it is no more their duty than anyone else's, and it is the responsibility of society to see that it is done without sanctioning special impositions on people of exceptional good will. (p. 237)

Narveson thus believes that from the perspective of those who suffer as well as those who seek to relieve others' suffering, it is preferable that the duty is assumed by society rather than individuals. And this presumably explains why, *as individuals*, we refuse to accept the duty to help poor strangers.

This explanation is not convincing. Narveson says that the duty to relieve suffering must be delegated to society in order not to place an unfair burden on "people of exceptional good will." But if the relief of suffering were a natural duty, then it would not require people of exceptional good will to fulfill it. Everyone is expected to carry out natural duties. Since it would not take a particularly moral person to throw a rope to save a drowning man, this action must be subsumed under our natural duty to help others. The rich stranger who paid for the surgery and the mortgage, on the other hand, would, I believe, be described as a person of exceptional good will. His action, then, is a supererogatory rather than a required duty. It is an action that this person believes he ought to do but that he cannot require others to do. It is an action demanded by a self-imposed duty consistent with a person's conception of right and wrong. Supererogatory duties bind only those persons who have a special commitment to others' welfare. Those who do not share this commitment are not morally delinquent. Yet Narveson expects these people to assume the duty to see to it that the society relieves suffering in order not to exploit those who are more virtuous. Why should they accept this duty? They might rightfully complain that society is demanding them to do what private morality does not require. State mandated welfare payments transform a supererogatory into a natural duty without any clear justification.

Another reason why the rich stranger's action is considered a supererogatory duty is that the very presence of the welfare state alters the moral rules that guide relations among private persons (Taylor 1976: 34-40). The American welfare system, through Social Security, Medicare, and Medicaid, has relieved children of much of the responsibility of caring for their elderly parents. People have come to rely so much on these programs that some now doubt whether children should be required to assume the duty to look after their aging parents. Before the establishment of the welfare state, this doubt would have seemed far more callous (Callahan 1983: 25). If a private person believes that the government, acting on his behalf, assumes the duty to care for those in need, he may feel far less personal responsibility. Expecting the government to intervene, our rich stranger may conclude that he has no duty to help. He shifts his duty to the state. If this were so, then one would expect different moral rules in the absence of the welfare state. Yet this is not the case. Even prior to the introduction of large-scale welfare programs, unilateral gifts to strangers were not taken for granted, required sincere thanks, and thus were not morally required. Today there is no effective international welfare system that looks after the indigent of poor nations. And if there is a general human right of beneficence, it imposes duties to help the poor no matter where they might live. Nevertheless, most Americans do not accept a moral duty to assist private, international relief efforts. Rich Americans do not risk moral condemnation by ignoring pleas from CARE or Oxfam America. Congressmen are not submitted to much pressure from their constituents to expand the relatively modest American Foreign aid program. Yes, many Americans do give; such giving warrants praise, but is not morally required.

Contracts and Duties

The moral duty to help poor strangers is, for some welfare advocates, based on a contractual obligation. Here reference is made not to a literal contract but to a contract model that is used to determine what actions in a given society are morally required. The model stipulates that people who enter a contract voluntarily to secure an advantage are morally bound to carry out the actions prescribed by that contract. Thus a particular action X is a basic obligation when it is, as G. R. Grice (1967) puts it, "in everyone's interest to make a contract with everyone else to do X" (p. 95). Contracts root duty in self-interest rather than benevolence. People accept the obligation to do X only if it is in their interest and if they know that everyone else is expected to do X as well.

In deciding what kinds of beneficent actions are morally required, Grice resorts to cost-benefit calculations not unlike those used by Lyons. For contracts to be made, he says, benefits must exceed costs, a formula that, not surprisingly, yields a duty of only *limited* beneficence. If you were to come across a diabetic in a coma, you would, Grice says, have an obligation to call a doctor. Grice seems to believe that it would be in everyone's interest to make a contract that would require such a modest gesture to save another's life. But Grice has no trouble imagining actions that not everyone would agree to do. If you happen to pass a stranded motorist, who is not far from a garage and who is filthy from an apparent futile attempt to repair his car, you would not, according to Grice, have an obligation to assist him (pp. 123-25). Given the inconvenience to the passing motorist, Grice seems to be saying, not everyone would want to take on this responsibility. People who know who they are and what their interests are would assume the obligation to assist the diabetic but not the stranded motorist. Would such people be willing to assume the more general obligation to help poor strangers? Grice does not address this question fully; he does say, however, that the rich have a special obligation, presumably because the cost of assistance would be trivial for them. Yet he does not explicitly explain why the rich would have an interest in making a contract to assist the poor.

Grice intimates that he appreciates why the rich might not eagerly acquiesce to such a contract. He concedes, for example, that it may not be in the interest of the destitute to enter a contract to forego stealing. But this does not mean, he says, that no contract is feasible or that the contract grounded on obligation must be abandoned. Instead, he recommends that the contract should be drawn to include sufficient compensation for the destitute so they would have an interest in accepting it (pp. 109-10). Thus to induce the rich to form a contract to help poor strangers, some compensation may be required, though Grice does not specify what form this compensation should assume.

Jan Narveson 1967, using reasoning similar to Grice's, does spell out the kind of compensation he would offer the rich. He draws on the well-known Kantian position that one cannot will neglect of the needy as a universal law for one would be willing indifference to oneself if one should ever need assistance (p. 236). Narveson argues that it is to everyone's advantage to assume the duty to relieve suffering because it assures assistance to anyone who might fall on hard times. If the well-to-do should face distress, they, too, would receive assistance. The bargain Narveson strikes with the rich is simple: in return for helping others, they are compensated with security. Ultimately, then, the obligation is justified in terms of everyone's self-interest, for when an obligation is imposed by society ". . . each individual gains more from having the obligation (provided everyone is seen to have it as well) than he loses" (p. 236).

But it is surely *not* self-evident that the imposition of this obligation would make everyone a winner. The rich might correctly calculate that they would be better-off not to assume this obligation. It would be expensive for them to guarantee their own security by agreeing to help people who are far more likely to require relief. It would be far less expensive if they would fend for themselves. They could save, buy insurance, hire private professionals to attend to their needs in hard times. And the level of material comfort they could guarantee through their own savings would be far greater than what society could provide in the form of welfare. Given a choice, affluent Americans would not be swayed by Narveson's argument to sign the contract he proposes. By grounding the obligation of mutual aid in personal gain, Narveson allows people to abdicate their responsibility by simply showing that such an abdication is in their self-interest. This difficulty does not plague all social contracts. Agreements that merely prohibit assault on persons and property would, for example, be more acceptable to all prospective members.

There may be other, more enticing forms of compensation. The poor could propose to the more affluent: "If you agree to provide poor relief, we will agree to abide by the social rules that allow you to accomulate and protect your wealth." This bargin may be sufficiently attractive to induce the affluent to give welfare. But it also blurs the distinction between moral duty and social control; after all, the affluent accept the duty only to assure social calm. The moral duty strategy, justified in this way, loses its alleged value, for the right to welfare becomes ineluctably precarious when it ultimately depends on the providers' interests. Thus the rich might not agree to the proposed contract if the poor were too few and feeble to pose a serious threat, or if the poor were conditioned to eschew violence or crime, or if it were less expensive to punish the recalcitrant poor than to provide aid to all the poor. Thus if the duty to help is rooted in contractual arrangement, the right to welfare is a reality *only* when social conditions are perfectly propitious.

Of course, it would be far easier to come up with an acceptable contract if we asked people to negotiate behind the Rawlsian veil of ignorance. Given that in the original position everyone has a potentially equal chance of requiring welfare, the obligation to provide it would be far more palatable. Even behind this veil, however, some might still reject this obligation, for, as many of Rawls' critics have noted, there is no reason to assume that people in the original position would be so cautious as to protect themselves against the chance of calamity, or to assume that should calamity strike, government would be the only reliable source of relief. From a more practical point of view, Rawls' argument, and more particularly the concept of the veil of ignorance, is not likely to have widespread popular appeal, and, therefore, its impact on ordinary, everyday moral sensibilities is bound to be modest. Rawls' theory of justice, despite its profound and deserved influence among academics, has had little direct bearing on popular moral and political discourse. This may be so because it is couched in such arcane language. It is unlikely that even educated laymen are familiar with such key Rawlsian terms as the difference principle, original position, or veil of ignorance. But his theory is also inaccessible because it asks people to sever their ties with reality. And this may be asking too much. The reality most people construct for themselves simply would not allow that justice requires people to deny their existential traits and then act to avoid an uncertain worst possible fate. Nor for that matter could most people's moral world incorporate other crucial Rawlsian positions such as that 1) one's personal success is based on conditions that are arbitrary from a moral point of view, or 2) one is entitled to rewards only if everyone else benefits. While the veil of ignorance may make the difference principle an integral element of justice as fairness, it also makes Rawls' theory too remote and obscure to have much effect on popular moral values.

Social Rights and Duties

A simpler and more direct way to get people to assume the duty to help others is to persuade them that the right to welfare is no different from other rights, such as civil and political, that already enjoy widespread legitimacy. If persuaded, people would have no other choice than to guarantee the right to welfare just as they guarantee other rights. Then the question becomes how to link these different kinds of rights. Let's consider two efforts.

First, Rodney Peffer (1978) claims that a crucial shared feature links the right to well-being with other moral rights. This feature, as described by H.L.A. Hart (1970: 63-64), is that to protect a moral right, one person may justifiably constrain another person's freedom. Rights permit legal coercion, and this, more than anything else, distinguishes rights from other moral concepts. Hart maintains that legal coercion can enforce *special* rights against particular persons who have made promises or contractual agreements and general rights against all persons who would unjustifiably interfere with what another person should be allowed to do or have. General rights, Hart says, encompass traditional rights such as free speech but not rights to well-being. Peffer sets out to dispute this last point. He claims that, in certain instances, the protection of a person's right to well-being can justify coercion. To make his case, he considers two hypothetical examples. First, to save the life of a celebrated violinist, a person who has the right blood type is compelled to be plugged into the victim for nine years. Peffer concedes that such coercion is not justified because no one should be forced to give up nine years of one's life. Second, "But what if a person need only walk across a room and touch the violinist in order to save his life?" (p. 76). Now, Peffer believes that coercion is permissible. He explains: "Surely, in this case, we would be justified in forcing an obstinate or amoral person to do this one small thing. After all a life is at stake!" (p. 76). Peffer then triumphantly concludes: "Thus, contrary to Hart and most other liberal theorists, there do exist situations in which, though no traditional rights to freedom are at stake, coercion is justified. It is these moral situations that make attractive the proposal to recognize rights to well-being" (p. 76).

The moral situation cited by Peffer is an extreme one in which the cost is so ludicrously trivial and the benefit so obviously great. If we extend Peffer's analysis to cases that are more similar to those covered by welfare programs, his argument becomes less convincing. Let's amend slightly Peffer's pivotal illustration. Now the "obstinate or amoral person" is a millionaire who must give $10,000 to save the violinist's life. A life is still at stake and the sacrifice is still small. Yet it is no longer clear that coercion is justified. If the millionaire refuses to help, he probably would be denounced as selfish and cruel. But to take so much money from a particular person against his will is not something that most people would tolerate. What kind of coercion is acceptable is highly subjective, and people who would not hesitate to force a person to cross a room to save another's life might be reluctant to take $10,000 from a millionaire for the same purpose. Surely, one might respond, society could help the violinist, for by spreading the cost among all taxpayers the burden on each would be trivial. This would be fine if only the violinist would require help; but if we have more donors we also have more would-be recipients. And when society must pay for, say, kidney dialysis, heart transplants, and one day, artificial hearts, the cost to each taxpayer would no longer be trivial.

Second, Gregory Vlastos (1969) attempts to make the connection between different rights by showing that they share the same moral premise. This premise is that human beings have equal worth. Despite all the obvious differences that distinguish one person from another, Vlastos explains, people share a common human capacity to experience well-being and to decide how to pursue their own well-being. This capacity, he says, is not earned, not achieved through individual merit or accomplishments; it is instead a necessary condition of human existence, defining what it means to be a human being; as such, it characterizes the humble as well as the grand. Through their ability to experience well-being, he says, humans give value to other objects which would have no value unless some person valued them. Only man has an intrinsic worth that exists independent of others' judgments.

Vlastos' debt to Kant is evident. Kant notes: "All objects of the inclinations have only conditional value since, but for their inclinations and their respective wants, their object would be without value" (1949: 176-77). Only a rational being, Kant claims, who alone can will his actions according to universal laws, has absolute value, and, therefore, may not be the object of another's inclination. And this is why man must always be treated as an end and never merely as a means. Kant thereby underscores the autonomy of each person and the respect with which each person must be treated.

Vlastos' effort to trace civil and political rights back to the premise of equal human worth is simple, and, from a Western, liberal perspective, rather uncontroversial. If humans have equal worth, he begins, then people's free choices to say, do, and think what they want must have equal value regardless of the outcome of their choices. This being the case, he continues, people have an equal right to freedom, a right that serves as the basis for such specific and familiar rights as freedom of speech, thought, and religion (Vlastos 1969: 147-51).

Vlastos uses the same reasoning to justify the right to welfare. Just as people's freedom has equal value, no person's well-being has more or less value than anyone else's. He recognizes that the welfare of a statesman who could benefit others may have more *instrumental* value than the welfare of an unskilled worker. But he also believes that the welfare of the two men has equal *intrinsic* value. This belief yields a similar if more controversial set of propositions:

— "in all cases where human beings are capable of enjoying the same goods, we feel that the intrinsic value of their enjoyment is the same."
— *"one man's well-being is as valuable as any other's."*
— "one man's (prima facie) right to well-being is equal to that of any other's."
— ". . . this is the basis of various welfare-rights, such as the right to education, medical care, work under decent conditions, relief in periods of unemployment, leisure, housing, etc." (pp. 150-51).

Despite the efforts of Vlastos and others to place the right to welfare on an equal footing with more traditional rights, many people, I suspect, still find the duty imposed by this right more intolerable than the duties required by most civil and political rights. Such people continue to reject the right to welfare.[4] They are among Ronald Reagan's most ardent supporters, who apparently endorse Reagan's effort to limit government welfare and then to define this more limited aid as an expression of collective compassion rather than the fulfillment of a collective moral obligation. For rejecting the poor's right to welfare, Reagan's supporters are not condemned as morally bankrupt, though they are occasionally labeled as heartless. Anybody who would challenge the right to, say, religious freedom would not go so unscathed. While there may be much disagreement over whether school prayers violate the right to religious freedom, there seems to be no disagreement that such a right exists. There is simply less consensus over the right to welfare than over other rights. This is not to say that this absence of consensus is justified. I do not intend to pass judgment on this issue. Instead, I merely want to speculate on why this right is not as widely accepted as the more traditional rights. There are a number of good reasons why this is so given the intrinsic structure of the right to welfare that distinguishes it from other rights.

1. Positive and Negative Obligations

Civil and political rights, as has been so often noted, can be protected if people simply do not interfere in each others' lives. Such rights impose the *negative* obligation of forbearance, of non-interference. A right to welfare, on the other hand, can only be protected if people accept the *positive* obligation to give part of their resources to others; it demands, as do other social and economic rights, a collective reallocation of resources.

This distinction ultimately foils Vlastos' attempt to draw a parallel between the two kinds of rights. If we accept the principle that one man's freedom is as valuable as anybody else's, we would quite naturally not interfere with Smith's right to become a carpenter or to worship in a Methodist Church. But from the principle that each person's well-being is as valuable as anybody else's we would not agree to buy a BMW for a person who enjoyed driving this expensive car as much as those people who actually own one. It is so much easier to permit another to satisfy his wants than it is to assure that another's wants are satisfied.

This distinction between positive and negative obligations does not, as others have argued, necessarily diminish the moral claim of a right to welfare (Cranston 1967: 43-53). Yet, if we believe that people are at least to some degree self-interested, it would not be surprising if they would define their morality, private as well as public, so as to avoid positive obligations,

[4] A 1982 Roper survey, for example, asked respondents whether an adequate standard of living was a "privilege that a person should have to earn" or a "right." Only 38 percent of respondents earning more than $30,000 a year and 48 percent of those earning between $20,000 and $30,000 believed it was a right. Even among people earning less than $10,000 a year, 35 percent thought it was a privilege. Reported in *Public Opinion*, June/July, 1982, p. 27.

to minimize the sacrifices they must make for the sake of others (Fishkin 1982). They would be likely to eschew the more expensive, burdensome positive obligations in favor of the less demanding duty of forbearance. Such an attitude is consistent with Lyons' and Grice's view that the more difficult it is to carry out a given action, the less likely that action will be considered a right. Since it is easier to forbear than to give, civil and political rights are more popular than the right to welfare. And when it becomes more difficult to protect civil or political rights, they, too, lose favor with the public. When forced busing became necessary to permit black children to attend racially integrated schools, an integrated education ceased to be, for many, a right. To lighten their moral burden, people fall back on moral principles that challenge rights that impose positive obligations. One might, for example, deny the right to welfare by claiming that "people get what they deserve," a common notion of equity. Yet no matter how people explain or express their distaste, rights that exact sacrifices are bound to be less popular than those that do not.

2. The donor-recipient bond

One might object, however, that the rigid distinction I have drawn between the right to welfare and other rights is contrived, for, in a certain sense, all rights call for positive obligations. After all, the right to vote would not be protected unless the government spent taxpayers' money to print ballots. Refusing to accept that only social and economic rights entail positive obligations, David Watson points out that "the courts, legislatures, police force, defense services, and administrative services involved in government do not compare unfavourably in terms of expense and effort with provision for the social and economic rights in question" (Watson 1977: 44). Raymond Plant, Harry Lesser, and Peter Taylor-Gooby make a similar point. "Traditional rights — life, liberty, property, etc., clearly require forbearance on the part of others to be met. However, such forbearance cannot just be legislated into existence — the right not to be killed (the right to life) will require protection by police forces, defense forces, etc., all of which are going to involve capital expenditures" (Plant et al. 1980: 77).

All this is undeniably true. How, then, can I claim to explain the more limited support for welfare rights than for other rights on the grounds that the former entail resource transfers? The reason is that stressing how money must be spent to guarantee all rights blurs the crucial uniqueness of the right to welfare, a uniqueness that lies in the bond between donor and recipient whereby some people are asked to pay for others' welfare. Donors give and receive nothing (tangible) in return while recipients receive and give nothing (tangible) in return. Given this asymmetry, the more affluent are apt to complain bitterly that they are stuck with obligations but have, in reality, no right to welfare at all since they do not expect to apply for Food Stamps or AFDC payments. Cynically, they might say that the right to welfare is reserved for the poor who have so little in the way of obligations. Such cynicism may be unjustified but not surprising when a right asks some people to support strangers. (This should not be the case for more universal social insurance programs such as Social Security in which donors eventually become recipients. Yet even here the focus is so often on the tensions between donors — the active labor force — and recipients — the elderly.) Thus the resistance to the right to welfare stems not so much from the fact that money must be spent to fulfill the right, but rather that money must be transferred from one group to another.

Supporters of civil and political rights do not face this kind of resistance. People do not believe that they are assuming obligations to protect other people's rights. Recipients' reliance on donors, so crucial for the right to welfare, is largely, though not entirely, irrelevant for more traditional rights. Such rights do rely untimately on forbearance, the enforcement of which is funded by people who agree to pay for the protection of everyone's rights, including their own. This arrangement conforms to the contract model posited by Grice and Narveson. People pay for courts, defense, and police services to guarantee everyone's right to life, property and freedom of speech and religion. Civil and political rights, unlike the right to welfare, are not intended to improve some people's condition at the expense of others. But, one might object, is it not the case that the rich benefit most from resources spent (on national defense and police and fire departments) to protect property rights? Yes, just as journalists and the articulate and opinionated benefit most from efforts to assure a free press and free speech. But the crucial point is that such expenditures are not generally perceived as transfer payments from one group to another. Money spent to protect traditional rights is not normally seen as part of an effort to affect income redistribution. In contrast, welfare payments are invariably linked with income redistribution schemes. These perceptions may be neither fair nor accurate, but they are consistent with popular images of these rights.

It is true, however, that when some civil and political rights are first introduced or extended there are clear winners and losers. When obstacles to black voting were lifted, for example, the political advantages gained by blacks diluted whites' political power. Yet once established, the perpetuation of such a right is not seen as an ongoing transfer of power. To maintain welfare rights, in contrast, is to prolong the unilateral transfers from the haves to the have-nots. Even in good times, the elderly, sick, handicapped, and single-parents with small children will need help.

It is also true that the enforcement of some civil rights entail transfers very similar to those that assure economic rights. Such enforcement usually permits the poor to do what they would not be able to do without public assistance. Legal aid, for example, protects the right to equal treatment before the law by permitting the poor to use the judicial system to safeguard their interests and rights. Here again, the obligation to provide such aid benefits only the poor. And here again, consistent with my position, there has been much resistance to assume this duty. As a rule, there will be more enthusiasm for funding efforts to enforce non-interference than there will be for giving people what they would not have on their own.

3. Compassion versus obligation

Another reason why the right to welfare is less widely accepted is that it is not essential — if there were no such right, welfare would not necessarily be neglected. The poor can be helped without it. There is another morally acceptable way to provide care. Private, voluntary, compassionate charity offers help to the poor without granting them any rights. Indeed, it denies the poor the right to welfare while attending to their well-being. It is the rival to rights. What distinguishes it from the right to welfare is not only the amount and kind of aid offered, but, more important, how it allocates power to donors and recipients. It permits donors to decide whether, how much, and to whom to give, thereby leaving recipients powerless. In contrast, the right to welfare gives to recipients control over a share of donors' income. Not surprisingly, then, many affluent citizens perfer charitable to obligatory giving. Not only do they help the needy, but they also retain control over their income, derive satisfaction from the act of giving, and bask in the gratitude their generosity elicits. Such donor benefits are jeopardized when the right to welfare is introduced. So why introduce it if donors can rely on charity?

There is, on the other hand, no obvious morally acceptable alternative way to assure the more traditional rights. Take away these rights and there is a moral vacuum. Charity is irrelevant. Altruism is not the basis of forbearance. Our opportunity to speak, worship, or vote depends on no one else's kindness, nor do we thank anyone for not harming us or for not destroying our property.

When we describe actions that allow us to speak, we normally use terms that reveal our acceptance not only of the right to free speech, but also the justification of this right offered by Vlastos. Suppose Ambassador Jeane Kirkpatrick is scheduled to speak on a campus where there is much opposition to the Reagan Administration's policy in Central America. Suppose further that despite this opposition, no attempt is made to disrupt her speech. In reporting this event, we would not, I believe, describe the audience as benevolent, nor would we say that Ambassador Kirkpatrick was allowed to speak because the audience admired her. Insterad, the audience's reaction would most probably be described as respectful, tolerant, considerate, or polite. This respect is special, for it is extended to a person for whom many in the audience have no respect; this respect is given to a person who as a person should have an equal opportunity to express herself. Based not on affection, sympathy, or admiration, this respect is demanded by the speaker's right to free speech, a right based on her worth as a human being.

One might object, however, that free speech can be preserved by a charitable act even when the speaker has no right to speak. Let us say, for example, that a member of the audience does interrupt Kirkpatrick's speech. In response, she might instruct the security guards to remove the disrupter from the auditorium. But if she allows him to express his views, then his free speech rests on her kindness, for under these circumstances, he has no right to speak. Here then is a case where, contrary to my claim, free speech is protected by a charitable inclination rather than by a right. But to use free speech in this way is odd, given how most Americans consider the term. Thus if Jones can only speak his mind if it suits Smith's preferences, we would say that Jones does not enjoy free speech. When in non-democratic regimes some people are allowed to say what they want because it serves the rulers' interests — interests that could include sympathy and affection for the speakers — we would still not conclude that the people enjoy free speech. Restraints on speech must assume the form of legal rules, applied universally, and beyond such restraints, free speech prevails regardless of others' charitable impulses.

Welfare rights are therefore more precarious because given ordinary moral sensibilities and language there is a way to attend to welfare in the absence of rights. There is, then, a choice, a choice not available to those who want to protect people's opportunities to speak, worship, or vote.

4. Desert and Duty

In describing income transfers among private persons (setting aside those that take place within families) we normally say that if a person deserves payment someone else must have an obligation to pay. An employee deserves his wage that the employer is obligated to pay. The depositor deserves his interest that the bank is obligated to pay. A person normally deserves payment for having fulfilled his end of a contract.

Desert is also used to describe welfare recipients. In this context, however, it has a somewhat different meaning. We distinguish between the deserving and undeserving poor. While they both have in common the need for assistance, they presumably require help for different reasons. The undeserving poor, able-bodied adults who are allegedly lazy, deserve their fate and therefore do not deserve our help. They exhibit qualities that deserve not reward but contempt. It may be difficult to convince people that they have an obligation to help those who may need but do not deserve help. The deserving poor, the young, aged, and handicapped, do not deserve their fate. What do they deserve? Not compensation in the sense that the employee and bank depositor deserve compensation; after all, the deserving poor have not made any contracts with taxpayers. (One might claim that welfare legislation represents an implicit contract between the public and welfare recipients. Such a contract is surely legally legitimate. But, for many, it is not morally legitimate because the reciprocal element normally associated with contracts is missing; most welfare recipients allegedly enjoy benefits without having made any contribution to the public good.) What they do deserve (and this is why they are called the deserving poor) is our compassion, and it is this compassion, and not a moral obligation, that inspires the assistance. The undeserving poor, who are not even entitled to our compassion, have a far more tenuous claim to our help. The important point is that in everyday moral thinking, people assume obligation through contracts. So the cynical taxpayer might wonder why he is obligated to provide welfare to poor strangers when he knows that all his other obligatory payments result from contractual agreements.

Desert does not affect other rights in the same way. True, we recognize that convicted felons may not deserve their basic freedoms. But besides this, we do not normally think that some people deserve freedom of speech and religion while others do not. The more traditional rights are far more universal and far more clearly linked to the notion of equal human worth.

Concluding Remarks and Speculations

Welfare programs help poor strangers. When private persons do the same voluntarily it is morally praiseworthy but not required. And if they choose to ignore poor strangers, it is not morally wrong. Welfare programs thus compel people to do what private morality does not require. People are told they *must* help when they know that, as individuals, few would condemn them for not helping. This makes no sense. This may be why there is so little enthusiasm for public assistance. And this is why the moral duty strategy is bound to fail.

How can I claim that this strategy is bound to fail, when, in fact, the poor are still being helped with funds provided by the non-poor? Despite my pessimism, welfare programs are still with us. In response, I would point out, first, that the mere presence of welfare does not mean that the strategy is working; welfare, after all, can be justified in terms other than the state's duty to protect the poor's right to well-being. Governments do provide services (libraries, museums, parks, loans to small businesses, farm subsidies) even though they have no clear moral duty to do so. Second, welfare, compared to most other government programs, is held in low esteem. According to the 1982 National Election Study, 54 percent of respondents believed that the government is spending too much on welfare. In contrast, only 13 percent of the respondents shared the same concern about spending for Social Security, a far more expensive program (Miller 1982: 188-89). Probably the most important cause of this disaffection is the disdain people feel for welfare recipients, who are commonly regarded as lazy, proligate, and promiscuous. Another possible, if less obvious, explanation for this disenchantment is that the principle that the state has a duty to care for the needy is not a morally acceptable justification for welfare. This is, of course, my thesis.

Assume, for the sake of further speculation, that this is the case. What then is to be done? Set aside the moral duty in favor of the state charity strategy. This proposal invariably alarms welfare advocates who fear that it would ineluctably deny welfare recipients their security as well as their dignity. Perhaps these fears are warranted. I am not sure. Yet, I believe a case can be made to assuage the critics' anxieties and to encourage them to postpone their final verdict.

To adopt the state charity strategy is *not* to abdicate public responsibility for the poor; the burden would not be returned to private charities; the government would remain the primary source of poor relief. It would mean instead that public officials would recognize that taxpayers supporting welfare are acting beyond the call of duty, expressing their generosity and not fulfilling an obligation. It would mean further that public officials would attempt to make taxpayers feel sympathy for the truly needy, good about themselves for helping, and confident that welfare programs are becoming more efficient. At least in tone, if not in detail, this has been the message presented (half-heartedly) by Ronald Reagan. This message, if pressed more vigorously and imaginatively, might serve well the interests of the poor. I do not mean to suggest that Ronald Reagan is a friend of the poor. Yes, he cut welfare rolls during his first term, and yes, his proposed 1986 welfare outlays are not magnanimous. Nevertheless, by promoting efforts to curb welfare abuses and by shifting the focus from taxpayers' duty to taxpayers' generosity, he may be performing a useful function; he may be setting the groundwork for a more favorable public image of welfare. Thus, the anti-welfare hysteria that developed in the early 1960s and continued under Republican as well as Democratic Administrations through the 1970s has certainly abated under Reagan. This offers welfare advocates a wonderful opportunity; instead of attacking Reagan as a heartless friend of the rich, they should affirm the importance of generosity among Americans and energetically convey a more benign view of welfare recipients and programs. There is, of course, no guarantee that such a strategy would work; but it is surely worth trying given the apparent failure of the moral duty strategy to engender enthusiasm for welfare. If the strategy were even moderately successful, and, as a result, welfare were to become more legitimate and popular, generosity could be translated into more generous benefits; there is, after all, no natural ceiling to what Americans would be willing to give to those needy poor who are not entitled to help.[5]

Higher benefits would be a hollow reward, critics might complain, if recipients' dignity were compromised. Just as charity stigmatizes the poor, this view charges, so too would the state charity strategy. This fear is based on an image of charity that has haughty donors lording over groveling recipients. Is such a fear reasonable? Perhaps not. Even if the state charity strategy were implemented, donors and recipients would remain strangers, benefits would still be distributed by social workers and bureaucrats, and the expression of personal gratitude would still be inappropriate.

As far as I know, there is no evidence showing that the poor receiving welfare now suffer greater humiliation than did poor welfare beneficiaries in the past. Indeed, the poor may feel less humiliation if Reagan convinces the American people that only the truly needy are being helped and if the

---

[5] This charity strategy assumes that citizens' concern for the well-being of strangers is a preference, no different from, say, consumer preferences. As such, it can be kindled, nurtured, and strengthened. To do this, one must understand what makes people compassionate and generous. Social psychologists for example, have demonstrated that imitation is an important source of altruism; people are thus far more likely to drop a coin into a Christmas kettle if they see someone else do the same. It has been argued that the British emulate the model of unilateral giving to strangers in distress, represented by the welfare state and more particularly by the National Health Service. And this, for some, explains why as of the early 1970s the British were able to rely exclusively on voluntary donations for their supply of blood while in the United States blood from commercial banks had to supplement voluntary donations that failed to meet the demand (Obler 1981). The charity strategy calls on welfare advocates to "market" welfare, to make their product as attractive as possible, to stimulate "demand" for the product. If done crudely, the consequences could be grotesque. But if handled delicately and tastefully, the result could be greater and more long-lasting support for programs that help those who cannot help themselves.

negative publicity that has tainted welfare in the past begins to fade away. Recipients' dignity may depend more on the popularity of welfare than on how it is justified.

In the best of all possible moral worlds, it might be preferable if all Americans had a right to a decent standard of living. But contemporary America simply falls short of this moral ideal. Those who care about the poor's well-being should recognize this, and stop insisting that Americans *must* help and begin persuading them that they *want* to help.

REFERENCES

Callahan, Daniel. 1983. "Supporting Parents." *New York Times*, April 11, 1983.

Cranston, Maurice. 1967. "Human Rights, Real and Supposed." In D. D. Raphael, ed., *Political Theory and the Rights of Man*. Bloomington: Indiana University Press.

Fishkin, James. 1982. *The Limits to Obligation*. New Haven: Yale University Press.

Gallup Report. 1981. August.

Grice, G. R. 1967. *The Grounds of Moral Judgments*. Cambridge: Cambridge University Press.

Hart, H. L. A. 1970. "Are There Any Natural Rights?" In A. L. Meldon, ed., *Human Rights*. Belmont, CA: Wadsworth.

Hochman, Harold M., and James D. Rodgers. 1969. "Pareto Optimal Redistribution." *American Economic Review* 59 (September): 542-57.

Kant, Immanuel. 1949. *Metaphysical Foundations of Morals*. Translated by Carl J. Friedrich. New York: Modern Library.

Lemann, Nicholas. 1984. "The Culture of Poverty." *The Atlantic* 254 (September): 26-41.

Lyons, Daniel. 1969. "The Odd Debt of Gratitude." *Analysis* 29 (January): 92-97.

Miller, Warren E., Arthur H. Miller, and Edward J. Schneider. 1980. *American National Election Studies Data Sourcebook 1952-1978*. Cambridge: Harvard University Press.

Miller, Warren. 1983. *American National Election Study 1982*. Ann Arbor, Michigan: Inter-University Consortium for Political and Social Research.

Narveson, Jan. 1967. *Morality and Utility*. Baltimore: John Hopkins University Press.

Obler, Jeffrey. 1981. "Private Giving in the Welfare State." *British Journal of Political Science* 11 (January): 17-48.

O'Connor, James. 1973. *The Fiscal Crisis of the State*. New York: St. Martin's Press.

Peffer, Rodney. 1978. "A Defense of Rights to Well-being." *Philosophy and Public Affairs* 8 (Fall): 65-87.

Piven, Frances Fox, and Richard A. Cloward. 1971. *Regulating the Poor: The Politics of Public Welfare*. New York: Random House.

Plant, Raymond, Harry Lesser, and Peter Taylor Gooby. 1980. *Political Philosophy and Social Welfare*. London: Routledge and Kegan Paul.

Raphael, D. D. 1981. *Moral Philosophy*. Oxford: Oxford University Press.

Rawls, John. 1971. *A Theory of Justice*. Cambridge: Harvard University Press.

Silver, Morris. 1980. *Affluence, Altruism, and Atrophy*. New York: New York University Press.

Taylor, Michael. 1976. *Anarchy and Cooperation*. New York: Wiley.

Tinder, Glenn. 1979. "Defending the Welfare State." *New Republic* 180 (March 10): 22-25.

Urmson, J. O. 1969. "Saints and Heroes." In Joel Feinberg, ed., *Moral Concepts*. Oxford: Oxford University Press.

Vital Speeches of the Day. 1965. XXXI (February).

____________. 1980. XLVI (September 15).

____________. 1981. XLVII (February 15).

____________. 1984. L (September 15).

Vlastos, Gregory. 1969. "Human Worth, Merit, and Equality." In Joel Feinberg, ed., *Moral Concepts*. Oxford: Oxford University Press.

Watson, David. 1977. "Welfare Rights and Human Rights." *Journal of Social Policy* 6 (1): 31-46.

Justice and Charity*

Allen Buchanan

The distinction between justice and charity is thought to be fundamental in ethical theory. Yet remarkably little has been done to develop the distinction systematically or to articulate the role it is to play in ethical theory. Four theses about the difference between justice and charity are widely held and rarely argued for: (1) Duties of justice (with the exception of those which correspond to special rights generated by promising or special relationships or reciprocal group undertakings that generate obligations of fair play) are exclusively negative duties (duties to refrain from certain actions); duties of charity are generally positive duties (duties to render aid). (2) Duties of justice may be enforced; duties of charity may not. (3) Duties of justice are perfect duties; duties of charity are imperfect. (Perfect duties are determinate both with regard to the content of what is required and with regard to the identity of the individual who is the object of the duty; duties of charity are indeterminate in both senses: the kind and amount of aid, as well as the choice of a recipient are left to the discretion of the benefactor.) (4) Justice is a matter of rights; charity is not (duties of justice have correlative rights; duties of charity do not), and what is one's right is owed to one, the lack of which gives one justified grounds for complaint that one has been wronged.

It is far from clear how claims 1–4 are supposed to be related to one another. Although all four purport to characterize differences between justice and charity, we shall see that not all are equally plausible candidates for answering the question, What makes something a duty of charity rather than a duty of justice, and vice versa? Moreover, it will become clear that some of these claims are thought to be derivable from the others, although the connecting assumptions are often either not made explicit or not argued for.

By analyzing theses 1–4 and by articulating and assessing the grounds for asserting them, I shall explore the distinction between justice and

* I would like to thank Andrea Witte for helping me to work out the implications of the view that certain forms of beneficence, including not only the provision of a decent minimum of income but also the practice of rescuing strangers, can qualify as public goods. I am also greatly indebted to Jody Kraus, Ronald Milo, and Holly Smith for helping me to untangle a number of confusions that afflicted an earlier draft of this essay. Finally, I am also grateful for excellent comments by G. A. Cohen, Deborah Mathieu, and the editors of this journal.

Ethics 97 (April 1987): 558–575

charity and advance some conclusions about its importance—or lack of importance—for ethical theory. The analysis offered here not only illuminates the question of how we are to draw distinctions between duties of justice and duties of charity, it also has some rather surprising implications concerning the nature of rights and our grounds for ascribing them to individuals.

Each of the four theses refers to *duties* of charity. To some this may seem misleading, if not inaccurate. But I hasten to emphasize that 'duty' here is being used in a very broad and innocuous way, simply to refer to whatever is expressed by a moral imperative, a judgment about what ought or ought not to be done, what is in any sense morally required. In particular, it is not assumed that duties may be enforced or that they have correlative rights.[1]

I

The view that duties of justice are always negative,[2] while those of charity are (generally) positive,[3] is perhaps the least satisfactory attempt to distinguish justice from charity since it simply begs one of the most hotly disputed questions in the theory of rights, the question of whether there are positive as well as negative (general) rights.[4] Anyone who seeks enlightenment on where to draw the line between justice and charity or who wants a principled justification for drawing the line where his intuitions tell him it should be drawn is unlikely to find much solace in the claim that justice concerns only negative duties since this latter claim is as controversial and in need of justification as the very judgments about

1. It might still be objected that there are some cases in which charitable acts cannot properly be called duties because they are in no way morally required, being clearly "beyond the call of duty," as when a person rushes into a burning building to save a stranger. See, e.g., R. Epstein, "A Theory of Strict Liability," *Journal of Legal Studies* 2 (1973): 189–204. This objection is based, I believe, upon a confusion between charity, as it is ordinarily understood, and extreme generosity. It would be a case of ungrateful understatement to thank a person who rescued you from the flames for being charitable. To avoid confusion, the term 'superogation' might be usefully reserved for acts so generous that they are clearly "beyond the call of duty" in the sense that one who does not perform them is subject to no moral criticism at all.

2. Perhaps the most influential contemporary exponent of the extreme view that all (general) duties of justice are negative is Robert Nozick (*Anarchy, State, and Utopia* [New York: Basic Books, 1974]). Others who espouse this position include P. Foot ("Euthanasia," in *Medicine and Moral Philosophy*, ed. M. Cohen, T. Nagel, and T. Scanlon [Princeton, N.J.: Princeton University Press, 1981], pp. 276–303), and J. Narveson ("Equality vs. Liberty: Advantage, Liberty," *Social Philosophy and Policy* 2 [1984]: 33–60). Judith Jarvis Thomson also seems to be committed to it in her widely read article, "A Defense of Abortion," in *The Problem of Abortion*, ed. J. Feinberg (Belmont, Calif.: Wadsworth Publishing Co., 1973), pp. 121–39.

3. It may be correct to call some omissions charitable, as when one's opponent in a public debate refrains from pointing out a humiliatingly gross fallacy one has committed.

4. Henceforth I shall drop the qualifier 'general.' Throughout this essay I am concerned only with general rights and duties, not those that arise through promising or from special relationships, such as that between parent and child.

charity and justice it is supposed to support and explain. Since an adquate theoretical justification is currently lacking for the thesis that all rights are negative,[5] some who distinguish between justice and charity in the first way, like Nozick, argue in indirect fashion that all rights are negative by attempting to show that the enforcement of positive rights must lead to unacceptably frequent and severe disruptions of individuals' activities as rational planners or to intrusions that are intuitively unjust.[6]

It is clear that the establishment of certain rather ambitious positive rights—such as the right to an equal share of income or a right to be aided whenever one needs help by whomever is able to help, regardless of costs—would require frequent and severe disruptions. But it is extremely implausible, as more moderate libertarians such as Hayek have admitted, to hold that the establishment of more modest positive rights, such as a right to a "decent minimum"[7] of income or a "right to easy rescue,"[8] will always or even generally result in unacceptable intrusions into individuals' lives. As Hayek observes, well-publicized, long-standing tax laws can provide funding for a legal right to a "decent minimum" of income without shattering that stable framework of expectations which is properly valued by the champions of the individual freedom. Further; as several philosophers and legal scholars have recently noted,[9] a right to easy rescue—a limited right to be rescued from great harm—by a person who can do so without unreasonable cost or risk to herself, cannot be dismissed as either intuitively unjust or as unacceptably disruptive of individuals' expectations. And as these same writers have also pointed out, the problem

5. In this essay I make no attempt to support the claim that no adequate theoretical grounding is available for the thesis that rights are exclusively negative by canvassing the work of negative rights theorists, though I believe there is now a broad consensus that such a grounding is lacking. Like many of their opponents, negative rights theorists often rely on moral intuitions that are not as widely shared as they would like to think. It is not an accident, I think, that Robert Nozick, perhaps the most influential recent negative rights theorist, frankly acknowledges that he provides no systematic justification for the list of negative Lockean rights he espouses in *Anarchy, State, and Utopia.* For this reason, Thomas Nagel has aptly labeled Nozick's view "libertarianism without foundations" ("Libertarianism without Foundations," *Yale Law Journal* 85 [1975]: 136–49).

6. This is Nozick's aim in the famous Wilt Chamberlain example (pp. 160–62).

7. F. Hayek, *The Constitution of Liberty* (Chicago: University of Chicago Press, 1960), pp. 223–58.

8. Without attempting to list necessary and sufficient conditions for an act of aiding being an 'easy rescue,' the basic idea is intuitively clear enough and can be illustrated by a familiar example from the philosophical literature on 'Bad Samaritan' laws. Simply rising from one's poolside chair and lifting an infant's head from the water to prevent it from drowning would (for a person of normal physical abilities) be an easy rescue. An *easy* rescue is one which can be effected without significant cost to the rescuer. The term 'rescue' implies that without aid there is a high probability that the individual will suffer great harm or death.

9. For perhaps the most thorough critical analysis of the arguments for and against a duty of easy rescue, see J. Feinberg, *Harm to Others* (New York: Oxford University Press, 1984), pp. 126–86. See also an excellent article by E. J. Weinrib entitled, "The Case for a Duty to Rescue," *Yale Law Journal* 90 (1980): 272–75.

of drawing a line between reasonable and unreasonable risks or costs here seems no more difficult than that of applying a "reasonableness standard" in other areas of the law, including not only the law of torts but also the law that establishes the most basic negative rights. For example, self-defense is a recognized defense in the law of homicide, and a successful defense of this sort requires that the defendant acted reasonably in the circumstances.[10] In general, the concept of reasonableness employed in limiting duties to aid seems no more a matter of degree and no more unworkable than in other areas of the law.

There is an even more basic reason for rejecting the attempt to use the distinction between positive and negative duties to draw the line between justice and charity. Until now the theorist who holds that all (general) rights are negative—that is, the libertarian—has been allowed the offensive, and arguments have been adduced to show that he has failed to undermine the hypothesis that there are positive duties which have correlative rights. The libertarian can be put on the defensive by one simple but powerful observation about what is at the heart of morality: morality is fundamentally (though not exclusively) concerned with avoiding states of affairs that are harmful for individuals. Such states of affairs, clearly, can be avoided not simply by refraining from harming but also by preventing harm. After all, a great deal of what makes harmful states of affairs a matter of moral concern is their *harmfulness,* whether or not they were the result of someone's harming. For this reason there is at least a *presumption* that there are some positive moral rights—rights to aid that prevents harm—if it is assumed that rights principles express what is central to morality and if, as the libertarian believes, there are rights not to be harmed. The burden of argument, then, lies initially on the libertarian to show that even though the harmful state may be the same, there is a right not to be harmed by another but never a right to be aided in such a way as to prevent harm.

In addition, at least part of what makes harmful states a matter of moral concern, namely, a regard for the well-being of individuals, must make beneficial states morally important as well.[11] But if this is so, then

10. T. C. Grey, *The Legal Enforcement of Morality* (New York: Alfred A. Knopf, 1983), p. 159.

11. D. Mathieu, "Individual Liberty and the Duty to Prevent Harm" (Ph.D. diss., Georgetown University, 1984), chap. 1, and "Respecting Liberty and Preventing Harm: Limitations on State Intervention in Prenatal Choices," *Harvard Journal of Law and Public Policy* 8 (1985): 19–55. A libertarian might reply that what is of moral concern is not the states of individuals but the *intrusions* (by other individuals) that affect those states. This reply, however, does little more than restate the negative rights only view since it seems difficult to imagine a satisfactory account of why intrusions are morally significant that would not rest on the tendency of intrusions to affect well-being in some way. Otherwise, the significance of intrusions seems mysterious. But even if intrusions can be shown to have moral significance independent of their tendency to affect well-being, this would do nothing to show that *only* this consideration is sufficiently important to ground rights and that rights do not also have a foundation in concern for well-being that is sufficiently powerful to make a prima facie case for positive rights.

strong arguments will be needed to deny that if there are rights to be aided so as to avoid harm, there are also at least some modest rights to be benefited. None of this *proves* that there are positive rights, of course, but it does bring home the initial strangeness of the view that there are only negative rights and makes it clear that the libertarian needs powerful arguments to support his position. In sum, absent a more adequately supported theory of (exclusively) negative rights than is now available, any attempt to ground an analysis of the distinction between justice and charity in the thesis that justice is restricted to negative duties is unconvincing.

II

There are, it seems, two quite different reasons given for the thesis that duties of justice may be enforced while duties of charity may not. The first is that, since duties of justice, but not duties of charity, have correlative rights, only duties of justice may be enforced because only duties for which there are correlative rights may be enforced. The second is that duties of justice, being perfect duties, may be enforced, while duties of charity, being imperfect, cannot. Imperfect duties are indeterminate both with respect to the recipient of aid and the amount and kind of aid, and the idea is that attempts to enforce them would prove arbitrary and subject to abuse. This second reason will be taken up in Section IV; the first is criticized in the present section. In Section III I shall examine the view that duties of justice have correlative rights while duties of charity do not. But at this point in the argument I shall show that even if that view is true, thesis 2 (that duties of charity need not be enforced) must be rejected.

The thesis that only those duties having correlative rights may be enforced is a very sweeping yet too rarely questioned claim about the sole condition under which coercion is morally justified. Perhaps the most serious challenge to it rests on the recognition that enforcement is sometimes necessary to secure contributions to *collective goods*, that in some cases, at least where the collective good in question is extremely important, such enforcement seems morally justified, and that its being justified does not appear to depend upon any assumption that the individuals in question have a moral right to the good in question.[12] Enforcement of a duty to contribute is sometimes necessary for the provision of important collective goods (such as clean air, energy conservation, or national defense) owing to the fact that voluntary contribution may be blocked because some individuals attempt to take a free ride on the anticipated contributions of others. Successful collective action may also fail to occur if enough individuals refrain from contributing because they

12. A classic exposition of the nature and pervasiveness of problems of collective action is found in M. Olson's *The Logic of Collective Action* (Cambridge, Mass.: Harvard University Press, 1965).

lack assurance that others will contribute, even though they have no desire to take a free ride.

It is true, of course, that collective goods[13] problems can in some cases be overcome without recourse to enforcement through the force of moral exhortation of personal example, through the assignment of property rights, or by making the process of contributing sufficiently valuable in itself (through the goods of solidarity or community, for example). Nonetheless, enforcement of a duty to contribute is sometimes the only effective means for securing some collective goods. Hence, unless one is willing to advance the very sweeping and implausible thesis that the need to achieve important collective goods *never* provides an adequate justification for enforcement of duties for which there are no correlative rights, one must conclude that it is false that only rights principles may be enforced.

It is important to emphasize not only that the need to secure certain important collective goods is widely recognized as a sound justification for enforcing positive duties of contribution but also that the force of such justification does not appear to rest either implicitly or explicitly upon the assumption that there is a right to the good in question. Once such justifications are recognized, it may be advisable, in order to provide individuals with incentives to report failures to contribute, to establish legal rights for individuals to the good in question; but this does not show that the moral justification for enforcing contribution presupposes either legal or moral rights to the collective good. Indeed, it is rather odd—perhaps somewhat hysterical—to say that by not contributing each noncontributor has thereby *violated the rights* of each potential beneficiary of a collective good, including himself.[14]

13. Although coercion can solve both the free-rider and assurance problems, it is inaccurate to say that both problems are *public goods* problems. A public good problem exists only where there is an *externality* (a neighborhood or third-party effect) which encourages attempts to take a free ride on the contributions of others. The assurance problem can occur even where there is no externality and is not the result of anyone's attempt to take a free ride. Consequently, it is best to reserve the term 'public good' only in reference to the free-rider problem and the broader term 'collective good' to refer to goals of collective action that may fail to be achieved *either* because of the free-rider problem *or* the assurance problem. A collective good is simply any state of affairs whose production requires the efforts of many individuals and from which at least all who contribute will benefit.

14. It is somewhat more plausible to maintain that after the potential good is actualized, those who benefit from the contributions of others but refrain from contributing themselves wrong the contributors or violate their rights by taking unfair advantage of them, but even this will not always be so. If, as in cases of paternalism, the benefit was imposed upon one, it is far from clear that one must either try to avoid enjoying it or contribute to its provision. It might be said that even though no *individual* need have a right to the benefit (for enforcement to be justified), nevertheless, the *group* that benefits has a right to enforcement, a collective right against the *government*. Whether or not this is so is irrelevant to my argument for two reasons. First, I am concerned to refute the assumption that enforcement is appropriate only where there are *individual* rights to the good in question. Second, my claim is that the case for enforcing contribution to collective goods is not *based upon* the

Whether or not a share of it is *owed to* each individual and regardless of whether those who fail to contribute could rightly be said to have *wronged* all potential partakers of the good, some collective goods are of sufficient importance that enforcement seems justifiable if that is what it takes to secure them. If we are *ever* justified in enforcing such non-rights principles, then we must reject any attempt to distinguish between duties of justice and duties of charity that is based on the assumption that only the need to enforce rights principles can justify coercion.

Furthermore, it is not simply that there are plausible non-rights-based arguments for enforced contributions to collective goods that do not assume antecedent moral rights to the goods in question; there are in fact plausible arguments of this sort for enforcing duties of *charity* under the certain circumstances because some important forms of charity are themselves collective goods.[15]

Without an effective enforcement mechanism, strictly voluntary compliance with duties to aid may founder due to the fact that a system of aid for the needy is a collective good. Even if rational individuals agree to a system of duties to contribute to the good, they may find it rational to defect from it so long as compliance is voluntary. The situation has an incentive structure similar to that of a many-person Prisoner's Dilemma. Each individual may reason as follows: "Either enough others will contribute to the good in question, regardless of whether I do so, or they will not. Since my contribution is a cost to me, the rational thing for me to do is not to contribute so long as I will be able to partake of the good regardless of whether I contributed."

The last condition, that noncontributors will not be excluded from partaking of the good if it is achieved, will generally be satisfied in the case of at least some important duties to aid the needy. In the case of a duty to rescue, it will not be feasible to try to determine, in situations calling for prompt action, whether a particular individual (or which individuals among a group of endangered persons) has already "contributed" to a system of mutual aid by already having performed acts of rescue. But more important, in a society in which acts of rescue are fairly infrequent, a system in which I can count on being rescued only if I have myself already established that I am a contributor by having rescued others

---

assumption of a right, and the thesis that *if* there is a case for enforcement *then* the group has a right against the government to enforce does not entail that the latter right is the *basis* for enforcement. On the contrary, the collective right against the government is derivative from the argument for enforcement, not vice versa.

15. The idea that collective charity is a public good is not new. Milton Friedman floats it in *Capitalism and Freedom* (Chicago: University of Chicago Press, 1962), chap. 12. See also A. Buchanan, "Revolutionary Motivation and Rationality," *Philosophy and Public Affairs* 9 (1979): 67–68; R. Sugden, "On the Economics of Philanthrophy," *Economic Journal* 92 (1982): 341–50, and "Reciprocity: The Supply of Public Goods through Voluntary Contributions," *Economic Journal* 94 (1984): 772–87; and D. Collard, *Altruism and Economy* (Bungay, Suffolk: Chaucer Press, 1978).

would be vastly inferior from a strictly prudential point of view to one in which I can count on being rescued by whoever is in a position to do so, regardless of whether I have already proven that I have made my contribution. Moreover, even if there were some ready way of identifying those who either *have* aided or of predicting accurately who *will* aid those in need, it will often be impractical to attempt selective rescue of just those individuals from the midst of endangered groups. Rescue efforts, in other words, often involve externalities or "spill-over effects."

It might be replied that in fact individuals will not behave thusly (that is, will not be free riders, who defect from agreements to contribute) because their desire to maximize their own utility will be constrained by altruism. Now the extent to which individuals observe moral constraints on their individual utility-maximizing behavior is an empirical issue, but this much seems clear: since altruism is generally limited, the *scope* of duties to aid which we can expect people to fulfill voluntarily is probably considerably narrower than that of duties they would discharge if those duties were enforced.

The free-rider problem arises on the assumption that the good at which each individual aims is accurately described as 'the provision of aid to the needy.' If this is his goal, then as we have seen the individual may withhold his contribution if he believes that the needy will be provided for by others or that they will not, regardless of whether he contributes. There are several different ways in which one may benefit from the attainment of this good without having contributed to it. Some may derive satisfaction or avoid discomfort simply by knowing that the needy are provided for. Others may view the provision of aid to the needy as instrumentally good: it makes for a more stable social structure, in which those who have wealth and power may enjoy them in greater security, and increases overall productivity by enabling more people to work. Indeed it is often said that the major social welfare programs initiated in western Europe in the late nineteenth century were motivated chiefly by the latter sorts of considerations rather than by a sense of justice or a direct concern for the well-being of the needy.

However, the free-rider problem will *not* block successful collective action if a sufficient number of people desire *to provide for the needy* rather than simply desiring *that the needy be provided for.* If I regard the good to be attained as 'a system of aid to the needy *to which I contribute,*' then, of course, I cannot partake of that good without contributing to it.

Whether or not a sufficient number of people to achieve a particular goal of collective charity will be effectively motivated by the desire to be charitable (rather than simply by the desire that charity be done) is an empirical question whose answer will vary from case to case, depending upon the psychology of the individuals involved. But even if an individual does not himself wish to take a free ride on the contributions of others to a system of aid to the needy, he still may be unwilling to render aid to the needy unless he has *assurance that others* (with resources as great as or greater than his) *will also render aid* to himself or to others in similar need. He may be unwilling to contribute without assurance that others will do so for either or both of two distinct reasons. (*a*) He may conclude that it is better to expend his "beneficence budget" on an act of independent charity toward some particular person in need rather than risk contributing to a collective charity in which the threshold of contributions needed for success is not reached. (*b*) His commitment to being charitable may be limited by a requirement of fairness or reciprocity.[16] That persons who are strict individual utility-maximizers may fail to achieve systems of aid that are public goods is hardly surprising. What is striking is the more general conclusion that collective action to create and maintain systems of aid may falter even if some individuals are significantly altruistic.

Whether or not enforcement will be necessary to achieve goals of collective charity does not appear to admit of a general answer. Under certain rather strong conditions, strictly voluntary contributions may suffice. However, in the case of systems of aid that are collective goods, as with collective goods generally, there seem to be no strictly voluntary strategies which will work in all circumstances.[17] If this is so, and if enforcement is justified in *any* such case, then it is *not* the case that enforcement of a duty to contribute is justified only where there is an antecedent moral right to a share of the good in question, whether it be national defense or a system of aid.

Why does the negative-rights-only theorist, that is, the libertarian, hold that enforcement of duties to aid is justifiable only on the assumption that there is an antecedent moral right to receive aid? Perhaps the libertarian reasons as follows: "Everyone has a basic moral right against coercion (i.e., right to negative liberty). The only thing morally weighty enough to justify infringement of this right against coercion would be another moral right. Therefore, if enforced contribution is ever morally justified, then its justification presupposes that individuals have a moral right to the good in question."[18]

Elsewhere I have criticized this view in detail.[19] The claim that there is a general moral right against coercion (or to negative liberty) strong enough to rule out *all* enforced contribution to collective goods (including systems of aid) is non-question-begging only if the right in question is

16. Sugden, "Reciprocity," pp. 773–74. For related work that also challenges the current emphasis on justice by taking duties of beneficience seriously, see T. D. Campbell, "Humanity before Justice," *British Journal of Political Science* 4 (1974): 1–16; and B. Barry, "Humanity and Justice in Global Perspective," in *NOMOS XXIV: Ethics, Economics, and the Law*, ed. J. R. Pennock and J. Chapman (New York: New York University Press, 1982), pp. 219–52.

17. See, e.g., D. Mueller, *Public Choice* (Cambridge: Cambridge University Press, 1970), chap. 4.

18. This libertarian argument was suggested to me in conversation with Jan Narveson.

19. A. Buchanan, "What's So Special about Rights?" *Social Philosophy and Policy* 2 (1984): 71–73, and *Ethics, Efficiency, and the Market* (Totowa, N.J.: Rowman & Allanheld, 1985), chap. 3.

viewed as a presumptive moral claim (i.e., a prima facie right), not a justified moral claim (i.e., a right all things considered). In other words, if the libertarian supports his premise that there is such a strong, virtually unlimited right against coercion (or to negative liberty) merely by an appeal to our moral intuitions but views the rights as a justified moral claim rather than as a prima facie right or moral presumption, he begs the question against the nonlibertarian who maintains that in some cases duties to aid may be enforced so long as costs are not excessive and are distributed fairly. For the nonlibertarian can simply point out that his moral intuition is that a virtually unlimited moral right against coercion is simply too unlimited a right to be plausible. In other words, the nonlibertarian can say that though he finds a strong presumption against coercion to be intuitively plausible, he does not find intuitively plausible the much stronger claim that there is a moral right against coercion if this latter claim entails that the only thing morally weighty enough to justify coercion is a moral right. Yet if the libertarian admits that an appeal to our moral intuitions only supports a prima facie right against coercion, then he cannot assume that the *only* consideration morally weighty enough to defeat this presumption would be a moral right to (receive a share of the good).

Indeed, the nonlibertarian can even admit that there is a right against coercion (not just a prima facie right) but hold that so far as the existence of this right can be supported adequately merely by an appeal to intuition, its scope and content are not sharply specified. He can then argue that when it comes to specifying the scope and content of this right, one morally relevant consideration is the need to overcome barriers to successful collective action for providing certain morally important goods, such as aid to the needy, or for preventing certain morally important harms. Once the proper content and scope of the right against coercion have been determined, it may *then* be correct to say, with respect to the *specified* right, that only the need to respect another moral right could justify its infringement. But what the libertarian overlooks is the possibility that in moving from the intuitively plausible assumption that there is a moral right to negative liberty or against coercion to a specification of the scope and limits of that right, certain non-rights-based considerations—including the need to use coercion to secure certain important collective goods, and, in particular, systems of aid—may be decisive.

In sum, the premise that there is a general moral right to negative liberty, that is, against coercion, may be understood either as a claim about a prima facie right or as a claim about a right simpliciter, that is, a right all things considered. If the former, then the premise is intuitively plausible, but it does not follow from it that the only thing morally weighty enough to override the (merely prima facie) right to negative liberty is a moral right. If the latter, then it may be true that only a moral right would be weighty enough to override the (justified) moral claim to negative liberty, but the thesis that this moral right to negative liberty is broad enough to rule out *all* arguments for enforced contribution is not something which the libertarian can support simply by an appeal to intuition. It appears, then, that the libertarian cannot support his assumption that coerced contribution is justified only when there is a right to the good in question by an intuitive appeal to a right to negative liberty or against coercion.

To admit that some enforced principles requiring contributions to systems of aid or other collective goods are morally justifiable (even in the absence of a moral right to the goods in question) is not to say, however, that whenever a problem of collective action exists, enforcement is justified. First of all, since enforcement, even if not always a great evil, is never a good thing, the need to overcome the free-rider or assurance problems justifies enforcement only if the good cannot be attained by other, less undesirable means (e.g., moral exhortation, leading others to contribute by one's example, etc.). Second, and perhaps even more obviously, enforcement is not justified if the cost of enforcement surpasses the benefit of attaining the good in question. Third, even when the preceding two conditions are satisfied, further limitations may be needed to restrict the scope of collective goods arguments for enforcement simply because the class of collective goods is so large that overuse of this type of argument for enforcement may result in dangerous concentrations of coercive power.

A libertarian might raise the objection that such non-rights-based arguments for enforced contributions fail to recognize a fundamental qualification. While acknowledging that there may be some rules of social coordination, including some principles specifying obligations to contribute to important collective goods that rational individuals would wish to see enforced, even in the absence of corresponding rights, the libertarian will point out that enforcing them is permissible *only if* enforcement does not itself violate important moral rights.

This qualification is in order. However, if the qualification is to become a sound criticism either of non-rights-based, collective goods arguments in general or of the enforced charity arguments set out above, the libertarian must discharge two difficult tasks, the second of which no one has yet achieved. First, he must clearly specify *which* basic moral rights would be violated by all attempts to enforce any duties to contribute to important collective goods or to enforce duties of beneficence, even the relatively undemanding duty of easy rescue or the duty to contribute to a collective effort to provide a decent minimum of goods and services for those who cannot provide for themselves. Second, he must provide a coherent and plausible *justification* for the claim that these moral rights do exist. To rule out in principle all enforceable principles requiring contribution to collective goods and all enforceable principles of beneficence, the libertarian would have to specify and then justify either (*a*) a virtually unlimited general right of negative liberty (or against coercion) or (*b*) a virtually unlimited right to private property. The great obstacle to supporting *a*, as I noted earlier, is that he must do so without begging the question by appealing to intuitions that his nonlibertarian opponent does not share.

Similarily, even if the view that there is *some sort of* moral right to private property has considerable intuitive appeal to many people, the much stronger assertion that there is a virtually unlimited moral right to private property clashes with many persons' intuitions, as the widespread support for at least minimal welfare rights shows. So in the absence of broad consensus in intuitions, the assertion of such an extremely strong moral right to private property is just as much in need of theoretical support as an extremely strong right to negative liberty. Granted that a sound theoretical justification for a virtually unlimited right either to negative liberty or to private property is currently lacking, the burden of proof is on the libertarian to defend the sweeping hypothesis that *every* non-rights-based argument for enforced contributions to charity or to other collective goods violates important moral rights.[20]

III

Ethical theorists as diverse as Kant and Mill have shared the view that duties of justice are perfect, while duties of charity are imperfect.[21] Those who hold this view also typically offer it as a reason for the thesis that duties of justice, but not duties of charity, may be enforced. The idea is that the indeterminacy of imperfect duties (what Kant calls their "play room") makes them unsuitable for enforcement since attempts to enforce them would be afflicted by abuse and arbitrariness and would lead to highly unpredictable intrusions.[22]

20. For a critical survey of arguments for a strong right to private property, see L. Becker, *Property Rights: Philosophical Foundations* (Boston: Routledge & Kegan Paul, 1977).

21. I. Kant, *The Metaphysics of Morals*, trans. J. Ellington (Indianapolis: Bobbs-Merrill Co., 1964), p. 48; and J. S. Mill, *Utilitarianism*, ed. O. Piest (Indianapolis: Bobbs-Merrill Co., 1957), p. 61.

22. Kant also holds that what he calls duties of virtue, which include those of charity, are unenforceable because they require not particular actions but, rather, the adoption of an end. If this point holds at all, it does so only with regard to the duty to *be* charitable, i.e., to have a certain disposition of character. In this paper I am concerned with duties of aid as imperatives to act, not with the development of moral character traits. Kant also attempts to provide a theoretical basis for the distinction between duties of justice and duties of virtue by claiming that the former are "determined" by the "contradiction in conception" version of the Categorical Imperative's universalizability test, the latter by the "contradiction in willing" version. This way of distinguishing between justice and charity seems unfruitful, however, because the "contradiction in the conception" test is both too strong and too weak to generate plausible moral principles. For a discussion of the problems with the "contradication in conception test," see A. Buchanan, review of *Acting on Principle* by O. Nell, *Journal of Philosophy* 75 (1978): 332–33. Even if the "contradiction in conception" test could be salvaged, however, Kant's attempt to correlate duties of virtue with it and duties of virtue with the "contradiction in willing" test seems arbitrary and ad hoc.

In criticizing thesis 2 (the view that only obligations with correlative rights may be enforced), I presented arguments for enforcing duties to aid the needy that did not justify enforcement on the grounds that there is an antecedent moral right to the aid in question. There are two quite different ways to construe such arguments. According to the first, these non-rights-based arguments are properly described as arguments for enforcing duties of charity, and even after an appropriate enforcement mechanism is in place the duties in question remain duties of charity, without correlative moral rights. According to the second way of construing them, these non-rights-based arguments justify the establishment of institutional arrangements for fairly specifying, distributing, and enforcing duties to aid in the absence of a moral right to aid, but once such institutional arrangements are in place a revision should take place in our conception of what others have a moral right to aid. To put it rather crudely, according to both interpretations, we begin by assuming the existence of a duty, but not a right, to aid; in the first we end up with no right to aid but only an enforceable duty of charity, while in the second we end up with a right to. If the first way of construing the non-rights-based arguments is correct, then the view that duties of charity are imperfect is simply false. For what the arguments show, on the first interpretation, is that appropriate institutional arrangements for specifying and distributing duties to aid can eliminate the indeterminacy that is definitive of imperfect duties without altering their status as duties of charity. Such institutional arrangements can specify the amount, kind, and recipient of aid.[23]

In addition, if the first way of construing the non-rights-based arguments for enforcing duties to aid is correct, the circularity of the argument that duties of charity may not be enforced *because they are imperfect* becomes starkly apparent. If duties to aid can be made determinate by appropriate institutional arrangements, which will include provisions for enforcement, then lack of determinacy cannot itself be a reason for not enforcing them.

If, however, we view non-rights-based arguments for enforcing duties to aid according to the second interpretation—as leading to the conclusion that once the appropriate institutional arrangements are in place there is a right to receive aid—then these arguments do not contradict the view that duties of charity are imperfect. This is so because the duties in question, though no longer imperfect since they are made determinate by the institutional arrangements, are also no longer duties of charity but, rather, duties of justice. However, even though the second way of construing the non-rights-based arguments for enforced duties to aid is *consistent* with the thesis that duties of justice are perfect and those of charity are imperfect, there is a sense in which it also *trivializes* that thesis. For what those arguments show, on the second interpretation, is that the distinction between perfect and imperfect duties is in no way a fun-

23. E. Weinrib suggests this point, though he approaches the issue in terms of legal duties to aid rather than in terms of a distinction between justice and charity (p. 291).

damental distinction in ethical theory, but, rather, a shifting one which changes as our institutions change or as we move from one type of society to another. So regardless of which way we interpret the non-rights-based arguments for enforced duties to contribute to the needy, thesis 3 is of little value for understanding the distinction between justice and charity or for establishing the alleged importance of that distinction in ethical theory.

Although nothing in my argument hinges on choosing between the two interpretations, it is worth pondering for a moment the implications of the second, according to which the *existence* of certain rights can depend upon the availability of appropriate institutional arrangements for fairly specifying, distributing, and enforcing duties of aid. If this view is correct, then two rather surprising conclusions follow. First, which moral rights individuals have are not determined exclusively by the ethically relevant features *of those individuals*. On the contrary, for at least some important moral rights, whether or not an individual has the right depends not only upon whether the individual possesses certain characteristics (such as certain important interests or the capacities associated with personhood) but also upon the availability of institutional arrangements which may or may not exist in a particular society at a given time. It is important to note that the moral rights which (according to the second interpretation of the enforced charity arguments) correspond to duties to contribute to collective charity are *not* identical to any of the three types of rights usually considered to be covered by the term 'special rights.' They are not (1) rights that arise from special personal relationships (such as that of parent to child). Nor are they (2) special rights that are generated by promises or contracts. Finally, since none of the enforced charity arguments utilizes premises about fairness, they are not the same as (3) those special institutional rights that are said to be the correlative or "fair play" duties to contribute to cooperative institutions from which one benefits. But if so, then there are some moral rights that are neither special in either of these three senses nor general in the sense of being ascribable to all human beings (or all persons) regardless of the type of society in which they find themselves. Yet it has generally been assumed that the distinction between special and human (or natural) rights is exhaustive. Second, if there are some (nonspecial) moral rights whose existence depends upon the availability of social arrangements that may or may not be present, then the principles specifying these rights will in an important sense be conclusory, or derivative, rather than premissory, or basic. In other words, such rights principles will not be derivable from any more basic rights principles but will require for their justification contingent premises about the existence of certain social arrangements. Thus if there are such rights, no plausible ethical theory can be exclusively rights-*based.*

IV

The fourth approach views duties of justice as having correlative rights and duties of charity as lacking them. Those who assert it take the first half of thesis 4 to be uncontroversial, and I, too, shall assume, for purposes of the argument, that all duties of justice have correlative rights. Now many who take the distinction between duties with correlative rights and those without them to be fundamental also hold that justice includes only negative duties. But if, as I have already argued, the thesis that justice includes only negative duties is unjustified, then they must argue, not assume, that only negative duties have correlative rights in order to conclude that positive duties of charity lack correlative rights.

The prevailing view is that what distinguishes duties that have correlative rights (and hence qualify as duties of justice) from those that do not is that the former, but not the latter, are *owed to* someone.[24] Thus a person's failure to perform a duty for which there is a correlative right gives one grounds for a *justified grievance* that one was *wronged*. Everything hangs, then, on *how* we are to determine what one is owed, the lack of which grounds a justified grievance or a claim that one was wronged.

B would be wronged if A failed to do his duty to aid B only if B (or B's interests or needs) is not only the *focus* but also the *source* of A's duty. If I ought to advance your interests or satisfy your needs only because doing so will advance someone else's good, then *you* are not the *source* of my obligation, though you are the *focus* of it. The distinction between the focus and the source of duties to aid is not sufficient to distinguish duties of charity from duties of justice, however. If I have a duty of charity to help Jones when he is in need, it is my duty to help him because *he* is in need, not because helping him serves others' interests.

What, then, *in addition* to the condition that B is the source, not just the focus of the duty, is needed to justify the judgment that failure to perform the duty wrongs B? One suggestion is that if A's failure to do his duty wrongs B, then A's not doing his duty itself creates a presumption that A must offer restitution or compensation to B.

The thesis that there is a connection between justice and restitution or compensation is distinct from the more general thesis, considered above, that justice may be enforced. It is true that enforcement, understood broadly as the provision of coercive sanctions, includes restitution and compensation since the prospect of being required, on pain of coercion, to compensate or provide restitution is one kind of coercive incentive. But the point of the present discussion is not to focus on the role that restitution and compensation play in enforcement. Instead, our topic here is the way in which restitution and compensation, which are always restitution *to someone* and compensation *of someone*, are supposed to give content to the idea that duties of justice, unlike duties of charity, are directed toward someone, the right bearer, in a distinctive way.

That nonfulfillment of duties with correlative rights creates a presumption for restitution or compensation may well be true, but it is of

24. R. Wasserstrom, "Rights, Human Rights, and Racial Discrimination," in *Rights*, ed. D. Lyons (Belmont, Calif.: Wadsworth Publishing Co., 1979), p. 57.

little help in deciding *whether* a duty is a duty of charity or of justice. If we already knew that A's duty toward B is a duty of justice, then the thesis that only duties of justice have correlative rights would enable us to conclude that A owes restitution or compensation for failing to do his duty. But if we are uncertain whether A's duty is a duty of justice or of charity and hence also unsure of whether B has a right to what it is A's duty to do, we are likely to be at least as hesistant about whether A owes B restitution or compensation.

The question of whether someone ought to be required to provide compensation or restitution, like the question of whether it is morally justifiable to enforce a duty, is not in general the sort of question which can be answered by an appeal to intuition, much less intuitions about what is charity and what is justice. These are highly theoretical questions: answering them will require a weighing of complex and sophisticated considerations. And in fact there has been considerable controversy in recent years over *what kinds* of factors should be taken into account in determining how or whether one should be compensated for certain sorts of acts and omissions. Much of the debate in the literature on the economic analysis of law has centered on the question of how much weight considerations of efficiency should be given in the justification of claims to compensation.[25]

If the distinction between duties of justice and duties of charity can only be made by distinguishing between duties that have correlative rights and those which do not, if we can only determine which duties have correlative rights by ascertaining whether failure to fulfill them justifies compensation, and if the justification of claims to compensation is the complex matter it seems to be, then the judgment that something is a duty of justice rather than charity is a highly derivative, theoretical statement. And if it is, then the distinction between duties of charity and duties of justice will not itself be of any use in tackling any of the issues whose resolution was presupposed in drawing the distinction. Moreover, even if, after the resolution of these complex issues in ethical theory is achieved, we can then distinguish duties of justice as those that have correlative rights and duties of charity as those that lack them, this will have rather limited significance, especially because knowing that a duty is a duty of charity will not itself settle the question of whether enforcing it is morally justifiable. At most such a judgment will serve to *sum up* the results of the various arguments that led to the conclusion that for some failures to perform duties compensation or restitution is required while for others it is not.

There is another feature associated with the concept of rights which might be thought to provide a way of distinguishing between duties of

25. J. Murphy and J. Coleman, *The Philosophy of Law: An Introduction to Jurisprudence* (Totowa, N.J.: Rowman & Allanheld, 1984), chap. 5; and M. Kuperberg and C. Beitz, eds., *Law, Economics, and Philosophy* (Totowa, N.J.: Rowman & Allanheld, 1983), pt. 2.

justice and duties of charity (granted the assumption that duties of justice have correlative rights and that duties of charity do not). Ronald Dworkin and others have stressed that what is distinctive of justified rights claims is that they "trump" or override mere appeals to what would maximize utility.[26] If it is true that only rights claims "trump," then it might be thought that only duties with correlative rights may be enforced at the expense of failing to maximize utility. Hence, if we knew which duties may be enforced even though enforcing them would preclude maximizing utility, then we would know which are duties of justice and which are duties of charity. However, unless one takes rights principles to be self-evident (in which case one could distinguish between justice and charity without recourse to the trumping feature), one will need arguments—perhaps very complex ones—to determine whether certain obligations ought to be enforced even at the expense of maximizing utility. Here, too, the judgment that a duty is a duty of charity rather than a duty of justice will not be a starting point for theorizing about important issues in ethical theory but, rather, a conclusory, summing up statement that rests on vigorously contested assumptions.

V

I will make no attempt to summarize the various arguments of this essay. The main conclusion of the analysis, however, can be succinctly stated: Each of the four most widely accepted theses concerning the difference between justice and charity is either unjustified or false, or it renders the distinction between justice and charity both difficult to draw and of limited significance in ethical theory.

I would like to suggest that this conclusion receives some independent confirmation from the fact that a distinction between justice and charity seems to play no role in two of the most prominent competing models for deriving basic ethical principles. It has long been known that in utilitarianism the distinction between justice and charity is not of fundamental importance: the ultimate justification for both principles of justice and principles of charity is that acting on them maximizes social utility. Principles of justice are simply those whose utility is so great as to outweigh whatever disutility attends enforcing them.[27] Thus in utilitarianism the important distinction is between those duties to aid others that may be enforced and those that may not, 'duties of charity' merely serving as a convenient label for the latter.

Similarly, the distinction between justice and charity appears to have no place in Rawlsian hypothetical contractarianism. Although Rawls suggests that this method of deriving ethical principles can accommodate

26. R. Dworkin, *Taking Rights Seriously* (Cambridge, Mass.: Harvard University Press, 1977), pp. 184–205.

27. J. S. Mill is representative here (p. 53).

the traditional distinction between justice and charity,[28] he does nothing to substantiate this claim. Moreover, the main elements of Rawls's initial choice situation that are said to determine the selection of ethical principles—namely, the veil of ignorance and the preference for primary goods—seem to ensure that the parties will simply choose a set of principles governing the distribution of expectations of primary goods without considering whether they are to be understood as principles of justice or principles of charity. Indeed, nothing in the description of the original position either reflects or seems capable of generating a distinction between principles of justice and principles of charity. The same seems true not only of Rawls's theory but of hypothetical contractarian theories generally, including, most recently, David Gauthier's.[29] Kant, as we have seen, does draw what he takes to be an important distinction between justice and charity, but it is not internal to the conception of hypothetical choice in an original position. Rather, it is anchored, quite independently and inadequately, in a distinction between perfect and imperfect duties.

The description of the choice the parties are to make could be modified, of course, so that they are to choose two different sets of distributive principles, those which are to be enforced and those which are not, and it could be stipulated that the distinction will be marked by the terms 'principles of justice' and 'principles of charity.' But here, as with utilitarianism, the real issue would be, Which principles are we morally justified in enforcing? Introducing the terms 'justice' and 'charity' would add nothing to its resolution. Though I will make no attempt to do so here, I believe that the same point can be made with respect to universalizability procedures and ideal observer theories. Across a broad spectrum of competing models for generating basic ethical principles, the distinction between justice and charity is conspicuous by its absence. If my arguments in this essay are sound, this omission is not a defect.

28. J. Rawls, *A Theory of Justice* (Cambridge, Mass.: Harvard University Press, 1971), p. 109.

29. D. Gauthier, *Morals by Agreement* (Oxford: Oxford University Press, 1986).

DUTIES, RIGHTS, AND CHARITY

Keith Burgess-Jackson

For rights theorists who hold that every right is logically correlated with a duty, and vice versa,[1] charity poses a problem. There is a duty, it seems, to perform charitable actions, and yet there is no correlative right. That is to say, no person, however needy, has a valid claim on any other person to be the beneficiary of a charitable action. The dilemma can be put formally as follows:

(1) For all persons P, if P has a right, then some other person, Q, has a duty; and for all persons Q, if Q has a duty, then some other person, P, has a right. (Let us call this the "correlativity thesis.")

(2) Some person has a duty to perform a charitable action (where "some" means "at least one").

(3) No person has a right to be the beneficiary of a charitable action.

This triad of propositions appears to be inconsistent. If (1) and (2) are true, then (3) must be false. If (1) and (3) are true, then (2) must be false. If (2) and (3) are true, then (1) must be false. But since some people wish to maintain all three propositions, the appearance of inconsistency must be shown to be appearance only. In this essay I show how one group of theorists, including Kant and Mill, has attempted to deal with the dilemma. I go on to show that their attempt to do so is unsatisfactory and that there is an alternative solution to the dilemma which (a) does not rest on the nebulous distinction between perfect and imperfect duties, (b) leaves the correlativity thesis intact, and (c) preserves our pretheoretical intuitions about charity. I conclude with a brief analysis and critique of Mill's conception of imperfect duty.

I

The traditional solution to the dilemma of charity rests on a distinction between perfect and imperfect duties. Kant defines "perfect duty" as "a duty which permits no exception in the interest of inclination."[2] By implication, a Kantian imperfect duty is a duty which *permits* exception in the interest of inclination. To illustrate the distinction. Kant describes four cases, two for each kind of duty. In the first case of imperfect duty, the duty is to oneself. One has an imperfect duty, Kant says, to develop one's talents. In the second case, the duty is to others—to be loving, to sympathize, and to render assistance when they are in need.[3] Kant, despite much criticism, apparently thought that his categorical imperative gave the right result in these cases, for his theory entails that it is wrong to let one's talents rust and to fail to render assistance to others when they are in need.

The first two Kantian duties are said to be imperfect because the occasions for acting are left to the agent. My Kantian duty is to develop my talents, but this duty can be discharged by a number of activities (painting, playing soccer, writing poetry, building exquisite clocks, and so forth) performed at different times and places. Similarly, my duty to be sympathetic or to render assistance to others can be discharged at my discretion. If I am inclined not to render assistance on a particular occasion, I am free, according to Kant, to refrain from doing so, as long as I perform at least some acts of that kind on other occasions. Unfortunately, Kant's distinction between perfect and imperfect duties was never fully developed, so it is hard to do more than speculate about what he had in mind.

Mill drew what appears to be the same distinction, but his analysis of the concept of imperfect duty rests on an ambiguity. Duties of imperfect obligation, he says, are "those in which, though the act is obligatory, the particular occasions of performing it are left to our choice, as in the case of charity or beneficence, which we are indeed bound to practice but not toward any definite person, nor at any prescribed time."[4] The problem with Mill's analysis is the reference of the word "it." Contextually, it must refer to "the act." But this generates the following claims: first, that "the act" is obligatory; and second, that the particular occasions of performing it ("the act") are left to our choice. Now, there are two interpretations of what Mill meant by "the act." On the first, "act" means "act-type"; on the second, "act" means "act-token." The first interpretation renders Mill's claims vague, while the second makes them self-contradictory and incoherent. I will discuss the difficulties with Mill's analysis of imperfect duty later in the essay.

Let us assume for the moment that the distinction between perfect and imperfect duties is sound. If so, the dilemma dissolves. It becomes:

(1a) For all persons P, if P has a right, then some other person, Q, has a perfect duty; and for all persons Q, if Q has a perfect duty, then some other person, P, has a right.

(2a) Some person has an imperfect duty to perform a charitable action.

(3) No person has a right to be the beneficiary of a charitable action.

Propositions (1a) and (2a) no longer yield the denial of (3), for (1a) speaks of perfect duties only, while (2a) speaks of imperfect duties. Moreover, (3), when conjoined with (1a), does not yield the denial of (2a). So a rights theorist, by adopting the distinction between perfect and imperfect duties, has salvaged the three propositions. This, as I say, is the traditional solution to the dilemma—a solution which, incidentally, brought together two moral philosophers (Kant and Mill) who are often set against one another.

To recapitulate, the traditional solution to the dilemma of charity is to distinguish between perfect and imperfect duties. Only the former, it is said, entail correlative rights.[5] Thus, it does not follow from the correlativity thesis and the fact that we have duties to perform charitable actions that any person has a right to be a beneficiary of a charitable action,[6] for the duties that we have with respect to charity are imperfect. This result strikes many people as a happy compromise, a way to reconcile our pretheoretical intuitions about charity with our theoretical beliefs about the logical relation between rights and duties.

II

I would now like to suggest an alternative solution to the dilemma which does not rest on the distinction between perfect and imperfect duties. The solution rests instead on a distinction between two types of duty: a duty to do (or refrain from doing) such-and-such an action, and a duty to be (or refrain from being) such-and-such a person.[7] In the charity context, the distinction is between performing a charitable action on the one hand and being a charitable person on the other, or between charity as an action and charity as a disposition of character. Let us define "charitable person" as follows:[8]

(CP) "Person P is charitable" = df. P is the sort of person who would, in appropriate circumstances, perform a charitable action.

Paradoxically, nothing in this definition requires that a charitable person perform charitable actions. The appropriate circumstances may never arise. Robinson Crusoe, for example, could have been charitable before Friday arrived on the scene, if he were a person of a certain kind. Moreover, one can perform a charitable *action* without being a charitable *person*. Suppose I am not charitable, but that in a momentary lapse of character—a fluke—I flip a quarter to a beggar. I am not charitable because, by hypothesis, I am not the sort of person who would, in a situation of that kind, perform a charitable action. Nonetheless, I did (arguably) perform a charitable action.[9]

Still, there has to be *some* connection between being a charitable person and performing a charitable action. The connection seems to be this. Since charitableness is a disposition of character, it cannot be observed by empirical means. But dispositions tend to manifest themselves in behavior,[10] so particular charitable actions provide *evidence* of a person's charitableness. The proposition that P performed a charitable action, in other words, provides evidence for, or creates an inference to, the proposition that P is a charitable person. Even Mill, I think, would accept this characterization. "[I]n the long run," he says, "the best proof of a good character is good actions."[11] So in the case described, my charitable action (flipping a quarter to the beggar) provides *evidence* that I am a charitable person. Indeed, if my charitable actions are regular enough, or fall into a pattern, one might be *justified* in inferring my charitableness. But by hypothesis, I am not charitable.[12]

We can distinguish, then, between two types of duty in the charity context: a duty to perform a charitable action and a duty to be a charitable person. The latter presupposes that dispositions of character are (to some extent) within our control, but this seems plausible enough. At any rate, I shall not argue the point here. Given this distinction, the dilemma of charity can be reformulated as follows:

(1) For all persons P, if P has a right, then some other person, Q, has a duty; and for all persons Q, if Q has a duty, then some other person, P, has a right.

(2b) Some person has a duty to be charitable.

(3) No person has a right to be the beneficiary of a charitable action.

From (1) and (2b), it follows that someone has a right that another be charitable. But this does not constitute a denial of proposition (3), for (3) speaks of beneficiary rights, not a right that others be persons of a certain kind or be disposed to act in certain ways. In other words, it is possible for *everyone* to have a duty to be charitable (that is, to be the sort of person who would, in appropriate circumstances, perform a charitable action) and yet *nobody* to have a right to be the beneficiary of a charitable action. Notice also that (1) and (3) entail the following: that no person has a duty to perform a charitable action. This, however, is distinct from, and consistent with, (2b), which speaks of the disposition to be charitable rather than the performance of charitable actions.

The only difference between the original dilemma and the reformulated dilemma is the second proposition. Proposition (2) held that some person has a duty to perform a charitable action. Proposition (2b) holds that some person has a duty to be charitable. In both cases the word "some" means "at least one," so this cannot ground a difference in acceptability. Moreover, both propositions are consistent with all of us, or some significant subset of us, having the same duty (see below). The question is therefore this: Which proposition, (2) or (2b), best captures our pretheoretical intuitions about charity? For my part, the second does. I come to this conclusion by considering my reactions to two hypothetical situations, in one of which there is a failure to perform a charitable action and in the other of which there is a failure to be a charitable person.

In the first situation, I observe an affluent-looking person walk by a beggar without contributing so much as a penny to the beggar's cup. My reaction is one of indifference. Although it would be a good thing for the person to contribute, I conclude, there is nothing wrong with not doing so on this occasion. Perhaps the passerby was on his or her way to an important engagement. In the second situation, I am told that the affluent-looking person *never* performs charitable actions, and indeed believes that giving to charity is wrong (it does not matter why). Assuming that I have reason to believe this report, my reaction is different. I now know something definite about the person's character, and judge that the person has violated a duty of some sort. While it seems permissible to forbear from performing particular charitable actions, it is impermissible to forbear from being a charitable *person*. I doubt that I am alone in having these intuitions.[13]

So much for the intuitive attractiveness of proposition (2b). I now wish to point out certain theoretical advantages of the alternative solution. First, it does not rest on the vague and problematic distinction between perfect and imperfect duties. The perfect-imperfect duty distinction has been formulated in many ways by many theorists (as we saw) and has led to much confusion in ethical theory. It also strikes some theorists as an *ad hoc* solution to the dilemma of charity. What we want, in the charity context, is an *explanation* and *reconciliation* of two intuitions: first, that we have duties with respect to charity; and second, that no person can claim discharge of those duties as his or her due. If anything, the perfect-imperfect duty distinction obscures these intuitions; it does not explain them. It also forces us to abandon the correlativity thesis, which we may want to retain for other reasons.

Second, the alternative solution rests on a commonsense distinction between being a person of a certain kind and performing actions of a certain kind. This distinction is at home in many contexts, ranging from competitiveness to generosity to maliciousness. We distinguish easily and naturally between generous persons and generous actions, as well as between malicious persons and malicious actions. Why not similarly distinguish between charitable persons and charitable actions? I see no reason in principle or practice why this cannot be done.

Proposition (2b) raises an interesting question. Granted that some person has a duty to be charitable, we should ask: Who? Which of us? It seems to me that the natural answer is "all of us." Each member of the community has a duty to be the sort of person who would, in appropriate circumstances, perform a charitable action. It follows that any one of us who failed to be charitable would be subject to censure by any other. We would, and should, be indignant at those who fail to inculcate charitable character traits. In other words, each of us is a correlative rightholder with respect to the duty of others to be charitable. As for what ultimately grounds this duty, there are many possible answers, ranging from a hypothetical social contract to utilitarianism to the Kantian categorical imperative. Nothing in my argument, however, hinges on this broader claim about the extent or basis of rightholding. The dilemma is solved by the more modest claim that some person has a duty to be charitable.

III

Let me return, in the remainder of this essay, to Mill's attempted solution to the dilemma of charity. As we saw, Mill's solution rests on the distinction between perfect and imperfect duties. Only the former, he says, entail correlative rights. Since the duty of charity is imperfect, it does not entail that anyone has a right to charity, and this, he thinks, solves the dilemma. But as I suggested earlier, Mill's analysis of the concept of imperfect duty is ambiguous. He uses the word "act" without specifying whether he means "act-type" or "act-token." Let us assume for the moment that he meant "act-type." Then he makes the following pair of claims: (a) the act-type (in this case, charitable actions) is obligatory, and (b) the particular occasions of performing that act-type are left to us, the agents.

The problem with this interpretation is that claim (a) is vague. What does it *mean* to say that an act-type (that is, an act of type T) is obligatory? What does it *mean* to say that a person is obligated to perform charitable actions? That we must perform at least one action of that type, period? That we must perform an action of that type at regular intervals? If so, at what intervals? Have we discharged our duty to perform charitable actions by performing one charitable action? Two? A dozen? One per year? Ten per year?[14] This problem aside, one might question whether obligations attach to act-types at all. The natural thing to say is that one is obligated to perform act-*tokens* (that is, concrete actions), not act-types (generic actions). Of course, whenever one does perform a concrete action, one also performs many generic actions, but this does not save Mill from the difficulty at hand.

Let us assume, alternatively, that Mill meant "act-token" when he said "act." Then he makes the following pair of claims: (a) the act-token (in this case, a particular charitable action) is obligatory, and (b) the particular occasions of performing that act-token are left to us, the agents. The problems with this interpretation are twofold. First, a given act-token, *by definition*, is not performed on "occasions." It is performed exactly once, at a particular time and place. Thus, claim (b) is incoherent. But more importantly, claims (a) and (b) contradict one another. Claim (a) makes a particular action obligatory, while (b) (its incoherence aside) grants discretion to the agent whether to perform it. According to (b), the agent gets to *choose* the occasions on which the act-token is performed. But if obligatoriness means anything, it means that certain options are foreclosed to the agent. Can one be both obligated to perform a given charitable action and still have discretion whether it gets performed? The logical tension is obvious.

It might be asked, given these difficulties, whether the defects in Mill's analysis are general or specific. Is his analysis problematic only in the charity context, or more generally? The answer is that his analysis is generally defective. The problem is that Mill conflates the concepts of particular, spatiotemporally locatable action and types of action. As we saw, there is no single interpretation of his phrase "the act" which provides a clear, coherent conception of imperfect duty. Consequently, Mill's distinction between perfect and imperfect duty is useless as a solution to *any* dilemma, not just the dilemma of charity. It remains possible, of course, for some other analysis of imperfect duty—Kant's, for example, if adequately developed—to withstand scrutiny. I leave that possibility aside, for it seems to me that while possible, no such analysis is forthcoming.

It might also be asked whether the alternative solution to the dilemma of charity is general or specific. It appears to solve the dilemma of charity, but does it solve other dilemmas? The answer is "no." Recall that the dilemma of charity arose because there seemed to be duties of charity that were uncorrelated with rights. Let us take another example of a duty which is often thought to be uncorrelated with a right: obedience.[15] If we are to preserve the correlativity thesis and still maintain that no person has a right to be the recipient of anyone else's obedience, then we cannot hold that there is a duty to be obedient on particular occasions. But this is counterintuitive. As Feinberg points out in the article cited, a motorist has a duty (or so it seems) to obey a police officer who orders him or her to stop. But it would be odd to say in such a case that the officer (or anyone else) has a *right* to our obedience.

In the case of charity, the strategy was to distinguish between (a) having a duty to be a charitable person, and (b) having a duty to perform a charitable action. Can the same distinction be used to solve the dilemma of obedience? It seems not, for it would require us to say that there is a generalized duty to be obedient, though not, perhaps, a duty to perform particular obedient actions. I, for one, am unwilling to postulate a generalized duty to be obedient, whatever the authority in question. So there are two strategies available to the theorist. First, he or she can limit the analysis of this essay to charity, thus preserving the correlativity thesis at least in that context (this is my preferred strategy); or second, he or she can apply the analysis elsewhere—for example, to obedience. The latter strategy produces counterintuitive consequences, as the obedience example shows, but it at least has the virtue of maintaining the correlativity thesis in other contexts besides charity.

IV

To summarize, the traditional solution to the dilemma of charity rests on the distinction between perfect and imperfect duties. Both Kant and Mill drew this distinction, though in different ways. In examining Mill's distinction, we saw that his analysis of the concept of imperfect duty is flawed. On one of two plausible interpretations, it is hopelessly vague, while, on the other, it is incoherent and self-contradictory. To avoid these difficulties, I proposed an alternative solution to the dilemma of charity. Rather than distinguish between perfect and imperfect duties, as did Kant, Mill, and others, I distinguished between having a duty to perform a particular action and having a duty to be a person of a certain kind. This distinction has the following virtues: First, it solves the dilemma of charity; second, it leaves the correlativity thesis intact (at least in the charity context); and third, it makes sense of our pretheoretical intuitions about charity.[16]

The University of Arizona

Notes

[1]See, e.g., Rex Martin and James W. Nickel, "Recent Work on the Concept of Rights," *American Philosophical Quarterly* 17 (1980): 165-80. Like the others in this series, this article contains an extensive bibliography. It also contains a brief discussion of the relation between rights and duties, including the claim that they are necessarily correlated.

[2]Immanuel Kant, *Foundations of the Metaphysics of Morals*, trans. Lewis White Beck (Indianapolis: Bobbs-Merrill, 1959), p. 39 n.10 (original pagination: p. 421 n.10).

[3]The four examples can be found *ibid.*, pp. 39-41 (pp. 421-23). For a discussion of Kant's examples and what he may have meant by the terms "perfect duty" and "imperfect duty," see Fred Feldman, *Introductory Ethics* (Englewood Cliffs, N.J.: Prentice-Hall, 1978), pp. 106-14.

[4]John Stuart Mill, *Utilitarianism*, ed. Oskar Piest (Indianapolis: Bobbs-Merrill, 1957), p. 61. For a discussion of Mill's conception of imperfect duty in the context of bad samaritanism, see Joel Feinberg, *The Moral Limits of the Criminal Law: Harm to Others* (New York: Oxford University Press, 1984), pp. 133-34, 143-48.

[5]See, e.g., Mill, *Utilitarianism*, p. 61: "In the more precise language of philosophic jurists, duties of perfect obligation are those duties in virtue of which a correlative *right* resides in some person or persons; duties of imperfect obligation are those moral obligations which do not give birth to any right" (italics in original).

[6]Indeed, Mill explicitly denies this conclusion. He says that "No one has a moral right to our generosity or beneficence because we are not morally bound to practice those virtues toward any given individual." *Ibid.*, p. 62; cf. Joel Feinberg, *Rights, Justice, and the Bounds of Liberty: Essays in Social Philosophy* (Princeton: Princeton University Press, 1980), p. 144:

> Duties of charity . . . require us to contribute to one or another of a large number of eligible recipients, *no one of whom can claim our contribution from us as his due*. Charitable contributions are more like gratuitous services, favours, and gifts than like repayments of debts or reparations; and *yet we do have duties to be charitable*.

(Italics added.) This passage contains the seed of the distinction that I go on to draw between having a duty to perform a charitable action and having a duty to be a charitable person.

[7]Something like this distinction, if not the distinction itself, is drawn by Alan R. White, *Rights* (Oxford: Oxford University Press, 1984), pp. 26-27:

> A duty is always a duty *to do* so and so or a duty *to* such and such. Duties *to do* so and so include duties *to act*, for example to chair a meeting, to clothe one's children, or to keep records; or *to forbear* from acting, for example not to interfere, not to carry offensive weapons; or *to achieve*, for example to ensure that nothing is lost, to find a replacement, or to arrive early; or, perhaps, *to be*, for example impartial, helpful, or vigilant.

(Italics in original.) One might add "charitable" to the last three items on White's list.

[8]Cf. *The Compact Edition of the Oxford English Dictionary* (Oxford: Oxford University Press, 1971), 1:382 (original pagination: 2:288): (a) "Showing Christian charity or the love of God and man"; (b) "Tender-hearted: loving, kindly; well-disposed; benevolent"; (c) "Full of active charity to others; *esp*. liberal in almsgiving to the poor"; (d) "Connected with or devoted to a recognized object of charity, *esp*. as defined in the various statutes on the subject; of the nature of a charity"; (e) "Inclined to think no evil of others, to put the most favourable construction on their actions, etc." (italics in original).

Of these definitions, (b) seems closest to what I have in mind, for it focuses on the disposition to be charitable rather than on particular charitable actions.

[9]There are two rather obvious problems with (CP). First, it leaves open the force of the counterfactual "would"; and second, it leaves unspecified the phrase "appropriate circumstances." I assume that these problems can be solved. In any event, nothing substantive hinges on the definition. So long as there *is* a satisfactory definition of "charitable person,"

the point made in the text is sound. I use this definition only to illustrate the distinction between charitableness as a property of persons and charitableness as a property of actions.

[10]Indeed, this assumption underwrites the very plausibility of the claim that we have duties to be charitable. The assumption is that by *being* charitable, we will, or are more likely to, perform charitable *actions*. At a minimum, we are more likely to get charitable actions by inculcating charitableness than by inculcating noncharitableness.

[11]Mill, *Utilitarianism*, p. 26.

[12]This should come as no surprise. On any plausible epistemological theory, one can be justified in believing that p without p being the case. That is, on any plausible epistemological theory, justification is distinct from truth.

[13]Tom Regan, for example,says that "though we have a duty *to be charitable*, charitable organizations themselves have no right to our contributions, and they have no right to this because they have no valid claim-against us in this regard." Tom Regan, *The Case for Animal Rights* (Berkeley and Los Angeles: University of California Press, 1983), p. 272 (italics added).

I assume, of course, that Regan was speaking literally, and not, for example, saying that we have a duty to perform charitable *actions*.

[14]In short, Mill owes us a theory of act-type obligatoriness. I will not speculate here on the likely success of such a theory. As pointed out by an anonymous reviewer, the concept of a charitable person suffers from the same sort of vagueness as Mill's concept of an act-type. The reviewer asks: "How many charitable actions must a person perform before he can be called a charitable person?" To answer this, of course, one needs a theory. It has not been my goal to offer such a theory, though I admit that one is necessary. But I see no reason why an adequate theory cannot be put forward. Unfortunately for Mill, as I go on to argue, vagueness is not the only defect in his analysis.

The reviewer also raises an epistemic question: "How does one know whether a person has a disposition to be charitable?" Again, one needs a theory. I sketched such a theory earlier in the essay when I discussed the possibility of inference from particular charitable actions to a disposition of charitableness. So while I admit that this is a problem, it is not an insuperable problem. Nor is it a problem peculiar to charity. How does one go about in general ascertaining dispositions of character? In principle, it seems no more difficult to know that one is charitable than to know that one is competitive, avaricious, or bold. It seems clear that we can have knowledge of all of these character traits.

[15]See, e.g., Feinberg, *Rights, Justice, and the Bounds of Liberty*, p. 138.

[16]I would like to thank two anonymous referees for commenting on an earlier version of this essay. I am also indebted to my teachers, Allen Buchanan and Joel Feinberg, for piquing my interest in (a) the nature of rights and duties, and (b) the relation between them. I owe a different sort of debt to Alan R. White, who, in his book *Rights* and other publications, made me rethink my muddled views of rights, duties, and other moral concepts. Needless to say, none of these people is responsible for the result.

CHAPTER 15

The Great Maxims of Justice and Charity

Onora O'Neill

Near the beginning of his *Second Treatise of Government* Locke speaks approvingly of Hooker's derivation of two fundamental principles of human obligation, 'the great maxims of justice and charity'.[1] The Law of Nature obliges us not merely to deal justly with others but to preserve them.[2] Charity is concern for the needs of others[3] it is not a marginal matter of discretionary philanthropy. Like justice, charity is a serious obligation, whose violation might in certain circumstances amount to murder.[4] The status of charity here is strikingly different from its status in recent liberal thinking. Modern liberals, who are agnostic about the good for man and uncertain about human needs, typically depict charity as institutionally and intellectually marginal.

Utilitarian liberals urge us to maximise subjective good. They demand action that satisifies human desires. Concern to meet claims of need is then submerged in generalised beneficence. This has two results. First, charity may be less urgent than fulfilling strong desires for unneeded items. Those whom need reduces to apathy register faint claims on consequentialist scales. Second, since any open-ended commitment to beneficence generates an alarming 'overload' of obligation,[5] utilitarian liberals often compromise and settle for quite a limited conception of beneficence.

Deontological liberals also marginalise charity.[6] Since they are agnostic about the good for man they have nothing to say about virtues, not even about the virtue of justice. They seek principles for building institutions rather than characters. Plato had hoped that good men would need no laws; deontological liberals hope that good laws will work without good characters. They make few, sometimes unflattering, assumptions about human nature. Human beings are seen as bearers of intrinsically arbitrary but rationally ordered desires or preferences, which just institutions accommodate and arbitrate. Modern deontological liberals do not even argue that private vices may be public virtues, nor that greed can have fortunate economic consequences. They are not concerned whether preferences are greedy or generous, selfish or altruistic. Those are the debates of another age which demanded an account of the good for man, took character as seriously as institutions and still looked for a doctrine of virtue. If liberalism is only about institutions that will justly mediate conflicting preferences, it will have nothing to say about character, about virtues and vices, or about charity and greed.

Deontological liberals are then inclined to picture charity as no more than individual philanthropic activity, whose commitment to meeting needs or preserving mankind may without fault be not merely selective but capricious, and which will certainly be insufficient to see needs met. They differ over how much activity that might formerly have been classified as charitable can properly be brought within the sphere of justice. They agree that charity, understood as philanthropy, is not obligatory, and most classify philanthropy as supererogatory. However, those who think this typically mean only that philanthropy is not a matter of obligation; they offer no account of the good for man to explain why we should take seriously principles that we have no obligation to follow.[7] If charity is supererogatory and supererogation reflects no more than personal preference, a principle of charity can hardly be a great maxim, on a level with the principle of justice.

There is little point in arguing whether the identification of charity either with a 'great maxim' that binds us as strongly as the principle of justice or with optional private philanthropy is correct. Many differences of framework and method separate the protagonists of these two interpretations of charity. Neither will be convinced by any merely conceptual claim that charity is essentially what the other asserts it is. I shall therefore try a more historical and speculative approach to the disagreement.

I begin by asking how and why charity, once a great maxim, was marginalised. I shall sketch one account of the matter, which is quite widely accepted, but which I shall query. I will go on to suggest that the modern reconstrual and marginalisation of charity is less deeply grounded than this received view of its decline suggests. Finally I shall argue that there is no intrinisic reason for liberals to think of obligations to meet the needs of others as peripheral.

A Conventional Story?

A conventional account of the marginalisation of charity might run like this. The Thomist synthesis always was a patch up job. Despite the antiquity of the project,[8] the union of Stoic Natural Law and the new law of the Gospels remained programmatic. Justice was one of the cardinal virtues of antiquity; charity the greatest of the theological virtues. The reconciliation of the City of Man and the City of God may be impossible. Within Christianity the more pessimistic Augustinian tradition looked askance at it. So it should be no surprise that justice and charity met separate fates when the Christian synthesis fell apart. On this view all that we learn from an attentive reading of Locke, such as Dunn provides for us, is that he is less modern than interpreters such as MacPherson—let alone appropriators such as Nozick—suppose. Locke still thinks within a theological framework, so still thinks that charity is obligatory. Modern liberals drop the theological framework, and in doing so lose the basis for any doctrine of virtue or specifically of charity.

This conventional liberal story can have a second, forward-looking chapter. Once we discard the theological framework we can revise Locke, extract the sound core of deontological liberalism and concentrate on principles for building institutions rather than characters. We can have a universal theory of justice and bracket a concern with virtues. Any further discussion of the virtues will have to be reoriented; for example, by locating them within a naturalistic account of human motives, which construes them as dispositions which are important in discussions of moral education or of psychology. The link between obligation and virtue may be severed, but a revised, reduced and relocated discourse of the virtues can still be available.

This story is accepted, in part if not in all its aspects, in many quarters. The libertarian right are generally pleased to be agnostic about the good for man, although some of them regret having nothing to say about the good life, or at least nothing that goes beyond the consumer-preference vision of the Sunday colour supplements, because this makes it hard to know what to say about education. For libertarians charity (construed as philanthropy) remains an option, but is suspect because it may damage recipients' self-respect.[9]

Welfare liberals too think that the boundaries of obligation are the boundaries of justice; but they worry that too much not be left beyond the pale. They argue that justice untempered will not be cold and harsh because it includes welfare rights. On this view much that used to be thought charity is indeed a matter of obligation, not because charity is a matter of obligation but because at least part of what used to be thought charity is more correctly seen as a matter of justice. Justice demands more than libertarians suppose; it includes obligations to provide the means of life and to secure others' agency.[10] However, libertarians and welfare liberals agree that we can have only a theory of justice but no doctrine of virtue. Charity is not the only virtue that modern liberalism has revalued, or rather devalued. It marginalised the entire tradition of the virtues.

Those who aim to revive that tradition also present justice and charity as alternatives. They typically reject and criticise liberalism and abstract ethical reasoning, and the very aspiration to give a universal account of justice; they prefer a relativist or historicist, or more recently "communitarian" framework.[11] Recent Neo-Hegelian works depict abstract liberal accounts of justice and rights as expressive of a social order which eroded the communities which made sense of particular configurations of virtues. They insist that obligations can best be embodied in characters and traditions rather than in formal institutions. Justice need not be abandoned, but must be domesticated. Justice too is specific to actual communities. International justice and the rights of man cannot be vindicated except within circles where these have become the prevailing outlook.

The diverging fates of justice and charity in the modern period are symptoms of deep social and intellectual changes. The liberal challenge leaves those who are still drawn to the virtues with profound dilemmas. On some accounts the virtuous person in modern times, at least in dark times, either may or must shun political involvement. Good characters can manage their lives, if at all, only on the margins of the institutions. In sunnier times those who pursue both social justice and personal integrity are still likely to be torn apart, not merely because of contingent factors but because universal justice and the virtues belong in different worlds.

The friends of virtue think we can have a contextualised doctrine of virtue but no universal theory of justice. Deontological liberals think we can have a universal theory of justice but no doctrine of virtue at all. Modern liberals and their critics apparently agree that we cannot have both a universal theory of justice and a doctrine of virtue. Both deny that justice and charity can be conceived as coordinate great maxims.

A Hypothesis: Natural Law to Natural Rights

These conventional stories cannot, I believe, explain the marginalisation of charity and other virtues in so much ethical thinking. I offer for the moment just two reasons.

First, the loss of theological foundations was a crisis not only for accounts of good character but for a theory of good institutions. Why was this *more* of a crisis for an account of good character? Why did the friends of virtue, but not those of justice, adopt historicist and relativist positions? Could not the friends of virtue too find a historical vindication? May not the friends of justice also need historicist vindications?[12] Unless we can understand what makes the case of justice and of charity so different, the loss of theological foundations cannot be the whole story.

Second, even where theological foundations are retained, charity and other virtues may be demoted. Many modern Christians, for example, take justice seriously, yet treat meeting the needs of others as a marginal matter; they do not see it as something that should make major inroads into their lives or pockets. Abstract theism, like abstract liberalism, is often inhospitable to a doctrine of virtue. If the loss of theological foundations is neither sufficient nor necessary to explain the diverging fates of the two great maxims, what can explain it? I shall propose a hypothesis.

The most striking theoretical difference between Lockean liberalism and contemporary deontological liberalism is not the loss of theological foundations. It is that for Locke the obligations of Natural Law are fundamental while for our contemporaries human rights are fundamental, and duties or obligations the corollaries of rights.

If rights and obligations were correlative this would not be a fundamental difference. It would be rather a matter of looking at one set of ethical relationships from two perspectives. One perspective would take the agent's view of the bearers of obligations, and the other the recipient's view of the holders of rights who could claim the performance of obligations from others. But if the two perspectives are not equivalent there may be some ethical relations which can be discerned and appreciated only from one perspective.

It is a matter of general agreement that there are no rights that lack correlative obligations. Such 'rights' would be unclaimable, mere rhetorical gesture. However the whole point about the obligations of charity, as traditionally conceived, is that these were meant to be obligations without correlative rights. Such obligations were traditionally said to be 'imperfect'. If we are to understand the diverging fates of justice and charity it may then be important to reexamine the status of imperfect obligations and the implications of treating rights rather than obligations as fundamental.

Imperfect Obligations

The term 'imperfect obligation' means simply 'incomplete obligation'. Since there are many ways in which an obligation might be incomplete, it is not surprising that the notion of an imperfect obligation has received various interpretations. However, one of these interpretations is particularly significant.

Sometimes obligations are said to be incomplete or imperfect because the act descriptions that they incorporate specify incompletely what ought to be done. However, *all* act descriptions underdetermine action in this sense. Even obligations of justice are expressed in general principles, whose application and interpretation needs judgement. That process of judgement is both a conceptual and an institutional necessity. It requires elaborate judicial and administrative procedures. The indeterminacy of act descriptions does not draw a line, certainly not a clear line, between obligations of justice and supposed imperfect obligations, such as those of charity. Indeterminacy cannot distinguish clearly between perfect and imperfect obligations.

Sometimes obligations are said to be imperfect on the grounds that they ought not to be enforced, or at least not enforced by legal sanctions. Perhaps obligations of justice ought to be enforced by law and other obligations ought not. However, it is not obvious that we should assume an exhaustive contrast between legal enforcement and non-enforcement: there are many modes of social regulation that can be effective and oppressive. At least at the start of ethical discussions it might be a good idea to be aware of the multiplicity of ways in which lives can be regulated and disciplined while legal sanctions are kept far in the background.[13] In any case, the claim that certain obligations ought not to be legally enforced can hardly be the *basis* for calling them imperfect. If obligations are dividable into those that ought and those that ought not to be enforced with legal sanctions, there must presumably be some other basis for so dividing them.

A third interpretation of the notion of an imperfect obligation is that it is an obligation whose performance is not, or not initially, allocated to specified right-holders. On this account obligations are imperfect if no right-holders have been defined and nobody can claim or waive a right. If the obligation is breached nobody will have been wronged, although wrong will be done. Seen from the perspective of recipience there is no ethical claim. From the perspective of agency, however, the claim is clear enough, although its allocation is undetermined. If there are obligations that are imperfect in this sense, a theory of rights can incorporate only part of a theory of obligations, the part that covers perfect obligations, which that are mirrored by rights. Perspective then makes a substantive difference.

If there are any obligations which are imperfect in this sense, it makes sense to think of them as embodied in characters and traditions rather than in formal institutions. Institutional relationships allocate agents to recipients, or provide procedures for determining allocations. They define roles and special relationships. Institutionalised claims can be grasped and pressed either by agents or by recipients. Claims that are appreciable only from the perspective of agents must be embodied in those agents and their ways of life rather than in the relationships between agents and recipients. This is what lies behind the traditional identification of imperfect obligations and the virtues: both categories grasp agent-centred rather than action-centred concerns.

A Proposal

Modern liberalism may have wiped charity off its ethical map not because it has lost its theological underpinnings but simply because it privileges rights over obligations, and there are no rights to charity. If modern deontological liberals cannot allow for imperfect obligations, it isn't surprising that they oscillate between classifying charity as mere personal preference, and seeing it as supererogatory. Yet either account of charity is disquieting. If charity is no more than personal preference, then callous and kindly action to others in need is equally permissible, provided justice is not breached. If charity is supererogatory then it seems that, ridiculously, mundane help to others in need will be in the same category as saintly or heroic action, of which deontological liberals in any case give no satisfactory account. It isn't surprising that liberals who think they face this dilemma often try to show that much that used to be thought charity is really a matter of justice.

Perhaps liberals can avoid the dilemma. Why should liberalism not be seen as one part of a theory of obligations, rather than of rights? By beginning with obligations one might at least discover whether any imperfect obligations can be established, rather than discounting them from the start by privileging a perspective that make them invisible.

This revisionary approach would have to confront the central question of deontological liberalism. If we do not appeal to Natural Law or Scripture, can we ground *any* obligations or rights? If we can, which are they? The interminable disagreements over the identification and interpretation of human rights are reminder enough that this problem is unsolved. Starting from the perspective of obligations, in which imperfect obligations too are possible, may worsen rather than resolve the disputes. However, since the debates that begin with human rights have not (I shall argue cannot) settle the central issues, it is worth seeing what can be done by approaching matters from another angle.

Maximal Equal Liberty

A well-trodden path into modern deontological liberalism is to construct an account of rights by taking seriously the equality and liberty of agents. Human rights are construed as those equal liberties (construed negatively by libertarians, and positively by 'welfare' liberals) which can consistently be assigned to all. Justice is a matter of securing the maximal or 'best' set of liberties that can consistently be enjoyed by all.

This type of construction can be developed in a way that eliminates the very possiblity of imperfect obligations. If the largest liberty is held to include an open-ended right to liberty that, so to speak, 'mops up' any space that is not absorbed in meeting obligations to respect others liberties, then there is no space for imperfect obligations. Such an open-ended right to liberty divides acts exhaustively into impermissible violations of another's rights and permissible uses of one's own. Obligations would be only what it took to refrain from violating other's rights, hence all obligations would be perfect obligations with correlative rights. Those who assume an open-ended right to liberty not merely give no account of imperfect obligations: they can allow for none. It is clear enough why such liberals must either construe charity as mere preference, or (if that is too uncomfortable) will assign it to the sonorous but ungrounded domain of the supererogatory.

Why should the largest set of equal liberties include an open-ended right to liberty? Some would object that any open-ended right to liberty will in practice make power, so rights, most unequal. Others will object more generally that the priority given to liberty is unvindicated. Both objections can be bracketed, because another, more fundamental difficulty undermines the whole project of making rights ethically basic. It is this. Many distinct sets of equal liberties could consistently be assigned to all: consequently the favourite deontological liberal construction is indeterminate.

The favoured resolution of this problem is to try to indentify the *largest* set of equal liberties that can consistently be held by all. Its difficulty is that liberty has no metric.[14] What makes one set of liberties larger than another, or any set maximal? Is liberty of access larger than freedom of speech? We do not know how to answer so specific a question. Still less do we know how to determine what rights and obligations are comprised within the largest liberty compatible with like liberty for all. A sufficient reason for bracketing issues about the priority of liberty is that we can see that no attempt to construct the largest set of equal and consistent rights will work, since it must assume a metric where there is none.[15]

If the construction of rights is indeterminate we have further reason to worry not merely about giving priority to liberty, but quite generally about giving priority to rights. We have already seen that privileging the perspective of rights marginalises or even undercuts imperfect obligations and virtues. We also know that concern for virtue need not be ruled out by concern for rights and liberty. A stress on justice and even on negative liberty and rights can be linked with rather than insulated from an emphasis on the virtues. The link between justice and charity that Locke affirms runs through many Natural Law writers. Skinner's writings on the tradition of civic humanism remind us of a tradition that insists that the practice of civic virtue is the condition of maintaining liberties.[16] Rousseau and Kant both argue for justice *and* virtue. Modern deontological liberals surely ought to explain fully why they cannot or should not any longer be concerned with virtue. For it may be true that failure to cultivate and practise the virtues and to recognise those obligations which are not mirrored in rights will eventually undermine liberty and rights.

The arguments offered so far have only a limited objective. They suggest that liberals rule out the possibility of imperfect obligations only by taking a recent and unnecessarily constrained view of their task. However, it is one thing to argue that there may be imperfect obligations and another to show that there are any. I have so far argued neither that there are imperfect obligations, nor that charity is one such. All I have claimed is that there are good reasons for constructing a liberal account of justice in ways that do not rule out imperfect obligations. If liberals could construct principles of imperfect obligation they might be able once again to offer an account of the virtues.

Prospect

How should such a construction proceed? What would it establish? Would it show anything about charity or about other virtues? Here I offer only a sketch.

The basic idea of the alternative construction is to focus in the first instance on obligations and not simply on rights. This allows for the possibility of imperfect as well as perfect obligations. Imperfect obligations, since they constrain agents rather than the relationships between agents and recipients, can be thought of as principles underlying and defining the virtues of agents, agencies or traditions.

The method of construction for imperfect as for perfect obligations is to consider what obligations can be had by all. This is parallel to the constructivist account of rights except in one respect. In constructing the set of human rights it was necessary to determine what the maximal set of equal co-possible rights is. That turned out to be the weak link of the construction. In constructing an account of obligations it is unnecessary to maximise. The aim is only to determine whether any given principle (on which an act, a life or an institution might be built) can be acted on by all; if it cannot, its rejection is a matter of obligation. The operative idea in the construction is modal not metric.

If we are looking to work out a set of universal obligations, principles of action that cannot be universally adopted must be rejected. One type of principle that can be adopted by one agent yet cannot be adopted by all is a principle whose enactment destroys or disables or undercuts agency in at least some others on at least some occasions and so renders those others at least temporarily unable to adopt that same principle. For example, principles of coercion or deception or violence undercut or destroy somebody's agency in some respect; so their rejection is part of any set of principles which can hold universally. What is going on here is a strict version of Kantian universalising. It identifies as principles of obligations those principles which must be adopted if non-universalisable principles are rejected.

Matters that are usually identified as central to justice—no violence , no coercion, no deceit—are components of the set of principles that must be adopted by rational agents *of any sort* who act on principles that can be adopted by all. The construction is just a way of identifying principles that must be adopted by any rational beings who do not organise their acts or lives or institutions on lines that cannot be shared by all of a plurality of agents.

This constitutes a method for constructing principles of perfect obligation, which can be universally adhered to in all interactions, and so can potentially be demanded by those who find themselves on the receiving end of action. Perfect obligations have corresponding rights. The discourse of rights, with its peculiarly powerful political impact, remains accessible to those who begin their systematic ethical thinking from the perspective of agency and obligation.

Although the approach can be used to identify rights as easily as to identify obligations, it does not propose any algorithm for just action. The construction determines only a set of principles: their application is a matter for deliberation and judgement. There are no algorithms for applying principles to cases. It follows that the exact demands of justice must vary with circumstances. For example, what constitutes coercion will vary depending on the vulnerability of those who would be victimised. Activity that might be normal bargaining or negotiating procedure in interaction with an equal may coerce the vulnerable.

The reason why metric notions can be avoided in this construction is that it does not aim to determine the total set of principles of obligation. It provides only a procedure for determing whether any proposed principle of action is one that could form the basis for action by all. If nobody were tempted to acts that violate a given principle of obligation, that principle would remain undiscovered: a theoretical but not a practical blemish. By contrast, standard constructivist accounts of rights must determine all rights if they are to determine any, since rights are individuated as mutually limiting components of the largest set of liberties compatible with like liberty for all.

This way of constructing an account of obligations allows that there may be an indefinite number of distinct principles of obligation. In many situations an act which violates none of them may be available; in others agents will find that there is no way to avoid all wrongdoing. Since no ethical algorithm is on offer there is no guarantee that painful and tragic dilemmas are even in principle avoidable.

So far the construction has been sketched only for the general case of unspecified ('arbitrary') rational agents, without any reference to the peculiarities of human rights. There may, of course, be further principles that could be universally acted on among pluralities of some sorts of rational beings, but not among pluralities of other sorts of rational beings.

The point can best be made by a couple of examples. Imagine in the first instance agents of a slightly idealised sort who without fail have well-ordered preferences, unerring capacities to calculate, excellent knowledge of options and outcomes and the capacities to exact their decisions. Could such beings universally act on the principle of refusing to help others in need? I take it that they could: nothing in the account of these beings shows that their capacities to act are at risk. We have no reason to think that they have needs, or that leaving needs unmet would destroy or undercut their agency. Among such idealised agents a principle of self-centredness could be universally adopted.

Among human agents things may be different. Here we are considering agents who are embodied in vulnerable form, are subject to illness and death and need regular nourishment and at times in their lives the care and attention of others. They need these things not merely for some arbitrary purpose but as conditions of becoming and remaining agents. Among such rational and needy beings, a principle of self-centred indifference to others needs could not be universally adopted. Its attempted adoption would erode or destroy the capacities for agency of some of their number, so guaranteeing that its adoption was less than universal. If rational and needy beings are to act only on principles they all can act on, they must eschew principles of undercutting or destroying one another's capacities to adopt principles. They must make it a matter of principle not merely not to coerce or deceive, but to reject self-centred indifference to others' needs insofar as this indifference threatens the other's agency. This means that they must make it a matter of principle to help meet at least some of the needs of at least some others. Among rational and needy beings, charity in the old sense of concern for the needs of others, is an obligation.

Welfare Rights and Imperfect Obligations

This line of thought has a good deal in common with that advocated by certain 'welfare' liberals who begin their argument from the perspective of rights.[17] It stresses the need to maintain the conditions of agency. Why then does it not lead to the same conclusion, namely that there is a right to have agency-threatening needs met? What shows that there is only an imperfect obligation to meet the needs of others? Why could we not come to the conclusion: non-coercion, non-deceit etc are matters of perfect obligation among all possible sorts of rational beings; help to those in need is a matter of perfect obligation among rational and needy beings? What shows that we are not dealing with perfect obligations and their correlative rights in both cases?

The assymetry between obligations not to coerce or deceive (and their like) and obligations to help those in agency-threatening need is in fact an obvious one. (And incidentally one much stressed by libertarians). It is just this. We can meet the universal demands of non-coercion, non-deceit etc by coercing and deceiving nobody. But we could not meet a universal demand for help for those in agency-threatening need. Helping others needs time, presence, effort and resources. Nobody can offer more than selective help. Hence obligations to help those in agency-threatening need cannot be owed to all in need. Yet obligations to help are also not merely special obligations owed to specified others in virtue of certain special relationships or agreements. Obligations to help are not merely institutionalised, positive obligations. They are in the first instance *unallocated* obligations. That they are obligations is established by the very argument by which obligations of justice are determined, subject to the restriction that we are considering rational beings whose vulnerable embodiment creates needs. That they are only *imperfect* obligations follows from the fact that the argument fails to establish who owes whom which sorts of help. It does not follow that obligations to meet needs cannot be allocated: indeed they often must be allocated before needs can be met. Among human beings the paradigm of needing help which no special relationship can supply is not the much discussed one of needing to be rescued by some present and competent stranger (the domain of so-called 'Good Samaritan laws'), but of needing support which could be supplied by others who are absent and numerous. It follows that the allocation of recipients to agents, a process of institutionalisation, is indispensable: but it is a separate and further move, which can be made only when principles of obligation have been established. Obligations here are clearly prior to rights, since the identification of rights to be helped awaits the allocation of recipients to agents, which itself presupposes the identification of principles of obligation.

Charity and Welfare

It may seem that we have strayed from standard paths of liberal debate to little purpose. For showing that charity, the duty to care for the needs of others is an imperfect duty seems to do very little to secure help for the needy (even in the sense in which arguments may help in practical tasks). What is the use to the vulnerable and needy of an obligation to help which they cannot claim? Isn't the intuition that we should worry only about justice, about claimable obligations and their correlative rights, a sound one?[18]

To be sure, justice and claimable rights are essential for everyone, including the needy and vulnerable. But it does not follow that we can afford to worry only about justice. In particular if the welfare liberal's aim of showing that meeting needs is a matter of perfect obligation cannot be achieved, we have reason to think hard about imperfect obligations as well as about justice. How important can unallocated obligations, and in particular an obligation of charity, be for those in need? Several considerations are relevant.

First, I have not identified charity with familiar forms of private philanthropy, which clearly are unable to meet all needs, and which may have built in difficulties such as those discussed under the heading of a 'culture of dependency'. An obligation to help meet the needs of others does not have to be discharged by means of private philanthropy. Its optimal enactment might demand that quite other sorts of institution be constructed. Second, I have not assumed or shown that it is part of the definition of imperfect obligations, or specifically of charity, that enforcement is wrong. It is clear that enforcement will require allocation of recipients to agents (or that procedures of allocation be established). Once allocation is achieved, enforcement is possible, and there may be reasons for thinking that it should take place. I have only argued that imperfect obligations, including charity, cannot be enforced until tasks are allocated. How if at all the legal sanctions should then be used remains a matter for discussion.

Third, I have argued only that an initial constructivist vindication of the principle of charity fails to determine any allocation of needy recipients to obligation bearers, hence (since the obligation cannot be universally performed) establishes no rights. The next step would be to consider how obligations to meet the agency-threatening needs of others might best be institutionalised. Often adequate institutionalisation would have to give the needy claims against specified others (perhaps both agents and agencies). The rights that would then be established would, however, be institutional rather than fundamental or human rights, although the obligations whose discharge these rights secured would be fundamental obligations and provide a standard by which modes of institutionalisation could be judged and vindicated. Adequate institutionalisation presumably takes different forms in different times and societies. In mass societies it may be that the most appropriate institutionalisation of an obligation of charity is some form of the welfare state. In saying this, one does not, of course, mean that nobody has rights to the services so established: but these rights are not vindicated merely by a fundamental argument that determines ethical principles but also by considerations for allocating and institutionalising that obligation. The missing element in the argument here is that nothing has been said about the legitimacy or otherwise of institutionalising imperfect obligations in forms that rely in part on legal enforcement. Rather than offer such an argument I merely note again that there may be reasons to discard a supposedly exhaustive contrast between that which is enforced by law and that which is simply voluntary.

Conclusions

In trying to link an account of justice with an account of the virtues I have been trespassing across some now well established boundaries. In the background lie various unexplored issues. Much of the point of attempting an account of justice along contructivist lines is that this is a way in which one can go when relying on conceptions of agency that do not hinge on preference, and on conceptions of moral reasoning that do not invoke a subjective conception of the good or rely on maximizing notions. The working parts of the construction I have sketched rely on modal notions, and specifically on the idea of determining what principles can and cannot be shared by all of a plurality of rational, or rational and needy, agents. The re-appropriation of the notion of an imperfect obligation has relied not on any determinate account of the good for man, but simply on identifying some modes of finitude which bear on the conditions for producing and maintaining human agency. These starting points, however, are economical rather than alien. They are, I suggest, weaker than the more luxuriant models of rational choice that are generally preferred, and they are embedded in ordinary conceptions of action and reason.

The conclusions offered are also in some ways economical. In arguing for a reconsideration of imperfect obligations and of charity I am well aware that no general duty of beneficence, such as utilitarianism may entail, has been established. Nothing has been said about obligations to please others or to make them happy, let alone to maximise happiness. In the sense in which the phrase is generally used there is here no 'overload of obligations' problem. Charity as here constructed is a much narrower duty than beneficence; it is concerned only with meeting agency-threatening needs.

In spite of this atmosphere of economy I shall put my largest conclusions quite extravagantly. First, if the liberal tradition is to salvage an account of justice from the shipwreck of the Natural Law tradition, then it can also take charity and other virtues seriously. It can vindicate an obligation not to neglect the agency-threatening needs of vulnerable and needy beings. Second, if liberalism is taken to be primarily a theory of rights, then a constructivist approach does not yield determinate results, and if it did could justify only those obligations whose recipients are allocated, i.e. the rights libertarians favour. Although that conclusion may be less harsh than its usual libertaraian interpretation, since I have argued that the determination of non-coercion and non-deception too must take account of the vulnerabilities of agents, a rights-based construction does not establish obligations to act to end agency-threatening need. Third, although the obligation to meet agency-threatening needs that can be established is only an imperfect obligation, this provides grounds for thinking not that charity is marginal or optional, or that it could be wholly embodied in voluntary philanthropic organisations, but that it is urgent to see how the obligation can best be embodied not only in characters and traditions, but in institutionalised social relations that put the needy in a position to direct claims to specified others.

NOTES

Thanks to Tim O'Hagan, Joe Schmitt, Nigel Dower, Sheldon Leader.

1 John Locke, '*Two Treatises of Government. . .*' ed. P. Laslett (Cambridge University Press, 1970) II, No. 5.

2 Ibid., No. 6.

3 See John Dunn, *The Political Thought of John Locke: An Historical Account of the Argument of the 'Two Treatises of Government'* (Cambridge University Press, 1969); James Tully, *A Discourse on Property: John Locke and his Adversaries* (Cambridge University Press, 1980); J. B. Schneewind, 'Ideas of Charity: Some Historical Reflections', unpublished.

4 John Locke, *Venditio*, p. 86, '. . . he that sells his corn in a town pressed with famine at the utmost rate he can get for it does no injustice against the common rule of traffic, yet if he carry it away unless they give him more than they are able, or extorts so much from their present necessity as not to leave them the means of subsistence afterwards he offends against the common rule of charity as a man and if they perish is no doubt guilty of murder', reprinted as appendix to John Dunn, 'Justice and the Interpretation of Locke's Political Theory', *Political Studies*, XV (1968) pp.68-87. For confirmation that Locke thinks those in dire need have rights to charity, see also *Two Treatises of Government. . .*, I. No. 42 where he writes: 'As *Justice* gives every Man a Title to the produce of his honest Industry, and the fair Acqusitions of his Ancestors descended to him; so *Charity* gives every Man a Title to so much out of another's plenty as will keep him from extreme want'.

5 James Fishkin, *The Limits of Obligation* (Yale University Press, 1982), S. Kagan, 'Does Consequentialism Demand Too Much? Recent Work on the Limits of Obligation', *Philosophy and Public Affairs*, 13 (1984) pp. 239-254.

6 Countless works could be cited: evidently John Rawls, *A Theory of Justice* (Harvard University Press, 1971) and Robert Nozick *Anarchy, State and Utopia* (Blackwell, 1974); also the writings of Alan Gewirth and Ronald Dworkin.

7 Cf. Alan Gewirth, 'the philanthropic relation . . . is one of supererogation. In its simplest form one person A freely gives another person B some good X . . . such that A has no strict moral duty to give X to B and B has correlatively no claim right to receive X from A. Thus, A's gift to B is an act of generosity or

charity', 'Private Philanthropy and Positive Rights', in Ellen Frankel Paul *et al.* *Beneficence Philanthropy and the Public Good* (Blackwell, 1987) pp. 57-78; also John O'Connor, 'Philanthropic activities are similar to supererogatory acts in that they are beyond duty', 'Philanthropy and Selfishness', Ibid, pp. 113-27. But see David Heyd on supererogation in liberal framework.

8 Cf. *Decretum Gratiani* 'Natural Law is that which is contained in the Scriptures and the Gospel', quoted in A. P. d'Entrèves, *Natural Law* (Hutchinson, 1951).

9 Cf. Robert Nozick, op cit., Ellen Frankel Paul et al., op. cit.

10 Cf. John Rawls, op. cit.; Ronald Dworkin, *Taking Rights Seriously* (Duckworth, 1977); Alan Gewirth, *Human Rights: Essays on Justification and Applications* (University of Chicago Press, 1979); Henry Shue, *Basic Rights: Subsistence, Affluence and U.S. Foreign Policy* (Princeton University Press, 1980).

11 These approaches may be Wittgensteinian, or more recently mainly quasi-Hegelian or revisionary Aristotelian. See, for example, Alasdair MacIntyre, *After Virtue* (Duckworth, 1981) and *Whose Justice? Which Rationality?* (Duckworth, 1988); Michael Sandel, *Liberalism and the Limits of Justice* (Cambridge University Press, 1982); Michael Walzer, *Spheres of Justice: A Defense of Pluralism and Equality* (Martin Robertson, 1983)

12 Various rapprochements have been tried. For example, John Rawls in 'Justice as Fairness: Political not Metaphysical', *Philosophy and Public Affairs*, 14 (1985) pp. 223-51 provides a communitarian underpinning for his liberal principles of justice: in the process he sheds claims to universal scope. Bernard Williams in *Ethics and the Limits of Philosophy* (Fontana, 1985) depicts liberal ideals, such as truthfulness and the meaning of individual lives, as emerging within determinate social orders.

13 Foucault's work is here a great corrective; it in turn may need correcting by consideration of the distinctive part state power can, perhaps in modern societies must, play in the revision and destruction of disciplinary regimes. Cf. Michael Walzer 'The Politics of Michel Foucault', in David Couzens Hoy, ed., *Foucault: A Critical Reader* (Blackwell, 1986).

14 If rights were based on a physicalist account of act individuation a metric would be available. Cf. Hillel Steiner, 'Individual Liberty', *Proceedings of the Aristotelian Society*, LXXV (1974-5) pp. 33-50. however, this approach has difficulty in giving a 'thick' enough account of liberty and its value to explain why it should be taken as ethically fundamental.

15 One reason why deontological liberals are preoccupied with determining a maximal liberty is that they are constantly seduced by preference-based accounts of practical rationality, where the possibility of finding a metric of value seems tantalisingly close. The reason it is close is that this account of practical reason meets the demands of consequentialism. Deontological liberals deploy it at their peril: in adding assumptions that secure the desired metric properties for actions and options they risk undercutting their reasons for rejecting consequentialism. Why try to ground rights without reference to other values if those values have been already been accepted? Rawls' discussions of rationality and Nozick's of compensation for rights-violations provide examples of this tendency.

16 Quentin Skinner, 'The idea of negative liberty: philosophical and historical perspectives' in R. Rorty, J. B. Schneewind and Q. Skinner, eds., *Philosophy*

in History: Essays in the historiography of philosophy (Cambridge University Press, 1984).

17 For example, in the work of Alan Gewirth and Henry Shue.

18 Thomas Nagel 'Poverty and Food: Why Charity Is Not Enough', in Peter Brown and Henry Shue, eds., *Food Policy: The Responsibility of the United States in Life and Death Choices* (Free Press, New York, 1977).

The Journal of Value Inquiry **25**: 203–216, 1991.

Articles

Generosity: A duty without a right

RICHARD STITH
Valparaiso University School of Law, Valparaiso, IN 46383–6493, USA

The rhetoric of rights permeates and dominates American legal thought today. Even ethics is often considered to involve fundamentally a mutual respect for "moral rights." Understanding human rights is taken to be a sufficient condition for knowing how we do and should order our life together.

I disagree. I think that with regard to rights, as to so much else, our modern modes of thought fail fully to capture the ways we still live, and therefore wrongly limit our choices concerning how we should live.

All this is commonplace. With some frequency in the academic literature, it has been noted that our times are peculiarly "rights infatuated."[1] And with similar frequency, this fact has been lamented.[2] There are many who do not agree that rights alone can provide an adequate basis for human community.

However, as explained below, recent analyses have been able to show only that significant normative values lie outside some sphere of immediate individual relationships which must still be relegated to rights.[3] I want to point out something more: that our practices reveal alternatives to rights even within that sphere. I think I have found something not only in addition to rights but also instead of rights. Some rights can and ought to be rejected in favor of what I call "duties of generosity." The practices to which I turn for models of non-rights-based relations are part neither of morals nor of law. They belong to what is called "manners" or "courtesy" or, more descriptively, "graciousness."[4]

Do duties imply rights?

One conceptually clear way to understand the limitations of rights begins with the commonly held "correlativity thesis." This thesis is that for every right there exists a correlative duty and that for every duty there exists a correlative right.[5] For example, if A has a duty to pay a debt to B, it is said to follow necessarily that B has a right to be paid by A. And likewise wherever B has such a right, A has such a duty.[6] "Such" is an important word here, because the correlativity thesis applies only to rights which are *claims* against another, not to rights which are merely *liberties*. A may well have a liberty-right to run his competitor B out of business without B having any duty to close up shop.

Perhaps the existence of liberty-rights could be said to weaken the correlativity thesis, in that certain significant rights are thus shown not to correspond to anyone else's duty. But, for our purposes here, the wrong side of the thesis is weakened. We are interested not in whether there is a duty for every right, but in whether there is a right for every duty.

Why so? Well, if there is a right for every duty, then it follows that the set of rights is equal to or greater than the set of duties. If every duty implies a right, then the modern primacy of rights talk is justified. Rights analysis covers the normative universe, in that it ends up describing all rights and all duties, according to this side of the correlativity thesis. On the other hand, if some duties do not imply rights, then thinking about rights must be supplemented by thinking about duties, if some of the latter are not to be overlooked. The adequacy of rights-based thinking is, therefore, appropriately attacked by pointing to duties which do not correspond to rights.[7]

Many scholars have, in fact, sought to discredit the thesis that every duty of one individual implies a right of some other individual, by pointing to apparently rightless duties. It is said, for example, that alleged duties to oneself cannot correspond to rights. Again, it has been argued that duties to God or to the State are not perfectly captured by rights language suitable for other human individuals.[8] Likewise, it is contended that many of our duties are to classes rather than to individuals and that here no one can be said to have correlative rights. I may have a duty to give to the poor, but no particular beggar has a right to my money.[9]

But none of these arguments, whatever their merits may be, points to situations where I have a duty to benefit a particular human being without that person having a right against me. These arguments thus appear to concede that our duties to benefit other human individuals are fully described in terms of rights. Yet it is just this implicit concession which I refuse. I want to discover ways to hold onto neighborly duties without invoking neighborly rights.

Some readers may fault me here for having failed to mention the many "will-based" theories of rights, which make the existence of rightless duties to individuals obvious.[10] Not every particular beneficiary of someone else's duty is a rightholder, so these theories contend, for in order to have a right one must have a legally recognized choice. Someone's duty to give me a cow does not *per se* imply that I have a property or a contract right to her. I have a cattle-right only if I have some remedy I can use effectively to obtain her if she is withheld, or perhaps also unless I have the ability to waive (or even to transfer) a claim to her. Such choices are not open to me, under English law for example, where I am a third-party beneficiary of a contract between my father and a rancher, or where the State has simply commanded the cattleman to redistribute his wealth under pain of criminal punishment. Criminal law duties, according to these theories, often impose duties on individuals without granting rights to other persons. Although you have a duty not to kill me, I have no full right not to be killed by you, because I cannot make the State provide me with police protection, nor can I or my estate force the State to punish an unsuccessful or successful attempt to murder me. And, of course, I cannot sell my right to life to some rich sadist in exchange for some preferred benefit to my family. Similarly, according to some theories,[11] no duties to infants and to the very senile (not to mention to fetuses and to animals) involve rights, because the beneficiaries of said duties are presently physically unable to exercise rational choice.

A moment's reflection will show, however, that this method of demonstrating the existence of duties without rights is not what we are seeking. It does not look for unnoticed duties which the catalogue of rights has missed. It simply takes the list of claim-rights and shortens it. Will-rights theory shows at most that a narrow definition of rights will not adequately bring to light all duties. It does not show that the commonsense notion of rights as legally or morally required benefits (which notion holds that both I and an infant have a right to life) is not sufficient. But it is this latter, popular notion that permits rights talk to dominate our thought. And so it is this that must be shown to give an inadequate account of duties.

Nor have benefit-based theories of rights surrendered entirely to will-based theories in the academic world, though they have been refined in response to some of the arguments made above.[12] A leading advocate of the benefit theory of rights has recently claimed that being a "direct, intended" beneficiary of a duty is sufficient for having a right.[13] It is theses of this sort which I shall oppose, not by redefining rights more narrowly but by calling attention to duties directly to benefit other individuals that cannot be translated into *anyone's* language of rights. In so doing, I attack the very core of correlativity and present the possibility of the rejection of rights in human relationships founded on duty.

Some duties of mutual generosity

Consider the following commonly accepted social rule for tea parties and the like: "No one may take the last cookie." Translated into our terms here, the rule becomes "Everyone has a duty to leave the last cookie on the table." There is a mutual duty[14] to leave the last cookie uneaten.

Although I shall appeal a bit to our shared beliefs and practices in analyzing this rule below, my primary purpose is not anthropological but logical. Even someone unfamiliar with this rule, or someone who disagreed with my more detailed description of it, ought to concede that the duty I depict is a possible one. That concession is all that I need in order to show that we may have duties intended directly to benefit others that do not correspond to rights possessed by those others.

Can this cookie-leaving duty be translated into the language of rights, as the correlativity thesis would demand? Certainly it cannot without contradiction be straightforwardly transformed into a statement of individual claim-rights. The rule "Everyone has a right to take the last cookie" is self-contradictory, if by it we mean that every person both has a binding claim in his or her favor and also has equally binding claims in opposition. Or, put another way, our normative practices do not permit us coherently to assert that A has a valid claim to the cookie, while B, C, and the rest also have identically valid claims. Rights in a conclusory or absolute sense must be exclusive, but any lesser degree of rights would not adequately represent the unequivocal duties of our original formulation. Moreover, even reducing the rights involved to non-absolutely weighted interests would not eliminate the antinomy, for even these lesser claims, being all identical, are incapable of leading to a resolution of the problem of what to do with the cookie. No one can eat the cookie without violating many other equal rights. Yet to leave it on the table would be worst of all, for this solution alone would violate *everyone's* rights. By contrast, there is no contradiction nor even any slight tension in the original duty formulation. The result is never in doubt. If everyone abides by his or her duty, the cookie simply remains uncontested and uneaten.

Even if we try to restate our duties merely as liberty-rights (rather than as claim-rights), we are unsuccessful. If everyone had a liberty-right to the cookie, it is true that all could, without logical or normative difficulty, make a grab for the cookie. The fastest or strongest would eat it, and no one else could claim that his or her rights had been violated. But everyone who made such an effort would have violated (or at least attempted to violate) the duty not to take the cookie. To be at liberty means, by definition, that one is under no duty, so liberty-rights obviously cannot express a situation where everyone is under a duty.

One's supposed cookie claim-right, too, could not be exercised without a violation of one's duty, so that yet another contradiction in a claim-rights translation has been shown. One cannot have a right to do that which one has a duty not to do – where, as here, the duties and rights in question operate on the same level within the same institution. (It is possible to say, for example, that one has a legal right to do X but a *moral* duty not to do X. But one cannot say that one has a legal right to do X and also a *legal* duty not to do X.) Rendering mutual duties not to take the cookie straightforwardly as mutual claim-rights to the cookie brings about insoluble antinomies both among rights and between rights and duties.

There is, however, one rights formulation which at first glance appears adequately to express everyone's duty to leave the cookie alone: "Everyone has the right to have no one else eat the cookie," i.e. to have the cookie go to waste. Under this latter formulation, no one could claim the last cookie, but each could feel properly aggrieved and could rightfully complain if someone else took the cookie. I must agree that this translation is not self-contradictory in any way, nor does it contradict the original duty rule. But to state it is to reveal the incompleteness of our original rule statement. Those who practice the duty rule would surely also find it most impolite and ungracious for anyone seriously to complain when someone else ate the cookie. So let us temporarily reformulate the original rule as follows: "Everyone has a duty to leave the last cookie *and not to object if someone else takes the cookie*."

Furthermore, the proposed translation of the duty to leave the cookie into the right to see that the cookie goes to waste seems to miss the intent of those who do their duty. That intention is to have someone else eat the cookie, not to have it left over. The whole point of rule compliance here, as it might be explained to a child learning it, is generously to grant other people's appetites precedence over one's own. To complain when one's wish is fulfilled would be to contradict that intent. We can thus combine the idea of non-complaint and that of the intended beneficiary into a simpler and final duty formulation: "Everyone has a duty to leave the last cookie *for someone else*.[15]

Is it possible, however, that this duty to let others eat the cookie is but the indirect reflection of some other duty, which duty possibly could be expressed in terms of rights? For example, it has been suggested to me[16] that the duty here might really be to the host: Guests might leave the last cookie in order to keep the host from worrying that he or she had not provided enough food. This attractive idea, however, is open to several objections. For one thing, if such a duty to the host exists, it, too, does not correspond to any host rights. It would be absurd for a host to insist that no one eat the last cookie so that he or she could imagine all to be satisfied.

Furthermore, the duty-to-the-host idea does not fully capture the practice we have already described. If the host were the real intended beneficiary, then surely it would be within the rights, and even the duties, of each guest tactfully to stop others from eating the cookie. But this is not done.

Moreover, if by some chance all other persons have left the room without eating the cookie, I know of no rule still forbidding one to eat the cookie. Similarly, it is common (though quite difficult because politeness discourages candor) to attempt to determine whether in fact anyone else present really wants the cookie. If no one else does, then one is free to eat it. This fact shows that others as intended beneficiaries are absolutely essential to the original rule. When they are absent, or when they are already satisfied and so cannot benefit, the rule has no application. Therefore, the rule does not aim at waste nor at pleasing a host. Even when rule compliance makes the cookie go uneaten, it remains on the table as a symbol of our mutual care for one another.[17]

Nor, let it be emphasized, is the duty an ascetic one, meant to combat self-indulgent gluttony or to encourage self-sacrifice for its own sake, for, if it were, it would remain in force when one were alone as well as among others.

We have discovered, then, a duty directly to benefit other individuals which cannot be translated into rights, no matter how rights may be defined. What name should be given to this newly discovered creature? "Graciousness" seems almost correct, but a bit too broad and too connotative of style rather than of substance. "Deference" may be too small spirited. While I own that the title is not perfect, I would contend that the mutual duty we have unearthed is appropriately called one of "generosity" because it involves an obligation to relinquish potential possession to someone who has no right to possession. And it involves a *duty*, rather than a supererogatory act of generosity, because one does wrong in taking the cookie for oneself.

There is something quite odd in all this. Someone who takes the last cookie, when others might want it, not only has no right to possess it. He or she also violates a duty to leave the cookie for others. Yet others at the table not only should not object, but should be pleased – since the cookie is being consumed by an intended beneficiary. The last cookie is left precisely for someone who does not do his or her duty. Our duty is to leave the cookie for someone whose appetite is so imperious that duty's command is ignored. This mutual duty of generosity is a duty to benefit precisely and only those who do wrong. Such duties are nearly unheard of in legal[18] and moral systems, but they abound in manners and in religion.

Consider another example: "A host has a duty to provide as many towels as a guest might desire. A guest has a duty not to request any towels which a host might desire." Here we are dealing no longer with identical duties incumbent upon all participants in a practice of graciousness. (The guest has no duty to provide towels for the host.) The prior example envisioned only one role, that of potential cookie-eater, while here there are two, those of host and of guest. It is important briefly to consider this variation on mutual duties of generosity, since it would seem to be rather more common. Complementary duties are more frequent than identical duties in human interactions.

The problem in essence is, however, the same. Just as we previously wondered what to do with a mutually wanted cookie, here we ask ourselves, as host or as guest, what should be done with mutually desired towels. And the answer, as a matter of duty, is equally clear: The towels should be left for the other, who (if he or she in fact retains or obtains the coveted towels) is violating a duty.

Can these duties be coherently translated into rights? No, for the same reasons we have already explored. A guest cannot have a right to towels desired by a host and the host at the same time have a right to towels desired by the guest. Such a translation incohrently pits one's rights against another's rights and against one's own duties. Yet from duties there results no contradiction and a clear if rough solution: The host should provide as large a pile of towels as a guest could possibly wish, even to the point of skipping his or her own bath if towels are scarce, while a guest who suspects such a scarcity should take few if any towels from the pile (insofar as, but no further than, the guest has reason to hope that the towels left behind might end up being used by the host).

A variant practice also exists: The original towel possessor (the host) offers additional towels to a bath-hungry guest who graciously refuses to take them. The host then "insists" and the guest continues to refuse until one or the other gives in. This resolution occurs either because one has been convinced that the other truly does not desire the towels, or because one has breached the duty to be towelless. (Perhaps, however, the latter has done so not out of a desire for towels but rather out of a desire to respect the other's sense of duty to relinquish towels, of which more later.) This variant has the obvious advantage that the towels do not go to waste, but it does not involve any essential alteration of duties.

Note that this practice, again, does not demand self-sacrifice for its own sake. It is perfectly all right not to offer towels (and also all right to request and use towels) that the other person cannot possibly desire – which is not to deny that at some point an additional duty not to be gluttonous or ungrateful might come into play to limit absolutely the number of towels one should hoard.

There seems little point in multiplying examples further. Courtesy duties of generosity are so common and important to our life together that I would suppose they take more instructional time than do morals in educating the next generation, perhaps precisely because young children find it hard to grasp the fundamental point that such duties are not to be translated into rights. A child, in my experience, immediately converts the duty to let others play with the toys in his or her possession into a right to play with toys possessed by others. Indignant outrage follows, and must continue to follow, such a translation – because in terms of rights this rule is self-contradictory. Only when the mutual duty of generosity has been grasped can there be peace (which may not occur until toys become no more important than towels in the child's life).

A theory of generosity duties

The special character of mutual duties of generosity, and its distinction from that of rights, can be further brought out in a real property metaphor.

The phenomenology, the *feel*, of a right is that of a rule-protected power (insofar as one has secured that to which one has a right) and of a rule-supported claiming or demanding such power (insofar as one is not yet in possession of that to which one has a right). As spheres of potentially absolute and arbitrary power, rights are litigious by nature, one might say, so that there can be no peace as long as rights seem to overlap or, *a fortiori*, as long as they actually do overlap (as in the translations of cookie, towel, and toy duties). A normative system of rights requires *exactitude*. There must be precise and known boundary lines between Whiteacre and Blackacre if incoherence and squabbling is to be avoided.

By contrast, mutual duties of generosity involve "buffer zones" extending back a bit from the boundaries to which rights would press. Each property owner has a duty to relinquish the use of these zones to the other. That is, each has a duty both not to use the buffer strip and also not to object to the use of the strip by the neighbor. The result is that litigation is lessened. Trespass does not trigger conflict. Minor infractions of duty are accepted, and even welcomed in the best of all worlds. Only major intrusions are brought to court (just as there might properly be objections if someone ate *all* the cookies).

It is essential to ask here whether property still exists in a practical sense in the buffer zones. That is, is there any difference (from the point of view, say, of the owner of Whiteacre) between the yardage the frontier zone intrudes into Whiteacre and the yardage it intrudes into Blackacre? I think not, though from a certain formal point of view the first remains the "property" of the owner of Whiteacre, while the second remains alien.

Similarly, the cookie duties and the towel duties were not significantly different, despite the fact that, by hypothesis, the last cookie was the property of none of the potential eaters, while the towels were the property of the host. What we have along the border is, therefore, a realm without property *or* rights, a realm of what one might call "lawless altruism."

We may observe in passing that private property is thus not necessary to generosity, a conclusion frequently disputed.[19] Wherever one, without being coerced, relinquishes *de facto* possession of a good to someone who has not a right to possession, one is being generous. This statement remains true even if one is under a duty so to act, as we have seen. Note that it is not essential that one be giving up one's own property. Generosity is possible even among thieves and even in a Hobbesian state of nature. And, from the point of view of the recipient who had no right to what he or she obtained (and may even have had a duty to refuse it), gratitude is called for.

Is a world without property, a world of "lawless altruism," any more stable or desirable than one of "lawless egoism"? The simple answer is that two people can sacrifice the same object more easily than two can acquire the same object. As long as we are willing to put up with waste, or are willing to see the buffer not as waste but as a symbol of mutual regard, peace would seem to ensue. It must be admitted that, in the most gracious of all worlds, each side would actually plead with the other to use the entire zone (the "I insist" we noted before). And the other side would wish to use the zone not in order to obtain some personal gain, but in order to please his or her altruistic neighbor. Since both sides would feel the same, at each level and *ad infinitum*, a kind of good-natured "battle" might occur. Still, a dialectical synthesis might be found in which *both* sides could come to sacrifice themselves for the other: the one by deferring to the other's territorial desire and the latter by occupying the territory in deference to the former's desire to be duty-observing. The first sacrifices land and the second sacrifices virtue. In any event, the defects of such a system are an important strength. Waste or generosity-battle is in fact not likely to occur because people are not going to be wholly duty-minded, and the system has anticipated this fact. Minor violations of duty are expected and promote efficiency, while extreme violations are checked by rights as well as by conscience. "Lawless altruism" is, therefore, clearly preferable to "lawless egoism."

In all our analysis so far, we have presumed mutual identical or complementary duties. Indeed, it is the fact of mutuality which has enabled us to prove that duties can exist without correlative rights. Can this presupposition be removed? Can one have duties of generosity toward those who have neither rights nor duties toward one?

I do not see why not. If I can dutifully leave a cookie for a rational adult who ought to do the same for me, why cannot I leave a cookie for a small child not yet subject to duties? If the rational adult has no right to the cookie, why need the child have a right? I think that nothing requires the child to have any right (or at least any claim-right) to the cookie, though no wrong is done when the child eats it.

The reason we began with mutual duties is that the benefit-theory of rights could otherwise easily have argued that a duty to another person must by definition, as it were, involve a right on the part of that person. We can now see that this is not the case. To say the child has a right to the cookie *adds* something, phenomenologically, to the statement that I have a duty to let the child have the cookie. It adds an imaginary or real claiming of power over the cookie on the part of the child, a vain or effective appeal to rules to force me to give the cookie. The language of rights militantly reduces rules from an object of common loyalty to the status of security guards at the beck and call of the child. And I am likewise reduced from a servant of the law to a servant of the child. This phenomenological reflection shows, by the way, that will-based theories are nearer than benefit-based theories to the essence of rights. Rights always involve self-centered (which may not be equivalent to "selfish") acts of will – at least in the imagination. A duty not to make such an appeal is perhaps the easiest and most effective way to prevent a rights consciousness from arising, but it is not strictly necessary. What is necessary is only that no reductionist appeal by the beneficiary be imagined or realized.

Professor Joel Feinberg has used the language of aristocracy to call a world without rights, even one in which most people conscientiously do their duties, "servile."[20] Property and rights are needed, it would seem, in order to promote human dignity. But do our experiences in this rightless realm of graciousness bear him out? I think not. Rights subject us to each other, while duties subject us only to a common law. One might say that rights convert that law itself into something which can in part be privately owned. Rights, not duties, are the baser way to order our life together. To be generous and self-sacrificing on the one hand, and gratefully to accept benefits recognizing that one does not have a right to them on the other, is the more noble life.

A final touch should be added to this sketch of duties of generosity. Note that no mention has yet been made of the inculcation of the virtue of generosity nor of the enforcement of the duties pertaining thereto. The simple reason for this omission is that our purpose has been normative and logical, not genetic. How to bring about and maintain generous ways of living together is an empirical and psychological question separate from the question of how to describe the inner logic of a system of duties without rights.[21]

But mention should be made here of the peculiar logical irrelevance of enforcement mechanisms to the system which has been described. Neither party to a cookie dispute has any rational self-interest (other than envy) in violating the duty of non-complaint by appealing to higher powers. If such powers were to step in, they could do so only in order to remind *all* parties that *none* may have the cookie – not to allocate the cookie to anyone. This is what children finally learn after many futile attempts to make parents enforce their rights to toys.

Note, too, that even the intervention of higher enforcement authority does not recreate the exactitude of a system of rights. An enforcing power would require *both* property owners to move back from the buffer zone. It would not be interested in the erection or protection of a boundary fence (except insofar as this might be required for the definition of the buffer zone). The duty-enforcing state or community is not interested in total and exact control of the world, in deciding precisely who eats the cookie or farms the land. Unlike the Christian tradition in which there is a duty to turn the other cheek, the realm we have discovered is not simply one where individuals are duty-bound to submit to injustice, while a higher ideal of justice remains available and perhaps enforceable by God or by a civil authority. *There is no just allocation* of the cookie or the towels or the toys or the borderland. There is no "right" answer. There is only the possibility of possessing and the duty not to do so.

Notes

1. R.B. Louden, "Rights Infatuation and the Impoverishment of Moral Theory," *Journal of Value Inquiry* 17 (1983): 87–102. Among the best, albeit short, histories of the modern idea of rights are John Finnis, *Natural Law and Natural Rights* (Oxford: Clarendon Press, 1980), pp. 205–210 and accompanying notes; and M.P. Golding, "The Concept of Rights: A Historical Sketch," in *Bioethics and Human Rights*, ed. E.L. Bandman and B. Bandman (Boston: Little, Brown, 1978), pp. 44–50. See also Golding's more refined treatment: "Justice and Rights: A Study in Relationship," in *Justice and Health Care*, E.E. Shelp ed. (D. Reidel, 1981), pp. 23–35.
2. See, e.g., Louden, *id.*; Theodore Benditt, *Rights* (Totowa: Rowman and Littlefield, 1982); Karl Marx, "On the Jewish Question," in *Early Writings* (New York: Random House, 1975), pp. 211, especially 230–231; J. Narveson, commentary on Feinberg's essay "The Nature and Value of Rights," *Journal of Value Inquiry* 4 (1970): 258–260; "Law and Ecological Ethics Symposium," *Osgood Hall Law Journal* 22 (1984): 281–348; J. Raz, "Rights-Based Moralities," in *Utility and Rights*, ed. R.G. Frey, (Minneapolis: University of Minnesota Press, 1984), pp. 42–59; Michael Sandel, *Liberalism and the Limits of Justice* (New York: Cambridge University Press, 1982); and Ch. Taylor, "Atomism," in *Powers, Possessions and Freedom: Essays in Honour of C.B.*

Macpherson, ed. by A. Kontos (University of Toronto, 1979), pp. 39–61. Not to be neglected is the seminal, if controversial, work of the late Michel Villey, especially as found in his "Droit Subjectif I" *Seize essais de philosophie du droit* (Paris: Dalloz, 1969), pp. 140–178, originally published in *Archives de philosophie du droit* 9 (1964): 97–127.

3. See especially works cited in notes 7–10 *infra*.
4. So far as I have been able to determine, recent normative theory has been curiously uninterested in the structure of modern manners, as opposed to that of modern morals or of modern law. Ronald Dworkin has used "philosophy of courtesy" as a foil, but I know of no one who has seriously taken up this task. *Law's Empire* (London: Fontana Press, 1986), pp. 45–86.
5. Alan White, for example, asserts the commonness of this view, though he does not himself share it. *Rights* (Oxford: Clarendon Press, 1984), p. 85. Those who have proposed the thesis appear to include S.I. Benn and R.S. Peters, *The Principles of Political Thought* (New York: The Free Press, 1959), pp. 102, 107, and Charles Fried, *Right and Wrong* (Cambridge: Harvard University Press, 1978), p. 81. John Finnis, note 1, at 210, seems implicitly to hold such a view when he states "The concept of rights is not ... of less importance or dignity [than the concept of duties]: for the common good is precisely the good of those individuals whose *benefit*, from fulfillment of duty by others, is their *right* because *required* of those others in justice." See also Carleton Kemp Allen, *Legal Duties* (Oxford: Clarendon Press, 1931), 156–220; R.W.M. Dias, *Jurisprudence*, fourth edition (London: Butterworth's, 1976), 36–39; George Whitcross Paton, *A Textbook of Jurisprudence* (Oxford, Clarendon Press, 1972), p. 285; other philosophers have denied the second half of the thesis, as explained later in the text.
6. The analysis of correlativity is, of course, that of Wesley N. Hohfeld *Fundamental Legal Conceptions* (New Haven: Yale University Press, 1919).
7. Benditt (*supra*, note 2), Louden (*supra*, note 1), and Raz (*supra*, note 2) all point out that we may well have rights which we ought not to exercise. This "ought" is something else which rights talk misses. I do not mean to deny or minimize this important critique of rights, but it is not germane to the present part of our analysis. It is a critique as much of the "must do"'s of duties as of the "must have"'s of rights, for it points out that both duties and rights may miss the more subtle "oughts" and "shoulds" of human relationships. By contrast, my first interest is to demonstrate that rights are inadequate even to convey all the strong and clear imperatives of duty.
8. John Austin calls these rightless duties "absolute." II *Lectures on Jurisprudence* (New York: Burt Franklin, 1861), pp. 66–75. Cf. the critiques by Allen, *supra* note 5, and by Paton, *supra* note 5.
9. Besides Austin, *id.*, and Benditt, *supra* note 2; see John Stuart Mill, *Utilitarianism*, ed. H.B. Acton (London: J.M. Dent and Sons, 1972), pp. 46–47. Joel Feinberg, *Rights, Justice, and the Bounds of Liberty* (Princeton University Press, 1980), pp. 135–139, 144, mentions these "duties of charity."

   Feinberg, *id.*, also refers obscurely to rightless "duties of self-sacrifice" and exemplifies them by acts of heroism taken from H.B. Acton, "Symposium on 'Rights,'" *Proceedings of the Aristotelian Society* (1950), Supplementary Volume 24, pp. 107–108. Feinberg, Acton, and Benditt (*supra* note 2, p. 7) may be calling attention to duties without rights similar to those discussed in this essay. But their duties of heroic self-sacrifice are unlike the ones I discuss below in that theirs are far more rare than mine. Moreover, at least some of theirs seem construable as duties without rights only because of a confused juxtaposition of two different subjective points of view. A hero may feel under a duty while his beneficiaries do not feel a right to his services. But within this own subjective world, a hero might well say that those who are aided have "a right" to his help, though they do not realize it. Finally, none of these writers draws attention to the mutuality of rightless duties which is the focus of the present work.

10. H.L.A. Hart is the leading figure here: "Bentham on Legal Rights," in *Rights*, ed. D. Lyons (Belmont: Wadsworth Publishing Company, 1979) pp. 125–148. See also Allen, *supra* note 5, Dias *supra* note 5, Finnis *supra* note 1, Golding *supra* note 1, and Paton *supra* note 5.
11. See, e.g., P. Montague, "Two Concepts of Rights," *Philosophy and Public Affairs* 9 (1980): 372 and 384.
12. See, e.g., the telling response to Hart by Neil MacCormick, "Rights in Legislation," in *Law, Morality, and Society*, ed. P.M.S. Hacker and J. Raz (Oxford, 1977), pp. 189, 198.
13. David Lyons, *Rights, supra* note 10 at 63, 73. I am referring to duties specifically to benefit certain other persons, not to so-called "useful duties."
14. Some readers may object that the term "duty" seems too strong here. I have two responses. The first is that our language permits the word "duty" to designate all behavior mandated by a non-optional social institution. Only so long as an institution is felt to be optional does the word "duty" seem excessive. For example, it strikes us as odd to say that a man has a duty to dance with a woman, but a dancing instructor of young people might well say "A gentleman has a duty to ask a woman sitting by herself to dance," because he and his audience are at that time committed to the conventions of social dance. Similarly, if we take proper cookie-behavior as something the breach of which would be unthinkable, the word "duty" seems appropriate. My second response is that nothing turns on the word "duty" anyway. My point is not to rank such behavior highly or lowly, in a normative hierarchy, but to discern its inner logic. I want to ask whether and when sentences in the imperative form referred to by the word "duty" entail correlative rights. I have chosen the word solely for this purpose, not for its connotations nor as part of any wider axiological assertion.
15. One could adduce less rich examples where the impossibility of waste as a goal would be still more obvious. Consider what happens when two similarly-situated persons reach a closed door simultaneously. Each has a duty to open and hold the door for the other, while neither has a right to have the door held open. It cannot be that the purpose of this mutual duty is to have the benefit of first entry go to waste, i.e., to have each refuse to go through the door until the other has done so, leaving both permanently outside.
16. By Professor James Albers
17. I owe this felicitious expression to my secretary Pat McRae.
18. I say "nearly" unheard of, because there are a few examples or near-examples in our law of such duties without rights, not counting the criminal laws already mentioned. Included would be juridical refusal to rectify *de minimis* duty violations, intra-family absence of rights to sue in tort when duties are violated, and the general civil and criminal lack of a right not to be endangered by another's failure to adhere to his or her duty of care (except in the exceptional

case where harm actually occurs). There may be more such one-way duty relations in foreign law. See, e.g., Inga Markovits, "Pursuing One's Rights under Socialism," *Stanford Law Review* 38 (1986): 689–761; and George P. Fletcher, "Human Dignity as a Constitutional Value," *University of Western Ontario Law Review* 22 (1984): 171–182, 180. See also Richard Stith, "New Constitutional and Penal Theory in Spanish Abortion Law", *American Journal of Comparative Law* 35 (1987): 513–558.

19. Feinberg puts it this way "... consciousness of one's right is *necessary* for the supererogatory virtues, for the latter cannot even be given a sense except by contrast with the disposition always to claim one's rights," *supra* note 9 at 157.
20. Feinberg, *id.* at 156.
21. I would suspect that all duties must sometimes be enforced if they are to be firmly entrenched, and if expectations of originally wrongful benefits are not to develop into assertions of rights. It is probably important that last cookie grabbers sometimes not be invited to the next tea party.

The Southern Journal of Philosophy (1991) Volume XXIX, No. 1

FAMINE AND CHARITY

John M. Whelan, Jr.
Lycoming College

Glancing through my favorite magazine I read: 'Five things you can do for 72 cents or less . . . 1. Enjoy a cup of coffee. 2. Pick up a newspaper. 3. Buy a few stamps. 4. Have a soft drink. Or 5. Make a lasting difference in the life of a child and family overseas through Foster Parents Plan'. I opt for the soft drink. Is my purchase of it and consequent failure to help the family a failure to do something that I am morally required to do, as for example a failure to save a child from drowning would be? Or is it a failure to do something that I morally ought to do even though I am not morally required to do it, as for example a failure to hold the door for someone carrying a heavy package would be? Or is it just a failure to be as generous as I possibly could be, and therefore, merely a matter of doing less than the ideal? Or is there some other possibility?

The view I will try to defend is that, on the one hand, no purchase of mine, no matter how frivolous, can be faulted morally for being a failure to give to charity; and on the other, that giving to charities like the Foster Parents Plan is not morally optional in the way that, for example, giving to the local symphony is.

My view is closely related, obviously, to the traditional view about charity. And both views face two problems. The first is suggested by the customary phrase 'duty of charity': it seems contradictory to say that anyone has a duty to do what she does not have to do. And my conclusions seem to be similarly paradoxical: how can it be true, as my view seems to suggest, that giving to charity is both optional and also something that ought to be done? Second, many philosophers and others believe that my first claim is false; they believe that many of our purchases can be faulted morally for being failures to give, for example, to famine relief.[1] In support of this they note that the world has changed radically since the traditional view was formulated;

John M. Whelan, Jr. teaches at Lycoming College; and has begun to publish somewhat regularly in the area of ethics.

disparities in wealth are much greater; and it is possible to prevent terrible suffering in other parts of the world by giving to charity. As a result, they believe that many of our more frivolous purchases *can* be faulted morally for being failures to give to charity.

In the remainder of this essay I will try to show, first, that the line of reasoning I just sketched is fallacious, so that whatever else can be said about our more frivolous purchases, they are not morally defective for being failures to give to charity; and, second, that we ought to give to charity, even though we do not have, in any serious sense, a duty or obligation to.[2]

I.

The questions with which I began this essay distinguished what I am morally required to do from what I morally ought to do even though I am not required to do it. And in my opinion discussions of charity are hampered by not attending to this distinction. In particular it is commonly assumed that if I am not morally required on some occasion to give to charity, then it must be the case that giving to charity on that occasion is strictly optional: a nice thing to do, but not something that ought to be done.[3] It is important to be clear that this assumption is false, so I want to say a bit about the distinction.

Let me begin with two definitions: Jones is morally required to do x on some occasion if and only if there is a *moral requirement* on Jones to do x on that occasion and there is not a more important reason for Jones to refrain from doing x. Jones ought to but is not required to do x on some occasion if and only if there is a *moral reason* for Jones to do x on that occasion, the moral reason does not amount to a moral requirement, and there is not a more important reason for Jones to refrain from doing x.

Some examples of moral requirements. Moral requirements can be specified against assault, theft, lying, cheating, breaking promises, failing to do your duty, and so on. Examples could easily be multiplied, but each would be an example of an obligation voluntarily taken on, as in the case of a promise, or of a duty associated with some particular social role and (for the most part) voluntarily assumed, as when someone becomes a parent or policeman or professor, or of what are traditionally (and in my view misleadingly) called 'natural duties', like the requirements against assault, theft, cheating, lying, and so forth.

Some examples of moral reasons that do not amount to requirements (hereafter I will refer to these simply as moral reasons). Jones can easily open the door for someone who is carrying a large package; so there is a moral reason for her to do so, but not a requirement. Smith can give candy to all of the Halloween 'trick-or-treaters'; consequently there is a moral reason for him to do so, but he does not violate a requirement even if he refrains out of prejudice from giving candy to the one black child. Brown coerces (but does not force) her teenage son into dressing and grooming as *she* chooses. There is a moral reason for her not to do this, but it does not amount to a requirement. White tells Smith a true, but embarrassing story he has heard, let us say at twelfth hand, about Jones. There is a moral reason for him not to gratuitously hurt Jones's reputation like this, but it is not a requirement. Blue goes out of his way to do a favor for Green; there is a moral reason for Green to express his gratitude to Blue, but he is not required to.

Two comments. In saying there is no moral requirement against doing (or failing to do) any of these things, I do not mean to imply that doing any of them is morally acceptable. On the contrary, if there is a moral reason against doing something, then it ought not to be done unless there is a more important reason in favor of doing it. And I do not mean to imply either that moral requirements ought always to prevail over moral reasons in our deliberations about what to do.

So what do I mean to imply? Giving a full answer to this question, every point clarified and defended, would take me too far from my main topic; however, the most important part of that answer would be this: if there is a moral requirement on Jones to do x and there is not a more important reason for Jones to refrain from doing x, then someone may *demand* that Jones do x; whereas if Jones merely ought to do x, then, although Jones is liable for moral criticism for failing to do x, no one may demand that she do it. Further, if Jones is required to do x and she fails to do it, then someone may demand that Jones offer an apology, explanation, compensation, or rectification (whichever is appropriate); but if Jones fails to do what she merely ought to do, then no one may make such a demand.

This condition fits my reaction to cases: for example on the occasions when Jones is required to keep her promise, Smith may demand that Jones keep it, and if Jones breaks it, and Smith does not know why, then Smith may demand an explanation, and depending on what the explanation is perhaps also an apology. And if Smith suffered a serious loss as a result, then possibly he can demand compensation as well. However, if Jones fails to do what she ought but is not required to do, then perhaps explanations or apologies will be *expected*, but they may not be demanded. For example if Blue does a big favor for Green, then, as we say, Green 'owes Blue a debt of gratitude', but this "debt" is precisely unlike a debt incurred as a result of a contract in that payment cannot be demanded. Reactions diverge with respect to Smith and the Halloween candy: some share my reaction that Smith has not violated a requirement; others disagree. But to the best of my knowledge reactions do not diverge about this: *if* Smith violates a requirement by refusing to give the black child some candy, then others may demand that he rectify the situation.

The expression 'may demand' of course means is permitted morally to demand, and on my view the permission to demand compliance with it is essentially involved in the justification of any moral requirement; so the permission is justified in whatever way the requirement is justified. By contrast no one is permitted morally to demand that I do what there is merely a moral reason that I do: persuasion and criticism are the only "weapons" we may use to get people to do what they ought but are not required to do.

I am aware that what I have just written raises all sorts of questions, but for present purposes I hope this much can be conceded: 'Jones morally must do x' is stronger than 'Jones morally ought to do x'; and therefore there may be circumstances in which it is true that Jones morally ought to do something even though it is not true that she must do it, and similarly that it may be true that she ought to do something even though it is not true that she is required or has a duty or obligation to do it.

If I am right about this, then we should expect to find circumstances in which Jones, for example, is required to prevent harm, and also circumstances in which she ought to prevent it even though she is not required to. I believe this expectation is met. For example, most people believe that there is a moral requirement to save someone from drowning when it would be easy to do so, and most believe that there is a moral reason to hold the door for someone whose arms are filled with heavy packages. Roughly speaking, what distinguishes the first sort of case from the second is this: there is a requirement on Jones to prevent harm to Smith when there is sufficient reason to believe that the harm she can prevent is serious and undeserved, when there is also sufficient reason to believe that she can prevent this harm at little or no cost to herself, and also that preventing the harm will benefit Smith; and when, in addition, there is *not* sufficient reason to believe that Smith or anyone else will prevent the harm if she does not prevent it. By contrast the conditions under which there is a moral reason for Jones to prevent harm to Smith are much looser. The harm need not be serious, the cost to Jones need not be small in absolute terms only small in relation to the seriousness of the harm that Jones can prevent, and it does not matter whether others will help if Jones does not. What matters is whether Jones's failure to help favors her own relatively unimportant interest at the expense of an interest of Smith's which is much more important; whether, in other words, Jones favors her own interest in an objectionably selfish way. Very roughly and in sum: Jones *must* prevent harm to Smith when the harm she can prevent is serious, and it will not get prevented unless Jones prevents it; whereas Jones ought but is not required to prevent harm to Smith when it would be objectionably selfish not to.

II.

Now I can take up two of the main questions of this essay: Does it follow from the fact that there are occasions when I am required to prevent harm that there are occasions when I am required to give to charity? And does it follow from the fact that there are occasions when I ought but am not required to prevent harm that there are occasions when I ought but am not required to give to charity? In my view the answer to both questions is 'No'. And I will try to show that this answer is correct by showing that there are no occasions when anyone *ought* to give, since if there are no occasions when the loose conditions described above are met, then there can be none when the more strict conditions for a requirement are met, and so none when anyone has a duty to forego some purchase and give the money she thereby saves to charity; and, if it is assumed that rights and requirements are connected, then this will also show that no one has a right against anyone that she forego some purchase and give the money to charity.

However, I must admit that a strong argument can be made for the opposite conclusion. Informal reasoning for that conclusion might go something like this. Suppose after reading the advertisement for the Foster Parents Plan, I head off for the Coke machine with fifty cents in my pocket, and when I get there, a child is standing next to it who manifestly needs money for food much more than I need the Coke. Not that she will die if she does not eat soon, and not that she may not be able to get food somewhere else, but she is very hungry now, and I can easily buy her something to eat at no sacrifice to myself. In circumstances like these it seems obvious that I ought to give her my Coke money, though of course I am not required to, have no duty to, and the child has no right against me that I do so. And it can also seem obvious that it is only my callousness and lack of imagination which prevents me from seeing that the actual situation when I buy a Coke is often in all morally relevant ways exactly like this hypothetical situation. After all, it is often true that my need for the Coke is small, and a starving child's need for food is always great. If this is correct, then what follows is that *I ought to use the need of a starving child as a kind of yardstick whenever I buy anything*. Before each purchase I ought to ask myself: is this purchase objectionably selfish given that I could send the money to a charity which will help people who are starving? And if the answer is 'Yes' and I make the purchase anyway, then in making it I will have done something just as wrong as turning my back on the hungry child at the Coke machine. I will not have violated a requirement or failed at any duty that I have, but I will have done something I ought not to have done.

These informal reflections lead to the following argument: 1. No one ought to do anything which constitutes an objectionably selfish failure to prevent harm. 2. A purchase constitutes such a failure if the money spent on it could be used to prevent harm, and preventing that harm is much more important than the benefit produced by the purchase. 3. Many of our purchases are for relatively unimportant things, the money spent on them could be sent to charities which prevent hunger and disease, and preventing those harms is much more important than making those purchases. Therefore, 4. many of our purchases ought not to be made.

This argument seems to me to be both radical in its implications and difficult to fault. Radical in its implications because not many of us think that each and every one of our purchases ought to be justified by comparing its importance to us with the importance of food to a starving child, nor do we think that it is wrong to make purchases which cannot be justified in that way. Difficult to fault because, as I will show in the next section, none of the objections typically made to roughly similar arguments undermine this one.

But before I get to that let me make two comments by way of clarification. First, a defender of this argument need not claim that many are now to *blame* for the objectionably selfish way they spend their money. Not many realize they are being objectionably selfish when they buy a Coke, and perhaps they are not to blame for failing to realize it. However, this does not invalidate the conclusion that they are spending their money in a way that they ought not to spend it.

Second, as should be obvious, the argument above is indebted to Peter Singer's well-known article 'Famine, Affluence, and Morality'.[4] That article elicited a powerful response when it was first published in 1972. Why? Certainly not because Singer argued that we ought to give money to charities designed to help people who are starving: that conclusion has been a commonplace in our moral tradition for a long time. Rather it was because Singer's article suggested this different conclusion: no purchase is morally justified unless the money spent on it brings about a benefit which is at least as important, impartially considered, as the harm that could be prevented if that money were used to prevent people from starving. Singer derived that conclusion from this premise: 'if we can prevent something bad from happening without sacrificing something of comparable moral significance, then we ought to do it'. Many philosophers would now reject that premise because they believe that we need not act based on the result of this sort of impartial comparison: doing so, in their view, demands too much of us.[5] These philosophers believe that it is acceptable morally to give our own projects and desires weight out of proportion to the weight they have when considered from an impartial point of view.[6] However, my argument shows that this objection can be avoided. Someone is objectionably selfish only if she favors herself *too much*. And a defender of my argument can admit (even insist) that there are irresolvable differences about when that point is reached. These differences arise on account of differences in the relative importance people assign to preventing various sorts of harm as opposed to making particular purchases, and also to differences about how great people think the gap between the two needs to be before it is objectionably selfish to make the purchase. For this, and other reasons, judgments about which purchases are objectionably selfish may differ somewhat. Be that as it may, all but the most heartless egoist must admit that there comes a point where favoring her own relatively unimportant interest over someone else's much more important interest is objectionably selfish, and consequently ought not to be done. My argument would therefore seem to demonstrate not merely the commonplace that we ought on occasion to give something to charity, but also the unsettling conclusions that some and possibly many of our purchases can be faulted morally for being failures to give to charity, and also that each and every one of them ought to be justified in the light of a starving child's need for food.

III.

It would be wrong not to buy food for the child by the side of the Coke machine, why would it not therefore be wrong for someone to purchase a Coke when she could easily do without it, and could then send the money to charity which would prevent children from starving? And more generally, why does it not follow that we ought to measure each of our purchases agains the need of a starving child for food?

Some think the reason is distance: one child is far away, the other is close at hand.—'Out of sight out of mind' is undoubtedly a psychological truth, and for that reason perhaps we ought not to blame those who do not give, but it is not a moral truth, so it is hard to see that it has anything to do with whether we ought to give.

'If the child is close at hand, we can be *certain* that our money will do her some good; if we send it to a charity in another part of the world, who knows? Perhaps the food will rot on the dock; perhaps it will be used for political purposes; perhaps the charity will be run by unscrupulous men for their own profit'. Perhaps. But there are reputable charities, and with respect to them, these risks are slight.

'The sick and starving are to blame for their poverty; so we should not help them'. This is dubious (though many people believe it) but suppose it were true . . . . Suppose a child was drowning because she ignored a warning sign, would it then be morally acceptable to allow her to drown?

'Giving to famine relief will only lead to more children, and therefore to more of a problem in the long run'. This is probably not true as a matter of fact, but suppose it were . . . . What follows is that we ought to give to charities which provide more than food, not that we ought not give to charity.

'Others with much more money can give more easily than I can'. True, but not enough money will be given; I can sometimes give without sacrificing anything important, my money will do some good, so it would seem that I ought to give it.

Many philosophers identify morality with what they are required to do, obligated to do, with what it is their responsibility or duty to do, with what others have a right against them that they do. So they make objections like this: 'Maybe it would be *nice* if I gave to charity, but it is not something that I *have* to do; therefore it is not something that I am wrong for not doing'. But this simply does not follow. True, it is not the case that I *have* to give, but it does not follow that it is not the case that I *ought* to give. And certainly it is wrong to fail to do what I ought to do. Put another way: to be objectionably selfish is not merely to fail to be nice.

'My money is just a drop in the bucket; I cannot help everyone'. Suppose there are more hungry children by the Coke machine than I have money to help, does it follow that I should not help any of them? What would seem to follow is that, on that occasion, I ought to help as many as I can up to the point where it would not be objectionably selfish to fail to help more.

And if this is what I ought to do on that occasion, then this is what I ought to do on every occasion; I ought to monitor each of my purchases with the thought of a starving child: before each purchase I should ask myself, would it be objectionably selfish to buy *this* given that the money spent on it could prevent a child from starving? And what follows from the argument in Section II is that no purchase which it would be objectionably selfish to make in the face of the need of a starving child ought to be made, and the money saved thereby ought to be sent to a charity designed to help people who are poor and suffering.

IV.

Arguments of the kind I described in Section II are basically arguments from analogy which lead to the conclusion that many of our purchases are currently unrecognized instances of a familiar pattern: I do not hold the door for someone whose arms are filled with packages when I easily could; I do not give the starving child by the side of the Coke machine money for food when I have no important use for it; my wife and I do not eat at the cheaper restaurant for $45, but eat instead at the extravagant one for $70 when the difference in our enjoyment is not great, and the $25 saved could buy food and make a significant difference in the lives of starving children. The conclusion seems inescapable that this last purchase, and potentially many others, is objectionably selfish.

I will criticize this sort of argument in two stages: first, I will show that it is impossible, by contributing to any actual charity, to prevent people from starving in the way that those who argue as I described above typically suppose; second, I will show that the actual benefit paid for by giving money to a charity cannot unfavorably be compared with the benefit paid for by any frivolous purchase.

In moods when I am troubled by the argument above, I dimly imagine something like this: my $25 is sent to some charity and starving people get to eat $25 worth of food; my money is not sent and these people continue to starve: I imagine that my money can make this significant difference in the life of these starving people, and I wonder how, in the face of their need, I can use it to bring about small pleasures.

But these thoughts are a delusion; my money cannot make that difference. No charitable organization will alter the amount of money budgeted for food because my $25 does or does not arrive. Furthermore, it is senseless to think that my money could be, so to speak, "tracked" and we could thereby determine what effect its arriving on some particular day has or lacks. Finally, charities need to pay for all sorts of things—salaries, vacations, paper, advertising, equipment, and so forth—so my $25 cannot be said to make the difference between no food or $25 worth of food for people who are starving. If I do not send my money to some charity, then that charity will have that much less money to pay for all of the things that it needs to buy; it's ability to help people who are starving will be slightly less because I will have failed to pay for a fractional share of all the kinds of things the charity buys.

These considerations are enough to prove the following: I cannot send $25 to a charity and bring it about that starving people will get to eat $25 worth of food that they would not have gotten to eat otherwise; therefore, if it is objectionably selfish to eat at the more expensive restaurant, it is not because by doing so I fail to make this significant difference in the lives of the people who are starving. If there is a comparison which calls my purchase of the expensive meal into question, it is not this one.

But perhaps that purchase is objectionably selfish for another reason; perhaps it is selfish because it is a failure to pay for a fractional share of everything that a reputable charity needs to buy in order to help people who are starving.

In order to get a feel for what this benefit might amount to, consider CARE. In 1989 CARE USA employed approximately 7500 people in 36 developing countries. These people helped provide emergency relief assistance: flood in Bangladesh, earthquake in Armenia, hurricane in the Caribbean, drought and civil war in the Sudan, Ethiopia, Somalia, and Mozambique; CARE claims to have distributed approximately 230,000 tons of food; estimates vary about the number of people who got the food, but the number is certainly in the millions. In addition CARE employees helped vaccinate 600,000 children, helped build water systems, distributed food supplements, helped plant 29 million trees, taught farmers about safer more efficient growing techniques, helped thousands of people start and sustain small businesses, and many other things. The cost for doing all of this was $325 million. This means that each failure to contribute $25 to CARE in 1989 was a failure to increase by about one thirteen millionth the net benefit produced by CARE in that year. However, each failure to contribute $25 to charities which help people who are starving was not just a failure to contribute to CARE: it was a failure to contribute to each of the charities which do more or less what CARE does; so it was a failure to increase a much larger benefit by a much smaller fraction. Nonetheless, for my purposes it will be enough to focus on this question: is one thirteen millionth of the just described benefit significantly larger or smaller than the benefit produced by spending $25 for a more extravagant meal?

In my view the answer to that question is completely obvious: it has no answer. And if I am right about this, then it follows that no purchase of mine is objectionably selfish because it is a failure to give to a charity like CARE because there is no way to make the comparison which needs to be made if any purchase is to be called into question for being a failure to give to CARE. Note: my conclusion is *not* that the benefit brought about by my contribution is small in relation to the benefit brought about by my purchase of the meal; my conclusion is that there is no way to make this comparison.

Suppose someone disagreed with me about this, suppose she thinks it is obvious that one thirteen millionth of the benefit produced by CARE is vastly more important than the benefit produced by the more expensive meal. Or suppose she thinks the benefit brought about by a contribution to CARE is less important, could she defend her assertion? And in general, how do we defend claims of this kind?

Consider: someone disagrees that the benefit brought about by holding the door for someone whose arms are filled with heavy packages is more important than the exertion she would have to make to bring it about, what could I say to her? For one thing I could ask her to consider what she would want if roles were reversed. But suppose she is a self-reliant egoist . . . then I could ask instead which of these two things would be worse if it happened: you have to struggle through some door with your arms filled with heavy packages or you have to make the exertion necessary to open that same door (not the emotional exertion necessary to open it *for* someone, just the exertion necessary to open it)? The answer, I take it, is obvious. And again: which would be worse, that you have to forego the enjoyment of a Coke or that you have to continue starving? Again obvious. And now compare: which is worse, that you have to give up the pleasure of a more expensive meal or that each of the people who benefit from CARE in a year have to give up one thirteen millionth of the benefit?

With respect to this last question, it seems obvious to me that we have absolutely no idea what the answer is, and no idea how to find out. And this feeling of mine can be supported like this: our normal use of predicates like 'objectionably selfish' presupposes that we can confidently sort comparisons of individual well-being into one of three categories: that x happens to A is worse than that y happens to B, or that x happens to A is better than that y happens to B, or that reasons can be given for either answer, and so we must agree that the answer is uncertain. For example, I can remember as a child arguing about whether it would be worse for someone to lose his sight or his hearing. The argument was interesting because we could think of reasons to argue both sides: it was possible to try to extend our experience; to imagine and compare. But nothing like this is even *possible* when what we are trying to compare is some individual benefit with the result of the following psuedo-calculation: add the roughly estimated number of benefits of a roughly "estimated" magnitude that CARE, for example, brings about in a year, then subtract the roughly estimated number of losses of the roughly "estimated" magnitude that CARE also produces in a year, divide the result by 325 million, and then multiply by the cost of the frivolous individual benefit.

To call something objectionably selfish, to say that it belongs in the same category as the refusal to give a starving child money that was to buy a Coke, is to make a serious charge of immorality. If the charge is to be defensibly made, then it must be anchored in comparative judgments of well-being that almost all of us can immediately appreciate. That is why people are troubled by the (delusory) thought that the money spent on their more frivolous purchases could make a significant difference in the lives of people who are starving. And that is also why the charge cannot defensibly be made when it depends on a comparison between some individual benefit and the fractional part of a net benefit paid for by a contribution to, for example, CARE.

At this point someone might make the following objection: "True, each person's failure to give may only make a slight difference; so no one of those failures is objectionably selfish. But if everyone reasoned as you do, then no one would give to charity, and that would make a large difference to the well-being of lots of people."[7] This would be a good objection if I were arguing that it is not the case that people ought to give to charity because failing to give only makes a slight difference. But that is not what I have been arguing. My conclusion so far is only that a particular argument is defective; an argument which has the quite radical conclusion that many of my purchases are objectionably selfish for not being contributions to charity, and also that each of my purchases ought to be justified in the light of a starving child's need for food. It is one thing to show that this argument is defective, and that these conclusions are unsupported, and quite another to show that it is not the case that we ought on occasion to give to charity.

In my view philosophers equate attempting to refute this argument with attempting to argue that it is not the case that we ought to give to charity because they assume that people will give to charity only under the delusion that their contributions will make a significant difference in the lives of some of those who are starving—certainly advertisements of the kind that I mentioned at the beginning of this essay aim to keep that delusion alive. Nevertheless, the fact that people give to, for example, cancer research, shows that they will give to charities even if they are well aware that their contribution will have no individually important effect.

Furthermore, I made two criticisms of the argument of Section II and neither of them had anything to do with claiming that contributions to charity only make a slight difference: I claimed first that my, for example, $25 contribution cannot make the difference in the lives of people who are starving that the purchase of $25 worth of food could make; and I claimed second that there is no way to compare the effect that my contribution in fact does have with the benefit I would have to forego in order to make it.

To summarize: the argument I sketched in Section II is unsound; as a result it does not follow that I ought to think about what to give to charity by comparing the importance of each of my purchases with the importance of the harm I could prevent by foregoing it. And it also does not follow that what I ought to give in a month (day? year?) is what is left over after all of my not objectionably selfish purchases have been made. However, it does not follow from either of these conclusions that it is not the case that I sometimes ought to give to charities which aim to help people who are starving.

V.

Before going on to the final part of this, let me try to put what I have argued so far into a larger perspective. In the background of the debate over consequentialism, understood as the doctrine that agents ought to perform the act with the best consequences impartially considered, has been the thought that if consequentialsim is true, then many of our purchases can be faulted morally for being failures to give to charity; and if consequentialism is not true, then our current attitudes toward charitable giving are justified.[8]

I have tried to challenge both of these assumptions. In Section II I showed that a strong argument can be made for the conclusion that many of our purchases can be faulted morally for being failures to give to charity without assuming that consequentialism is true: a much weaker premise calls many of our purchases into question. And in Section IV I showed why that argument failed. An implication of what I had to say in that section is that it does not follow that I ought to give to famine relief even if consequentialism is true: the idea that it does follow assumes that giving and failing to give to charity have effects on the well-being of individuals which these acts cannot have.

VI.

I said at the beginning of this essay that we ought to give to some charities, and now let me add, to charities which effectively attempt to prevent various sorts of serious harm. Giving to charities like these is not merely nice; it is something that we ought to do. In view of the foregoing, I need to clarify this last clause. Obviously I do not mean that any particular purchase can be faulted morally for being a failure to give to charity. And if moral evaluation were ultimately only a matter of evaluating acts and failures to act, then my view would be paradoxical because I would be saying about some act both that I ought to perform it, and that performing it is optional. Further, if acts and failures to act were the only objects of moral evaluation, then the dissatisfaction many morally sensitive people feel at the amount of their charitable giving would have to be attributed to confusion: no reasonable person ought to feel dissatisfied about failing to do what is, after all, optional, strictly speaking.

But despite what many moral theorists assume, acts and failures to act are not the only objects of moral evaluation. And despite what others assume, acts, failures to act, and dispositions to act are not the only objects either. When people feel dissatisfied at the inadequacy of their response to famine relief, for example, they are not dissatisfied with themselves for failing to give on some particular occasion when they ought to have given—as someone would doubtless feel dissatisfied with herself for not saving someone from drowning when she easily could have. Nor are they dissatisfied with themselves for lacking some disposition to act. Rather they are dissatisfied with a set of their expenditures when that set is viewed in the light of the world's need; and so perhaps they say to themselves, "I ought to give more."

Those who believe moral evaluation has only to do with acts and failures to act must believe that our expenditures either succeed or fail to pass moral muster one by one. And I tried to show in Section IV that from that point of view none of our expenditures, not even the most frivolous, can be faulted morally for being a failure to give to charity. Nonetheless, I also believe that if I do not work enough charitable giving into my budget, then an entire set of my expenditures is morally defective in an important way; and therefore, giving to some charities is something that I sometimes ought to do.

In sum, the paradox I have mentioned is resolved like this: each of my charitable contributions is, strictly speaking, optional; however, giving to a charity at least once within an indeterminate period of time is not optional. Put another way: I am not blamable morally for failing to give to charity on any occasion, but if a large enough set of my purchases lacks a contribution to charity, then I *am* blamable morally for that.

This last conclusion needs defense from at least three points of view. First, it might be claimed that the effect of my earlier arguments is to undermine the only reason anyone could have to give to charity. I have already responded to this objection. People do not need to believe that they personally are preventing harm to anyone in order to be motivated to give to charity: many of us find that the desire to marginally improve the ability of institutions to prevent hunger and starvation is a completely adequate motive. People do not need the illusion that their contributions are individually important when they give to cancer research, and they do not need it when they contribute to CARE or Oxfam.

Second, it might be claimed that my conclusion is much too weak: it is not merely that we ought to give to certain kinds of charity from time to time, but that we ought to give a determinate amount, or that we ought to forego particular purchases and give to charity instead. I tried to defeat the only plausible argument for these conclusions that I know of in Section IV. I will not repeat those arguments here.

Third, it could be argued that my conclusion is too strong; it is not the case that we *ought* ever give to charity: giving to charity is a nice thing to do when we do it, but there is nothing bad even about never giving.

I have already conceded that there is no obligation to give, and also that failing to give on a particular occasion is not objectionably selfish. But it does not follow from either of these conclusions that there is nothing bad about not giving ever. Further, if anything is bad about not giving ever, it would appear to be this: such a failure would constitute, among people who have money to spend on inessentials, complete neglect of the suffering of other people. Therefore, the following argument would appear to justify the conclusion that many of us ought on occasion to give to charities which help people who are poor: 1. Completely neglecting the suffering of other people when you can do something about it at small cost to yourself is a bad thing. 2. Not giving at all to institutions which reduce the suffering of other people constitutes complete neglect of that suffering. 3. Therefore, those who have money to spend on inessentials ought to give some of that money to charities which reduce suffering.

Obviously this argument will not convince everyone. If someone does not accept 1., I have no general arguments guaranteed to convince her that she should. Two things can be said in favor of 2. One is that most of us hold people liable for blame if they do not sometimes give to charity, and I do not believe that conclusion can be supported without accepting something like 2. The other is that holding someone liable for blame because some set of her acts lacks a particular element is not confined to the case of charity. Parents have no duty to play with their children, and each time they do, they are doing something optional; but that parents sometimes play with their children is not optional. Friends have no duty to do favors for one another, and each time one friend does a favor for one another, what she has done is optional; but that friends sometimes do favors for one another is not optional.

What do we owe the poor? If the question means what are we obligated to give to private charities which benefit the poor, then the answer is nothing: no one and no government may demand that we contribute to charity. But if it means what ought we to do about hunger and poverty in addition to paying taxes, then the answer is that most of us ought to give to charities which are trying to eliminate it.[9]

NOTES

[1] Among philosophers, Peter Singer is notable for producing a careful argument for this conclusion. But roughly the same argument has regularly been made from one or another pulpit for a long time. Versions of Singer's argument appear in the following places: 'Famine, Affluence, and Morality', *Philosophy and Public Affairs*, v1, (1972); 'Reconsidering the Famine Relief Argument', *Food Policy: The Responsibility of the U.S. in the Life and Death Choices*, Peter Brown and Henry Shue (eds.), (New York: The Free Press, 1977); *Practical Ethics* (New York: Cambridge, 1979) pp. 158-181. In this last he explicitly mentions stylish clothes, color televisions, second cars, private schools, and expensive meals as examples of purchases that probably ought to be foregone in favor of charitable giving.

[2] Let me emphasize here that my essay has a quite specific focus: are any of our purchases morally defective for being failures to give to charities which try to help people who are starving? This focus is quite different from, for example, Onora O'Neill's in *Faces of Hunger* (London: Allen and Unwin, 1986). In that essay she argues for "far reaching political activity which transforms the basic principles of economic and social structures." (*op. cit.* p. 145.) Perhaps such a transformation is needed, but meanwhile each of us must confront the question of whether he or she has an obligation to do something about poverty and starvation by contributing to charity.

[3] To cite just a few examples, in a book devoted to this topic, William Aiken and Hugh La Follette (eds.) *World Hunger and Moral Obligation* (Englewood Cliffs, New Jersey: Prentice Hall, 1977) the following authors explicitly assume that if there is no duty or requirement to give to charity, then giving is, strictly speaking, optional: Aiken and La Follette, 'Introduction', pp. 2-3; John Arthur, 'Rights and the Duty to Bring Aid', p. 48; Jan Narveson, 'Morality and Starvation', p. 52; William Aiken, 'The Right to be Saved from Starvation', p. 86.

[4] *Loc. cit.*

[5] Bernard Williams' name is most often associated with this claim, but many philosophers echo it. See for example, Bernard Williams, 'A Critique of Utilitarianism', J. J. C. Smart and Williams, *Utilitarianism: For and Against* (New York: Cambridge, 1973); 'Persons, Character, and Morality', and 'Utilitarianism and Moral Self-Indulgence', both reprinted in his *Moral Luck* (New York: Cambridge, 1981). For a dissenting view, see Shelly Kagan's intricate and comprehensive discussion of these issues in his *The Limits of Morality* (Oxford: Clarendon Press, 1989).

[6] This way of putting the point derives from Samuel Scheffler *The Rejection of Consequentialism* (New York: Oxford, 1982).

[7] My consideration of this objection is prompted by reflection on "Five Mistakes in Moral Mathematics", Chapter 3 of Derek Parfit's *Reasons and Persons* (Oxford: Oxford University Press, 1987). Parfit tries to show there that I may have a reason to contribute to some project *because of the effect that contribution has* even in circumstances where that effect is imperceptible. I agree.

He considers a case where I have to choose whether to add the water in my one pint water bottle to 999 other pints which have already been poured into a water cart which is about to go into the desert to help 1000 thirsty men. This case would be analogous to the actual situation when we have to decide whether to give to charity if it were changed in at least the following ways: people are always thirsty and always in the desert, the water cart is always leaving, there are lots of uses, though many of them are frivolous, to which the water might be put by those who have to decide whether to donate, one pint donated does not mean one pint received, there are costs associated with getting the water to the thirsty men which those sending the water have to pay, and finally those sending the water have to decide *not* whether they would have a reason in these circumstances to donate their water (I believe they would), and *not* whether in these circumstances they ought sometimes to donate their water (I believe they sometimes should), but whether not sending some particular pint and using it for something else is objectionably selfish on some particular occasion.

[8] This thought is explicit on the first page of *The Limits of Morality.*

[9] Many people helped me with this essay, but let me single out A. P. D. Maritninch for assistance with an early draft; Richard Brook, Owen Herring, and Oliver Larmi similarly for a more recent draft; and J. L. A. Garcia similarly for a still more recent draft.

JUSTICE TO CHARITY

By Loren E. Lomasky

I. Introduction

Despite what one may be led to believe by breathless reports in the media, the acme of misery in America is not the woes, financial and otherwise, of Donald Trump and Michael Jackson. People lose their jobs, have their assets drained by reversals of fortune, suffer from illiteracy, malnutrition, lack of shelter, and other mishaps. The circumstances in which they find themselves are genuinely distressing. It would be an odd understanding indeed that failed to find these circumstances directly relevant to what morality asks of us. If morality is to count for anything, then surely it must take notice of exigent need. This is not merely the deliverance of a late twentieth-century Western moral consciousness massaged by the blessings of comparative affluence and graced with a newfound awareness of social justice. All traditional ethical codes of which I am aware, sacred and secular, demand that one take the distress of one's neighbor as bearing on one's own activities. "Am I my brother's keeper?" is the question; the well-nigh universal answer is "Yes." The disposition to be moved by and respond to distress is the virtue of *charity*.

It would, then, seem undeniable that among the moral duties that confront us are duties of charity. The proper recipients of such duties are those who are, either locally or globally, unfortunate[1] and for whom relief from distress is not countermanded by other moral considerations.[2] The proper bearers of the obligation are those who are situated so as to be able to respond to the misfortune and who would not be unduly burdened by doing so.[3] The precise contours will, of course, be determined

[1] By *global* misfortune I mean a set of circumstances that, taken together, render a person's life miserable on the whole. A *local* misfortune is one that disadvantages an individual at some particular time or with regard to some particular aspect of her doings while having little or no effect on the remainder of her affairs. So, for example, destitution is a global misfortune, while being hot, tired, eight months pregnant, and unable to find a seat on the bus is a local misfortune. What counts as appropriate charitable relief will be a function in part of whether the misfortune one aims to alleviate is global or local.

[2] E.g., it is not (under ordinary circumstances) an instance of charity to pass a hacksaw to a justly imprisoned felon.

[3] Sometimes we teach our children: "Be charitable to those less fortunate than yourself." This may pass muster as elementary moral pedagogy, but as a general prescription concerning when and toward whom to be charitable it is deficient for at least three reasons: (i) If you are *very fortunate*, then some of those less fortunate than yourself will be far removed from the domain of eligible charity recipients; multimillionaires are not obliged to bestow

by the circumstances in which the recipient and bearer of the duty find themselves. Much remains to be specified, but at least this much seems clear: unless morality recognizes strict duties of charity, it is insufficiently responsive to the plain fact that the woe of other persons *matters*.

In what follows I shall argue that this way of putting the matter is mistaken. One can maintain both that an adequate morality takes the misfortunes of other people to be a salient datum and that positing a duty of charity is a misconceived way to underscore that salience. That misconception is, however, deeply embedded in the strain of ethical thinking that has dominated the modern era, what I shall call the "jurisprudential paradigm." Briefly, if morality is modeled on law, such that its subject matter is taken to be individuals' rights and duties, then all moral concerns will be parsed in those terms. Morality will speak in a stentorian voice concerning what *must be done* and what *must not be done*; and with regard to that which is neither, it will adopt a discrete silence. The absence of command is *permission*, and how one chooses to behave within the zone of permissions is a matter of personal preference removed from the imperatives of morality-as-justice. If I am neither morally obligated nor forbidden to play golf, then it is simply not a matter of legitimate moral concern—not for me, not for anyone—whether or not I elect to golf. Similarly, if I am merely permitted but not obligated to relieve the distress of other persons, then whether I do so or not is beyond the purview of moral concern. Because the consequent will seem false to all but the doughtiest surviving Social Darwinists, the antecedent must be rejected. Ergo, duties of charity.

Note that the preceding argument presupposes what I have called the "jurisprudential paradigm" of morality. If, however, the language of morals is more capacious than a discourse of rights and duties, it remains an open question whether acknowledging the salience of other people's distress is best rendered by positing rights to receive charity and duties to provide it.[4] I shall, after disposing in Section II of a superficially appealing argument, contend in Sections III and IV that the jurisprudential par-

largesse on mere unimillionaires. (ii) If you are *very unfortunate*, then you are not generally obliged to assume further burdens in order to lighten the load of those even worse off than yourself. (iii) Because misfortunes are local as well as global, charity may call on you to respond to a (local) misfortune of someone who is (globally) more fortunate than yourself.

A complete taxonomy of the duty of charity would require additional qualifications and distinctions beyond those of this and the previous two notes. Because the aim of this essay is not to explicate but rather to cast doubt on the notion of a duty of charity, I abstain from such labors.

[4] Whether (i) each right has as its shadow a duty resting on some individual or set of individuals to satisfy that right, and (ii) all duties derive from the rights of some individual(s), are discussed in the philosophical literature under the rubric of the *correlativity of rights and duties*. Note that these are two logically independent theses; (i) may obtain even though (ii) does not. (The reverse is also logically possible, but I am unaware of its advocacy in the literature.) In Section IV, I examine the claim that duties of charity are *imperfect duties*, duties for which correlativity does not obtain.

adigm is impoverished. Rights and duties are the shell of morality, the hard and inflexible casing that safeguards the soft tissue of our vital practical concerns. Absent the protection provided by that tough exterior, we would be unable to give effect to that which matters to us as moral beings. However, the shell taken by itself is lifeless. Less metaphorically, I shall argue that morality should be understood as extending to the zone of permissions, and that this is where most questions of aid to the less well-off are located—most but not all: Section V investigates the case that can be made for welfare rights. It is acknowledged that, under a limited range of circumstances and to a limited extent, there may exist rights to receive aid and duties to provide it; but, for reasons adduced there and in Section VI, these are relatively minor adjuncts to the virtue of charity. Section VII offers brief concluding remarks.

II. Why There Can Be No Duties of Charity: A Bad Argument

Someone might try to short-circuit duties of charity in this way: To be charitable toward someone entails more than transferring needed goods. It additionally requires that one do so from the appropriate sort of motive. One must give, it is said, "from the heart." When the United Way volunteer comes round and extracts from the office curmudgeon a grudgingly tight-lipped, tight-fisted pledge, the curmudgeon gives to a charity but does not give charitably. Thus, if there is a duty to be charitable, it is at least in part a duty to act from appropriate feelings and attitudes. These, though, are not under our voluntary control. I can directly will to give ten dollars, but not to do so with an open and loving spirit. By an application of "ought implies can," it follows that there can be no general duties of charity.

There are two respects in which the argument is defective. First, and most obviously, it assumes that duties of charity are necessarily duties to be charitable. We can, however, distinguish between charitable *persons* and charitable *acts*. A charitable person is one who is disposed to be moved by the needs of others and who, in virtue of that disposition (and not some incentive external to it), regularly acts to relieve those needs. The virtue manifested is the biblical quality of *agapê/caritas*, the third term in the triad "faith, hope, and charity" (better: "love"). A charitable act, by way of contrast, intends the melioration of another person's misfortune but may or may not take that melioration to be intrinsically desirable.[5] So, for example, if the office curmudgeon makes his pledge

[5] Reference to intention is necessary because one who inadvertently or accidentally advantages another has not thereby performed a charitable act. If the remains of the pizza I toss into my garbage pail are subsequently scavenged by a hungry family, I have not performed the charitable act of feeding them, let alone acted charitably toward them. This is true, I believe, even if I am aware when I toss out the pizza that there is a very high likelihood that it will be discovered and eaten.

because not to do so would be to make himself an object of unfriendly gossip, he has nonetheless performed a charitable act. To borrow a locution from Aristotle, he has done what the charitable man would do, though he has not done it as the charitable man would do it. Even if it is not the duty of anyone to be charitable, one can have duties to perform charitable actions.[6]

Second, and more speculatively, it is questionable whether all "oughts" do imply "cans." If my entire fortune is nine dollars, that fact is a decisive counter to the claim that I ought to give ten dollars. It is less clear that my being of a cold and haughty temperament renders it false that I ought to give cheerfully. That I am unable through an act of will to feel charitable toward my fellows has less the character of an excuse than a moral indictment. There are not only certain things that I ought to do but also ways I ought to be. If I fall short of those ways, then I am, other things equal, morally deficient. The insertion of the *ceteris paribus* clause is to acknowledge that external happenstance can mitigate or eliminate one's responsibility for character defects. But the mere fact that I am not able to reform my character through a simple act of will is not itself an excusing condition.[7]

I may be culpable for the current deficient state of my character in virtue of antecedent voluntary actions that led to my current disability. If, for example, habitual self-indulgence has deadened me to the distress of others, then my absence of feeling is a condition for which I bear responsibility. Had I then chosen to act differently I would now be a different sort of person, one who is not only capable of performing charitable actions but also of being charitable. So construed, this is an instance of "ought implies could have done."[8] But even if no causal chain is traceable between past performances and current dispositions, it does not follow that the latter are a matter of moral indifference. It may be inappropriate for others to blame the individual whose actions are acceptable though his character is deficient, but it surely is appropriate for the agent himself to

[6] Arguing similarly, Kant declares: "[L]ove as an inclination cannot be commanded. But beneficence from duty, when no inclination impels it and even when it is opposed by a natural and unconquerable aversion, is practical love, not pathological [!] love; it resides in the will and not in the propensities of feeling, in principles of action and not in tender sympathy; and it alone can be commanded" (Immanuel Kant, *Foundations of the Metaphysics of Morals*, 400, trans. Lewis White Beck [Indianapolis: Bobbs-Merrill, 1959], p. 16).

[7] Sidgwick comments: "I agree that it cannot be a strict duty to feel an emotion so far as it is not directly within the power of the Will to produce it at any given time. Still . . . it seems to me that this emotional element is included in our common notion of Charity or Philanthropy, regarded as a Virtue: and I think it paradoxical to deny that it raises the mere beneficent disposition of the will to a higher degree of excellence, and renders its effect better" (Henry Sidgwick, *The Methods of Ethics*, 7th ed. [1907; reprint, New York: Dover, 1966], p. 239).

[8] Aristotle writes in *Nicomachean Ethics*, trans. Terence Irwin (Indianapolis: Hackett, 1985), 1114a20–23: "It was originally open to the person who is [now] unjust or intemperate not to acquire this character; hence he has it willingly, though once he has acquired it he can no longer get rid of it."

reflect, "I should be more open in my giving; I would be a better man if I were to do so." This is to offer a straightforwardly moral assessment, but it does not invoke any precondition of causal possibility.

The upshot is that one's inability to exercise direct control over one's feelings is no logical bar to the existence of duties of charity. One may, at a minimum, be morally obligated to perform charitable actions and, maximally, to be a charitable person.

III. An Alternative to Charity as Right or Duty

I noted in Section I that the jurisprudential paradigm presents a dilemma: either the misfortunes of others are not morally salient considerations or they generate duties to render aid. Why, though, should this understanding of morality be embraced?

With very few exceptions, modern moral theory has taken as its fundamental project the derivation of rationally acceptable means for the resolution of interpersonal conflicts. Individuals' interests collide; that is why morality is both possible and necessary. In the absence of some peaceable means through which differences can be brokered, the denouement is a perpetual state of war in which life is, Hobbes tells us, "solitary, poor, nasty, brutish, and short."[9] And so, from Hobbes onward, it is the quest for appropriate articles of peace to which philosophers have bent their efforts. An ethic of rights and duties is the inevitable product. If some item is contested between two parties, then a resolution of that conflict must of necessity indicate which of them has a right to that item and which a duty to withdraw. Just so long as rights and duties are acknowledged, the parties can live peaceably together. What more can be asked of a theory of ethics?

Considerably more, or so was the prevailing view of premodern moral philosophy. For the ancients, the primary practical question was not "What are my duties?" but "How may I live well?" Though answers differed in particulars, the common theme is that the good life is one informed by the *virtues*. A moral virtue is understood to be a settled disposition to feel and act in intrinsically good ways. "Why be virtuous?" is a question that admits only of the question-begging answer: "Because virtues are those good-in-themselves components of a life that is itself inherently good." Less easy to supply but more informative is a specification of which traits are virtues and how these may be inculcated, harmonized, and sustained. An examination of classical responses to these questions would be out of place here, but what is worth considering is the rationale underlying this conception of ethics.

[9] Thomas Hobbes, *Leviathan* [1651], ed. Michael Oakeshott (New York: Macmillan, 1962), Part 1, ch. 13.

Moral inquiry in the ancient world begins with the assumption that each of us has as a core interest the achievement of *eudaimonia*, a flourishing life. Thus, it is of considerable urgency for an individual that she identify and come to possess its components. Because we are social animals, it is undeniably the case that one such component of *eudaimonia* is a facility of avoiding conflicts with others and settling those conflicts more or less amicably when they do arise. Therefore, justice—the natural home of rights and duties—is among the virtues. The Greek world is in many ways distant from our own, but it was one in which there existed a well-developed conception of the importance of law as an arbiter of the affairs of contentious human beings. The Greeks' horror of the disorder that would ensue in the absence of law was at least as great as our own, and thus the conditions of justice receive considerable attention in their philosophical thought.

Nonetheless, Greek ethical inquiry extends considerably beyond the search for an interpersonal conflict-resolution device. There is more to the achievement of *eudaimonia* than scrupulously fulfilling one's duties to others and claiming from them one's rights. Indeed, of at least as much interest to these philosophers as *inter*personal conflict is conflict waged *intra*personally. They observed that individuals often prize in an ineffectual sort of way goods that their conduct routinely contravenes. One who recognizes that temperance is integral to living well may simultaneously choose to eat and drink more than he should; a man who realizes that he ought to confront a danger may instead flee from it. *Akrasia*, "weakness of will," is inimical to *eudaimonia* insofar as it thwarts pursuit of one's own good (and not, say, because it thwarts the "greatest happiness of the greatest number"). The primary problem is not right relations with others but rather the establishment and maintenance of an appropriate balance within oneself,[10] and this problem was typically depicted through a set piece in which different "parts of the soul" war with each other, "appetite" confronting "reason" with directive mastery of the self at stake.

That is not to maintain that other-regarding conduct is of merely peripheral or instrumental concern. Because the good life is a life lived among others, right relations with them is a constituent of living well. An individual without friends or with the wrong kind of friends, or with inappropriate affections toward them, is handicapped; and thus Aristotle devotes two books of the *Nicomachean Ethics* to an examination of the conditions of friendship. One who lives as a wolf among men thereby renders himself bestial, and thus a disposition to act justly toward one's compatriots is similarly prized as a constituent of *eudaimonia*. Note,

[10] It is the absence of such an internal balance that we overhear the Apostle lamenting in Romans 7:15 when he confesses: "That which I would I do not, while that which I would not I do."

though, that the value of duties and rights is not simply a given from which ethics commences, but instead flows from an appreciation of the personal value to an individual of leading as good a life as she can. Given this conception, it would be thoroughly misleading to say that one has a "duty to be virtuous." That would suggest that virtue is something onerous, the price of admission to civil society.[11] It would be better to say that the virtuous person is *privileged* with regard to enjoying the necessary preconditions for living a fully human life. Virtue is its own reward, not in some prissy, otherworldly sense, but insofar as it is manifested in a flourishing life in this world.

I shall not offer here an extended argument concerning the respects in which the ancient conception of ethics may be judged more satisfactory than that which infuses the modern, primarily liberal tradition, or, for that matter, those respects in which liberal thought importantly supplements its predecessor.[12] The purpose of the preceding excursus into the history of moral thinking is to remind ourselves that a framework of rights and duties is not the only structure within which we can find a place for the moral salience of the misfortunes of others. A humane individual who esteems living decently among others heeds their distress irrespective of an alleged duty to aid. He does so because he understands that he has a good, that they have a good, and that these are largely complementary rather than ingredients of a grim zero-sum game. The visage of the mean-spirited, miserly man is unlovely, and not only as viewed by others; those of us who have a tolerably adequate conception of what it is to live well would not wish to become such a person. The liability of misanthropy is not only that it showers negative externalities on others but that it precludes one from experiencing the range of goods that are enjoyed only through successful sociality.

Eudaimonia, therefore, incorporates "liberality" or "magnanimity." These virtues are not quite the same as charity; they incorporate a sense of *noblesse oblige*, the open-handedness a superior shows to an inferior. Charity, by way of contrast, is expressive of a relationship between individuals who, despite differences in fortune or rank, are seen as being in some fundamental sense equals.[13] The reflection "There but for the grace of God go I" exemplifies that disposition. This may be why classical Greece and Rome lacked a precise equivalent to the concept of *charity*; it

[11] The price-of-admission view is embraced with characteristic bluntness by Hobbes and, disclaimers and qualifications aside, is adopted by most of the tradition of modern moral philosophy.

[12] A more extended statement is offered in Loren Lomasky, *Persons, Rights, and the Moral Community* (New York: Oxford University Press, 1987), especially ch. 3, "Projects and the Nature of Ethics."

[13] The paradigmatic relation in which natural equals stand is, for classical philosophy, friendship, and Aristotle explicitly observes that, while friendship of a sort can obtain between persons who differ markedly in their stations and virtues, true friendship is feasible only between equals.

emerges within scriptural religion as a corollary of the doctrine that all men partake of a brotherhood within God's creation. From that viewpoint equality is basic, differences in position adventitious. Thus, the classification by the Church of charity as a *theological* virtue. But whatever the origins of the concept may have been, charity does not necessarily presuppose a theistic orientation. Other stances can offer a surrogate basis for the equality on which charity rests, e.g., Kant's insistence that persons, unlike things, are ends in themselves who equally are imbued with worth.[14] Nor is it the case that, in common usage, "charity" invariably attaches itself to a presupposition of equality: we speak nonmetaphorically about acting charitably toward children and even animals. Fine points of semantics aside, there is broad recognition within both the Greco-Roman and biblical traditions that openness to the needs of others is a virtue.

IV. Charity as an Imperfect Duty

Once the jurisprudential paradigm becomes dominant, it is not surprising that a corresponding shift in the conception of charity follows. Philosophers as distinct as Kant and J. S. Mill invoke the category of *imperfect duty* to maintain that charity is prescribed by morality yet is a matter for the free, uncompelled performance of individuals. A perfect duty is characterized as one in which the manner, object, and occasion of performance are precisely specified, while imperfect duties are "those in which, though the act is obligatory, the particular occasions of performing it are left to our choice, as in the case of charity or beneficence, which we are indeed bound to practice but not toward any definite person, nor at any prescribed time."[15] Thus, while it is a strict obligation of morality to be charitable (or: to perform charitable acts), the mode in which the obligation is discharged is to be chosen by the agent.

This attempt to combine duty and discretion is, for at least four reasons, awkward. First, there is no clean line that can be drawn between duties whose manner of performance is specifiable and those whose manner of performance is not. If Mark has borrowed five dollars from Martha, then it is a perfect duty (of justice) that he repay the sum; but, at his

[14] "In the realm of ends everything has either a *price* or a *dignity*. Whatever has a price can be replaced by something else as its equivalent; on the other hand, whatever is above all price, and therefore admits of no equivalent, has a dignity. . . . Thus morality and humanity, so far as it is capable of morality, alone have dignity" (Kant, *Foundations of the Metaphysics of Morals*, 434–35, p. 53). For Kant, humans are equal most fundamentally as beings who are capable of being motivated to moral action.

[15] John Stuart Mill, *Utilitarianism*, ed. Oskar Piest (Indianapolis: Bobbs-Merrill, 1957), p. 61. Mill goes on to remark: "In the more precise language of philosophic jurists, duties of perfect obligation are those duties in virtue of which a correlative *right* resides in some person or persons; duties of imperfect obligation are those moral obligations which do not give birth to any right."

option, he may repay by cash or check, a little earlier or later, with a smile on his face or a frown. The contractual arrangement between them may be specific with regard to any or all of these conditions, but that is to note that specificity is a matter of degree among perfect duties rather than a criterion distinguishing perfect from imperfect duties.

Second, to the extent that imperfect duties lack specificity, it becomes difficult or impossible to determine whether they have been fulfilled. Suppose that charity is indeed an imperfect duty; then it is unquestionably the case that someone who lives out her entire life without ever once coming to the aid of another has failed to discharge the duty. Suppose, however, that at age seventeen she had extended aid and then decided that she had had enough of that sort of thing, thereafter keeping her wallet tightly shut. (Or, alternatively, she lives an initial sixty years entirely unblemished by a single charitable act but resolves to perform a few once she is pensioned off.) Has the duty of charity been discharged? "No," one may respond, "that's too little of a good thing." But if that is too little, what, then, is enough? We might, to pick a number, hold that an individual is obligated to take advantage of no fewer than 25 percent of the opportunities for charitable action that come her way. Ignore the objection that any such ratio is thoroughly arbitrary and unmeasurable in practice; it suffices to note that the proposal seeks to eliminate the intolerable vagueness of imperfect duties by transforming them into perfect duties. A duty to be charitable 25 percent of the time is as determinate as a sharecropper's obligation to give 25 percent of his produce to the landlord. The attempt to transform imperfect duties into "real" duties is akin to the military tactic of saving the village by destroying it.

Third, it is not usually the case that any special regard or esteem is due to one when he fulfills his duties. If Mark pays Martha the five dollars he owes, perfunctory thanks would be an appropriate response. Should she fulsomely laud him for this act and praise him to others, Mark would have reason to feel miffed. Such extravagance in praise suggests that he is the sort of man who cannot be expected routinely to settle his trifling debts. If charity is a duty, then its performance is no occasion for special mention; one is simply doing what one is obliged to do anyhow. Charity, though, is meritorious. We not only approve but admire the charitable person.[16]

[16] It can be argued that charity becomes admirable only to the extent that it is supererogatory, above and beyond the call of duty. There is a baseline, the objection continues, below which charity is merely the fulfillment of duty and is to be approved no more than other dutiful acts. Charitable performances above the baseline are, however, meritorious.

There is, no doubt, some truth to the suggestion. We will not be inclined to esteem the person who only occasionally chooses to aid others. However, this reflection only marginally buttresses the imperfect-duty model. We lack the ability to ascertain where the hypothesized baseline lies; and if we could do so, we would then have to find some analytical category other than imperfect duty for charitable acts that fall above it. The attempt to assimilate charity within the jurisprudential understanding will have been de facto abandoned.

Fourth, and most serious, imperfect duties lack a proper beneficiary. They are not duties to anyone in particular, and thus if I fail to discharge an imperfect duty, there is no one who can justifiably complain that I have thereby wronged him. If I owe ten people one dollar each (a perfect duty), then should I fail to pay any one of them, that person has been dealt with unfairly. But if it is alleged that I have a duty (imperfect) to pay ten dollars to any one of ten people (my option which), a failure to comply is a moral wrong that wrongs no one. Had I given Anderson rather than Jones the entire sum, Jones would have had no complaint at getting nothing; but then my paying no one leaves Jones no worse off than he would have been had I discharged the duty. Symmetrical reasoning applies to each of the ten.[17] The conclusion is that these duties are imperfect in the colloquial sense, that they are *luft*-duties detached from the interests of assignable individuals. Lacking a point, their status within the overall moral economy is mysterious.

Note that charity understood as a virtue does not suffer from the liabilities itemized above. That there is no sharp line separating charitable from uncharitable individuals is not a theoretical defect; dispositional traits are naturally understood as being arrayed on a continuum rather than on/off. To be charitable is to be possessed of the appropriate beliefs and attitudes about how one ought to respond to the misfortunes of others, and to be disposed to express these through appropriate action. It would be an absurd mischaracterization to identify as charitable someone who only on rare occasions extends aid to another, or who, when he gives, does so grudgingly. It is similarly absurd to regard the charitable person simply as someone who is punctilious about the fulfillment of his duties. To be charitable is not merely to do what one (morally) must but to evince a commitment to pursue one's own good in a way that meshes with the good of others. That is why the charitable man is a proper object of esteem. Conversely, the complaint properly lodged against an individual deficient in charity is not that he has withheld items he is not at liberty to keep but rather that, by grasping too tightly onto that which is his, he thereby evinces disdain for the well-being of others. We do well to avoid forcing charity into the Procrustean bed of duty. It does not fit. The construction of ersatz imperfect duties multiplies rather than solves philosophical problems. Charity—and here is meant charity conceived as a

[17] It is tempting to retort: "*All* of them are wronged because what I owed to each was a 0.1 probability of receiving the entire amount." The objection misfires. Suppose that my strategy for discharging imperfect duties is always to give preference, if possible, to someone whose name begins with a vowel. Given the presence of Anderson, Jones had no chance of receiving my largesse, yet I have complied with my duty. "Jones can complain that the vowel selection-strategy itself constitutes unfair treatment of him." That is true only if what is owed Jones (and each of the other nine) is an equal chance of getting the money, as with a fairly conducted lottery. That is to say, however, that the duty owed is not an imperfect one at all, but rather a perfect duty to each that he enjoy an *ex ante* 0.1 probability of receiving the amount (coupled with the perfect duty *ex post* to pay the winner ten dollars).

social virtue—is a richer notion than can be paralleled by a legal model of rights and duties.

V. Charity and Welfare Rights

Although the concept of charity cannot be amalgamated without considerable loss into the jurisprudential paradigm, it does not thereby follow that there is no place whatsoever in the moral lexicon for rights to receive aid—welfare rights—and corresponding duties to provide it. Charity is a virtue we have reason to prize in ourselves and others irrespective of what we judge individuals' rights to be, but just as it is a misapplication of Ockham's razor to attempt to reduce all morally salient considerations to rights and duties, so is it mistaken to hold that a virtue ethics is complete unto itself. Our view of morality will be misshapen if we dispense with either.

The proper home of virtues is human *distinction*. To possess a particular virtue is to excel in the domain in which the virtue is operative. So understood, virtues include but extend beyond the realm of morality. The Greek term *aretê*, which we usually translate as "virtue," is more accurately rendered by "excellence." Thus, Aristotle can speak without any hint of paradox of the *aretê* of a shoemaker, a horse, or even a knife, and not simply the virtues of a human being as such.[18] Our use of the term "virtue" has largely become confined to morality (and, under the influence of Victorian sensibilities, specifically to sexual morality), but even contemporary usage allows us to say of Barry Bonds that he exemplifies to a high degree the virtues of a consummate baseball player insofar as he hits, fields, and runs with distinction.

When we attempt to improve ourselves or educate our children, we take as a model for emulation (I do not mean simply mimicry; creative flexibility is a component of excellence) the virtuous individual. That person is the incarnate standard of high-level achievement. To learn what it is accurately and coolly to appraise and confront dangers, we observe the courageous man and school ourselves to behave similarly; if we aim to develop skills in scientific or scholarly endeavors, we take our bearings from those who possess theoretical wisdom. No set of rules in a copybook can encapsulate what is required for mastery in an area of practical endeavor. That is not to say that rules are entirely without utility, but to note that how, when, and where one is to apply them is not something that can be learned by rote. A kind of apprenticeship is required, and that incorporates empathetic identification with those who have already

[18] Within the class of virtues that pertain to human beings as such, Aristotle recognizes two distinct subclasses, moral virtues and intellectual virtues. Just as the man who is temperate or magnanimous displays a characteristic human virtue, so too does the skilled solver of scientific problems.

achieved excellence, coupled with a regimen of habituation designed to make their traits one's own. To some extent this can be done vicariously; history and literature contribute at least as much to moral education as do tomes of moral philosophy.

Some virtues have wide-ranging application. Regardless of what ends we seek, we will do better if we act with steadfastness, temperance, and prudence. Others are more narrow in their scope, such as the specific virtues of the baseball player. Because of differences in scope, we have reason to prize some virtues above others: compassion counts for more than baseball-hitting skill.[19] Still, to the extent that we take some trait to be a virtue, we esteem the individuals who possess it—Barry Bonds as well as Mother Theresa. Were we to do what they do, we would be pleased if we could do it as they do it.

Rights and duties operate within a different sphere. Persons' rights impose what Robert Nozick calls "side constraints" on action.[20] They do not mandate ends to be achieved, but rather limit the means that may permissibly be employed to realize whatever ends one might have. It is in that sense that "Do not violate rights!" acts as a constraint on goal-directed action. Rights generate correlative duties. Depending on the right in question, these duties can be held "against the world" or against some specifiable individual. If Martha has a right to speak her mind freely, then everyone has a duty not to prevent her from doing so. If, by way of contrast, she has a right that Mark repay the five dollars he borrowed, then Mark (and no one else) has a duty to remit that amount.

While virtues aim at distinction, rights establish a moral minimum. The *least* that is permissible in one's conduct is to respect others' rights. I may—and should—do much more than merely avoid transgressing rights, but I *must not* do less. That is why no special appreciation is due to someone merely for compliance with duties. "You've gone a whole day without stealing so much as one thing from me; thanks a lot!" is either a joke or an insult.[21] We rarely invoke the category of rights when considering relationships that by their nature presuppose considerably more than minimal decency between the parties: proper conduct of friend with friend, lover with lover, or parent with child is not adequately expressed

[19] If an activity is judged to be unworthy in its own right, we will not admire mastery of it. Carlos the Jackal is notably more talented as an assassin than is John W. Hinckley, Jr., but we do not hold him up as a model for emulation. But one who thinks differently about the propriety of assassination—who is, say, engaged in the business of training junior hit men—may quite reasonably within that context assign *The Life and Times of Carlos* as required reading for his students.

[20] See Robert Nozick, *Anarchy, State, and Utopia* (New York: Basic Books, 1974), pp. 28-35.

[21] If circumstances render respect for rights exceptionally difficult or are such as would lead many people to give short shrift to rights, then gratitude becomes appropriate. We praise the person who makes an effort to return the cash-filled wallet found on the sidewalk because we recognize that most other finders would have pocketed the money. Here compliance with rights merges with moral excellence, and it becomes appropriate to import responses at home with the latter into the former.

in the language of rights and duties. When we do resort to that language it usually indicates that the relation has entered a pathological state. I do not mean to say that there are no rights and duties obtaining, say, between spouses, but rather that success in a marital relation entails far more than the minimal deference of respect for rights that is owed to a stranger.

Rights, then, are both maximally weighty and minimally demanding moral claims. The two aspects go together. I am obliged to respect the rights of individuals for whom I have no great sympathy, for whom I even have an active distaste. "Love your neighbor" may be a sustainable injunction when the neighbor is inherently lovable, but to love someone who is clearly odious demands a moral heroism that few of us possess. To *commend* heroism is one thing, to *insist* on it another, and a morality that aspires to be practical necessarily eschews the latter. (It is different for religions. There the telos is not harmonious relations among human beings, but an imitation of the divine perfection.) Grandiose manifestos of "basic human rights" undercut themselves by pitching the demands they would place on us at a level higher than that with which we can reasonably be asked to comply. They mistakenly conflate the language of virtue with the language of rights. Such conflation has become unfortunately frequent in recent years; it sometimes seems that no individual or group is able to formulate a moral agenda (for better working conditions; for kindness to animals; for courteous behavior toward those of a different race or those who are prone to unconventional sexual practices; for whatever) without an announcement proclaiming the discovery of a heretofore unknown "right" that is henceforth to be zealously maintained. This rights inflation is yet another unwelcome consequence of the hegemony of the jurisprudential paradigm.

Even if we set such extravagance aside, there is room for considerable controversy concerning just what rights there are, who has them, and why. As crucial as these questions are, it is beyond the capacity of this essay to develop a theoretical response.[22] I shall instead offer a few remarks to show why it is at least plausible to believe that an adequate accounting of rights and correlative duties will locate them somewhere within the territory that has been marked out by the tradition of classical liberalism. By "classical liberalism" I mean the view holding that the preponderance of basic rights[23] individuals possess are negative, man-

[22] I attempt to do so in *Persons, Rights, and the Moral Community*.

[23] The term "basic rights" is meant to pick out roughly the class of rights that have sometimes been denoted "moral rights" or "human rights." They are to be distinguished from (i) special rights, such as those established by a contract between two parties or that might obtain between individuals enjoying a special relationship such as parent and child; and (ii) rights created by particular enactments of a government or another collectivity capable of originating rights. I prefer the term "basic rights" because it is less question-begging than the alternatives: "moral rights" may suggest that special rights are something other than moral, while "human rights" implies that all and only human beings are the beneficiaries of rights claims while, for example, animals are not and incurably comatose people are.

dating forbearance on the part of others but not active provision of aid. "Libertarianism," as I understand the term, is the view maintaining that *all* basic rights are negative. Libertarian theories, therefore, constitute a subclass of classical liberalism but are not coextensive with it.

Why should we suppose that morality needs to recognize the existence of rights? After all, rights are awkward things, blocking the reformist agendas of those who are persuaded that they could cook some wonderful omelets if only they were permitted to break a few eggs in the process. The answer immediately suggesting itself is that rueful experience has taught us to be suspicious of the culinary credentials of these would-be chefs. Many of the greatest paroxysms of misery human beings have known, not least those that have marred the twentieth century, were brought about by reformer/revolutionaries confident in their ability to engineer Heaven on Earth. What they brought us instead were living hells. If we can maintain a rule of rights, we may be able to thwart their worst excesses.

Rights so understood are indeed plausible, but they are also superficial. They are no more than a concession to human fallibility. Were we better able dispassionately to judge the effect of our designs, so as to ensure that they actually are conducive to the greatest happiness of the greatest number, we could entirely dispense with the category of rights. Since our judgments are unreliable, especially when passions or interests are engaged, rights serve as handy "rules of thumb," generally reliable signposts by means of which we can more efficiently advance overall welfare. They are superficial because, as rules of thumb, they play second fiddle to general utility. We are to respect the rights of Jones (and Anderson, and Smith, and so on) only because we thereby do better with regard to overall welfare, not because of any special moral status enjoyed by Jones. Were we more gifted social engineers, we would be granted carte blanche to sacrifice any or all of Jones's interests whenever opportunities to enhance overall utility beckoned.

What is left out of the preceding paragraph's account is how things present themselves specifically to Jones. He might complain with no little justice against those proposing to sacrifice him to the great god Utility: "I understand that by quashing my interests you will be able to achieve benefits for others, benefits which, in terms of your impersonal standard of value, score greater than what I forfeit. But that's not good enough to satisfy me. What I have primary reason to value are those ends that are distinctively mine, those that I deeply care about. From the perspective of my *personal* standard of value, I lack sufficient reason to go along with your notions of what is socially optimal." That is to say, while annihilating Jones's interests may be justifiable according to the criteria of an abstract theory of social good, *it is not justifiable to Jones*. The result is easily generalized. Each other person has equivalent reason to object to a moral schema that would leave her own deepest concerns dispensable, that would render her a mere means to the achievement of high overall utility totals rather than an end in herself. Correspondingly, each has reason to value the secure enjoyment of moral space within which she is able to act on behalf of the conception of the good that is distinctively her own.

Rights emerge as the boundary markers of moral space. They establish a regime of mutual and reciprocal forbearance. Individuals who are rights-holders are not obliged to be the sacrificial victims or servants of ends distant from their own, but are instead acknowledged to possess a moral entitlement to devote themselves to projects that individually matter to them. Rights are responsive to the urgency from the perspective of an agent of carving out a life rendered coherent and meaningful in virtue of persistent attachment by him to his own directive ends. The rational acceptability of assuming the duties generated by the rights of others derives from recognizing that they too have reason to demand provision of moral space. Basic rights, then, can be characterized as "those moral constraints that impose minimal demands on the forbearance of others such that individuals can pursue projects amidst a world of similar beings, each with his own life to lead, and each owing the same measure of respect to others that they owe to him."[24]

As noted above, classical liberals have traditionally understood rights to be predominantly negative in character. One should not suppose that this is symptomatic of a moral myopia that blinkered an earlier, less "socially enlightened" age. Rather, it is a strict corollary of the logic of rights. If what people have reason to demand from others and to cede to them in return is moral space, then the primary moral right is to be let alone. One may do more than respect the liberty of others, but one must not do less. This is not, as critics of liberalism have often charged, arbitrarily to place liberty above all other values. Instead, it is to recognize that whatever it is that one may value, one needs liberty to pursue it, and one needs it from others in the form of their noninterference. Rather than enthroning one value above all others, liberalism decentralizes questions of value, leaving their resolution to the private initiatives of individuals. Freedom from interference is the freedom to direct one's affairs in accord with one's own judgments concerning what is to be cherished and what is to be to spurned.

A requirement of noninterference minimizes the involuntary implication of individuals in each other's designs. To require that I not violate your liberty to pursue the ends that matter to you is less invasive than to require me actively to further those ends. The former requirement represents the acknowledgment that pursuit of your ends is primarily your business and not, as utilitarianism would have it, a free-floating onus incumbent alike on all moral agents who are in a position to bring about the ends' advancement. This can, with some qualification, be understood

[24] Lomasky, *Persons, Rights, and the Moral Community*, p. 83.

as a judgment about relative costs: I shall likely regard as a lesser burden an obligation not to interfere with you than a requirement to render aid. For better or worse, though, that is not a universal truth. One encounters Pecksniffians and Puritans who find it intolerable to be precluded from foisting their conceptions of the good life on everyone, and when they are too numerous or too powerful the stability of a liberal order is imperiled.[25] That is why "liberal" denotes not only a political credo but also a temperament, and why an ethic of virtues must supplement an ethic of rights and duties.

But though the logic of rights indicates that they are primarily negative, it does not entirely rule out the existence of welfare rights. What each of us needs from all others is, first and foremost, noninterference, but for those who are unlucky this may not be enough. Whenever it is feasible for individuals to act on their own behalf to secure the goods they need to live decent lives, the responsibility to provide is theirs. There is, however, no assurance that liberty will universally guarantee to all persons the requisites for living as project pursuers. For one situated on the margin of exigency, adherence to an order of mutual noninterference can be extremely costly. If the choice confronting one is either to fall below a baseline of minimally satisfactory existence or to encroach on the moral space of others, one may lack sufficient reason to acknowledge a duty of noninterference. A moral hero will, we may believe, even then respect rights, but recall that what rights entail is minimal forbearance, not heroism.[26]

If a regime of rights is to be robust, it cannot demand of individuals more than they can reasonably be expected to provide. It cannot reasonably be demanded of a man that he forbear when to do so comes at the cost of all his prospects for living as a pursuer of personally valued ends. Thus, reciprocity dictates that individuals precariously perched on the edge of exigency can be obligated to respect the liberties of others only if they are simultaneously ensured a sufficiency of material goods.[27]

So conceived, welfare rights are not at odds with the program of classical liberalism. Instead, they render it justifiable at the margin. If all are entitled to a decent minimum below which they need not fall, the ben-

[25] An important recent investigation of the conditions of stability for a liberal order in which people profoundly differ with regard to their basic religious and ethical conceptions is John Rawls, *Political Liberalism* (New York: Columbia University Press, 1993). Although I believe that Rawls's account is hobbled by excess attachment to the jurisprudential paradigm, I cannot pursue that argument here.

[26] Hobbes, no enthusiast for heroes, observes: "When a man is destitute of food, or other thing necessary for his life, and cannot preserve himself any other way, but by some fact against the law; as if in a great famine he take food by force, or stealth, which he cannot obtain for money nor charity; or in defence of his life, snatch away another man's sword; he is totally excused . . ." (Hobbes, *Leviathan*, Part 2, ch. 27, p. 223).

[27] Two recent arguments to essentially the same conclusion are Allen Buchanan, "Justice and Charity," *Ethics*, vol. 97 (1987), pp. 558–75; and Jeremy Waldron, "Welfare and the Images of Charity," *Philosophical Quarterly*, vol. 36 (1986), pp. 463–82.

efits of an order of rights are withheld from no one. This conclusion is accepted by virtually all major classical-liberal theorists. Locke, for example, declares: "As justice gives every man a title to the product of his honest industry, and the fair acquisitions of his ancestors descended to him; so charity gives every man a title to so much out of another's plenty, as will keep him from extreme want, where he has no means to subsist otherwise."[28] Such contingent claims to provision by others do not undercut the primacy of negative rights. The latter are the norm; the former kick in only under exceptional conditions.[29]

I conclude that welfare rights (not properly referred to as "rights to charity") are, within strict limits, justifiable. It does not follow, of course, that these are to be identified with the grab-bag of benefactions typically put forth under the banner of "welfarism." All of the following qualify the legitimacy of welfare rights:

(1) That which individuals enjoy as a matter of right is a decent minimum. The formula is vague, but not infinitely expandable. As Locke notes, it is "extreme want" that demands melioration, not relative deprivation. Welfare rights are not a blank check that may be cashed in for whatever fosters a commodious existence.

(2) Again following Locke, it is only against "another's plenty" that individuals can press justifiable claims. Redistribution that impinges significantly on those obliged to provide is unwarranted.

(3) The claim against others to welfare goods is contingent. Those who are able to supply through their own efforts the requisites of a decent life are not to be granted a place at the public trough. Being forced to starve is tragic, but choosing to do so because one finds work unpleasant is culpable imprudence.

(4) Noninterference is the primary right, and much of the indigence we actually observe is the product of unwarranted interference. In a regime in which individuals enjoy full liberty to meet their own needs, it will not often be the case that they are unable to do so. No minimum-wage or occupational-licensure laws will restrict access to employment; zoning ordinances and housing codes will

[28] Locke, *First Treatise*, Book 1, ch. 4. Where Locke speaks of charitable relief, Hobbes explicitly turns to politically authorized welfare measures: "And whereas many men, by accident inevitable, become unable to maintain themselves by their labour; they ought not to be left to the charity of private persons; but to be provided for, as far forth as the necessities of nature require, by the laws of the commonwealth. For as it is uncharitableness in any man, to neglect the impotent; so it is in the sovereign of a commonwealth, to expose them to the hazard of such uncertain charity" (Hobbes, *Leviathan*, Part 2, ch. 30, p. 255). (I do not hereby mean to be seen as taking sides in the scholarly debate over whether Hobbes is or is not to be considered a proto-liberal.)

[29] I offer a more extended discussion of rights at the margin in "Rights without Stilts," *Harvard Journal of Law and Public Policy*, vol. 12 (Summer 1989), pp. 775–812.

not restrict access to housing; and opportunities to profit will not be ruled out of bounds by "victimless crime" statutes. Nor will an ethos of welfarism spawn an army of bureaucrats whose livelihood rests on the perpetuation of generational cycles of dependency within a welfare class.

(5) Welfare rights do not supplant private charity. Even though, in a strict sense, there is no duty to be charitable, many individuals voluntarily elect to respond to the misfortunes of others. To the extent that charitable provision is forthcoming, coercive redistribution is illegitimate.

Although rights to welfare are theoretically well-grounded, I am inclined to believe that the preceding stipulations, especially the fifth, render their interest largely theoretical in a different sense. A social order graced with individuals disposed to act compassionately toward their unfortunate fellows will be one in which persons only infrequently need resort to welfare rights—and one in which compassion is lacking will be unlikely to sustain a structure of rights at all.

VI. Wide and Narrow Philanthropy

The preceding argument has identified two respects in which charitable provision is superior to reliance on welfare rights. First, while rights are pitched only at the level of moral minima, charity as a virtue is situated within the realm of human distinction. Second, because there is a standing presumption against coercion, voluntary subscriptions are inherently preferable to mandated transfers. To these we can add a third: charity admits of discretion and imaginative application that is both improbable and inappropriate with regard to welfare rights.

Individuals can properly be taken to enjoy as a matter of right no more than the basic requisites for living as independent pursuers of ends that are their own. Mandatory transfers are, therefore, restricted to goods that are neutral among persons' possible projects. John Rawls calls these "primary goods," characterizing them as "things that every rational man is presumed to want," because "they normally have a use whatever a person's rational plan of life."[30] Not all primary goods are tangible; among the primary goods that have a prominent place in Rawls's theory are rights and liberties, powers and opportunities, and the social bases of self-respect. Whatever their importance in that context, however, intangible goods have limited applicability to questions of transfers and redistribution.[31] Money is the most fungible and thus the most project-neutral of

[30] John Rawls, *A Theory of Justice* (Cambridge, MA: Harvard University Press, 1971), p. 62.

[31] Affirmative action policies do raise such questions insofar as they aim at restructuring the network of social opportunities.

goods, and therefore justifiable redistributive measures will largely be confined to cash transfers. Of more dubious legitimacy are in-kind transfer programs. A case can be made for public provision of housing, food, and health services insofar as these are judged to be goods that people need irrespective of whatever else they want. That case will, however, rely to an uncomfortable extent on paternalistic rationales, and it is likely to conceal hidden agendas. (The construction industry will offer abundant support for public housing, agricultural interests for food stamps, and so on.) Although there may nonetheless be some legitimate role for in-kind provision, it is less by orders of magnitude than what is observed in the actual functioning of welfare states.

But while state-operated redistributive programs are required to maintain neutrality among competing ends, private philanthropy operates under no such constraint. Individuals who proffer aid are not simply responding in mechanical fashion to the misfortunes of others. Rather, they are giving effect to their own conceptions of how to live well among others. In this respect charitable provision is not unlike market transactions. When buyer meets seller in the market, each brings to the transaction her own subjective valuations; and the bargains into which they enter are predicated on the achievement of mutual satisfaction. Similarly, voluntary charitable giving centrally incorporates the preferences of donors as well as the needs of recipients. One chooses not only whether to give but also in what amount, to which beneficiaries, in what way, and for the sake of which ends. Private judgments concerning questions of value are thereby given fuller expression than could ever be achieved through mandatory, monolithic governmental programs.

This aspect of private charity is especially observable in morally contested domains. Planned Parenthood and right-to-life agencies compete for "clients" much as do Pepsi and Coca-Cola, and the competition is imbued with moral significance for their respective supporters. In the United States there exist thousands of foundations, large and small, dedicated to advancing particular conceptions of the good. To invoke the market metaphor again, these are key players in the marketplace of ideas. They purvey not only cash but values. Their giving intrinsically incorporates advocacy and thus enriches public discussion.

Much philanthropic activity is, of course, distant from controversial policy matters. To the best of my knowledge, there exist no consequential pro-cancer or anti-literacy factions.[32] Feeding the hungry, sheltering the homeless, clothing the naked, and healing the sick are consensus values. Still, even these charitable functions are morally rich. The choice of giving to one cause has an associated opportunity cost of alternative chari-

[32] Although these blights are spread in copious abundance by, respectively, tobacco companies and the public schools, in the spirit of this essay I shall charitably assume that furtherance of these evils is not their primary intention.

table giving (or noncharitable expenditure) forgone. A dollar donated to the Cancer Society is a dollar not given to literacy projects or to any of the myriad of other potential claimants on one's resources. Thus, to provide support even for uncontroversial causes is to make a morally significant choice in a way that writing out a check to pay one's taxes is not. That is not to make the preposterous claim that every donor does – or should – deliberate at length over each potential benefaction. Time and energy spent on deliberation also come attached to opportunity costs, and the individual who dithers endlessly before dropping a quarter into the street-corner Santa's kettle presents a ludicrous figure. Umbrella agencies such as United Way are a reasonable way to economize on scarce nonmonetary resources. Still, even nondeliberated, uncontroversial acts of charity are manifestations of moral character. They are a means through which one identifies oneself with certain ends above others and expresses convictions about the sort of society in which one wishes to live and how to be a contributing member of it.

Even where ends are uncontroversial, the manner in which they are served can express a particular moral stance. Most American hospitals and private colleges were founded by religious denominations. In part, this can be explained as a service function to communicants who might otherwise have been underprovided along the relevant dimension, but it also incorporated judgments concerning what it is to live decently as a Catholic or Methodist or Jew. Institutional variety encouraged responsiveness to the diverse preferences of different clienteles. Even today, in the wake of considerable homogenization, attending Brigham Young University is noticeably different from pursuing studies at Notre Dame. Diversity would be yet greater if not for restrictive state regulation and direct service provision. The optimal extent of parochial diversity in these areas is disputable, and I do not claim that more is always better than less. Note, though, that even a determination on the part of an eleemosynary agency and its supporters to blend in rather than provide markedly distinctive services is itself a morally considerable decision.

Private charitable providers are at liberty to innovate and experiment to an extent that public bureaus are not. They do not await a legislative mandate to come into existence and are not hobbled by the terms of their enabling legislation or an encrusted civil service. Most important, they are not obligated to tender their services to all comers on an impartial basis. A public agency that withholds aid from some persons who meet formal eligibility criteria, or that provides significantly different services to different beneficiaries, thereby violates a core principle of political justice. States are required to be *neutral* among citizens, and the stipulation that they not advantage some persons or conceptions of the good above others sharply limits their discretionary authority. But that which constitutes impermissible discrimination on the part of a public agency can be entirely benign when exercised by private parties. The latter are not constrained to serve everyone alike, but may instead determine for themselves how their efforts can most effectively meet the interests of clients and supporters. If a private foundation finds that it has a comparative advantage in serving one subclass of potential beneficiaries, it is at liberty to specialize in what it does best. When old programs are seen to be of diminishing effectiveness, they can be supplanted by new ones. Experiments will be undertaken and new directions charted without fear of violating duties of neutrality.

Governmental programs are not altogether fossilized. Their administrators do not simply carry out a legislated algorithm. Programs can be modified in the light of experience, and occasionally—but only *very* occasionally—they are even allowed to die. The differences between private and public programs with regard to flexibility are matters of degree, but when these are sufficiently pronounced they amount to differences in kind. Public welfare mechanisms are simply incapable of generating knowledge to the extent that private philanthropic agencies routinely do. This is yet another reason why even the most scrupulous attention to welfare rights is incapable of substituting for the functions of private charity.

VII. Conclusion

The misfortunes of others *do* matter. Attention to this evident datum has fueled the claim that, just as we have duties not to interfere with others, so too do we have duties to provide charitable relief. The hegemony during the previous three centuries of the jurisprudential paradigm adds further impetus to this presumption and promotes the metastasis of conceptions of "social justice" that are fatal to the preservation of a realm of discretion in which individuals are able to pursue various ideals of moral excellence. But if morality is primarily a menu of rights and duties, then there is no other plausible way to recognize the salience of individuals' misfortunes than to acknowledge the legitimacy of the demands of social justice.

Against the social-justice conception I have argued that relieving distress is morally important because charity is a virtue. Individuals who are not *obligated* to aid others nonetheless *should* do so. One lives more satisfactorily among others if one is alive to their weal and woe. This is not to advance the bald claim that one should be charitable because it is in one's self-interest to be such. Rather, it is to say something substantive about how one should conceive the relation between one's own interests and the interests of others. Unless one takes the well-being of others to be complementary with one's own, charity has no application. The rich might "buy off" the poor through transfer payments, but these transactions would not amount to charity.

Welfare rights *are* a species of buying off, but that is not to impugn their moral legitimacy. The whole of rights, negative as well as positive, can be understood as an elaborate system of quids being exchanged for quos. A person has reason to forbear in her dealings with others as the price of their forbearance toward her. No antecedent affection or sympathy is presumed. What is true of rights and correlative duties, however, cannot be extrapolated to the remainder of morality.[33] The social virtues, of which charity is one, resist modeling as bloodless transactions among mutually disinterested individuals. Instead, they represent a willingness to conceive of others' fates as not entirely external to one's own. Rights and duties are morality's carapace, valuable because they protect individuals' ability to direct their affairs according to their own lights, to forge relations of intimacy and trust, and to aspire to distinction.

Charity is an excellence because it manifests care for what is worth caring about. That proposition does not presuppose some one monolithic standard of value. There are an indefinite number of ways in which one can effectively display charity because circumstances and individuals' conceptions of the good are themselves various. This multiplicity stands in contrast with the fixity that rights and duties must have if they are to be practical. Contingent rights to welfare are theoretically validated because there is a baseline below which individuals cannot be obliged to fall without thereby jeopardizing the foundations of moral reciprocity. Philanthropic activity sometimes addresses itself to lifting people above that baseline, but it also serves the interests of individuals, givers as well as receivers, along numerous other avenues. Charity's responsiveness to different varieties of the good renders it an especially apt virtue for a free society. As etymology suggests and experience confirms, liberality fits well with a liberal order. Should the ministrations of the welfare state drive out private philanthropy, we will be the poorer for it.

Philosophy, Bowling Green State University

[33] That is why David Gauthier's *Morals by Agreement* (Oxford: Clarendon Press, 1986) is, at the very least, mistitled.

Acknowledgments

Maurice Cranston, "Human Rights, Real and Supposed," in *Political Theory and the Rights of Man*, D. D. Raphael (ed.), Bloomington, IN: Indiana University Press, 1967. pp. 43–53. Reprinted with the permission of Macmillan Publishers Ltd.

D. D. Raphael, "Human Rights, Old and New," in *Political Theory and the Rights of Man,* D. D. Raphael (ed.), Bloomington, IN: Indiana University Press, 1967, pp. 54–67. Reprinted with the permission of Macmillan Publishers Ltd.

Martin P. Golding, "The Primacy of Welfare Rights," *Social Philosophy & Policy* 1 (1972), pp. 119–136. Reprinted with the permission of Cambridge University Press (North American Branch).

William Aiken, "The Right to Be Saved from Starvation," in *World Hunger and Moral Obligation,* William Aiken and Hugh LaFollette (eds.), Englewood Cliffs, NJ: Prentice-Hall, 1977, pp. 85–102. Reprinted with the permission of Prentice-Hall Inc.

David Watson, "Welfare Rights and Human Rights," *Journal of Social Policy* 6 (1977), pp. 31–46. Reprinted with the permission of Cambridge University Press.

Rodney Peffer, "A Defense of Rights to Well-Being," *Philosophy & Public Affairs* 8 (1978), pp. 65–87. Copyright © (1978) by Princeton University Press. Reprinted by permission of Princeton University Press.

Allen Buchanan, "Deriving Welfare Rights From Libertarian Rights," in *Income Support: Conceptual and Policy Issues*, Peter G. Brown, Conrad Johnson & Paul Vernier (eds.), Totowa, NJ: Rowman and Littlefield, 1981, pp. 233–246. Reprinted with the permission of Rowman & Littlefield.

A. I. Melden, "Are There Welfare Rights?" in *Income Support: Conceptual and Policy Issues*, Peter G. Brown, Conrad Johnson & Paul Vernier (eds.), Totowa, NJ: Rowman and Littlefield, 1981, pp. 259–278. Reprinted with the permission of Rowman & Littlefield.

James P. Sterba, "A Libertarian Justification for a Welfare State," *Social Theory and Practice* 11 (1985), pp. 285–306. Reprinted with the permission of *Social Theory and Practice.* Copyright © (1985).

Raymond Plant, "Needs, Agency, and Welfare Rights," in *Responsibility, Rights, and Welfare: The Theory of the Welfare State*, J. Donald Moon (ed.), Boulder, CO: Westview Press, 1988, pp. 55–74. Reprinted with the permission of Westview Press.

David Copp, "The Right to An Adequate Standard of Living: Justice, Autonomy, and the Basic Needs," in *Economic Rights*, Ellen Frankel Paul, Fred D. Miller, & Jeffrey Paul (eds.), Cambridge: Cambridge University Press, 1992, pp. 231–261. Reprinted with the permission of Cambridge University Press.

Tara Smith, "On Deriving Rights to Goods From Rights to Freedom," *Law and Philosophy* 11 (1992), pp. 217–234. Reprinted with the permission of Kluwer Academic Publishers.

Peter Singer, "Famine, Affluence, and Morality," *Philosophy & Public Affairs* 1 (1972), pp. 229–243. Copyright © (1972) by Princeton University Press. Reprinted by permission of Princeton University Press.

Robert E. Goodin, "Vulnerabilities and Responsibilities: An Ethical Defense of the Welfare State," *American Political Science Review* 79 (1985), pp. 775–787. Reprinted with the permission of the American Political Science Association.

James W. Nickel, "Charity, Family Aid, and Welfare Rights," *Logos: Philosophic Issues in Christian Perspective* 6 (1985), pp. 71–77. Reprinted with the permission of Santa Clara University.

Jeffrey Obler, "Moral Duty and the Welfare State," *Western Political Quarterly* 39 (1986), pp. 213–235. Reprinted by permission of the University of Utah, copyright holder.

Allen Buchanan, "Justice and Charity," *Ethics* 97 (1987), pp. 558–575. Reprinted with the permission of the University of Chicago Press.

Keith Burgess-Jackson, "Duties, Rights, and Charity," *Journal of Social Philosophy* 18 (1987), pp. 3–12. Reprinted with the permission of Blackwell Publishers Ltd.

Onora O'Neill, "The Great Maxims of Justice and Charity," in *Enlightenment, Rights and Revolution*, Neil MacCormick & Zenon Banowski (eds.) Aberdeen University Press, 1989, pp. 297–312. Reprinted with the permission of Aberdeen University Press.

Richard Stith, "Generosity: A Duty Without a Right," *Journal of Value Inquiry* 25 (1991), pp. 203–216. Reprinted with the permission of Kluwer Academic Publishers.

John M. Whelan, Jr., "Famine and Charity," *Southern Journal of Phil*osophy 29 (1991), pp. 149–166. Reprinted with the permission of Memphis State University.

Loren E. Lomasky, "Justice To Charity," *Social Philosophy and Policy* 12 (1995), pp. 32–53. Reprinted with the permission of Cambridge University Press (North American Branch).